THE EDI HANDBOOK
Trading in the 1990s

Edited by

Mike Gifkins
&
David Hitchcock

with a Foreword by

The Rt Hon Lord Young of Grafham
Secretary of State for Trade and Industry

1988
Blenheim Online
London

British Library Cataloguing in Publication Data

The EDI handbook.
 1. Computer-telecommunication services
 I.. Gifkins, Mike   II. Hitchcock, David
 384.3

 ISBN 0-86353-148-2

ISBN 0 86383 148 2

Produced in the United Kingdom by Henry Ling Ltd, Dorchester

Blenheim Online Publications
Blenheim House, Ash Hill Drive, Pinner, Middlesex HA5 2AE, UK
The Publishing Division of Blenheim Online Ltd, London

CONTENTS

		Page
FOREWORD		v
PREFACE		vii
Mike Gifkins & David Hitchcock		

ELECTRONIC DATA INTERCHANGE — A FACT FOR THE 1990s
1	1992: Maintaining the UK's competitive edge in EDI	3
	Ray Walker	
2	The impact of EDI upon business organisation	11
	Paul Turnbull	

STANDARDS FOR EDI
3	A review of the relationships and roles of the standards making bodies	27
	Nigel Fenton	
4	Message standards for EDI	40
	Tom McGuffog	
5	Open communications standards: their role in EDI	56
	Paul Dawkins	

EXAMPLES OF EDI IN PRACTICE
6	EDI in freight forwarding: the ASTI story	77
	Terence Westgate	
7	The relationship between EDI and Electronic Funds Transfer (EFT)	85
	Christopher Eaglen	
8	UNICORN: EDI in a travel reservation system	104
	Anthony Allen	

TRADING ELECTRONICALLY
9	EDI development groups	117
	John Sanders	
10	Creating legal relationships with trading partners	126
	Bernard Wheble	
11	EDI in international trade: a Customs view	139
	Douglas Tweddle	

IMPLEMENTING EDI
12	Preparing the organisation for EDI	149
	David Jackson	
13	Selecting communications services for EDI	156
	Edmund Lee	
14	The enabling factors for EDI	165
	David Palmer	
15	How to build effective EDI links	175
	Keith Blacker	

VALUE ADDED AND DATA SERVICES
16   The IBM EDI service   187
       Ray Smithers
17   The INS EDI service   195
       John Jenkins
18   EDI services from Istel   201
       Phil Coathup

MAJOR TRENDS — CHARTING THE FUTURE
19   VADS interworking: a cloud on the EDI horizon   211
       Alison Bidgood
20   Meeting EDI user requirements with X.400, now and in the future   217
       Nick Pope
21   The challenges of EDI decision making   229
       Gil Patrick

FURTHER INFORMATION
22   Review of European EDI developments   241
       David Hitchcock
23   Classification of EDI developments in Europe   293
24   Computer data interchange: guidelines for users exchanging invoice
       and accounting information   295
       HM Customs and Excise

APPENDICES
A   Guide to UK EDI Suppliers   301
B   Guide to Interbridge   316
C   Authors' biographies   318
D   Selective bibliography and publishers' addresses   326
E   Guide to acronyms   329
F   Glossary of terms   335

FOREWORD

Electronic Data Interchange is an important element of business practice which offers considerable scope for cost-saving and improving competitiveness. The direct computer-to-computer exchange of information will not only automate the order-delivery cycle offering considerable savings in the cost of administration, but it will also enhance access to information such as stock levels, sales performance, product specifications, and market information. It will alter the nature of the supplier–customer relationship bringing them closer together. It should also encourage companies to look at their information systems strategies—to consider the ways in which information is used in their businesses, both internally and externally, and to ensure that information systems considerations are given their due weight in companies' strategic thinking. EDI is a development which no business can afford to ignore.

Although the UK can be pleased with its record of use of EDI, there is no room for complacency. The completion of the Single European Market in 1992 will spur the wider use of EDI. British companies must keep abreast with developments and my Department is playing its part in helping UK companies to do so. Under the Vanguard Programme, we have published through HMSO reports on major issues affecting the development of the market—use of EDI standards, interworking, training needs, EDI and X.400—with more to come. The Enterprise Initiative offers small and medium sized companies financial assistance in obtaining advice on their use of information systems, which includes external services such as EDI.

This book is probably the most comprehensive collection of information on EDI yet produced. It provides information on services available as well as articles on major issues. It should prove to be a useful work of reference. I hope it will also make a significant contribution to spreading understanding of the business benefits of EDI.

The Rt Hon Lord Young of Grafham
Secretary of State for Trade and Industry
London, September 1988

v

PREFACE

Mike Gifkins & David Hitchcock

Today we find computers at the heart of every business, whether large or small, and across all industrial sectors. Yet anyone in business who stands back for a moment can point to gross inefficiencies despite the use of so much automation.

Delivery dates gleaned from a telex are carefully re-typed into a computer terminal. A table of sales figures is received by facsimile and re-typed into a spread sheet. Invoices, delivery notes and purchase orders are generated by computer but are sent in the mail - often the first action upon receipt is to type the information into another computer system.

The EDI Handbook explains how Electronic Data Interchange (EDI) can cut through the gross inefficiencies associated with moving paper around in industry. The *Handbook* opens up the topic of computer-to-computer communications and makes the subject accessible to those in business who want the benefits of technology.

Based on a thorough introduction to EDI the book concentrates on the advantages which accrue from the technology and, perhaps just as importantly, discusses the changes in business practices which will be necessary for trading in the markets of the future. These changes will affect the very fundamentals of the way businesses are organised. At one level there will be changes in manangement structure as the techniques are adopted. There will also be redundancy amongst the white collar roles which are played by so many in today's paper-dominated environment.

The book has been developed both to serve as a definitive introduction to the subject and to offer practical help to the reader who wishes to proceed with an implementation. With this in mind we have organised the book into both editorial and information sections. This linking of two sorts of material in the one volume offers broad coverage of present and future issues allied to more pragmatic reviews of current initiatives.

We have brought together a collection of articles from individuals who are experts in their respective fields. We thank those authors for having penned such sound and thought-provoking papers. The book was conceived in response to the need for people in business to understand more of the possibilities offered by computer-to-computer communications available now. We hope it reveals some of the impacts which will result as we approach the next millenium. If we have met our goals for the book then it is the authors above all who are to be thanked.

The EDI Handbook includes sections treating:

Electronic Data Interchange - A Fact for the 1990s
An authoritative view of the point EDI has reached and how
it is likely to progress.

EDI in the business strategy

EDI brings changes in working practices which eventually impact large parts of an organisation. The use of EDI may be a competitive tool today. Tomorrow it will be a requirement for survival.

Standards in EDI

The distinction between communications and message standards, with a review of the major standards making bodies. An introduction to EDI messaging and to data communications, including OSI and X.400, with a discussion of the relevance to EDI.

Experience of EDI

Factual accounts of the experience of organisations which have used EDI. For some it is at the core of the business. For others it is an ancillary service.

The legal context

Business practice is at present most comfortable with paper documents. The technical means exist for replacing many of these with electronic equivalents. However, has the legal system caught up? How can trading partners incorporate EDI into their dealings?

Implementing EDI

A more detailed look at what the user needs, practically speaking, to get into EDI. An account of formatting and de-formatting software, of how to create interfaces to existing systems, and of the hardware needed.

Selecting communications services for EDI

There are already many vendors of communications services relevant to EDI, ranging from those offered by a Public Telecommunications Operator to the processing and clearing-house functions of a Value Added and Data Service. A review is made of the varied services which are already offered and their significance to the EDI user.

Major trends

Lively issues in EDI are interworking between suppliers of communications services and the integration of EDI with international telecommunications standards. The *Handbook* offers articles on both topics.

International EDI applications

A review of progess outside the UK, in Europe. A survey of European EDI development groups.

The views expressed in the papers are the author's alone. No attempt has been made by the editors to suppress any controversial opinions or ideas. While we have sought to minimise repetition, there is some and this reflects the freedom which each author has had to express his or her own viewpoint.

Finally we thank the many people amongst our colleagues, families and friends who have tolerated, advised and helped us during the months of preparation of this *Handbook*. We also owe gratitude to our employers, Scicon Ltd and Blenheim Online who have encouraged the venture.

MIKE GIFKINS — Scicon Limited
and
DAVID HITCHCOCK — Blenheim Online Limited
October 1988
London

Electronic Data Interchange — a Fact for the 1990s

EDI is a high growth activity. It is not usually of a very high profile in the public view. Rather than being high tech it is applied tech—the use of existing technology. However it is the application of two of our fastest-changing technologies, computing and telecommunications, that makes EDI special and gives it a variety which matches that of its parent industries.

As Europe approaches 1992, so international trade will become more and more free of both tariff barriers and non-tariff barriers. The seminal importance of EDI for the UK, and indeed for all of Europe, lies in the following question: "will international trade be facilitated or hindered by the many varied computer systems which traders use?" In the past the accent in automation has been upon intra-company developments. It is now becoming essential to move toward improvements in inter-company automation, and that is what EDI is all about.

We are privileged to have an opening paper by Ray Walker, Chief Executive of SITPRO. He has done much to introduce businessmen in the UK to electronic trading and sets the scene for the book.

In the past technologies have arisen at a gentler pace. The telephone and the car changed everything and each took perhaps 60 years to do so. EDI will not be so stately in its progress. Paul Turnbull takes a careful look at the likely impact upon organisations. Businesses constantly adapt themselves as conditions change and that means changing roles for people. Electronic trading is going to impact many working lives so it makes sense to try to understand the nature of the changes. Paul Turnbull does this, choosing as an aid in his complex task an emerging field of research called Information Economics which has been developed in the United States.

1
1992: Maintaining the UK's Competitive Edge in EDI

Ray Walker

It is a privilege to write the opening paper of *The EDI Handbook;* I would like to congratulate the editors, Mike Gifkins and David Hitchcock on their initiative. It will, I think, become a standard reference for all EDI users in the UK. The emergence of this book and of many other services associated with EDI that are being developed confirm, if confirmation is required, the arrival of EDI as a fact of business life in the UK today.

INTRODUCTION

As the Editors mention, EDI is a product of the growing integration of the related sciences of computing and telecommunications. As with many other of today's technologies, its roots can be traced back to the Second World War. Indeed, the general structure of EDI messages—Header, Detail, Trailer—is conceptually the same as that used by Morse operators on both sides during the war. Many of today's experts have graduated to EDI following early signals experience either in the services or telecommunications organisations.

Military logistics was also an early motivator of EDI. The complexity of organising the Berlin airlift led one of the pioneers of EDI, Ed Guilbert, then a Colonel in the US army, to develop the concepts which were later to emerge and be implemented in America as the TDCC standards. Since the Berlin airlift, speeding up the flow of goods has been a continual goal of EDI. EDI probably started with fixed format trials in the North American railway industry in the sixties. Then, as Doug Tweddle mentions in his paper in Chapter 11, the concepts were further developed during the introduction of the LACES system at Heathrow in 1971.

Indeed, the co-ordinator of the LACES project was the London Cargo Manager of Air France, none other than Etienne Dreyfous, now Vice President of the French trade facilitation organisation Simprofrance and Chairman of the United Nations Economic Commission for Europe's influential group of experts on EDP. It is within that committee that the GTDI syntax was developed (which now forms the basis of the ANA's TRADACOMS Standards). The same committee has been the driving force behind the development of the EDIFACT standards.

However it is clear from the experience of the USA and the UK that it is only when the three basic requirements of EDI—telecommunications, software and in particular, message standards—are available and stable, that widespread applications begin to develop. The UK has been at the leading edge of EDI precisely because we have devoted resources, expertise and enthusiasm to these basic technical requirements. Tom McGuffog, who has played such an important role in the development of EDI in the UK, describes in Chapter 4 the development of the TRADACOMS network, Tradanet. As he indicates, it was only when a stable set of message standards, capable of being securely transmitted over a store-and-forward network, was available, that EDI became a strategic tool for our leading high street retailers and their suppliers.

The UK has also led in the development of the major European EDI projects; for example ODETTE, the automotive industry's initiative and the first pan-European project, started in the UK. Further, we have also led Europe in the deregulation of telecommunications and our value added networks are well advanced compared with their continental competitors. Starting in 1975, my own organisation has made a substantial contribution to the development of message standards in Europe. Led by another pioneer of EDI, Don Trafford, the SITPRO syntax rules and data element directory were published in 1978, and sub-sequently became the basis of the UN/ECE GTDI. Recently we have been heavily involved in the development of the EDIFACT standards.

However as we approach 1992 and the Single European Market, we will need to consider how to maintain the UK lead in EDI. I indicate my own views later in this article but it is clearly a matter for some national debate. In that debate it is important to understand what EDI is, what it is not, and what the main developments are. I hope the following overview will assist in that process.

WHAT IS EDI?

EDI is a generic term covering a number of different categories of interchange. It can be defined as "the electronic transfer from one computer to another of computer processable data using an agreed standard to structure the data". EDI is not electronic mail or the information provided by the growing number of linked database services—sometimes called electronic trading. EDI is, however, paperless trading of the following three types.

* transaction data interchange, which can be sub-divided into
  two categories:

  i) general—normally related to a business or administrative
  transaction such as invoice, purchase order, credit note, payment
  instruction, freight booking, waybill, Customs entry;

  ii) specific—developed for a particular and special need.
  Electronic funds transfer, used widely in the banking industry is
  a good example;

* technical data interchange, used in design and engineering
  projects such as CAD/CAM; interactive interchange, which is
  being developed in the travel and tourist industries.

All have similar requirements, although one important distinction is whether the interchange uses fixed length or variable length formats. Variable formats are generally considered more efficient.

For clarity this overview deals only with variable format general transaction data interchange. This is the most widespread application of EDI and is what is meant by EDI in the rest of this article.

EDI REQUIREMENTS & The ROLE OF STANDARDS

EDI has three basic requirements:

> Firstly, a transaction message standard—a standard way of representing the data in each transaction.

> Secondly, translation software—software which interfaces with the in-house computer and which allows in-house data to be converted to the standard representation (message standard) or vice versa.

> Thirdly, communications—a method of transmitting the standard data from one computer to another. This can be physical, for instance the transfer of magnetic tape, but it is clear that the potential of EDI will not be achieved until the power of telecommunications is applied.

Standards play a vital role in all aspects of EDI but I would like to concentrate on the role of standards within messages. At its simplest, for example, two companies can each agree to accept the other's invoice format or message. Such bilateral arrangements are perfectly workable and have often been used. However as the number of trading partners increases the approach proves increasingly costly to support. With four companies wishing to exchange data, 12 different standards are required; with 12 companies, 132! Clearly, as more and more traders become involved a common standard for each transaction is required.

Message standards can be broken into a number of components:

> *Syntax*—the set of rules controlling the structure of a message and akin to the function of grammar in a language;

> *Data Elements*—the smallest indivisible piece of data (such as the date). Data elements are equivalent to the function of words in a language;

> *Standardised Codes*—required to represent each data element;

> *Segments*—a grouping of related data elements, such as name and address;

> *Messages*—a grouping of segments arranged according to both the message design guidelines and the syntax which represents a specific transaction, such as an invoice.

Message standards may be private, between two or more users; they may be those of a closed user group or trade association. They may be national or international. They may also be fixed format (that is, both data fields and records having a fixed length) or they may be variable format.

Fixed formats are traditionally where EDI started. For example nearly all computerised bank settlements employ fixed format messages. However, variable format messages are up to 70% more efficient from a transmission viewpoint, although they do require a more sophisticated syntax.

The UK has two main groups of message standards, one based on the ANA TRADACOMS standards and the other around the emerging UN-EDIFACT standards. Nigel Fenton reviews the standards in Chapter 3 so I do not propose to cover the differences here. Having two standards in the UK should not be seen as a problem or a competitive situation. Standards need to meet the functional requirements of the user, and it is perfectly reasonable for a user to start with one standard because it suits his requirements, and either to migrate to another as the requirements change or to adopt both standards, one for his national and the other for his international requirements. What is important is that the user understands the components of message standards, analyses current and future requirements and adopts an implementation strategy that allows some flexibility as circumstances change.

CURRENT UK & EUROPEAN DEVELOPMENTS IN EDI

Variable format EDI implementation first started in the USA in 1978 and has multiplied rapidly. The UK followed in 1982 and our growth pattern closely mirrors that of the USA. Today there are about 5000 variable format users in the USA and over 1200 in the UK. Continental Europe is somewhat behind the UK—about 250 variable format EDI users—but that number is growing rapidly.

Examples of EDI activities in the UK include the following (and they are expanded upon in later chapters):

the Article Number Association (ANA). The ANA was responsible for establishing in the UK the bar-coding for consumer products. Its EDI activities, based on the TRADACOMS standards, bring together major high street retailers (department stores and supermarkets) and their suppliers. The ANA is the UK's largest EDI group with about 1000 users.

major industries such as chemicals, electronics, motor manufacturing and construction. Nearly all of these major UK industrial sectors are participating in EDI projects within Western Europe (see below).

Government, HM Customs & Excise, the Property Services Agency (PSA) and recently the National Health Service (NHS) have all undertaken EDI implementations. HM Customs has been active in EDI since 1976 and a major computerised clearance procedure—the period entry scheme—is based on EDI techniques (see Chapter 11). A major EDI-related standardisation project called GOSIP (Government Open Systems Interconnection Profile) is also at an advanced stage of planning.

international trade, banking and insurance. In September 1987 the EDI Association (EDIA) (see Chapter 22) was formed to promote the development of EDI in international trade and the related service industries. Based on the experience of the Data Interchange for Shipping (DISH) and SHIPNET projects, the association has six sub-groups: Deep Sea, Short Sea & Surface, Air, Banking & Financial Services, Governmental Issues, Insurance. EDIA is quickly becoming a national forum for those involved in UK international trade and is expected to provide considerable user input into the newly formed West European EDIFACT Board.

Examples of EDI activity in Western Europe include the pan-European industry group initiatives CEFIC, EDIFICE, ODETTE and RINET.

> CEFIC brings together major multinational chemical companies in nearly all European countries. Although the project was only approved in 1986, it has already reached trial stage with the exchange of invoices and quality information and is based on the UN-EDIFACT standards.
>
> EDIFICE brings together companies in the electronics field such as Motorola, Texas Instruments, IBM and Hewlett Packard. Again rapid progress has been made and the project is moving to trial stage based on the UN-EDIFACT standards.
>
> ODETTE is the original and pioneering project being undertaken by the motor industry. It was born out of the Commission-funded Mercator project which took place in 1983/4 and for which SITPRO was the project leader. European EDI owes much to the ODETTE project because they have faced and solved many of the problems of a multinational, multilingual technical project. Its organisation has provided the model for others to follow.
>
> Currently using the UN-TDI syntax standards, ODETTE is committed to moving to UN-EDIFACT syntax and message structures as soon as possible.
>
> RINET is a new initiative in the re-insurance industry, bringing together many of Europe's largest insurance companies. Based in Brussels, it will adopt the UN-EDIFACT standards and also provide a dedicated telecommunications network.

THE EDIFACT BOARD

The EDIFACT Board was formed in January 1988 with the aim of co-ordinating and encouraging the development of EDI messages based on the UN-EDIFACT standards. It is endorsed and supported by the Commission for the European Communities (CEC) and by the European Free Trade Association (EFTA). It is an activity under the auspices of the UN/ECE with an expert appointed by the UN/ECE as rapporteur. He is charged with the responsibility for development, co-ordination, technical assessment and other support services. (The UN/ECE plays a major role in standards making which is not often recognised. For example the International Standards Organisation, which was responsible for developing the OSI seven-layer model, is also an activity supported by the UN/ECE).

The EDIFACT Board brings together representatives of European Community and EFTA Member States, the CEC and EFTA Secretariat, the European Standardisation Committee (CEN), active pan-European industry groups such as ODETTE, and international organisations such as SWIFT. The Board is supported by a Steering Committee and a technical secretariat. The Steering Committee manages and co-ordinates, on behalf of the Board, a number of specialist committees covering message development, technical assessment, maintenance, promotion and documentation. Message Development Groups already established cover: Trade (Purchasing and Supply); Transport (Road, Rail, Short Sea Ferry, Deep Sea and Air); Customs and Other Official Requirements; Finance (Banking and Insurance); Special Projects (Tourism and Construction).

Through these groups UN-EDIFACT messages are under development on a broad front. A draft invoice approved by the UN for trial use is already available. Other messages such as purchase order, confirmation of purchase order and despatch advice are at an advanced stage of development. In particular the Customs area has recently seen important developments.

Following the decision of US and European Community Customs authorities to endorse the UN-EDIFACT standards, work has started on a new standard Customs message which it is hoped will provide Customs clearance data for entry into both the USA and EC.

The UK input to these groups is currently being co-ordinated through SITPRO and the EDI Association in consultation with the Department of Trade & Industry.

GROWTH RATES AND BENEFITS

The authoritative Stanford Research Institute in the USA has predicted that EDI will grow at a rate of about 50% per annum until the year 2000. Input, another market research group, currently estimates that EDI in the USA is growing at 88% per annum and SITPRO's estimation, based on various sources, is for a current annual growth rate in the UK of about 100% per annum.

The list of new projects in EDI grows daily but it is possible to identify three main reasons for the spectacular growth. Firstly, once implemented EDI allows better customer service. Although this is sometimes difficult to quantify, there is no question that in an age where virtually no product is unique and competition is consistently fierce, improving customer service is a major target for many companies.

Secondly, EDI offers significant reductions in trading costs. At its simplest EDI avoids the re-entry of data and allows timely and error free transaction information to be passed from one computer to another. However, although these savings in themselves can be significant (a 97% cost reduction in producing and transferring international invoices has been observed) this is only part of the story. Providing error free information to the right place at the right time allows products to be delivered faster, shortening the delivery cycle. This means that lower stock levels can be held with confidence and valuable working capital released. EDI also usually brings the more certain and speedy payment of invoices thus generating cash flow. Taken together, reducing costs, releasing working capital and generating cash flow can markedly improve the return on the assets employed in a business.

Thirdly, EDI opens up a further and very potent opportunity for management—that of introducing new business strategies such as 'just-in-time' manufacturing. Until now paper has been the main medium for carrying information about business transactions. The procedures, timescales and constraints it has produced have been accepted subconsciously by management. Thus many companies are organised vertically into sales, production and finance and very little attention has been given to the opportunities which arise from lateral integration across the organisation. This is because lateral organisation requires excellent communication to be effective. EDI provides that and the integration of the supply, demand and finance chains within a company may yet be EDI's greatest achievement.

Certainly there is no doubt that EDI is a major new strategic tool for management. An American colleague of mine has called EDI "the key to co-operative computer systems" and I think he is right. It is the common denominator in improving business performance and I predict that its use will revolutionise national and international trading practices.

EDI & 1992

EDI has a critical role to play in the European Community for two main reasons. Firstly it is a strategic tool which sharpens competitive edge and secondly, it could be the solution to the problem of removing physical barriers to trade at the frontiers.

Whilst I have no doubt that a Single European Market will be fully established within the next fifteen years, it is unlikely that Lord Cockfield's plan will be totally realised by 1992 for a number of reasons. Not least amongst these are the political problems that a number of governments (including the UK) face in the proposals of tax harmonisation. However, without tax harmonisation significant problems will remain at border points—with all that means for lorry queues, delays and extra costs—unless an alternative can be found.

I believe that EDI offers that alternative. The near-instantaneous delivery of information to the relevant Customs points by linked networks carrying standard EDI messages is the solution. EDI is therefore a potential win-win situation for Europe as a whole. However will the UK still maintain its leading position?

Obviously the UK is well placed—we have all the techniques and skills that are required. However, as a nation we have had similar advantages in other fields and yet have failed to capitalise on them.

In two critical and basic areas of EDI—message standardisation and communications—we need to have a more focused attitude to the Single European Market if we are not to lose out to other Member States (Germany for example is catching up fast).

As Lord Young states in his recent White Paper, *DTI—the department for Enterprise,* "Differences in national standards, and testing and certification practices, can impose barriers to trade . . . Past experience shows that those countries which put most effort into European standards-making tend to secure Community harmonisation on terms most favourable to their industry and commerce." In this area we need to reconcile elegantly the problem of supporting both a *de facto* national standard and an emerging international standard. I believe that with thought, consideration and planning, this can be done. But it has not been achieved yet. Similarly we need to ensure that the UK speaks with one voice within Europe. Here I am much encouraged by recent events including the discussion between the BSI and SITPRO about fusion of their interests.

In communications we also need to take a number of actions. Firstly, we must resolve the commercial problems of the interconnection of networks or interworking to the benefit of the user. Alison Bidgood covers the issues in

Chapter 19 but the problem becomes even more critical in the context of 1992. A user in Bradford wanting to deliver a Customs clearance message to the Customs point at Gronau in Germany does not want to be told that he has to connect to, say, five different networks. He wants to connect to one and to know that his message will be quickly and securely delivered.

Secondly, we need to consider and resolve the outstanding issues of EDI and X.400. Nick Pope covers this in Chapter 20. I do not think the problems are difficult to resolve but, again, we need to take positive and planned action.

Finally, we need to support strongly the further deregulation of the European telecommunications industry. The best way for the UK to do that is to support unequivocally Michel Carpentier, the Director General of DG13 of the Commission, in his recent initiative and his Green paper. A freer telecommunications environment is clearly in all our interests. If we take these actions over the next two to three years we will face 1992 with confidence and our position as leaders in Europe will be reinforced. A win-win situation for Europe will become a win-win situation for the UK. The question is, will we take the required action?

2

The Impact of EDI Upon Business Organisation

Paul Turnbull

"The old hardware centralised families and businesses
The new software diffuses both into an information environment
Where the Gaugin maids
In the banyan shades
Wear palmleaf drapery"
*(Marshall McLuhan gives a contempory interpretation of T S
Eliot's 'Fragment of an Agon', in 'Culture is Our Business'— 1970)*

This paper examines the way in which electronic data interchange (EDI) alters the structure of industries and organisations. The early benefits of using EDI are primarily in the nature of cost savings which arise from performing existing business functions in more efficient ways. These cost savings are significant, but the future will see an increasing emphasis on using EDI to add value to goods and services. From this will emerge new functions, organisations and industry structures that are more suited to the exploitation of EDI and other communication technologies. The continuing success of UK industry will depend, to a large measure, upon the willingness of individual companies to look outside their own organisations and identify the opportunities for applying this technology. The potential gains from doing this are considerable but progress in most sectors, despite the early deregulation of telecommunications in the UK, has been slow. Much of the impact of EDI has been direct, anticipated and beneficial; however other effects, not all of which are desirable, will accompany the wider uptake of communication technology. These indirect effects will include function deskilling, information overload, decentralisation and the invasion of privacy. Finally, regardless of how one views the nature of change associated with EDI, there is no doubt that the future for those companies without experience of this technology can be compared with driving forward with eyes firmly fixed on the rear view mirror, blissfully unaware of what lies ahead.

ALTERING INDUSTRY STRUCTURES

EDI opens up completely new opportunities for supplier-customer relationships which bypass intermediaries, lock suppliers in or competition out. Market leaders who have adopted EDI and reaped the early rewards of cost reduction are now moving beyond this to create new trading structures. Marketing departments are benefiting from the ability to record the types of transactions passing through an EDI network, and from this to analyse buying patterns which may be local, national or global. Sales people are beginning to exploit the potential for EDI, particularly as it offers the opportunity to take the marketplace to the customer, who is but a keyboard away.

In the UK textile industry for example, the use of EDI has significantly reduced the lead-time of manufacturing, and provided an effective response to the shorter delivery times and increasing market share hitherto enjoyed by Eastern suppliers. Benetton, the clothing manufacturer with high street outlets, has progressed even further in its exploitation of this technology by using EDI to change its approach to weaving and distribution. This has been achieved by communicating sales data, recorded at retail outlets, through EDI to manu-facturing sites. There, buying patterns are analysed and goods subsequently dyed by style and colour in response to customer demand. This provides flexibility in matching supply to fashion demand, contains costs and delivers the right product to the market several months ahead of its closest competitor.

The business procedures incorporated in an EDI application offer new entrants to a market access to expertise they may not initially possess. Access, furthermore, from locations far removed from the geographical marketplace, as has happened in export. There, EDI applications such as the air-cargo freight forwarding system (ACP-90) in association with the electronic customs clearance system (DEPS) have given manufacturers on-line access to the business pro-cedures necessary for exporting goods. These systems have captured the expertise of freight forwarders, Customs and Excise and the major airlines in the form of instructions displayed on a computer terminal. As a consequence, companies which previously engaged freight forwarders to handle their exports are now entering the details of goods for export directly through EDI systems. This automates customs clearance and air-cargo forwarding and, in so doing, allows manufacturers to bypass the intermediary.

The aerospace industry provides an example of supplier lock-in with the attendant potential for competitor lock-out. Airlines procure those aircraft which offer a high fuel economy and a low servicing cost, particularly in the cost of replacing parts. The importance of this becomes apparent when you consider how long an aircraft design lasts. This can span 20 years or more, as in the case of the Boeing 727, and throughout this period the production of parts remains with the original design owner. Suppliers can therefore take a long term view of profitability, provided that the performance criteria are met and providing that their design is first to the market. A typical period for design and assembly takes around four years.

American air-frame assemblers such as McDonnell Douglas and Boeing dominate the design and assembly of fleet aircraft, including the activities of component suppliers such as Rolls Royce and Lucas. Payment terms are pegged to the US dollar to absorb any adverse movements in the exchange rate within their existing cost structures. The effect of this can be dramatic: in late 1987, the dollar moved 15 per cent in relation to sterling, and effectively reduced the revenue of all UK based suppliers by that amount. For them, the medium-term strategy may be to move their manufacturing bases to the US and remove any exposure to exchange fluctuations. This does, however, require a considerable period of qualification for the requisite certification by US civil aviation authorities in addition to incurring the problems associated with running a multinational company. A short-term solution, which is being adopted by suppliers, uses EDI to reduce the cost of holding safety stocks, retain the UK manufacturing base, exchange design information quickly, reduce procurement times and hence the lead-time for supply, increase the quality of design and production, and increase the responsiveness of service provision to demand. The airline industry provides a further example. Competitive pressure on airlines will continue to drive costs down the supply chain and require those companies without EDI to hold higher levels of safety stocks to meet ever shorter delivery periods. This will increase costs, reduce profits and eventually lock out those companies without the capability of exploiting EDI technology or the inclination to do so. Furthermore, US based EDI applications such as ATA 2000 already provide airlines with on-line access to information on the avail- ability of replacement parts around the globe. To be effective this system requires a critical mass of suppliers willing to enter and maintain this inform- ation. Progress towards achieving this state is locking-in suppliers to using this system in order to secure future business from airlines.

New businesses and products have also emerged from the adoption of EDI. This includes EDI network and application suppliers, consultancies and associ- ated service companies. The EDI network suppliers, for example, are inter- mediaries which supply and maintain core EDI networks and applications. They provide a service to trading communities that is independent of any user organisation, supporting interconnection between different computer equip- ment and provides a mailbox for the transmission of data between trading parties. The major players active in the UK include IBM, INS, and Istel.

ADDING VALUE

The early benefits of using EDI have arisen from performing existing business functions in more efficient ways. These benefits are primarily cost savings associated with automating highly repetitive tasks and amount to millions of pounds sterling. Automation by EDI saves costs in processing volumes of order forms, goods received notes and invoices throughout a trading chain. This has eliminated the reprocessing of information commonly transmitted between members of a trading community and reduced the number of errors in documents required to complete a business transaction. In turn this also delivers associated reductions in staff and the cost of using telephones, first class mail, telexes, facsimiles and couriers. Substantial savings in supply lead-times are realised by automating the administration associated with purchasing and sales. As a consequence a supplier can supply orders directly from production and rely less upon the need to hold safety stocks. This overall reduction in cost, although primarily a supplier benefit, is significant and in many industries delivers savings higher than some of the present industry profit margins.

In the short-term more companies will realise these cost reductions but for those with more experience of EDI there is the growing awareness of the opportunity for developing new approaches to business which add greater value to goods and services. Adding value is implicit in the competitive approaches taken by the world's major manufacturers, although the means for delivering this differ considerably. For example, Japan's manufacturers have adopted a strategy of low cost, quality and high volume. By contrast, the US and Europe have stressed quality, performance and delivery. Both approaches rely significantly on the ability to add value to the content of goods and services (Figure 2.1)

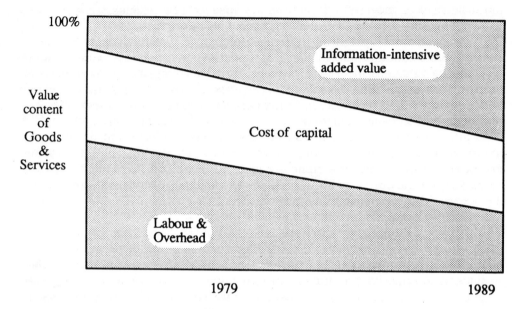

Figure 2.1 The value structure of the economy

At the same time, labour is being reduced in most industries, through automation and reorganisation. Indeed computer manufacturing reflects this with direct labour cost down to single figures as a percentage of sales. Capital is increasingly available on the international money markets as a commodity, at highly competitive rates, which reduces the cost of a company's working capital. In parallel with these trends is a growing realisation that what a company knows about its world and how it organises and manages this information—rather than its physical net assets—underpins its market value. This leaves the cost of capital plus information-dependent activities as the principal elements of adding value, and this is where corporate activity will increasingly be concentrated. To 'know what you know' and apply this to design, production, marketing, sales and service will move the management of information into the competitive arena in the years ahead. Within the scenario EDI will form an integral part of any future information infrastructure.

MEASURING THE VALUE OF INFORMATION

In the early justification of IT systems, value was synonymous with cost reduction, and benefits included staff savings which could be measured and validated by financial models such as cost/benefit analysis. This rationale is applied with increasing difficulty to new communication technologies such as EDI, which deliver significant benefits in the form of quality and time. It is evident from a recent study undertaken by OASiS into the major factors affecting the uptake of EDI, that early adopters felt that many of the benefits realised were qualitative in nature and as such were notoriously difficult to measure. This has resulted in many organisations accepting the results of a pilot implementation as the basis for understanding the benefits and costs associated with using EDI. By contrast, many other organisations have not been prepared to undertake a pilot and instead have deferred adoption in the absence of a business case capable of presenting the often highly qualitative benefits of using EDI.

A promising development in the measurement of qualitative benefits comes from the emergence of Information Economics. This applies economics rather than finance to assess the risk and value associated with the strategic use of information systems. This new field of analysis comes from the US where the work of Parker *et al* (publication in preparation) offers models to assess, *inter alia*: value by association, value by acceleration, and value by restructuring.

Value by association represents the ripple effect of incurring investment in one area which delivers benefits in another. For EDI, this typically involves the cost of data capture by one company and the associated benefit of reduced processing for parties elsewhere in a trading community. The initial registration of common details eliminates any further need for the community to re-input this data over the life of that product or service.

Value by acceleration causes benefits to be realised more quickly, by accelerating the rate of output from a department, business or trading community. This arises particularly in functions such as research, procurement, production and distribution. If you consider the pattern of resources committed during a product's life cycle (Figure 2.2), then it is apparent that the design phase commits significant forward-costs by predetermining the way in which costs are realised in the subsequent phases of development, commercialisation, marketing, sales and service support. For example, any flaws not detected in the design phase could impact on the time taken in development, the cost of selling, the reliability and hence cost of servicing in addition to the duration of the life cycle.

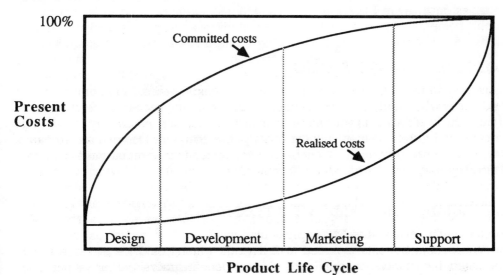

Figure 2.2 Resources committed during a project

The forward commitment of cost may represent as much as 80 per cent of the costs ultimately realised. EDI lowers the risk associated with this forward commitment of costs, by supporting the exchange of design information between supplier and system integrator/manufacturer. This collaboration increases the quality of knowledge and with it the chance of being 'right first time.'

In the subsequent phase of development, EDI also increases quality by facilitating the exchange of technical information and reducing lead times by eliminating paper chasing, and consequently releases capital for other purposes. It also affects market share by accelerating the delivery of products and services to the customer (first to market) and by providing a more responsive support service. The importance of this should be clear from the previous example in the aerospace sector. Incidentally, the Japanese have understood the significance of forward commitment of cost and that is why they apply a significant proportion of effort in quality assurance at the design stage.

Value restructuring assumes that because a function exists, such as quality assurance, it has some value. It follows that any change in the way a function is structured may of itself deliver greater productivity to other corporate activities. In this respect, EDI has given considerable support in realising new management philosophies that draw on restructuring. Procurement, for example, increasingly embraces value issues such as quality management which affect all the parties with which a company has dealings. In the US, this has advanced to the point where suppliers are rated each month, by the customer, on their ability to perform across a number of criteria including delivery, quality and service. Poor performers are dropped and overall quality increased. EDI for its part, automates much of this process and has thus enabled a wider vision of quality to be realised in practice, a vision that goes beyond the resource constraints of any single organisation.

Information economics does not seek to displace financial analysis but it does offer the prospect of providing a tool for management to assess the impact of communication technologies such as EDI, which deliver significant qualitative as well as quantitative benefits.

ORGANISATIONAL CHANGE

Automating by technology alone has, in the US experience, led to higher prices and of itself failed to stem an increasing cost differential in favour of the Japanese. It is through reorganisation in association with technology that the tide may be turned. It is essentially the organisation that wins the competitive battle, and not technology alone. To achieve this, senior management must champion the organisational change which accompanies automation and which is essential for the successful exploitation of EDI. This entails changes to business procedures, job roles, working practices, organisational structures, manning levels, and the flows and ownership of information. These are all very real issues consistently observed in EDI implementations.

Where office automation failed to deliver the paperless office and to impact in any significant way on organisational structure, the more pervasive nature of EDI which imports external influences and cuts across internal functions will probably succeed. These imported influences, such as competitive 'best practice', expose any comparative weakness in internal procedures and highlight the need for significant changes in business practice to operate more effectively and reap the benefits. This requires every person to change his or her behaviour with some degree of synchronisation. Managing this degree of change is something of which few organisations have experience today.

Some understanding of this can be gained from considering the first tier in a supply chain (Figure 2.3). The boxes represent functions such as tendering, R&D, procurement and production, all of which are common to an industry but never undertaken in quite the same way. For example, procurement and purchasing are performed in different ways by each of the organisations shown Even within procurement, each organisation differs in the way in which activities such as expediting, the process of chasing suppliers to meet delivery times, is performed. For some companies a buyer undertakes expediting, whereas in others a buyer may work in association with an expeditor, and for yet others a great number of specialist staff may perform this function who have no involvement in placing the order (buying). In this respect, EDI offers the opportunity to promulgate 'best practice' across the community. This not only reduces costs but, more significantly, allows each company to restructure a number of functions in line with the exemplar for that industry. This results in a matching function and activity across the trading community which in itself produces a marked increase in efficiency. Add to this automation through EDI, and the process goes even further. Restructuring functions in this way, by the use of automation (EDI) in association with reorganisation, eliminates some existing functions and creates new or hybrid functions.

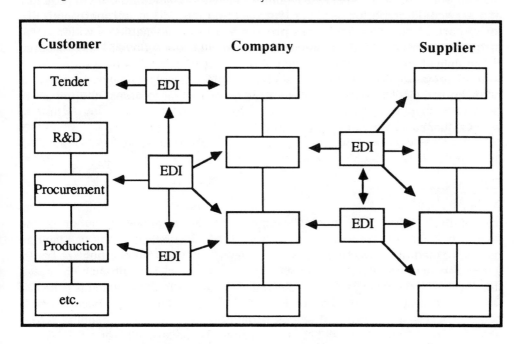

Figure 2.3   Information flows across a trading community

In the future, to remain competitive, organisations will need to view EDI in new ways and exploit the opportunity to accelerate decision making, direct information flows horizontally rather than vertically, and make information a right rather than a privilege. This will inevitably create new organisational structures, products and services affecting not only the people inside a company but also involving the wider business community. This will create the concept of 'virtual organisations' which will be formed as temporary or permanent associations with outside parties on the basis of functional or product collaboration. This is beginning to happen through EDI users taking opportunities to gain competitiveness in functions such as export, distribution, procurement and treasury management. This involves other companies, but in so doing delivers additional benefits to a community, so that the whole is greater than the sum of the parts.

An example of the opportunity for a virtual organisation lies in extending treasury management expertise to the wider community. This function presently serves large corporations in obtaining operating capital at interest rates more attractive that those offered by high street banks. To do this, the cash needs of operating companies are aggregated and a bulk purchase undertaken at discounted interest rates on the international money markets. Much of this process has been automated by using EDI. Should this application be extended across a trading community then smaller suppliers would receive considerable benefit. These non-corporate members, previously too small to access the preferential rates, could aggregate their cash needs alongside those of larger trading partners. The result would be a reduction in the cost of working capital which could lower their present interest rates significantly. Hence, as a result of the community pooling its expertise in treasury management and defining this as an EDI application, the industry becomes far more competitive. Furthermore because of the pervasive nature of EDI, the members of this virtual organisation need not reside in any single country or necessarily be in the same industry.

The management of organisational change is likely to be a limiting factor in obtaining the potential benefits from EDI. Research conducted by OASiS clearly indicates that most strategic information systems already cost two to three times more to implement organisationally than they do to buy or build. This imbalance is likely to become even more exaggerated with the advent of competitively priced EDI services, which are independent of vendor hardware, globally delivered and implemented to international or industry standards.

ACCELERATING DECISION MAKING

A different aspect of EDI which impacts on an organisation, arises from accelerating the decision-making process and taking days out of the business processing cycle. An extreme example of this comes from the finance sector where the frenetic activities of the dealing room shape the nature of the organisation and radically alter traditional notions of information ownership and decision making. Here, dealers demand information of high quality within very short time frames. Management has neither the time nor necessarily the expertise to debate its relevance or mediate in its distribution. The organisation is as a result lean, with information flows flattened to deliver what is needed to those who have the functional expertise to apply it.

By contrast, consider that most large international companies operate with more than five levels of management. A brief survey of managers' perceptions which OASiS has undertaken indicates that each manager's communication is represented by: 50 per cent information exchange to subordinates; 10 per cent with a boss; 10 per cent with peers; 10 per cent with customers.

There is only a very little left for value-added activities which might result in innovation. Organisations that fit this hierarchical model have several common characteristics. Predominantly, information flows upwards and management is empowered by virtue of its monopoly over information. Managers spend an inordinate amount of time debating its relevance and correctness, as well as miscommunicating it. For example, a company's information database of real customer and competitor knowledge often resides with a tiny proportion of its people and is limited compared with the potential for gathering data from wider sources.

As can be seen, much of a manager's information processing role is largely routine and in the future could be automated by using EDI in the form of distributed relational databases, conforming to international standards, and connected by networking technology. This will release time for managers to add considerably more in terms of value. Hence databases networked together could become the eyes through which an organisation see its world. To achieve this successfully, the management of information and its impact on organisation becomes a very real issue which requires a fundamental rethink of management roles. If however, management is able to adapt an organisation to harness the power of information then this will involve flattening the structure of information ownership to allow more staff to contribute greater value to business activities. This will in turn increase the corporate ability to respond to competitive pressure.

CORPORATE VULNERABILITY

Many large corporations have adopted a decentralised approach to the management of their operating companies. This has resulted in the centralisation of a few corporate activities such as procurement and treasury management, where it is accepted that economies of scale can be advantageous, although not at the expense of effectiveness. Control over activities ranging from business strategy to tactics is generally left to directors within each of the operating companies. As long as the business performs to agreed targets, individual companies continue to run autonomously. However, increasing aggressiveness on an international scale makes these corporations vulnerable to hostile takeover and the subsequent disposal of individual operating companies. This occurs in some cases because corporate activities add little value to the performance of the operating companies. Instead it concentrates on raising the overall share value by selling those subsidiaries with a low price/earnings ratio (P/E) and retaining or acquiring those which are higher.

The danger of this approach is its inability to make the whole greater than the sum of the parts and as a result the corporation is more vulnerable to predatory takeover and subsequent divestment. A defence against this is to use EDI to facilitate corporate-wide views of information, adding considerable value from identifying trends and opportunities not apparent in a decentralised company but able to be viewed from a central position. The added value from the central function would be threatened by any form of takeover which resulted in divestment and could therefore be used as an argument in a defence. Conversely, the divestment of an operating company would remove an important part of the corporate view and hence impair the 'sight' of that corporation. Furthermore the application of EDI in this way does not actively interfere with divisional management's right to manage.

EDI PENETRATION IN THE UK

Progress in the United Kingdom in the uptake of EDI varies from companies and individuals having a lack of awareness to sectors where usage is now growing. As can be seen in Figure 2.4 a few industries have now reached a ramp from which EDI uptake is expected to take off, the trajectory of which I leave to the pundits. These are not just the privileged few with massive data processing departments, but include sole-traders, partnerships, trade associations, and private and public companies.

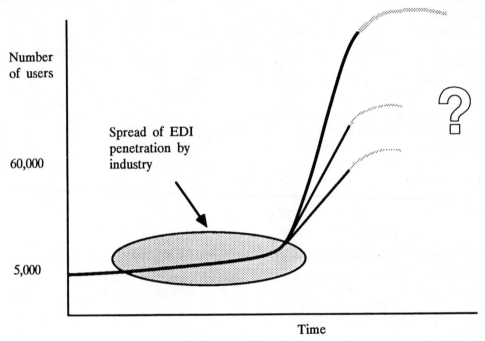

Figure 2.4   Present uptake of EDI in the UK

The successful uptake of EDI, along with other value added and data services (VADS), differs in several important ways from the adoption of other innovations and is characterised by the need to achieve a critical mass, a high degree of customisation, and a focus on implementation and use.

An accelerated rate of attaining a critical mass of users is important for realising the economic benefits associated with using EDI. In some industry sectors, there has been a delay in reaching anything like the critical mass needed to achieve economies of scale or to encourage the more laggardly companies to join an EDI community. The economic implications of this affect both the EDI supplier, looking for a return on capital, and the users seeking sufficient mass necessary to realise the full commercial benefits anticipated. The delay has been due in part to mismatch between the services marketed by the EDI suppliers and the potential users' inability to see or exploit any benefit, particularly where they perceive little value added to current business processes.

EDI incorporates a technological approach which can be applied in a variety of ways to business need. Typically, users seek to customise the application in the process of adoption. This customisation requires adjustment in both the organisation and the application to provide a better fit to corporate objectives. To achieve this absorbs significant resources in training and support. EDI users are dependent upon this support which to date has been provided through early adoptors, user associations, EDI suppliers and dealers. There is a question as to whether these organisations are prepared to absorb further EDI training and support as a cost of sales or of attaining critical mass. Failure to do this will slow down the rate of EDI uptake.

The ease of use and spread of EDI, rather than just the decision to adopt or the process of implementation, is the critical success factor in the long term. This is presently hampered by a lack of senior management and DP awareness of the strategic nature of EDI. This, in an increasingly commodity-oriented market-place for the provision of IT services, suggests the need for education in assessing the relative commercial value of packaged and bespoke solutions in providing EDI as a service to business users. Organisations without a pro-active IT infrastructure do, however, need a packaged approach to procurement which addresses the business, legal, organisational, implementation and tech-nical issues of buying an EDI service. The discussion so far has been on the direct impacts which are desirable and largely anticipated. I now turn to indirect unanticipated and perhaps unwelcome consequences which will inevitably arise from the adoption of EDI in the broader context of communication technology, namely: function deskilling and unemployment, information overload, decen-tralisation and invasion of privacy.

FUNCTION DESKILLING AND UNEMPLOYMENT

Automation lies at the heart of the information society and sociologists argue that this dramatically increases productivity while eliminating jobs on a massive scale. Industrial manufacturing is the chief target for computer automation with office administration close behind. The good news is that communication technology will generate new jobs: the bad news is that the uses to which this is put will displace proportionately more jobs. This imbalance for the US is projected at around ten to one and will be achieved primarily by function deskilling. This is the process by which EDI displaces a function with techno-logically-assisted cheaper labour. This can be compared with the impact of modern point-of-sales systems which are progressively displacing the function of check-out staff.

Whereas robotics and office automation are displacing manual and clerical skills respectively, it is likely that EDI will displace white collar skills such as bookkeeping, logistics and administration. This will no doubt be fuelled by the fire of international competitiveness which unfortunately takes no hostages. The more complex cultural nature of Europe may resist the ravages of deskilling, but some heed should be taken of the US where white collar employment is falling to the impacts of computers and communication technology. There is some comfort, however, in the fact that, despite a massive $40 billion spent on automation in the US manufacturing sector, the overall general level of unemployment remains at under six per cent.

INFORMATION OVERLOAD

Information gaps arise from a proportionately greater increase in the availability of certain information to part of the population. This gap widens over time, with the information rich getting richer, under the influence of new uses for communication technology. This is known by sociologists as the 'Mathew effect' in which: ''unto everyone that hath shall be given, and he shall have abundance; but from him that hath not shall be taken away even that which he hath'' (Matt. 25 v.29). A remarkable exception to this has been the free distribution by the French PTT of Minitel, an interactive videotex system which links homes throughout France to public and commercial information services. This is a far-sighted move which advances the French as an information society and distributes the privileges of information-access throughout society.

The information-rich may benefit from applying this information to their own gain, but with more information made available they will increasingly be faced with problems of 'information overload'. This is the state in which excessive communication inputs cannot be processed, leading to individual and organisa- tional breakdown. Symptoms of this are already evident in the financial sector where many dealers gain significant rewards from access to communication technology but experience information-overload and are burnt-out before reaching 30 years of age. This cannot be attributed merely to the general pressure of work but derives from the constancy of absorbing and analysing information to devise market tactics within the framework of a few seconds.

Given that Europe alone boasts over 4000 publicly-accessible databases, the prospect of sifting through the massive amounts of information they hold is bewildering. Yet this is the arena ahead, heralding a growing reliance on information and accelerating response times in decision making. This will be necessary to survive.

Scientists, engineers and managers who work in information-saturated en- vironments must filter increasingly larger amounts of information. Will senior management consequently be swamped with messages? (Within the broader context of VADS an example of this recently arose in the use of electronic mail. A colleague undertook an assignment for a major international company, where he was allocated an electronic mail box for the duration of a project. Unfor- tunately he was informed of this a fortnight after commencing work and on gaining access was confronted with the prospect of reading 160 messages.) The answer to this problem may be to use EDI to structure and hence filter the information. This, in association with information-based retrieval systems or knowledge-based applications, offers some means of coping with the problem of overload.

DECENTRALISATION AND INVASION OF PRIVACY

Optimistic predictions for the US estimate that by 1990 some five per cent of the workforce and 10 per cent of information workers will be telecommuters, working at least partly at home. Will such a pattern apply to Europe and does the removal of the constraining effect of physical distance between two individuals increase the volume of messages they exchange? Or by enabling employees to work at home will EDI, in association with on-line databases, increase the physical barriers to interaction among colleagues? Will senior management be overloaded with messages when employees are connected via a communication network?

Little research has been undertaken to understand these issues which are the meat of communication analysis. These issues reiterate the earlier theme of this paper which stresses the need to review organisational structures and culture in the light of the growing need for a wider view of information management.

With the inclusion of computers in communication systems, gaining access to the wider public, the disclosure of private information is no longer simply in the hands of individuals. A computer's capacity for memory and interaction, coupled with the pervasive nature of telecommunication, provides the possibility for invasion of privacy. An example of this is the use of communication to reduce absenteeism in American schools. There, a computer-based voice messaging system automatically contacts the parents of children who fail to attend, and requests that they discuss the absence with the Principal; it also records their responses. EDI can be applied in a similar way to monitor an employee's performance, as in the case of the administration of sales representatives, and is increasingly encroaching on the home. The boundaries between the work and home, private and public information are becoming distinctly fuzzy.

THE MANAGEMENT CHALLENGE

A report on the economic gains of the European Community from creating a single market by 1992 surveyed 11,000 companies across Europe and concluded, "It is neither a Christmas present nor an Easter egg. This is a potential which has to be used by the Governments of member states, Industry and other economic protagonists". These benefits amount to some £136 billion in savings and an increase of up to seven per cent in Gross Domestic Product (GDP) from: economies of scale, market integration, competition and collaboration.

There is no doubt that EDI will play a significant role in any progress towards achieving this, particularly in supporting competitiveness, economies of scale, rationalisation and collaboration in an increasingly international marketplace. EDI will provide a common business procedure which, depending how you view it, transcends or subverts political, cultural and geographical barriers and accelerates progress in achieving a common market, despite other constraints. This is already happening in the aerospace and chemical industries where pan-European EDI networks link organisations in many countries. Progress in the uptake of EDI for the United Kingdom is some 18 to 30 months ahead of continental Europe and potentially gives UK industry a competitive advantage. Consolidating this in terms of European ECUs requires urgent action by individual companies and whole industries in taking the initiative of adopting EDI. What is apparent is that the prospects for those companies which ignore EDI can be compared with driving into the future with eyes firmly fixed on the rear view mirror—blissfully unaware of what lies ahead.

Standards for EDI

Perhaps standardisation seems a dry topic. However, much of the story of EDI is synonymous with that of standards for data interchange. Agreed standards between users are a precondition for EDI.

The computer industry has spawned may proprietary protocols. 'Lock-in', through commitment of users to such protocols, has sometimes seemed an overt tactic of certain computer manufacturers. Perhaps the most exciting aspect of EDI, from a technological point of view, is the renewed impetus it gives to the implementation of open standards. Such published, widely agreed, conventions are the lifeblood of EDI. That is why this section is devoted to them.

Nigel Fenton, Executive Secretary of the Article Numbering Association, commences his paper with a valuable discussion of the distinction between message and communications standards. He then proceeds to give an account of the main standards-making bodies. This material forms an excellent introduction to the complex subject. Most of the organisations he mentions have provided more details which you may want to refer to later, in the *Further Information* section of this book,.

Subsequent papers in this section treat the two subjects of message standards and communications standards in more detail. Tom McGuffog treats message standards through detailed reference to the TRADACOMS story. As chairman of the TRADACOMS working party of the Article Number Assoication, he has been involved with the development of the standard messages and the Tradanet network since 1979.

Finally in this section Paul Dawkins, a communications consultant with Scicon Limited, writes about open communications standards. His main concerns are with the Open Systems Interconnection model of the International Standards Organisation and with the CCITT X.400 series of recommendations. Both these technical topics are treated in a clear, tutorial fashion: they are important to the future health of EDI.

3
A Review of the Relationships and Roles of the Standards Making Bodies

Nigel Fenton

INTRODUCTION

This paper is intended to provide a broad summary of current developments in the field of standards for electronic data communications. Further details concerning these developments are given in the section entitled *Further Information*. The paper attempts to cover most of the mainstream data communications activity affecting UK companies, but it is not all-embracing. Particularly, it does not consider the numerous closed user-group systems where these are not directly relevant to inter-industry commercial transactions.

It focuses on the exchange of data for commercial transactions between computers and is not directly concerned with interpersonal terminal-to-terminal text or messaging applications. The term Electronic Data Interchange (EDI) is now widely accepted to describe the applications covered by this paper. EDI may be defined as the electronic transfer from computer to computer of administrative and commercial or trade-related data in a standard structured format.

BACKGROUND: USER STANDARDS AND OSI

The term 'standards' is possibly the most used and abused word in the jargon-laden field of electronic communications between computer systems. In an environment where the possible permutations of computer devices, links, file designs, protocols, and data formats seems infinite, users are naturally anxious to achieve some semblance of order by agreeing and defining some common approaches. It is a measure of the eagerness with which users approach anything purporting to be a standard that the term has sometimes been applied when as few as two users are doing the same thing. The development and use of standards can broadly be defined as:

> *The harmonisation of communications between computer systems to allow interworking independently of the nature of the systems involved.*

The expression Open Systems Interconnection (OSI) is often used to embrace this objective. A system (of computers, software, terminals and data transfer mechanisms) is open if it can interwork with another system, using OSI standards.

OSI standards are being progressed on a worldwide basis by two bodies: the International Standards Organisation (ISO) and Comité Consultatif International Telegraphique et Telephonique (CCITT). These two bodies are endeavouring to work in step to achieve compatibility and in many cases the same people are involved with both standardisation efforts. Whilst ISO has formal responsibility for OSI standards, CCITT has done much practical work in the design of telecommunication equipment. In order to assist in an understanding of the objectives of OSI standards, a common reference model, the seven layer model, was developed to define a structure for communications between computer systems. Each layer represents separate communications-oriented functions and processing-oriented functions which go together hierarchically to build, ultimately, a completely open environment. Paul Dawkin's paper, later in this book, gives a tutorial view of OSI standards.

What OSI standards *do not* provide is a prescription for the nature of the messages to be exchanged between two partners wishing to communicate, for example, the format in which ordinary commercial data (such as orders, invoices, stock files and delivery information) and technical data (such as graphics) should be assembled for electronic transfer between different companies. In other words, even if every piece of hardware, every peripheral and every file were perfectly harmonised and compatible, the user would still have the problem of understanding the data sent to him in the absence of an agreed language. This is analogous to the telephone network, where the most sophisticated exchanges, satellite links and cordless phones will not assist if the callers cannot speak the same language, nor have a common understanding of the concept they are discussing.

In recognition of this, several bodies have set about defining standards for common data languages for a range of applications.

If a range of users can agree a common language and concept for their data communications, they can, by one means or another, surmount difficulties caused through the incompatibility of systems. This is why hundreds of companies in the UK are already conducting electronic data exchange, despite the absence of a full set of OSI standards. These user-built data languages or formatting conventions do not encroach upon the OSI approach. They are conventions for user data emanating from one, hopefully open, system for receipt into another system, in a structure agreed by the user. Figure 3.1 suggests one way of perceiving the relationship between such conventions and the OSI seven-layer model.

Just as the world accommodates many dozens of spoken languages despite the obvious theoretical benefit of having just one, so the computer world has developed, and continues to develop, different conventions for data formatting, depending on the application, its users, and the country of origin. Whilst born of necessity, this approach brings with it the same problems associated with the spoken word: there is a language barrier, which may only be overcome through a restriction in the number of different languages which are supported by a working community, and through the availability of good interpreters. The topmost level or Application layer of the OSI model may be considered as an absolute standard for a given data application: that is a standard for such things as in-house data structure or file design which, if adopted by every user, would allow true open systems interconnection. The difficulty is that standards of this type may not be practical in certain areas, an illustration being commercial

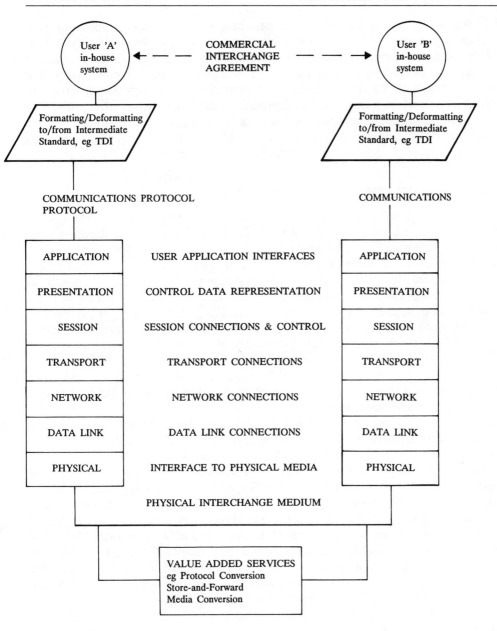

Figure 3.1 Perceived relationship between OSI standards and user-driven TDI-based systems

transactions where differences in business practice—for example taxation terms—across national boundaries may prove insurmountable.

In the absence of Application layer standards, the availability of an intermediate bridging format such as TRADACOMS or ODETTE, can provide a valuable working link between systems. The fact that users' own systems are based on different designs or infrastructures matters less because users can convert data received in the intermediate format into whatever structure their own application demands. Indeed, even if OSI solutions were never achieved,

EDI message standards would still provide a viable data processing tool, because they can so effectively bridge the gap between different systems.

This paper attempts to identify some of the principle areas of activity where user groups or industries are striving to achieve electronic communications through the use of available standards, or through the development of standards where none exist. In assessing some areas of activity, it is not always possible to distinguish absolutely between user-built standards and ISO standards, particularly since the former may develop into the latter if they are widely supported.

THE COMPONENTS OF EDI STANDARDS

The essential components or building blocks of EDI standards are an important issue. The working standards described in the following sections have varying degrees of commonality in the method they have adopted for standards design. The relative merits of these methods—for example the choice of syntax or the use of qualifiers—is a subject which often provokes lively debate, but should not detract from the underlying importance of EDI as an established practical tool.

Reference is made in the following sections to 'syntax rules'. These are the electronic data interchange equivalent of the grammar rules which are used in written language to structure communication. Until relatively recently most UK and European EDI users have based their standards on the United Nations Trade Data Interchange (UNTDI) syntax (United Nations Economic Commission for Europe: Guideline for Trade Data Interchange). This system is highly flexible and provides guidelines on syntax (character sets and transmission formatting rules) and on segment and message construction. There is also an associated directory of data elements, data elements being the basic components of an EDI message.

It should be noted that recent initiatives have been taking place to bridge the differences which exist between the UNTDI syntax and the American National Standards Institute's equivalent system known as ANSI X.12. The objective is to allow the building of EDI standards which will be valid for trade across international boundaries. The project began life as a joint effort between European and American EDI experts, and was christened Joint Electronic Data Interchange (JEDI). Following the agreements reached by the JEDI representatives on principles and syntax, the project has received widespread support from many countries and user communities and, importantly, from the EEC. It is known as Electronic Data Interchange for Administration, Commerce and Transport (EDIFACT).

The new EDIFACT EDI syntax has already been accepted as a full International standard: ISO 9735. The EDIFACT syntax is not greatly dissimilar from UNTDI, but there are some important differences which also have an impact on the method of standard message design. International standard messages (UNSMs) are now being developed as part of the EDIFACT project, which is coordinated by the EDIFACT Board and Steering Committee. Advanced drafts of the invoice and order files are already available. Other files are being developed as quickly as possible in order of perceived priority.

UNSMs are being based on the United Nations data element directory with new elements being created as necessary. They also use the concept of qualifiers, well established in ANSI X.12 standards. Qualifiers are codes used to confer a specific function or identify on a generic data element or segment. The effect of this is, in principle, to reduce the requirement for many specific data elements. Lists of approved qualifying codes do need to be maintained however.

The development of UNSMs is a time-consuming process, since the resulting message must take into account the genuine requirements of every country and industry which wishes to make an input. The price for great flexibility is one of complexity, and UNSMs are of necessity somewhat elaborate in their design and content. For example, some segments will be of critical importance to some industries and of no relevance to others. These segments will be of conditional status, and omitted from transmissions where unnecessary. Further details on the availability of UNSMs and on the EDIFACT project in general are obtainable from the UK Simplification of International Trade Procedures Board (SITPRO).

It should not be assumed that the EDIFACT standards or syntax will immediately or indeed ever supersede or outmode standards based on UNTDI, which have a large, established and successful user base. Nevertheless, there is growing support in principle for the evolution toward EDIFACT standards as the solution for EDI across national boundaries.

EDI MESSAGE/FILE DESIGNS

Data elements can be combined and assembled, using the appropriate syntax rules, into standard message designs. The standard message prescribes the accepted content and order of data elements for a particular application type—for example, invoice or delivery note. The objective of standards designers must be to achieve message formats which genuinely reflect the real business requirements of users. The meaning of an EDI message is what matters more to the user, in the working environment, than the underlying syntax or structure. Narrowly applicable, inflexible, highly customised messages will be of little value if they only suit the needs of a few companies. Conversely, standard messages which are so flexible and generic that they could mean anything to anyone will in practise mean nothing to everyone. Striking the right balance is not an easy task. In addition, multiple or competing message designs for a given application are against the interests of users. New EDI users searching for standards should realise the immense benefits of adopting existing standards wherever possible. Developing new messages unnecessarily is hard work, restricts the number of trading partners who can benefit and may limit the growth of EDI in an entire sector of business.

This said, the number of different application areas or industry sectors for which standards are required has meant that no single body could design all the necessary messages. The following section of the article lists some of the key areas where standards have been designed for and by user communities and details can be found in the section entitled *Further Information.*.

EDI STANDARDS—USER-COMMUNITIES IN THE UK

TRADACOMS: standards for electronic data communications

This is a complete system of data formatting specifications, message designs and component data elements for practical trading communication applications. The data elements, which have been designed by the Article Number Association (ANA) to meet the day-to-day commercial requirements of UK business, have alphabetic tags. The TRADACOMS standards are based on the United Nations Trade Data Interchange (UNTDI) syntax and message design method.

Formats are provided for transaction files: order; uplift notes; stock adjustment; delivery notes; uplift confirmation; invoices; delivery confirmation; credit notes; picking lists; statements; availability report; general text; stock snapshots; and the product, price, and customer information master files.

Over 1000 companies across the complete range of UK industries currently use the standards: the largest example of an EDI community in Europe. These include most multiple retailers, and suppliers from the grocery, hardware, pharmaceutical, electronic component, chemical, stationery, cosmetic, textile and service sectors. Maintenance Authority: Article Number Association (UK) Ltd, 6 Catherine Street, London WC2B 5JJ. Telephone: 01 836 2460.

H M Customs & Excise Period Entry System

H M Customs & Excise use some UN data elements and many application specific elements, all with mnemonic tags, as part of their Period Entry data communications system. The Period Entry standard is based on a forerunner to the UNTDI syntax and is used by large import/export concerns to send data to H M Customs & Excise.

Period Entry currently makes use of a SITPRO facility called Format Segments. This facility, which is an extension to the basic syntax rules, allows data elements in data segments to be defined explicitly within the transmission. This is achieved through the use of format segments which identify the tags of the elements to be included, and the order in which they will appear. Maintenance Authority: H M Customs & Excise Office, Dorset House, Stamford Street, London SE1 9PS. Telephone: 01 928 0533.

Organisation for Data Exchange by Teletransmission in Europe (ODETTE)

The objective of the ODETTE project is to progress the implementation of European standards to allow the transfer of data between suppliers and manufacturers, primarily in the motor industry. Because the provision of motor components may be from a variety of countries, into a manufacturing process which itself may be in several countries, a European-wide approach has been pursued. A number of working groups have been established to progress the specific areas of concern, for example syntax rules, data element and message design, transmission mechanisms, test programmes, inter-country exchange, and product identification.

Standard message designs originally based on UNTDI design principles, are well established for the following functions: delivery instruction; despatch advice; invoice. Further formats (including orders, credit notes, confirmation of delivery and ready for despatch advice) are also being established.

A large proportion of the data elements used in the ODETTE messages use UN data elements. Other new elements have been created, and submitted to the UN Trade Data Exchange Directory Secretariat for inclusion. In the UK and around Europe, live use of the standard ODETTE formats is underway amongst a number of motor companies and their immediate suppliers. ODETTE has expressed its intention to migrate towards use of EDIFACT messages (UNSMs) as rapidly as is practical, and is a major contributor to the EDIFACT project.

Within the UK motor industry as a whole, a range of EDI message standards are currently in use, including early national formats produced by SMMT, and it may therefore be some while before a totally coherent standards approach is attained. Maintenance Authority: SMMT Ltd, ODETTE (UK) Secretariat, Forbes House, Halkin Street, London SW1X 7DS. Telephone: 01 235 7000.

Data Interchange In Shipping (DISH)

A group of major shippers, forwarders and carriers, with the support of SITPRO, have developed a system of standards to cover: booking instructions; shipping instruction; maritime transport; contract information and other deep sea transport related messages. Live use of the messages is underway. Messages originally based on UNTDI are being redesigned using EDIFACT methodology. Further details can be obtained from: John Sanders, EDI Development Manager, Trafalgar House Group Services, PO Box 681, Southampton SO9 7PB. Telephone: 0703 552809.

United Nations (message) Concept Over Reservation Networks (UNICORN)

The UNICORN project is a collaborative venture between P&O European Ferries, Sealink and other companies in the holiday travel trade to develop a system of standards for on-line reservation facilities for travel agencies connected to participating travel operators. These standards will be based on UNTDI/EDIFACT syntax. An introduction to the venture is given in Anthony Allen's article in the section entitled *Examples of EDI in practice*. Further details can be obtained from: A D Allen, Sealink UK Ltd, Eversholt House, 163-203 Eversholt Street, London NW1 1BG. Telephone: 01 387 1234.

International Chamber of Shipping (ICS)

The ICS are working to produce EDI messages, covering the movement of cargo-related data between port of loading and port of discharge. The new EDIFACT syntax and message design methodology is being adopted. Further details can be obtained from: B Parkinson, General Council of British Shipping, 30/32 St Mary Axe, London EC3A 8ET. Telephone: 01 283 2922.

SHIPNET

An initiative by shipping exporters and freight forwarders to develop interactive EDI systems via network links, using DISH message standards. Further details can be obtained from: EDI Association, c/o SITPRO, 26/28 King Street, London SW1X 6QW. Telephone: 01 930 0532.

The EDI Association

An association has recently been formed which aims to bring together prospective and current users of EDI for *international* trade purposes. It will represent the UK in areas such as the formulation of standards and the way in which EDI is applied to international trade procedures. The association will be of particular interest to those involved in international trade and transport services, for example freight forwarders, air, sea and surface carriers and agents, ports, ICDs and airports etc. Projects currently being conducted under the auspices of DISH and SHIPNET are also likely to be embraced by the new association. Further details can be obtained from: EDI Association, c/o SITPRO, 26/28 King Street, London SW1X 6QW. Telephone: 01 930 0530.

Construction

The construction industry can benefit significantly from EDI for example to speed orders, deliveries and contractual transactions. An industry association, EDICON, has been formed to assist the industry in adopting and implementing EDI standards. Working groups have been established to explore areas such as the order and invoice cycle, exchange of bills of quantity information, and exchange of drawings. Further details can be obtained from: John Sanders, PO Box 681, Southampton SO9 7PB. Telephone: 0703 552809.

INTENDED APPLICATION AREAS OF ELECTRONIC DATA EXCHANGE STANDARDS

CAD/CAM

There is a widespread requirement for standards for CAD/CAM data transfer. Standards are needed, as with commercial transactions, for the contents of the transmitted data, which must be acceptable to all CAD/CAM systems at a high level. The requirements can be identified at three levels:

> *Graphical:* for example, contents of a graph or screen,
> coordinates, characters and graphical symbols.
> *Paper:* for example, engineering drawings, illustrated documents.
> *Application:* complex exchanges for example, curved surfaces,
> 3D models.

For the first level (graphical) the GKS Graphical Kernel System Standard is available. This is a full British Standard and a Draft International Standard (BS 6360, DIS 7942). Between the second and third level, a number of standards or interfaces exist. These include: Initial Graphics Exchange Specification (IGES); Standard d'Exchange et de Transfer (SET); Products Definition Data Interchange (PDDI).

Document interchange

This application covers the formats and encoding of office documents for exchange via electronic messaging systems. Developing standards in this area are:

> *ISO/TC97/SC18*
> Draft Proposal 8613 Information Processing—Text Preparation
> and Interchange—Text Structures.
> Draft Proposal 8505 Information Processing—Text
> Communication—Functional Description of Message Oriented
> Text Interchange System.

Draft Proposal 8506 Information Processing—Text Communication
—Service Specification for Message Oriented Text Interchange
Systems.
ECMA 93
Messages Interchange Distributed Application Standard (MIDA).
ECMA TC29
Office Document Architecture.
CCITT
A range of recommendations covering Basic Text Interchange
(Teletext) and the X.400 Message Handling Services
recommendations. It should be noted that the CCITT and ECMA
standards are being developed in conjunction with ISO, and
compatibility is therefore not an issue.

Cartographic

Ordnance Survey and other organisations involved in cartography have a
requirement for electronic exchange of digital map data. Ordnance Survey
believe IGES to be unsuitable and are not planning to adopt TDI. A specific
standard is being progressed in conjunction with European partners. Details are
available from: The Secretary, National Transfer Standards Group, Ordnance
Survey, Romsey Road, Southampton SO9 4DH.

Aerospace

A system of data-formatting standards to support projects for the design and
manufacture of aircraft is being progressed by the Commission Technical and
Industriel (CTI) of the Association Européenne des Constructeurs de Matériel
Aérospatial (AECMA).

The aim is to develop guidelines which will facilitate the exchange of
computerised data between partners on collaborative aircraft projects. Whilst
data is already exchanged electronically on most projects, the data structure
and mechanisms are never the same. The objective of CTI is to develop a data
dictionary of elements and messages and to publish guidelines on the exchange
of these messages. Details are available from: The Maintenance Authority ,
Computer Data Exchange Working Group, British Aerospace, Middleton,
Manchester M24 1SA.

Bibliographic/book ordering/publishing

A number of standards are in operation amongst publishers and libraries for the
exchange of bibliographic data. Determined efforts are currently underway to
rationalise these standards in the UK, primarily via the Book Electronic Data
Interchange Standards (BEDIS) Committee. Further details are available from:
David Whitaker, Chairman, BEDIS Working Party, c/o J Whitaker & Sons Ltd, 12
Dyott Street, London WC1A 1DF. Telephone: 01-836 8911

The existing standards include:

Machine Readable Cataloguing (MARC)
MARC is an implementation of ISO 2709 for bibliographic

information exchange. It is well established within the
international Library Community as the basis for bibliographic
EDI. It provides a record format with a leader directory, and a
range of fixed and variable length data fields. There are a
number of working versions, for example UK Marc and Library
of Congress Marc. The UK Maintenance Authority may be
contacted at: 2 Sheraton St, London W1V 4BH.

Book Industry Systems Advisory Committee (BISAC)
BISAC is a US standard, likely to be subsumed as an ANSI
standard. In its early version, BISAC provides fixed field formats
for purchase orders, invoices and confirmation messages. The
currently promoted version uses variable length fields and is
compatible with MARC. BISAC is used in the US, but not in the
UK. Maintenance Authority: BISAC, 160 Fifth Avenue, New York.

Serials Industry Systems Advisory Committee (SISAC) Standards
are under development for exchange of data on serial
publications, using BISAC methodology. It is worth noting that a
detailed comparison has been undertaken within the book trade
of the BISAC and TRADACOMS standards; this has, not
surprisingly, illustrated minimal compatibility or coincidence of
data elements. The UK book trade has yet to take a consolidated
view of its approach towards electronic exchange, but is actively
assessing the available alternatives.

Standard Generalised Markup Language (SGML)—Draft
International Standard 8879.
This standard provides a means of being able to separate the
contents of a document from its style of presentation. The
elements of a document, for example, headings, sub-headings,
paragraphs, are marked as such (a principle known as generic
markup). The font and other display characteristics are not
encoded. The standard is likely to be of value in electronic
publishing. For further information contact: BSI, 2 Park St, London
W1A 2BS.

TRADACOMS
For further information see Tom McGuffog's paper which follows
this chapter.

Banking

For financial transactions and data exchange, covering exchange via BACS, from
banks to customers, between banks, and between credit card companies and
retailers/banks, a comprehensive range of standards are published by the
Association for Payment Clearing Services (APACS). Because of the fairly static
content of financial transactions, these standards contain relatively simple
layouts for the data content. Work within ISO is also progressing in the
Banking/Funds Transfer area. Further information may be obtained from:
APACS, 32 City Road, London EC1Y 1AA. Telephone: 01 628 7080.

Insurance

The insurance sector has addressed the development of standards for electronic data communications. The British Insurance Association (BIA) established two working parties to examine methods of improving communications within the insurance industry. However, no standards were formally adopted or published: the industry has now redirected its attention to the provision of a mechanism (for example, a network) for data exchange with no ongoing work in the standards area. The British Insurance Brokers Association (BIBA) is also assessing the benefits of electronic communications. Again, no published findings are available.

A community of insurance companies working together with INS under the Brokernet project have developed a range of UNTDI-based message standards for motor insurance documents. Details are obtainable from: Brokernet, International Network Services, Station Road, Sunbury-on-Thames, Middlesex TW16 6SB. Telephone: 0932 761030.

KEY STANDARD SYSTEMS IN USE OUTSIDE THE UK

The standards described below, unlike EDIFACT discussed earlier, are unlikely to have a significant impact on UK traders.

ANSI X.12

The X.12 standards are produced by the American National Standards Institute. The syntax is not based on UNTDI, but bears some resemblance in terms of the segment and message design structure. The standards cover orders, invoices, despatch, advice and several other applications. A number of community-specific standards, such as Uniform Communications Systems (UCS), see below, are based on the ANSI X.12 syntax, which is regarded as the indigenous standards building methodology in the US.

Uniform Communications Systems (UCS)

This system of standards is maintained and published by the Uniform Code Council, the American National Numbering Authority (the US equivalent of ANA). The standards, which are based on an independent data element directory, contain formats for documents such as orders, invoices, statements and promotion announcements. They are currently used by around 120 companies in America.

The EAN numbering authority standards

Several other member countries of the International Article Number Association (EAN) have produced data formatting standards for commercial data. These include the Swedish 'Dakom' system, the German 'Sedas' system, and the Dutch 'Transcom' standards.

The New Zealand, Australian and South African numbering authorities are all developing EDI standards, generally using the EDIFACT syntax and TRADA-COMS message designs as reference models.

DISCUSSION

A great deal of activity is taking place in the standards-making world: the extent and diversity of this work is immense, and has raised concerns about the likelihood of, and indeed necessity for, total harmonisation. There appear to be two general categories of standardisation work. The first of these is the development by national and international standards bodies such as BSI and ISO of 'absolute' standards for structure and communication of data for a vast range of applications. These may be seen as providing standards for Layer 7 or 'application level' of the OSI model. The second general category is the production of bridging format or EDI message standards with which users can exchange data regardless of the nature of their individual application systems.

Users with a clear or urgent commercial requirement to establish electronic communications have shown that, by one means or another, solutions can be implemented relatively quickly. In a world where business pressures are paramount, these solutions may not accord with a more theoretical, wider-scale approach to national/international standards making. Furthermore, users who are achieving real benefits with implemented systems may need to be given very good reasons to change to a new standard. Altruism is unlikely to be a real motive.

In specialist areas, the production of standards may depend on the expertise of a small number of individuals, who are better equipped than other, more objective standards making bodies to develop working solutions quickly for their immediate needs. The most effective standards are achieved by business experts with technical guidance, and not *vice versa*. Communication between groups working in similar areas is not always totally effective, particularly where differences in approach, concept and objectives may be overcome less painfully (in the short term) through the production of multiple solutions than through compromises and changes in underlying business practise.

For these and many other reasons the production of standards does not follow a steady path. Moreover there are some who hold the view that total standardisation, in a world where there are so many variations in requirements, is impossible. Esperanto, despite all its attractions, never became established. Nevertheless, strong efforts must be made to restrict diversification, if only to make interpretation between different standards more practical. Certainly, a major educational effort is permanently required, so that divergent standards are not created merely through ignorance of what already exists. The emergence of the new EDIFACT standards offers real scope for international EDI. There remains much work to be done before EDIFACT messages are numerous enough and sufficiently tested to offer a definitive EDI solution, but the opportunity to use EDIFACT in import and export related EDI is now a reality.

However, the United Nations Data Element Directory does not, and perhaps cannot, make provision for data elements to cover every conceivable EDI application. Its main aim must be to provide elements for international trade which by definition is only one among numerous scientific and business activities requiring different data element directions. Moreover, it is question-able whether it is practicable to have a common set of EDI messages which apply internationally in a given context (for example in the motor industry, aerospace, or international trade) and which are also valid for internal domestic trade in a given country. This is because of wide variations in interpretation of terms which have similar names ('price', 'discount', 'net', 'recommended' are a few examples), and because export/import systems and transactions often differ significantly from their home trade equivalents. One can therefore envisage a situation where a proven national standard such as TRADACOMS can work in parallel with the EDIFACT messages being constructed to meet international trade requirements.

Given that user groups/industries will define the most appropriate EDI messages for their own needs, active efforts should be made to encourage them to follow a mainstream approach. In addition, it can be strongly argued that all businesses will benefit most from the existence of one set of standard messages for the electronic exchange of basic commercial trading data in the UK. Scientific, engineering, bibliographic, construction and other specialist areas may also need to develop their own sets of standards, to cater for their particular specialised applications.

There is no merit in pretending to the business community that two or more overlapping sets of standards are not going to cost more money than one set. Overlapping standards cost more to implement, maintain and enhance. They cost more money to support, and networks offering 'conversion' from one standard to another (even if this could be achieved without introducing ambiguity) must charge relatively higher prices.

The use of standards is a voluntary process, although commercial pressure within a trading community may lead to a rapid implementation of a working system. Would-be users of EDI must seek a standards solutions which has the widest possible support, internationally or nationally, and which has the least chance of leaving the user isolated from the trading community as a whole.

4

Message Standards for EDI

Tom McGuffog

THE NEED FOR STANDARD MESSAGES

The need for the electronic exchange of trading messages between companies became increasingly obvious as they reduced paperwork internally through computerisation. Sophisticated systems are continually being developed within companies to process orders received electronically from their salesmen, to route orders electronically to depots for assembly and delivery to customers, and to confirm deliveries electronically to head office for immediate invoice preparation by computer. However, the receipt of orders from customers' computer systems was by paper, as was the communication of invoices back to them. This resulted in delays in trading and increased errors and costs in administration.

Nevertheless, the electronic exchange of messages between companies has become increasingly common since the 1970s. Formatting a computer file so that it can be interpreted by another company is relatively straightforward. So too is exchanging that file by magnetic tape or even by direct computer-to-computer transmission, although this latter job can absorb a remarkable amount of technical energy when 'experts' put their minds to it.

Indeed, most EDI still falls into the category of communicating a file of data which is going to be printed out by the recipient or displayed on a computer terminal, before being actioned by a person. Even though companies are increasingly redeveloping their internal systems to ensure the automatic processing, routing and actioning of business messages, much of the external trading data is not yet in a form to be treated in a similar way. Since EDI can mean almost any exchange of data between companies, it is more exact to describe the subject of this chapter as Electronic Trading Data Interchange (ETDI): that is the exchange of well-defined, standard messages via an integrated network.

In the later 1970s some major retailers in the UK were keen to reduce the amount of administrative effort involved in processing delivery notes relating to suppliers' deliveries, pricing these, and then matching the priced delivery note totals against the totals of the subsequently received invoices. They wished to receive these invoices from suppliers on magnetic tape in a fixed format (unique to each retailer) so that there would not be the effort and errors involved in their staff keying and matching documents.

At that time, it was clear to the Article Number Association (ANA) that there would be major disadvantages to companies if each retailer continued to insist on its own unique format. The Trading Data Communication (TRADACOMS) Standards Group was set up by the ANA to agree a common format for such invoices on magnetic tape. However it rapidly became apparent to the TRADACOMS Standards Group that the real benefits from ETDI came not simply from all companies being able to receive all their electronic trading messages in a form which could be read into their computer systems automatically. Major additional advantages would come if these messages could then be automatically routed to precisely the point in companies' internal systems where action would be taken to fulfil the transaction, for example an order packed for delivery or an invoice cleared for payment.

Thus, the electronic passage of the trading message from company to company is only a limited, though important, part of the potential benefit of ETDI. The ultimate goal is the ability to be able to treat an external ETDI message as if it had been generated internally.

PROBLEMS OR OPPORTUNITIES?

There are in practice some inherent contradictions in trying to achieve this objective many of which are summarised in this section.

Many companies still have internal systems which are relatively simple, or partially computerised, or even badly designed: they will for some time not be able to take advantage of the automatic processing and routing of ETDI messages. They will, however, still wish to print out or display ETDI messages so the TRADACOMS messages have to allow for this.

Some industries will need particular ETDI messages which will be of very limited application in other industries. Some will feel that a competitive advantage could arise from the imposition of their particular message standards and will be less willing to recognise that most companies deal with a wide variety of industries. Thus, a company may sell most of its output within one industry, but buy its goods and services from a myriad of industries. Most companies buy supplies of engineering parts, stationery, food, clothing, electricity, local authority services, to name but a few. Consequently, standards should be multi-industry. Industry-specific ETDI standards would result in most companies having to support a series of ETDI standard messages, thus duplicating overheads unnecessarily. The TRADACOMS Standards are designed to support the general ETDI of most businesses large and small, in most industries. They recognise that there will be specialist message standards for certain specialist or technical data (scientific analyses, computer-aided design, graphics, bibliographies) but standard trading messages should be the same for most companies in most industries.

One international standard?

Given the argument in favour of one set of message standards for most industries, should the message standards have aimed to provide one international standard? We consciously rejected this approach for several reasons:

> The TRADACOMS Standards Group did not have the knowledge
> and experience to understand how each individual economy
> operates its business practices, for example what does 'discount'
> mean in Italy or 'recommended' in Japan? Trying to discover real
> business meanings and practices and then getting agreement

takes a great deal of time and effort in the UK. Effort grows exponentially beyond international boundaries. Also the further one delves into the international standards-making 'industry' the further one strays from the reality of business.

Most companies have separate home trade and international trade ledgers and computer systems. International trade is intrinsically more complex and is largely concerned with fewer, high value transactions, for example a ship load of iron ore or a container of toys. Even with the reduction of some customs barriers, exporting and importing is usually well differentiated from selling and buying in the home market. Therefore, different message standards are needed for most international trade. Having separate, though related, ETDI standards for home and international trading is believed to be a relatively small manageable overhead in comparison with the major business benefits of making rapid progress with ETDI.

The bulk of business transactions relate, and will continue to relate, to local and regional distribution. Sending a tanker of petroleum from Rotterdam to Immingham is one transaction. Breaking that load down to thousands of road tankers making tens of thousands of deliveries results in the majority of business transactions, which are now open to be converted from paperwork control to ETDI. Petrol stations should be able to order and be invoiced for their supplies—not only of petrol but also confectionery, tyres and shampoo—using one set of home trade ETDI standards.

The bulk of ETDI message transmissions will relate to home trade, and therefore message standards have to be particularly effective in meeting domestic needs.

ETDI message standards should reflect the real business practice of the firms and industries they serve, but be capable of automatic processing and routing. Therefore they should ideally represent the best of business practice, so that procedures which need people to interpret ambiguities—which would be obstacles to automatic processing and routing—are not perpetuated into ETDI. On the one hand, the TRADACOMS Standards have to reflect business reality if firms are going to find them useful. On the other hand, if the standards reflect archaic and idiosyncratic business practices they may become good for nothing. A wise compromise has to be found.

Some industries, for example, have one unit of measure for ordering (thousands) another for deliveries (cases) and another for invoicing (cartons). We refused to allow such practices to be codified into the TRADACOMS Standards. We have tried very hard to achieve consistency of logical business practice in the Standards.

SOUND BUSINESS PRACTICE

It would take a volume to describe the pros and cons of all the decisions which went into creating the TRADACOMS Standards in a form believed to represent sound business practice. Nevertheless, it is worth emphasising a few of the principles followed.

The relationships between transactions

A key principle covers the relationships amongst the main business trans-actions—the order, delivery notification and invoice. Orders may be created by companies in a variety of different forms, an example being that some will provide a breakdown by item first and then by location, indicating one or more dates of delivery for each location. The less precisely a message is structured when it leaves a customer, the more processing will need to be done by the supplier prior to actioning it. The TRADACOMS Standards are designed to minimise subsequent reprocessing. Therefore they assume that companies operate their businesses on the basis of the key transaction, being *one DELIVERY of one or more ITEMS to one LOCATION on one DATE.*

Therefore all orders, delivery notifications, and invoices should be in this form. The order can be set up in the outstanding order file of both customer and supplier in a form against which the subsequent delivery notifications and invoices need only be confirmation of complete delivery or relatively simple amendments. This represents good business practice for most companies.

Coding

One of the keys to successful ETDI is the correct coding of products and services and of trading locations. Unless trading partners can agree common identification for the item being traded and the locations involved in trading, it is not possible to have fully automatic processing of the electronic messages. Without common coding, the normal practice is to use the code ascribed by the supplier to the item being traded and the code ascribed by the customer to the delivery point.

Common item coding has been the goal of many industries for decades. These efforts have often foundered because of the enormity of the task of defining and categorising each item to be coded. With the development of the International System of Product Coding or Article Numbering known as EAN, the way is now open for all companies and industries to adopt standard product coding. All the EAN system requires is that each supplier of a standard product or service acquires a seven digit supplier code from his Article Number Authority. Then each supplier numbers all his products uniquely with a five digit code which becomes a suffix of his seven digit supplier code. A thirteenth check digit is calculated from the preceding 12 digits.

This provides unique codes for each traded unit of the form, 5000189 18176 2. All trading partners agree to use this code ascribed by each supplier to a specific pack of a product (in this case an outer of 48 x four-finger Kit Kat). It is 'meaningless' (there is no meaning within the code), and information relating to it is derived from reference to a product master file. This method of coding is the only practicable way to get all standard goods and services coded well and in time for effective ETDI. The only problem not solved in this way is that where exactly the same item is supplied by two different manufacturers it would have two different codes. However, these codes can be cross-referenced within the product master file of the customer.

Similarly, the TRADACOMS Message Standards contain a unique system of location coding. A 13 digit code is created by each trading partner for each of its own business locations and each partner agrees to use the codes assigned by the other trading partner for its locations. This code is distinguished from a 13 digit item code by the different algorithm used to calculate the thirteenth check digit.

Master files and transaction files

The ultimate ETDI message would be a simple stream of codes and quantities, as shown in Figure 4.1. All detailed data describing the items (prices, discounts, number of singles in an outer or case, dimensions of case, weights, storage and handling information) would have previously been exchanged in master files of product and price data, and of location data (delivery days and hours, handling equipment available, telephone numbers). Product and location codes would be cross-referred to the appropriate master files. Transaction files would, therefore, be simple and to the point. The EAN system of product coding naturally links the scannable symbol on the consumer unit in the shop (via EPOS) to the traded unit to be ordered from the supplier (via ETDI).

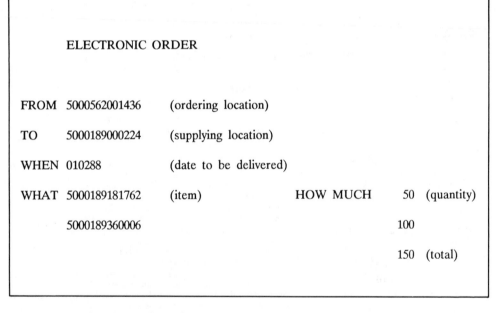

Figure 4.1   The electronic order

TRADACOMS STANDARDS

The objective of the TRADACOMS Standards Group was to produce a single set of UK ETDI message standards which most companies of any size could easily understand and use, but which would lead to automatic processing and routing and to the adoption of good business practices. It was also recognised that paperwork would not disappear overnight (if ever) and therefore the *Guidelines for Documentary Data Exchange* were published. These provide clear examples of agreed good business paperwork practices and they are now widely used in the UK.

From our study of paperwork practice and the collective knowledge of business practice, the TRADACOMS Standards Group developed the following structure of EDI Message Standards (see Figure 4.2).

BUSINESS NEED	SOLUTION
1 ELECTRONIC TRADE VOCABULARY	TRADACOMS STANDARD MESSAGES - Manual first published in 1982 - incorporates the best of business practice in electronic format and defines the data elements to be used.
2 ELECTRONIC GRAMMAR/SYNTAX	UNECE/GTDI - developed in the UK by SITPRO (Simplification of International Trade Procedures Organisation), and supported by the United Nations Economic Commission for Europe. The UNECE Guidelines for Trade Data Intercahnge syntax is widely recognised throughout the world and is supported by many National Customs authorities.
3 LETTER/MESSAGE DESIGN	TRADACOMS - the manual contains standards for TRANSACTION MESSAGES AND FILES: Orders, Invoices, Credit Notes, Statements, Remittance Advices, General Text, Delivery Notes, Delivery Confirmation, Uplift Notes, Uplift Confirmation, Availability Reports, Stock Snapshots, Stock Adjustments. MASTER FILES: Products, Prices, Trading Locations. When there has been a prior successful exchange of master files, the transaction files can become a simple stream of codes and quantities, thus substantially reducing the volumes of data to be transmitted, and also the scope for errors and queries.
4 ENVELOPE	TRADACOMS/UNTDI - The Manual defines how transmissions are constructed and addressed to ensure integrity.
5 PROTOCOL CONVERSION	TRADANET - The TRADACOMS Standards Group defined a specification for a secure, low cost network with which each company need only establish one communications link, using its own existing computers and protocols. No company needs to buy hardware or software to achieve protocol conversion with its business partners. TRADANET does this work, converting to and from the carrier standard of X.25.
6 ELECTRONIC POSTBOX/MAILBOX	TRADANET - each company fills its electronic postbox or empties its mailbox to suit its own processing convenience. Mail is sorted and forwarded securely to each intended recipient. Complete audit trails of all data movements are available to users.
7 ELECTRONIC POSTAL/SYSTEM NETWORK	TRADANET was constructed for the ANA and is currently operated by INS as a commercial venture, with standards being monitored and endorsed by the ANA. TRADANET makes use of INS's own high speed network, which adheres to published OSI standards (see Figure 4).

Figure 4.2 Standards for effective electronic trading communications
(reproduced from the TRADACOMS Manual by kind permission of the ANA)

Vocabulary

This is the definition of all the data elements involved in clear business communications. These are defined by the TRADACOMS Standards Group in close conjunction with user businesses. All data elements are listed in the TRADACOMS Data Element Directory.

Grammar

This is the syntax used to combine the data elements in unambiguous, structured form. TRADACOMS uses the UNECE-GTDI (see Figure 4.1) syntax which is well tried and tested. Using this common syntax means that the message standards are independent of media, machine or system. There is a software package available called Interbridge, developed by SITPRO, which converts internal files into and from this syntax (further information concerning Interbridge is given in Appendix B).

Message

These are the TRADACOMS Standard messages composed of the data elements above, structured according to the GTDI syntax. They have been designed to allow flexibility of use, efficiency of processing, and also ease of understanding. These now cover the following:

Master Files
* Products
* Prices
* Locations

Transaction Files

* Orders (simple, complex, multiple)
* Invoices
* Deliveries (notification, confirmation)
* Uplifts (instructions, confirmations)
* Credits, statements, remittances
* Stocks (snapshots, adjustments, availability)
* General communications

Figure 4.3 indicates some of the key data flows involving the main messages. A number of messages can be combined together into a file prior to transmission. This is highly relevant to domestic trade where a shop can have a number of deliveries each week which are summarised into one delivery or invoice file.

Many other messages are in testing or in preparation. Of particular significance are those relating to money transfers: companies are often involved in the collection of cash, for example, from diverse sites often via third party agents. In addition companies make payments via banks and financial institutions to suppliers and to employees. Hence, standards are being developed to meet needs such as credit transfers from a company's account to the accounts of its suppliers and employees.

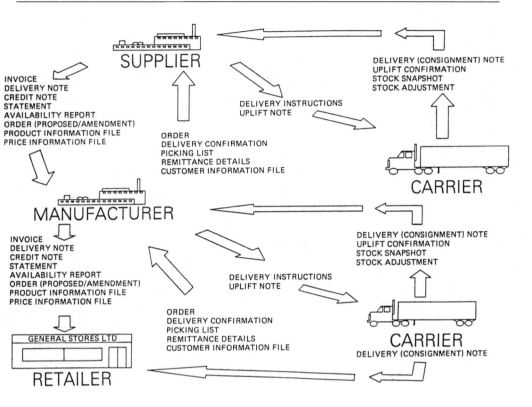

Figure 4.3   TRADACOMS data flow
(reproduced from the TRADACOMS Manual by kind permission of the ANA)

Message design

An example of part of a typical TRADACOMS message is shown in (Figure 4.4). This refers to an invoice message of which part of the invoice line detail segment is illustrated. Each segment is made up of data elements, which may be composed of a number of sub elements, which will be mandatory (they must appear) or conditional (they may appear). The data elements will be be fixed or variable in length, as shown. Practical guidance for use is then given. Where appropriate, lists of code values are defined to minimise the data to be transmitted and to reduce confusion.

TRADACOMS try to include all the elements that businesses really need, while keeping the structure of the messages as simple as is practicable. The message structures are relatively easy for users to follow. Irrelevant data are minimised, and conditional data which any two business partners do not need can be reduced to a minimum. In principle, pre-processing for simplification and standardisation is done by the sender of the TRADACOMS messages so that the recipient can re-process and route data for immediate action. Interpretation by the recipient is kept to a minimum. There is a never-ending battle in message design between providing a relatively simple standard message which all can understand and use given prior effort, and providing an all-embracing message which meets every conceivable need and hence is over-complex and difficult to use. The TRADACOMS Standards err on the side of simplicity and ease of use.

FILE: INVOICE FILE

Message	Type
INVOICE DETAILS	INVOIC
Page 6 of 10	

SEGMENT	DATA ELEMENT	DATA ELEMENT NAME	M/C	F/V	PICTURE	REMARKS: (See also General Remarks in Directory)
	+ AUCT	Unit Cost Price (excluding VAT) Cost Price (ex-VAT)	M M	>	9(5)V 9(4)	Cost of order unit including line discount. In pounds.
	:	Measure Indicator	C	>	X(6)	Mnemonic defining the measure, e.g. LBS, LITRE, LB/OZ, LB/DEC. Mandatory for variable measure items. Code Values List 4.
	+ LEXC	Extended Line Cost (excluding VAT)	M	>	9(7)V 9(4)	Includes line discounts. In pounds.
	+ VATC	VAT Rate Category Code	M	F	X	Code Values List 12
	+ MIXI	Mixed Rate VAT Rate Product Indicator	C	F	9	Value zero for the invoice item line for a composite product with component groups with different VAT rate codes. Starts at 1 and is incremented by 1 for each following invoice item line for the component. groups.
	+ CRLI	Credit Line Indicator	C	>	X(4)	Code Values List 9
	+ TDES	Traded Unit Description	C			Item description as it appears on the article, label or pack.
	:	Traded Unit Description Line 1 Traded Unit Description Line 2	C C	> >	X(40) X(40)	
	+ SPRI	Selling Price Manufacturers Recommended Selling Price Marked Price	C C C	> >	9(5)V999 9(5)V999	In pounds. Price marked on unit. In pounds.
	+ SRSP	Statutory Retail Selling Price	C	>	9(5)V 9(4)	Required for items such as drugs which must be sold at a regular price. In pounds.
	+ BUCT	Unit Cost Price (excluding VAT) before discount	C	>	9(7)V 9(4)	Cost of order unit excluding line discounts. In pounds.

Figure 4.4 An example of a typical TRADACOMS message
(reproduced from the TRADACOMS Manual by kind permission of the ANA)

STANDARDS DEVELOPMENT

The TRADACOMS Standards were first published in 1982, and have been very well received. They are now used by about 1000 companies in the UK and some abroad. The design of the messages has been followed by several other countries.

The industries using the TRADACOMS Standards in the UK include food, chemicals, pharmaceuticals, electronic components, textiles, clothing, shoes, do-it-yourself, building, books, records, furniture, white goods, gas, electricity, coal, railways, transport and distribution, local authorities, health, retailing, wholesaling, automotive and horticulture. New messages are being continually developed, and changes are made in a controlled fashion to meet the needs of other industries. A provisional message can be designed in a few months, and this is then released on a controlled basis for testing. Once all the practical problems are ironed out, the agreed message is formally published in the *TRADACOMS Manual.*

Updates are provided free to existing users. New users are charged a minimal cost of £50 as an ANA member and £90 as a non-member. Membership of the TRADACOMS Standards Group is open to all contributors. There are no bureaucratic hurdles. Hard workers with practical business experience are always welcome! One of the most difficult issues in ETDI standards control is how to keep them up to date and ensure that all users are working to the same version. It is very difficult to persuade a company which has settled down to use version five of the invoice, say, to move to version six if the changes are not seen to be beneficial, to be well managed, and to be infrequent. If all companies do not move to version six at about the same time, then we cease to have one set of standards, and degenerate back to an electronic Tower of Babel.

The TRADACOMS practice is to issue the new version of each standard free to all users. A few months are provided for study, and two dates are set—the first is six months thereafter, by which time all recipients of messages must be ready to receive to the new standard—the second is nine months thereafter (three months after the six months date) by which time all senders of messages must send to the new standard. In this way, no more than a maximum of two versions of each standard should be in use at any one point in time.

THE NEED FOR AN ELECTRONIC CLEARING HOUSE

It was difficult in the early 1980s to persuade many people that there was a need, or a viable market for, a clearing house which would sort and route all the TRADACOMS messages from sender to recipient. After all, those companies which wanted invoices on magnetic tape to the TRADACOMS Standards were already making rapid progress. Some cleared 75 per cent of all their invoices this way within a few years. Invoices could be sent on magnetic tape by express carrier without undue delay.

The demand for electronic ordering was growing more slowly and companies could always install a few direct communications links with major suppliers. Battling with different protocols, modems, lines and with employees of computer manufacturers and common carriers is a satisfying challenge for some DP professionals. Some people wanted to argue that we should wait for Open Systems Interconnection, when all computers would be made to the same communications standards, and all businesses would install such computers. The TRADACOMS Group felt that such a wait would stretch even its patience beyond the breaking point. Others suggested waiting for the full development and implementation of X.400, representing the ultimate in electronic mail. This seemed to the Group to be confusing the carrier standard with the fundamentals of an ETDI clearing house and network. These fundamentals are protocol conversion, postbox/mailbox facililties and network

Protocol conversion

Companies have different computers and different communications protocols, and different versions of these protocols. Each company wants to continue to use the protocol which best suits its needs to send all its ETDI messages. The ETDI clearing house has to be able to cope with all the most widely used protocols in such a way that no sender needs to worry about the recipient's computer communications practices.

Postbox/mailbox facilities

Companies have different and variable data processing timetables. They should be able to send their TRADACOMS messages to the ETDI clearing house whenever it suits their needs and to pull each type of trading message selectively from the clearing house whenever they are ready for processing. As ETDI develops, it becomes increasingly uneconomic to establish *ad hoc* links with each business partner, and creating and processing magnetic tapes starts to become a pain.

Companies need the electronic equivalent of the postal system, but with additional security and control. They need to be able to see that a message sent to a supplier has in fact been received and withdrawn from his mailbox. Companies need to be confident that they will only receive each TRADACOMS message type from an agreed source who is sticking to the rules. Security of processing and routing is fundamental to a commercial ETDI network.

Network

There needs to be a professional, well managed, effectively financed, securely run, network company which will provide computing facilities, and a hundred and one other services on which the large and small TRADACOMS users can depend. The network needs to be expandable without disruption to user service.

Having established these objective, the TRADACOMS Standards Groups 'merely' had to find such a clearing house. Unfortunately none existed. So in 1983, a Tradanet Network to carry the TRADACOMS Standard Messages was specified. Much to the surprise of the Group, many companies offered to supply such a facility. Unfortunately, most wanted to supply what they had available, and not precisely what the Group believed business needed. Only ICL was prepared at that time to build and operate the Tradanet clearing house and network envisaged (see Figure 4.5).

Tradanet was designed and developed during 1984. Extensive testing was carried out by a group of 10 companies in food, pharmaceuticals and retailing, and Tradanet was successfully launched as a public service in early 1985. Since

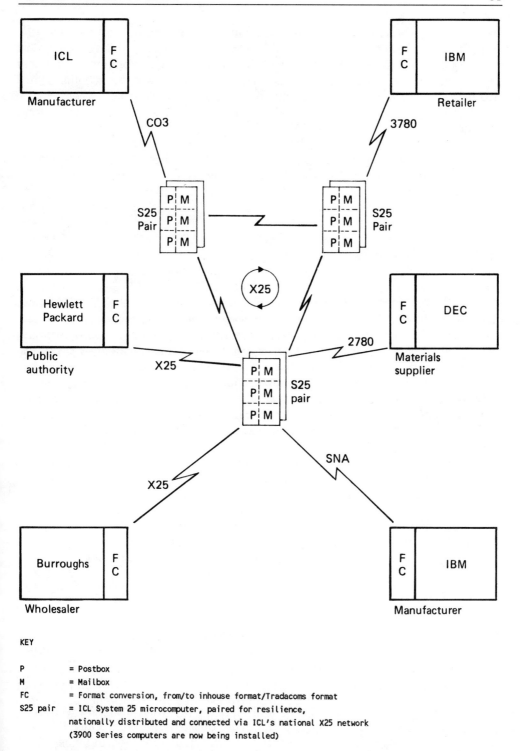

KEY

P	= Postbox
M	= Mailbox
FC	= Format conversion, from/to inhouse format/Tradacoms format
S25 pair	= ICL System 25 microcomputer, paired for resilience,

nationally distributed and connected via ICL's national X25 network
(3900 Series computers are now being installed)

Figure 4.5 A schematic of Tradanet
(reproduced from the TRADACOMS Manual by kind permission of the ANA)

then it has grown rapidly, probably because of the unique link between the effective electronic messages, TRADACOMS, and the secure, relatively low cost clearing house, Tradanet. There were 600 companies subscribing to Tradanet at the end of May 1988, with the volume of ETDI doubling every six months. There are many networks in the world and many message standards. It seems likely that ETDI has grown so fast and well in the UK because of the powerful bond between message standards and networks.

This is not to say that the TRADACOMS Standards are only used by the Tradanet network. Companies using the Edict EDI service also make significant use of TRADACOMS. Hence TRADACOMS is by far the most widely used ETDI message standard in the UK. With most companies using the one home trade message standard, a key barrier to the growth of ETDI is removed. The ANA welcomes the use of TRADACOMS by reputable networks. Since Tradanet was developed to the particular specification of the TRADACOMS Standards Group it is obviously the one we endorse. Tradanet is now run by International Network Services (jointly owned by ICL and GE Information Services Limited) and therefore has links to the rest of the world. The TRADACOMS Standards Group and INS work closely together on the development of the TRADACOMS Standards and the Tradanet Network. New facilities and services are discussed and agreed, as are charges. Agreement is not always reached on everything immediately, but both sides work hard together to ensure practical progress. Although there is a legal agreement which defines respective responsibilities, work is on the basis of mutual respect and joint learning.

Security is naturally a paramount concern, and ANA-TRADACOMS commissions a regular security audit of Tradanet by independent experts to satisfy everyone that all remains watertight and that the latest security features are being implemented.

The joint development of TRADACOMS and Tradanet is a fascinating process since so many of the issues are new and the rate of growth is exceptionally fast. It has been agreed to stick to sound, practical business principles, to make changes slowly and carefully, and to keep talking and listening to real users. What businesses want from an ETDI service are not subtleties of syntax or technical details, but a secure, reliable, low cost facility which they can use with confidence day in and day out to generate real applications benefits.

ETDI IN CONTEXT

TRADACOMS and Tradanet are concerned with the rapid (in minutes) exchange of well-defined and pre-agreed electronic trading messages, but in an off-line rather than on-line mode (normally store and call forward via electronic postboxes and mailboxes). Off-line systems are intrinsically easier and cheaper to provide. Nevertheless, for very urgent messages the recipient can leave a line open from his mailbox to receive defined messages from his trading partners almost immediately after they are sent.

To develop an on-line system is intrinsically more complex and expensive and is normally only justified when a direct financial transaction is involved—for example to check someone's account and clear for payment before a customer takes goods from the premises (as occurs with Electronic Funds Transfer at

Point-Of-Sale—EFTPOS). This is not the direct concern of ETDI, nor is access to electronic information. Videotex or viewdata systems can be powerful low-cost tools to make information available cheaply at remote locations (holiday booking vacancies, or stock availability) but they cannot cope with the secure exchange of large volumes of electronic trading data. It is possible that ETDI will be further developed to make access to information easier and quicker. At present however, it has plenty of potential work in handling standard trading messages between companies.

This paper will not go into detail on links between networks although further information concerning this is provided in Alison Bidgood's paper entitled *VADS interworking: a cloud on the EDI horizon.* Tradanet already links well with GE Information Service's overseas network, and the international exchange of trading messages will grow, especially with the development of EDIFACT standard messages for international trading. Obviously much remains to be done in many countries to put effective carrier networks and clearing houses in place. The TRADACOMS/Tradanet nexus would make a good model to follow if other countries are to experience the same rate of growth in ETDI as has occurred in the UK. Being realistic, however, the US scenario is likely to be repeated abroad, with many competing message standards and networks. In reality this means that companies have to maintain links to several networks and maintain a variety of standards. Large companies can do this, at a price: smaller companies find it expensive and off-putting. There needs to be more than one network to provide competition. However, the more links firms have to maintain with different networks the higher the cost and the less the use. In addition, passing messages through a number of networks raises considerable issues of security, responsibility and of added cost. Users only want to pay one low charge, and networks each want to recoup their costs, plus. It would take a brave man to forecast how all these issues will resolve themselves in the market place. Perhaps the major concern underpinning this paper is that we have to try to ensure that the UK maintains the advantages of its lead in ETDI. After all ETDI is not an end in itself. As in all computing, it is the business application which brings the benefit from message standards and networking.

LOGISTICS

Modern business depends fundamentally on logistics: the right product; in the right place; at the right time; at the right cost; and effective logistics depend on effective communications. Interfacing the logistics systems of companies profitably depends on sound communication links, and these are available now via TRADACOMS and Tradanet.

What can a company do with an order which is clearly understood, error free, and has arrived at its stock holding point minutes after the customer decided it was needed? It can fulfil it now. Customer demand is satisfied while it is still there, sales are maximised, stock can be reduced by the customer and the supplier, and products can be more fresh. The administration and distribution systems can be streamlined. If you want to know that all your trading partners have not only got the message but are acting on it, the TRADACOMS standard messages and the Tradanet ETDI network provide the secure system upon which you can depend. Once businesses appreciate that one installation of communication standards gives them an economic link to the UK business community, they can then confidently begin to restructure the business in a more economic form—to introduce just-in-time practices, to institute supplier quality assurance, to cut working capital, to improve customer service, to reduce administrative costs, and to exploit market opportunities.

In some senses, introducing ETDI with customers and suppliers via TRADA-COMS and Tradanet is the easy part of the job. The TRADACOMS Standards gives the messages which are relatively straightforward to understand and use, and are suitable for all trading partners. INS will help with the link to the Tradanet software packages irrespective of the user's computer types. The more complex problems arise when addressing the real business issues, such as:

> are your internal systems such that needs for the new supplies are immediately defined and communicated, in a standard format, to a file which can then be readily converted to the TRADACOMS format?

> have you agreed common product identification with your suppliers?

> is your order file updated hourly, or every 24 hours, or worse? There is usually quite a lot of work to be done to speed orders into the ETDI network as soon as the need has been identified. Stock cannot be cut to a minimum if orders hang around in files for days.

> is your supplier capable of responding quickly to the TRADACOMS order? Prior negotiations with trading partners for ETDI normally take a good deal of time and effort, but are essential for success. ETDI alone will not make a business responsive.

> are your delivery reception and testing facilities geared to handle the order quickly and get it to where it is needed? Stock doing nothing is waste.

> have you simplified or eliminated paperwork to support this new speedy way of doing business? Some paperwork will remain, particularly for signed receipt notes. Modernise your paperwork for the electronic era.

TRADACOMS and Tradanet can be viewed as the electronic bridges between trading partners. Moreover, they are catalysts for changing companies' ways of carrying out their business. They help companies to ask the correct questions about their internal and external systems development.

BENEFITING STRATEGICALLY

It is already becoming apparent which firms are going to benefit most from ETDI. They are the companies, large and small, which have clear business objectives and sound systems to support their achievement. Installing ETDI links without thinking fundamentally about the opportunities offered and the implications for internal systems is not only a wasted opportunity, but it will also eventually damage competitiveness. The leading High Street fashion retailers are installing TRADACOMS and Tradanet to link with their textile suppliers so that orders can be placed within minutes of the latest sales and stock figures coming from each branch, which tell them what the public are buying. One company is already linked to over 100 suppliers and will have a Tradanet link to 300 suppliers by June 1989. Its major competitor has similar plans. As a consequence, each supplier has only to install TRADACOMS and Tradanet once, and then it has a potential link to all its customers and suppliers. Similarly, a leading Do-It-Yourself retailer, which has installed electronic point of sale scanning, intends to link to all its suppliers via TRADACOMS and Tradanet, to ensure immediate stock replenishment with minimum working capital, but maximum response to consumer needs. It is easier to count the industries not affected by D-I-Y so the consequent ripple effects in our economy will be large—from this initiative alone.

It is far from being only retailers which have this strategic vision of the benefits of ETDI. The UK's major chemical companies, pharmaceutical companies and electronics companies have similar clear views of the fundamental importance of standard electronic data communications in the supply chain. So too do the Electricity Boards. Companies from all the sectors are using TRADACOMS and Tradanet.

Once it is known that it is possible progressively to send and receive all trading messages in a standard, fast, accurate and cost-effective form, then business can begin substantially to simplify the way it is run. Archaic trading practices and *ad hoc* procedures can be simplified and standardised and hence company action and reaction times can be substantially improved. To do this properly, a company must have business vision, for both its objectives and for its systems. The TRADACOMS Standards and the Tradanet network are the effective practical implementation of a vision, begun in 1979, of electronic communications between companies. Each company must provide its own vision at each end of the TRADACOMS/Tradanet line. The ANA has given all of British industry a fair advantage in the use of ETDI, if each company cares to take it. The more companies which do so, the more effective the total UK supply chain will become, leading to a far more competitive economy.

5

Open Communications Standards: Their Role in EDI

Paul Dawkins

REQUIREMENTS OF EDI

EDI has three basic requirements which are summarised below:

A transaction message standard that defines how data is to be represented and which must be understood by the trading parties;

Software which interfaces in-house systems to the EDI communications system and which will convert the message formats from the standard format to that used by the in-house systems and *vice versa* ;

A communications system to carry the messages, route them to their required destinations and provide an appropriate level of security.

The aims of EDI will only be realised if the EDI systems incorporate appropriate communications mechanisms. The following list represents the requirements of such communications systems:

The communications should be independent of machine, media and end system. This requirement allows the trading parties to operate within their own computing strategies without being restricted by the EDI system;

Do not affect existing Data Processing;

The EDI messages should not be affected by use of a particular communications protocol;

The communications must handle messages of appropriate format and standard. This implies that either the communications systems must handle messages of the particular format used by EDI, or that a general purpose communications system which can handle any format of message be used;

The communications must provide services that are required by the processes that are inter-working to provide EDI. These services will include definitions of what happens if the EDI message cannot be delivered to the receiving process (an incorrect address may have been given or the receiving machine may not be running).

Normally, it would be hoped that the messages transmitted would be independent of the communications system carrying them (just as the Royal Mail does not look inside the envelope surrounding a letter). This, however, is not always possible and sometimes there is the need for integration of the message format and communications service definition. This will have implications when the use of X.400 as a transport mechanism for EDI is examined in greater depth.

The communications system must also provide a number of services that are related to security of the interactions. There are four such services: authentication to ensure that both parties are completely assured of the identity of the other; non-repudiation to ensure that neither party can repudiate the transaction; confidentiality to ensure that the information is protected from unauthorised parties; integrity to ensure that the information cannot be altered by third parties.

Whilst it is the responsibility of the communications system to transport the interactions between the trading parties, the message itself must be constructed in a format that will be understood by the recipient. Standards for this are being developed, for example: ANSI X.12 and EDIFACT. It is sufficient to note here that the communications protocols used must be able to handle them.

EDI before open communications standards

When EDI is only concerned with the interactions between two parties, the management of the communication is a simple matter. The two parties only need to agree a protocol which both implement and then to agree a time when both their communications processes (and transaction applications) will be up and running. Then the EDI interaction can take place. There may be a problem of security (allowing an external organisation to have access to the corporate host machine) but this can be quite easily overcome by the user of a front end processor, physically disconnected from the host when external access takes place.

As the number of trading parties increases, however, it becomes more and more difficult to arrange these one-to-one communications sessions. In addition, not all the trading partners may wish (or be able) to use the same communication protocols. To get around such problems there emerged services provided by third parties—Value Added & Data Service (VADS) Providers. They acted as clearing houses for EDI messages. An organisation wishing to perform an EDI transaction would simply send the EDI message to the VADS provider, who would then take the responsibility of passing it on to the final destination. This offers the following advantages:

One-to-one communications

Each EDI party only needs to communicate with one other party,
the VADS provider, thus simplifying protocols and eliminating
scheduling difficulties.

Security

Each communicating party only has to provide access to the
VADS provider.

Additional facilities

The VADS provider may offer additional facilities such as interaction logging, message format conversion, and directory services.

The protocols used between the VADS provider and the trading organisation were based on *de facto* standards (although proprietary). The drawback to this operation is that an EDI community is limited to organisations subscribing to a particular VADS. It must be asked whether this is too restrictive and whether open systems interconnection might not unleash vast growth in EDI. It is with this in mind that a briefing on Open Systems Interconnection has been included in this paper.

OPEN SYSTEMS INTERCONNECTION (OSI) BRIEFING

Introduction

Open Systems Interconnection (OSI) standards have been designed to allow inter-working between collections of computer systems and terminals regardless of equipment manufacturer or geographic location. OSI standards have been developed and promoted by international standards bodies and are now achieving widespread acceptance. As the development of standards is a continuing and sometimes slow-moving activity it often happens that new communications applications are first implemented using expedient, proprietary protocols. As OSI standards mature, however, the advantages of using them become recognised not only by the user organisations, suppliers and service providers but also by legislative bodies. This is the status which OSI standards have reached today.

Aims of OSI

The purpose of OSI is to allow open connection and to enable any communications network to be used. This is to say that all the protocols used and provided by a network are public and published. Any computer vendor and communi- cations equipment supplier can implement those standards and thus enable its products to be connected. From the point of view of the user, there are three specific aims of OSI: inter-operability, network independence and vendor independence.

Inter-operability ensures that applications are able to communicate; they will be operating to the same protocol standards. Network independence means that applications will be able to communicate together irrespective of what underlying network is used to connect them together. The final aim is to provide a communications network which is independent of any particular computer vendor. This, in the first instance, allows an organisation to buy the most appropriate piece of hardware for a particular function, irrespective of the vendor. In the context of intercompany communications, such as EDI, it allows two organisations to exchange data electronically without having to find some proprietary protocol which is a lowest common denominator between them.

BASIC REFERENCE MODEL

One of the most striking complications of providing open communications is the vast range of communications options that must be provided to satisfy varying requirements, different levels of service and diverse communications technologies. To simplify this, the International Standards Organisation (ISO) developed the OSI Basic Reference Model which splits the business of communication into a number of manageable layers. Each layer (except the highest and the lowest) provides a service to the next higher layer and uses the services of the next lower layer to communicate with its equivalent layer in another system.

For two systems to communicate properly there is a requirement for 'protocols' defining what may be sent and when. In OSI, there is defined at least one standard protocol at each layer to be used between the two communication systems. For each layer there is also at least one standard service defined which the layer offers to the next higher layer.

The basic reference model is therefore a language which is used to describe communications, it defines the services provided by the network and it defines the protocols used for communications. The model defines seven layers as shown in Figure 5.1 and described below.

OSI Standards

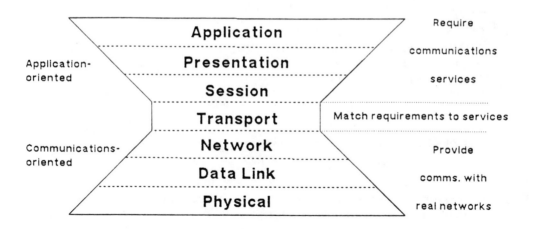

Figure 5.1   The OSI 7 Layer Model

Layer 1: Physical layer

The Physical layer is concerned with the transfer of bits across a physical communication link. It specifies the physical aspects of doing this including voltages, timing and even the plugs and sockets.

Layer 2: Link layer

Next, there is the Link layer, which has the responsibility for the transfer of data across the physical link. It is concerned with flow control ensuring that the sequence of data flowing is correct and that the transmission rate is matched to the processing capabilities of the ends. If the link is a physical wire or a local area network, then the two computer systems may be the 'End Systems' that wish to communicate; alternatively one of the systems may be an intermediary, such as a node of a packet-switched network.

Layer 3: Network layer

Above the link layer is the Network layer. In a simple case this has the responsibility for the transfer of the data between end systems across real data networks. Examples of such real networks include: X.25 packet-switching networks; Integrated Services Digital Networks (ISDN); and Local Area Networks such as Ethernet and Token Ring. It is also the Network layer's responsibility to allow end systems to communicate across concatenated networks.

Layer 4: Transport layer

The Transport layer takes the network service and provides the quality of service that the upper layers need. In particular, it is concerned with costs and reliability. The Transport layer protocol has five classes; which one is used will depend on the service sharing network connections. Improved error-protection can be obtained by doing error-checking at this level, in addition to whatever might be done in the lower layer. The five classes are:

> *0 Simple class*—with no error recovery. It is used when the underlying network is inherently error free (for example X.25 packet-switched networks).

> *1 Basic Error Recovery Class*—with minimal overheads but able to recover from networked signal error (disconnects and resets).

> *2 Multiplexing Class*—allowing several transport connections to be carried on a single network connection, but no error recovery.

> *3 Error Recovery and Multiplexing Class*—as 2, plus the ability to mask errors indicated by the network.

> *4 Error Detection & Recovery Class*—as 3 plus the detection of errors which occur as a result of low grade service from the network provider.

The Transport service is seen as the divide between dealing with communications and dealing with applications.

Layer 5: Session layer

The Session layer is responsible for organising the dialogue between applications. In particular, it is here that any necessary synchronisation between applications is done.

Layer 6: Presentation layer

The Presentation layer is responsible for ensuring that the two end systems agree and understand the organisation of the data being exchanged. Thus there are mechanisms for specifying the data representation and for negotiation of this representation, but not for data manipulation. While, to take a simple example, the Presentation layer allows two end systems to agree on the coding of characters, it does not do code conversion. It is not concerned with the semantic understanding that applications will have of the data.

Layer 7: Application layer

Finally, there is the Application layer which provides the interface between the OSI communications environment and the application processes using it. It provides a set of common application service elements (CASE) for management and activation of communications services in support of the application, that is the basic functionality that is needed for all communication in the distributed (OSI) environment. In addition there are a number of specific application service elements (SASE) which provide support for the context of communication. The following SASEs have either been specified or are in the process of being specified:

> *File Transfer Access and Management (FTAM)*—for reliable bulk data transfer and access to remote databases in real time.

> *Job Transfer and Manipulation (JTM)*—allowing batch jobs to be submitted on one open system and run on another.

> *Virtual Terminal Protocol (VTP)*—allowing communication between any terminal type and any host without concern for the application processes involved.

> *Messaging (X.400)*—X.400 is a set of standards developed by the CCITT for Message Handling Systems (MHS). Although they are mentioned here in association with the Application layer, they also define standards for the Presentation layer. The ISO has, however, defined a SASE which performs a function almost identical to X.400. This is known as Message Oriented Text Interchange System (MOTIS).

> *Transaction Processing*—this is still in an early stage of development but will provide communications for transaction processing environments.

Functional profiles

Although there are standards at every layer of the model, they do offer options, and it is unrealistic for any system to support them all. It is necessary to define which particular options are to be adopted and used. It should also be noted that the standards do not always specify practical constraints that must be placed on implementations designed for particular functions.

Several groups of interested parties have emerged, each of which defines a clear set of standards to be used in a particular technical or business environment. In essence these groups have selected from the set of OSI layers a protocol 'stack' (known as a functional profile) which provides the required communications service characteristics for the environment. The 'stack' and its options are published, and suppliers who wish to offer systems in the designated environment are required to demonstrate protocol conformance. There is a good deal of commonality between those functional profiles that have been proposed to date. The most significant functional profiles are:

> *The Standards Promotion and Application Group (SPAG)*—is jointly owned by 12 major manufacturers. They publish a book of functional profiles which are named, from the colour of the cover of their publication, the 'purple' profiles.

> *Manufacturing Automation Protocol (MAP)*—MAP was initiated by General Motors Corporation to allow computerised factory floor devices to communicate.

> *Technical and Office Protocols (TOP)*—TOP is a an initiative of a major group of computer systems purchasers led by Boeing which is aimed at the early provision of office systems that can inter-work effectively and based on international standards.

> *Government OSI Profile (GOSIP)*—GOSIP is a precise subset of international standards selected by the British Government (there is also a US Government GOSIP) to meet the needs of government administrative systems. Its quoted primary purpose is to facilitate systems procurement by government departments.

ADOPTION OF OSI STANDARDS

OSI standards are now supported by all the major computer vendors in addition to their own proprietary protocols. This take-up has come about because of several factors. Firstly, there was take-up by those computer companies who did not have strongly-positioned proprietary protocols (particularly the European manufacturers) and this was followed by those who had strong proprietary offerings but felt a need to provide connectivity to others. The second boost for OSI came from government support for OSI (particularly in Europe) through the mechanisms for procurement, a range of financial inducements for OSI and through OSI inclusion clauses in licence conditions. An example of this last point is provided by the UK VADS licence.

Under the new Class Licence for Value Added and Data Services there is a condition that within one year of an OSI standard being specified by the Director of OFTEL, it is necessary to provide access to new and existing services by means of the OSI standard. It will also be necessary to demonstrate how the service conforms to OSI standards. The service provider can continue to use proprietary standards but the OSI access must provide a broadly comparable service to that provided by the proprietary protocols.

X.400 BRIEFING

X.400 is a series of recommendations developed and published by CCITT. The stated aim of these recommendations is to:

*define message handling services that Administrations provide to
enable subscribers to exchange messages on a
store-and-forward basis.*

The word 'Administration' used above refers to a Public Telecommunications
Operator (such as BT or Mercury in the UK) and implies that X.400 is designed
for use in public services. In practice, however, in the same way as X.25 can be
used for private data networks, so X.400 can be used privately. As a result X.400
systems are being widely implemented by computer vendors, message switch
manufacturers and by system builders. As X.400 is widely implemented, it
enables the most appropriate computer to be employed for a particular function
and for this to communicate with other vendors' machines. It allows messaging
in a truly multi-vendor environment.

What is messaging?

In order to understand the capabilities of X.400 and why it could be appropriate
for use in EDI it is necessary to understand what is meant by the term,
'messaging' and how it differs from real-time file transfer. Messaging may be
defined as the passing of information from one computer process to another
where the communication is not in real-time. A computer network provides the
link between the communicating parties. The recipient does not have to be
connected to the network when the message is submitted by the sender. The
sender is only concerned with submitting the message to the network. It is then
up to the network to deliver the message when it can, or to take appropriate
action if it cannot be delivered.

Messaging is therefore particularly suitable for EDI where each party
operates autonomously from its trading partner.

SERVICES X.400 OFFERS

There are four services associated with X.400 messaging: message transfer
service, interpersonal messaging service, data conversion and directories.

Message transfer service

This is a general purpose store-and-forward messaging system that will handle
any message type provided that the message is wrapped-up in a suitable
'envelope' and is properly addressed.

Interpersonal messaging service

This is the equivalent of traditional electronic mail and allows an individual to
communicate with other individuals. The interpersonal messaging services
result in the creation of 'interpersonal messages'. These are one type of
message (the only one defined so far) which use the message transfer service
for routing and transmission. Although the service is called 'interpersonal
messaging service' this does not imply that the messaging must be between
people. It might equally validly be between computer applications or between
people and computer applications.

Within the specification for the interpersonal message service there is a definition of the structure of an interpersonal message. This is analogous in structure to a physical memorandum (see Figure 5.2).

It comprises a header, which contains address, subject and contents information and a body part that can contain any type of data. The X.400 recommendations define various types of information that can be included in the body: ASCII text, telex, voice, facsimile (Group III and Group IV), teletex and videotex.

These can either be used individually or in different combinations. X.400 also allows for nationally defined formats and private formats. The result of this is that an interpersonal message can contain any format of information. A private body type could in principle be used for private EDI transactions between collaborating trading partners. Also nationally defined body types or a new body type could be defined for EDI based on standards.

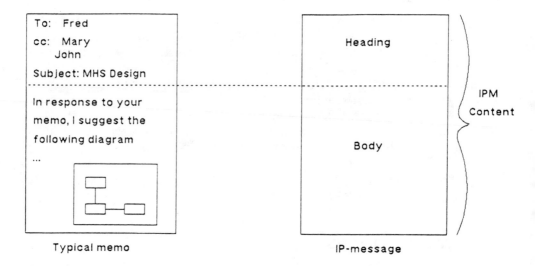

Figure 5.2 Interpersonal messages

Data conversion

X.400 defines a number of data conversion services. These are provided to allow otherwise incompatible formats to be exchanged. It includes sections for each body to be converted to each other body type. In virtually all cases, however, the detailed conversion rules have not been specified (in the 1984 recommendations).

Directories

This service is strictly outside X.400 but as it is so closely related it is worth mentioning here. In the 1984 X.400 recommendations the need to provide directory services was identified but the actual services were left for further study. In the 1988 recommendations it was recognised that directories were useful for other services in addition to X.400 and so it was decided to put them in a new series of recommendations, X.500.

X.500 defines what is in effect a globally-wide, distributed database that contains user directory information and the services needed to access it. Although X.500 can have implications for routing messages, it is unclear what impact they will have on EDI. At the present time, EDI participants have a good knowledge of their trading partners and they do not need to use directories on a message-by-message basis. It might be speculated, however, that a suitable directory service could open up the possibility of performing EDI transactions with completely new trading partners.

Architectural elements from which X.400 systems are constructed

X.400 defines two types of architectural element required to provide the Message Transfer and Interpersonal Messaging Services (see Figure 5.3), the Message Transfer Agents (MTAs) and User Agents (UAs).

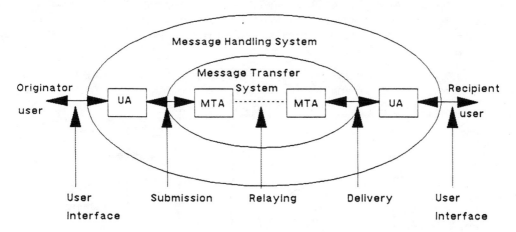

Figure 5.3   Functional model of X.400

Message Transfer Agent (MTA)

MTAs provide the Message Transfer Service. They route messages and deliver them in a store-and-forward manner. They are analogous to the sorting offices of the physical postal service and equivalent to the traditional message switches. Some MTAs only transfer messages to and from other MTAs. These are known as 'relaying MTAs' They may include facilities for data conversion and access to non-X.400 services (through 'Access Units'). MTAs are typically implemented on mini or mainframe computers. Some MTAs have, however, been built to run on top-end personal computers.

User Agents (UAs)

A User Agent is the mechanism that provides a user with the means to create, display and generally access messages and to submit them for delivery by the message transfer services. UAs are typically implemented on personal computers or on the same machine as the MTA. Multiple user agents could be implemented on a single host machine (see Figure 5.4)

PROTOCOLS

In the 1984 recommendations three main top-level protocols were defined (lower level protocols were also defined but they are outside the scope of this paper). These top-level protocols were:

Message transfer protocol (P1)—the protocol used for transmitting messages between MTAs.

Submission and delivery protocol (P3)—used by a remote user agent (one not built into the same machine as the MTA) for submitting messages to, and receiving messages from, the message transfer service (that is an MTA). In the 1988 recommendation this will, for practical purposes, be replaced with a protocol known as P7.

Interpersonal messaging protocol (P2)—defines the syntax and semantics of messages being transferred between IPM user agents. It is often referred to as the IPM envelope.

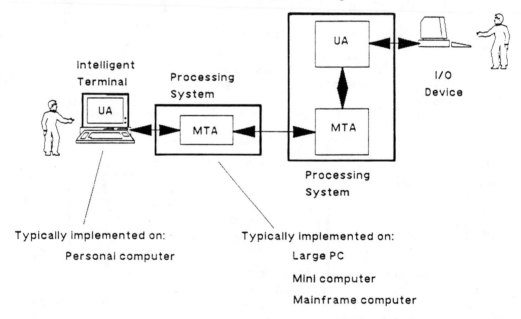

Figure 5.4   Co-resident and stand-alone UA and MTA

X.400 MANAGEMENT DOMAINS

Before X.400 addressing is discussed, it is important to introduce the concept of an X.400 'management domain'.

A management domain is the extent of control held by a particular managing authority. It will contain one or more message transfer agents and may contain a number of user agents. Two types of management domain are defined, administrative and private management domains. Administrative management domains (ADMDs) are operated by public messaging authorities. There may be one or more in one country (see Figure 5.5). In the UK British Telecom is responsible for an ADMD.

Private management domains (PRMDs) are operated by private organisations. They may be associated with one or more ADMDs but with respect to a particular interaction between a PRMD and an ADMD, the PRMD is considered to be associated with a single ADMD. The PRMD cannot act as a relay between different ADMDs. PRMDs, according to the Recommendations must be contained within one country. Thus a multi-national company should operate different private management domains in the different countries in which it operates. If messages are passed between these PRMDs, they should be relayed by the appropriate ADMDs. There is no technical reason why this restriction should be imposed. It simply gives extra traffic (and revenue) to the ADMDs. Whether it is enforced by statute or service contracts has yet to be determined.

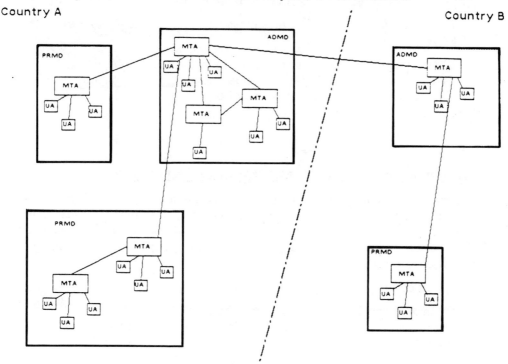

Figure 5.5   X.400 domains

ADDRESSING

The main objective behind X.400 addressing is to allow a descriptive name for each sender and recipient of the messaging service. The structure of the user name—known as the 'Originator/Recipient Name' ('O/R name') is hierarchical allowing a reasonable chance for a particular person's O/R name to be deduced from their real name and location. The O/R name includes such attributes as:

country, administrative domain, private domain, organisation name, organisation unit and personal name.

There are variations of this format which allow recipients to be addressed by numeric keypad and via telex. Whichever variant is used, the format is essentially designed for addressing messages to terminals. X.400 also defines a form of addressing that allows messages to be addressed to terminals. Within the addressing scheme, there is provision for what are essentially private attributes. These could be used to identify a particular computer process through which EDI transactions will take place.

Vendors have differing objectives for their products. The undefined aspects of a messaging leaving considerable freedom to the implementors. This has ensured a variety of types of system arising:

> *Gateways*—are typically provided by computer vendors who have existing proprietary messaging systems in order to provide access to external X.400 messaging services. The gateway looks to the external messaging service like an MTA.

> *Relay-only MTAs*—only provide message transfer between other MTAs.

> *IPM service*—users are provided with access to the MTA via user agents. They might be co-resident (running on the same machine as the MTA) or access may be provided for remote user agents.

ADVANTAGES OF USING MESSAGING AND X.400

An organisation can gain a number of advantages from adoption of X.400 messaging for the transfer of information. Some of these advantages are inherent in the fact that a messaging concept is used, others derive from the use of the X.400 recommendation itself. Considering the former group first, advantages of using messaging include:

> Speed compared with physical deliver mechanisms.

> Optimal network usage—messaging implies that if the communications network is busy, it is possible to delay the transmission.

> Receiving entity need not be present when the message is sent—this is particularly important for EDI where the sender may have no control over the operations of the communicating partner. Confidentiality—as no physical copies exist, a high level of security can be achieved. This can be enhanced by the use of encryption.

> Functionality—a wide range of mailing services can be provided relatively easily. These could include not only services one would expect from the physical mail, such as delivery notification, but other services such as message traces, different grades of service, hold for a period of time.

The advantages that come from using X.400 specifically include:

Multi-vendor support—all the major computer vendors are committed to supporting X.400 and thus multi-vendor networks of machines can be constructed. This is important for EDI where different companies will have different computing strategies and will buy from different vendors.

Public networks—public X.400 networks will be widely available thus facilitating the provision of connections.

Future support—unlike systems based on a proprietary protocol, which can be dropped and withdrawn, an international standard protocol will not disappear overnight. This ensures that investment will not suddenly be redundant.

It should also be added that the functionality that has been defined in X.400 is quite extensive and is as good as most proprietary messaging systems. It is certainly not the case of the standards adopting the lowest common denominator. Although there are quite compelling arguments for using X.400 for messaging, it must be recognised that there are some disadvantages. The most important of these is the potential cost of providing the X.400 services. The protocols are quite heavy and there are a large number of the services to be provided. In some simple application X.400 might simply be an over-kill. For EDI, however, where reliable, secure communications are paramount, the protocols and services are probably quite appropriate.

Another disadvantage of X.400 may lie in the way in which information layout is defined. X.400 uses the Abstract Syntax Notation 1 (ASN 1) but EDI standards such as UNTDI or EDIFACT are based on character streams with field delimiters. This difference may not cause significant difficulties. This is because ASN.1 is used to define the syntax of the message transfer protocol. It is not concerned with the message itself. That is the separate province of EDI standards.

HOW COULD X.400 BE USED FOR EDI?

There are essentially two ways in which X.400 can be used for EDI although as will be described later there are a number of different configurations. In the first way of using X.400, the EDI message is carried as an Interpersonal Message (IPM) body part. In the second approach the EDI message is treated as a new class of message.

The IPM method has a number of advantages. It is simple; all that is needed is a new body type. There is no need to define new services or protocols and changes to existing X.400 implementations will be minimal. Some of the existing IPM services are likely to be of great potential use for EDI, for example: receipt and non-receipt notification; originator and authorising users indication; primary, copy and blind copy recipient indication; cross-referencing, importance, obsoleting, sensitivity and subject indication; subject indication; body part encryption.

In addition to being able to transport the EDI message, the IPM approach also has the capability of carrying ordinary messages. These may be used for the ordinary correspondence that takes place between trading partners.

The alternative approach, in which a new message is defined, may become appropriate if the IPM user agent protocol, P2, imposes too high an overhead. This may be the case where trading partners are exchanging large volumes of data. The technique would require definitions of a new EDI message class and user agent, appropriate service elements and a user agent protocol equivalent to P2.

Whichever method is used, the X.400 message transfer level provides services which are of potential use for EDI. These include: delivery and non-delivery notification, time stamp; multi-destination delivery, grade of delivery selection, deferred delivery and hold for delivery.

POSSIBLE CONFIGURATIONS

There are three basic ways that an organisation may provide access to X.400 for its data processing applications. These are shown in Figure 5.6, and explanations for each are given below.

Option 1

An X.400 gateway may be installed on the host machine running the data processing applications. This method has the advantages that it requires no special hardware, which would need special management, and that such gateways are provided by many computer vendors. In spite of this, however, it is still necessary to implement the mechanism to ensure that incoming transactions are directed to the appropriate process and that outgoing messages are provided with the correct X.400 address and that any of the X.400 services that are required are requested.

There are a number of disadvantages with this configuration. The first is that external access is given to the mainframe which may be contrary to the security demands of the organisation. The second disadvantage is the availability of communications becomes tied to the availability of the host machine.

Option 2

Security of the host machine can be improved by placing an X.400 Message Transfer Agent between the host and the public carrier network. This has the additional advantage that the availability of communications is independent of the operation of the host machine.

The diagram shows a User Agent co-resident in the MTA. This is then directly connected to the host by a suitable link. An alternative arrangement might be to run the User Agent in the host machine and connect it to the MTA via the appropriate X.400 protocol (P3 or P7). The MTA in this configuration may provide a more general messaging role in the organisation.

Option 3

In this example access is provided directly by a user agent. It has the advantage of cheapness but until the appropriate P3 or P7 protocol is widely available it is likely to lead to restrictions in use. It may be appropriate, however, for a small organisation which only needs to interchange data with one other organisation.

If semi-proprietary protocols are used, then any suitable public network may be used; for example the public switched telephone network.

In all the examples only the connection to the public network is shown. There is no indication of the connection through the public network.

Option 1:   EDI using X.400: Gateway option

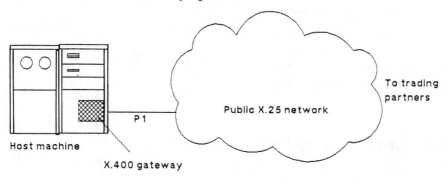

Option 2:   EDI using X.400: Security provided via an X.400 MTA

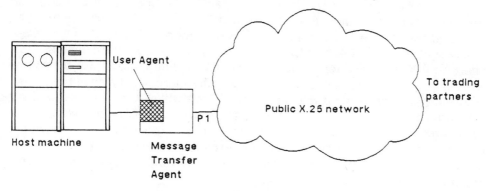

Option 3:   EDI using X.400: Access via an X.400 UA

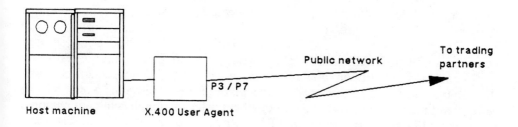

Figure 5.6   Three basic ways an organisation may   provide access to X.400

For the P1 options, there are several possibilities :

   to connect via the public packet switched data network to a
   public X.400 messaging system for onward routing. This has the
   advantage of removing responsibility for network level routing
   from the communicating party.

   to connect directly to each other communicant via a public packet
   switched data network. In this case it is necessary to provide
   network level address information.

   to route to a third party VADS provider which would operate as
   a clearing house (either via a public message handling service or
   directly over a public packet switch data network). There would
   only be an advantage in doing this if the third party were to
   provide some other service in addition to simple routing.

IMPACT OF X.400 ON VADS PROVIDERS

When considering the impact of X.400 on third party VADS providers, there are
two aspects to be considered. The first is what legal implications there are and
the second concerns the impact of widespread implementation of X.400. In the
UK, at least, the VADS licence stipulates that VADS providers must commit to
providing OSI communications within a specific time period. If a messaging
service is provided, then this implies that X.400 must be used. It must be
expected therefore that VADS providers will migrate to X.400.

   On the other hand, X.400 provides the store-and-forward and routing services
offered by VADS providers. It follows that PTOs, who provide X.400 services
will compete with VADS operators. It is likely therefore that they will be looking
for additional new services to compensate. There will still be the need (at least
for the time being) to provide communications with organisations that have not
migrated to X.400 but other services might include directory services, message
format conversion, a service to allow an organisation to communicate with all
companies in a particular sector—this might be used for invitations to tender—
and transaction logging.

OSI ALTERNATIVES TO X.400

X.400 is not the only OSI application service which could be used for EDI. FTAM
could be used to provide real-time file transfer for EDI messages with, for
example, a clearing house. JTM protocol could be used to transfer the EDI
message but in this case a suitable job would be invoked to process the
incoming message. In a similar way the new Transaction Processing service
could be employed. All these protocols do, however, lag behind X.400 in its
implementation. In addition they all require a more intimate interaction between
the communicants which may not be acceptable for organisations which have a
requirement for a high level of security or do not wish, for operational reasons,
to run their EDI processes continually.

   X.400 defines a communications system which because of its store-and-
forward nature makes it eminently suitable for transferring information between

different organisations. A party sending information only has to submit that information to the communications network, it does not have to consider whether the receiving process is up and running at that time. The network will deliver it when it can but if it cannot, then an indication of this is given. Furthermore, X.400 offers a range of services (such as indicating that messages have been received) which are useful for EDI. There are, however, still a number of issues that need resolving before X.400 achieves widespread use for EDI. The most fundamental of these is a) whether the message transfer service is used directly to carry the EDI message or b) whether the Interpersonal Messaging service is used with the EDI message, forming a special body type. For pragmatic reasons the latter is likely to become most widely adopted in the short term. In the longer term standards may be drawn up for use of the message transfer service.

As for alternatives to X.400, proprietary protocols are likely to reduce due to the pressure of the OSI conditions of the VADS licence, the wide-scale provision of X.400 by the computer vendors and the inevitable adoption of X.400 by user organisations. The consequences of the use of X .400 ought to be an accelerated growth in EDI as more organisations install an X.400 messaging capability. It is perhaps realistic to state that up to now, EDI has been performed between trading partners well known to each other. X.400 may present the possibility of EDI between unfamiliar parties and for new applications for data exchange. The major question remains however as to how the VADS providers will respond and whether they will offer a new range of services that cannot be provided directly through X.400.

Examples of EDI in Practice

In this section the editors have assembled more detailed accounts of several examples of EDI. All of these are operational—electronic trading today. They differ widely in their structures, their goals and how they are funded. They have made different choices of messaging standards and communications services. None of them is a 'text book' example: they show what has actually been done in particular sectors.

L'Association de Services Transports Informatiques (ASTI) provides support in the form of packaged software and networking expertise to a widely-spread community of freight forwarders. ASTI's customers make use of public networks but the complexities of doing so are concealed from them by specialist software. Terry Westgate's article is particularly interesting because he sets the ASTI initiative firmly in the context of his own experience of the history of tele-communications developments.

Bankers Automated Clearing Services (BACS) was created by a consortium of banks in the UK. Their princpal activity is to mechanise the UK's direct debit system. Christopher Eaglen examines, at a practical level, how businesses can use data structures defined by BACS to interface electronic funds interchange with their own EDI systems.

United Nations Interactive (message) Concept Over Reservation Networks (UNICORN) is an application standard for car ferry reservations and ticketing. Tony Allen, Systems Development Manager with Sealink, describes how a useful system has been assembled within this particular community of users.

6
EDI in Freight Forwarding: the ASTI Story

Terence Westgate

ASTI was founded in 1985 to help members of the freight transport industry make better use of computers for shipping communications. The low cost and high power of today's microcomputers and the wide availability of public telecommunications present attractive opportunities to even the smallest forwarding agent. It is possible to reduce the cost of communications, to improve information services to importers and exporters, to reduce the incidence of errors in documentation, and to save time in document preparation.

THE ORIGINS OF ASTI

Although it may be over 200 years since George Lesage sent the first electronic coded signals, 140 years since the Morse telegraph and 50 years since the first automatic telex exchanges, the combination of devices and facilities that ASTI is bringing to the international trade community is still no more than 15 or 16 years old—and the conventions of trade and the motivation of traders have changed not a jot over 2,000 years of recorded history.

The origins of ASTI can be traced back to 1968 when the author was working in the production control of aircraft electronics and the company made its first moves towards implementing a computer in that department. A major concern at the time was that the data processing department had little or no understanding of the dynamics of production—the thousands of permutations of events beyond the immediate control of the production department that needed to be kept in balance to satisfy the customers within the budgetary constraints of the business.

UNDERSTANDING COMPUTER FUNCTIONALITY

By 1972 in the role of a production manager, the author had implemented a materials management system. Whilst useful its functionality was restricted to extrapolating sales demand to component requirements and man hours. There was no attempt to automate purchasing or shop floor scheduling. Nevertheless the product of the simple logic of the computer was treated with suspicion and hostility. There seemed to be two underlying contributory factors to this resentment. The first was the rapid exposure of the implications of senior management decisons—basic financial modelling in fact. The second factor was less easily overcome and is still a major problem today. This is the lack of understanding of the capabilities and limitations of computers, and the restricted dissemination of this information by the data processing professionals. This factor was compounded in its effect by a general failure to explain the logic acting on the data to produce the results. There also seemed then, and still appears to be a psychological barrier whereby a fear exists of being unable ever to learn to understand the functionality of computers and their programs.

Between 1973 and 1975 the author developed and formalised a program of research in man-computer interaction. The sphere had by this time broadened to encompass data communications and interpersonal communications through computer networks. The first phase was an investigation into the various types of psychological stress that are generated by pressures to make decisions more rapidly. This pressure arises from the power of computer networks to make greater amounts of information available more quickly. The second phase involved the identification of the perceived uses and usefulness of interpersonal communications through computers to augment the information content of data transferred through the network. Although technical developments in computer communications had progressed rapidly and widely in the United States, the major body of knowledge in application research in telecommunications was developed between 1972 and 1976 by the Communications Studies Group in the UK. Their work generated research methods and templates for future research—in particular the Description and Classification of Meetings study (DACOM). The study factor-analysed meeting functionality with behaviour and was to form the basis for a comparative analysis of face-to-face meetings with computer mediated interpersonal communications that the author carried out between 1976 and 1979. The first series of experiments took place at the Cranfield School of Management, the second with Coopers and Lybrand in London and the third between the University of Quebec and McGill University in Montreal.

The principal purpose of these experiments was to identify what type of communication activities could and would be carried out through computer networks—to relate the logical benefits inherent in computer networks to the psychological acceptance of the medium by the users. The research methodology identified definite areas of rejection and acceptance of computer communications for business functions, the most significant of which were:

> *Acceptance*—the exchange of data where the context had already been established;

> *Rejection*—creating an interpersonal relationship, negotiation.

Now when EDI is analysed it seems it can be divided into two broad categories:

> *Type 1*—direct machine-to-machine transfer when the framework of decisions contingent upon the data has already been made, and;

> *Type 2*—machine-to-machine via a human intermediary when the decisions are not pre-programmed.

Examples of the first type of EDI are the call-off of dispatches against bulk purchase orders—in the grocery business or the motorcar industry for instance, and the automated submission of entries to Customs and Excise. The second type includes all broking and quasi broking activities—which includes the bulk of freight forwarders where most decisions are of a 'one off' nature even though the operational requirements are similar. A further difference is that in the first category, the data sets comprising the messages are defined and complete, while in the second category the data sets are random and more often than not incomplete. The data sets accumulate in the recipient's files until there are sufficient data to allow documents, transactions, or management information to be produced.

It has been the ASTI experience that Type 1 EDI is sandwiched between various activities of Type 2 in the complete chain of a business transaction and that Type 2 is also surrounded by a variety of *ad hoc* information transfers before a data structure to allow EDI to take place can be established and accepted.

Although ASTI is involved with both types of EDI, it is Type 2 which demands the most skill and attention to the human factors to achieve useful implementation—and it is not simply a matter of ergonomics. The human vagaries that dominate and override technical systems have their roots in issues ranging from international politics in standards committees to near paranoia in data processing management, and to the commercial interests of marketing obsolescence by equipment manufacturers and telecommunication companies.

So there was clear understanding of the market niche for ASTI, but before it could be set up in its present form there had to be publically accessible data communication.

THE DEVELOPMENT OF PACKET SWITCHING

Packet switching had been invented at the National Physical Laboratory (NPL) in Teddington at the end of the 1960s to enable different computers on the NPL site to communicate through a common protocol. By the early 1970s the NPL was employing the data transfer routine and also a basic computer-based interpersonal message service. During that period, however, the wide scale developments in data transfer and interpersonal messaging through computer networks were mainly concentrated in the United States; through the Advanced Research Projects Agency network of the American Defense Department (ARPANET), and the public commercial networks of Telenet and Tymnet.

ARPANET's principal function was to link remote and diverse university computers thus enabling the transfer of research programs between different machines through a common network protocol. The first computer based interpersonal message system was developed—to pass on and explain operating instructions for the computer programs being transferred through the file transfer routines of ARPANET. ARPANET stretched from Hawaii to Scandinavia and had a node at University College London which at that time, together with the National Physical Laboratory, was the base for the author's research.

By 1975, the United States not only had wide-scale international data networks, but routines for transferring files of data and a variety of message services available to the general public. By comparison, in the United Kingdom, there was a primitive experimental packet switched system (EPSS) and computer-based message services were illegal. The position was broadly similar across Europe.

THE CONTEXT FOR DATA EXCHANGE

Creating the context for data exchange generally fell into the Type 2 EDI functions and activities perceived as not suitable for computer based communications.

During the period that the DACOM experiments were being conducted, X.25 had been ratified and there was a gradual relaxation of the regulations concerning the use of data networks for interpersonal messaging. Notwithstanding the almost impossible task of policing a policy that differentiated between data transfer intelligible and not intelligible to humans, the Telecommunications Authorities (PTTs) were reluctant to encourage computer messaging. This reluctance was based on their unpreparedness to offer this type of service themselves and a perceived conflict with their telex generated revenues. In the event, it was British Telecom that broke the mould and in 1980 commissioned a market study into the business prospects for a public electronic mail service. The author was instrumental in both the market research and the selection of the system to be installed, Dialcom. The result was the introduction of Telecom Gold in 1982. Shortly after the licensing of British Telecom by Dialcom to operate the service in the UK, Dialcom expanded its licensee base to Hong Kong and Canada before being acquired by ITT later in the following year. ITT Dialcom continued to attract new licensees among the companies in a further 10 countries before being itself acquired by British Telecom in May 1987.

At this stage of the paper it would be instructive to return to the history of data networking. In 1979, the inaugural meeting of Working Group 6.5 of the International Federation for Information Processing (IFIP WG 6.5) took place in Montreal. The purpose of the group was to formulate the basis for standards for interpersonal computer-based message services. What started life as question 5 in Study Group VII of the International Consultative Committee for Telecommunications of the International Telecommunications Union (CCITT) at the beginning of the 1980 four-year study period, emerged as the X.400 series of recommendations in October 1984.

Therefore by the end of 1984 there was not only a 15 year period of practical experience in transferring data through worldwide networks, but a network of public message services operated by PTTs as well as the proprietary systems that had been steadily developing at the same time: General Electric's GEISCO, I P Sharp's Mailbox, OnTyme II, Infonet and others. In the private network domain, the Society for Worldwide International Financial Telecommunications (SWIFT), and the Society for International Airline Telecommunications (SITA), had both shown over the previous seven years that a concerted effort by members of a common industry group with agreement on applications and data structures could produce dramatic increases in efficiency with corresponding economic and operational benefits. The technical, commercial and regulatory infrastructure for the international electronic interchange of data between public subscribers was in place—tried and tested.

THE GROWING COMPUTER DEPENDENCE

While the networks were being established a further development was taking place in the mass production of semiconductors and the price of computers was plummeting. The computer functionality that had cost £100,000 in 1975 was by 1984 available for a little over one fiftieth of the price. Modems had become more generally available, transmission speeds had increased and realistic tariffs were established for the public data networks. In terms of data communications

Europe was beginning to reach the position of the US seven or eight years previously—with one major exception; during the intervening period the increasing use of first telex, and secondly facsimile had produced established habits that would be difficult to change.

At the same time, however, a growing dependency on computers was increasing the need for homogeneity of data interchange—fax to ASCII to Baudot to voice was not an efficient mix of media. In certain areas of commerce, a clear return on investment could be demonstrated for capital equipment to automate data capture and communications—in particular Optical Mark Readers in the grocery and automotive businesses. But in general trading and shipping areas, there was a need for a different type of data communication, an organisation and a style of data handling more akin to SWIFT, but with an Open Systems Interconnection (OSI) potential, and a facility to overcome psychological barriers thereby ensuring the effective use of computer communications in business.

ASTI grew out of system development assignments within the East Asiatic Group in Denmark and the National Freight Consortium in the UK during the period 1981 to 1983. The concept was simple enough—the SWIFT of shipping, but using publicly available facilities under private management, thus removing the need for massive central investment in computers and networks. (Remember that there were no such public facilities when SWIFT and SITA were established). Technically there was a need for network management and interconnection on a worldwide scale, and data standards to allow files to be transferred meaningfully. There was also the need to set realistic tariffs which would fund the management, education and user-support tasks essential to the establishment and maintenance of a computer communication user group. It now seemed that the theories of man/computer/application interaction generated 10 years earlier would have a part to play in the implementation of data communicatons on a global scale.

The operating company of ASTI is Services Transports Informatiques SA (STI). As a first step to providing a single source of network services, it was necessary to draw up contracts with national telephone companies and data network providers. Simple though it may seem, writing international communications contracts goes against the principle of a telephone company only opening accounts with co-residents of the operating country. For shipping companies with branch offices and agencies scattered around the world STI was thus already able to offer a useful service. Its contractual arrangements with many PTTs worldwide facilitated data communications by removing a non-technical but nonetheless significant obstacle. STI provides a single bill for international users of a variety of services—including telex.

INTEGRATION OF EXISTING SYSTEMS

As was clear from experience in the East Asiatic Group, there was a vital need to integrate telex with data communications. Telex was then the backbone of shipping communications. Telex had become a communications culture and user expectations were entrenched. Telex was and is considered a legal document. Although it has now been supplemented by facsimile, there are more than 1.5 million telex terminals in the international directories and the growth of telex installations and traffic has only just reached its peak after 50 years of gradual growth. Whatever ASTI would provide in terms of data communicatons had to integrate with the telex network, or its impact in shipping would be negligible.

International trade movements are enabled by three types of information about the goods: information about the physical properties and movement of the goods; information about the value and ownership of the goods; information for regulatory, statistical and bureaucratic purposes. The handling of information by the parties to the trade is characterised by a fragmented distribution of data and a variety of collection and collation methods which lead to the production of forms—which in turn authorise and regulate the movement of goods, title and money.

In more than 90 per cent of international movements, a freight forwarder is at the centre of the cobweb of information about the consignment and will handle the production of forms, declarations to customs, insurance and the details of physical transport. At the centre of the forwarders' operations is the consignment, or job file. A job file contains most of the data concerning a consignment, and all of the data required to enable its transport. A complete job file represents about 2,000 characters. Whether or not the freight forwarder has a computer, a significant part of his operation is the capture and consolidation of data prior to the preparation of documents. It is important to understand that this function is unlikely to change.

At the early stages of a shipment it is not unusual for the only information on file to be the name of the customer, or consignor, the country of destination and a broad outline of the nature and volume of the goods to be shipped at a certain time. But this information is enough for the forwarder to start booking space with a shipping or airline and to alert his correspondent in the country of destination. A job number will be allocated and if the forwarder has a computer then a data file will be initiated. In a manual operation, the data file is likely to be a manila folder. In either case the intake of data is through the telephone, telex, facsimile or by mail.

A LACK OF JOB CONTROL?

The Cranfield experiments indicated that initial contacts would most likely continue to be made by telephone, as would any negotiations concerning the job. The same research methodology, but in the operational environment, indicated that a lack of job control would be perceived if the data path was direct from the customer's computer to the forwarder's data processing system. On the other hand shipping lines, and certainly the customs authorities, need computer-to-computer bulk file transfers.

The ASTI approach is therefore to separate these two types of data transfer; firstly, the man-computer-man leapfrogging of small parcels of data on which decisions can be taken and, secondly, the machine-to-machine file transfers on which any decisions to be made have already been pre-programmed. The two components of the ASTI network are communication channels and users with common expectations of the type of data being transferred. The policy of maintaining universal access to the service via public networks has already been discussed. The issue of creating common data sets is currently the subject of much discussion and debate, in the main devoted to defining messages containing predetermined sets of standardised data records. The dictionary of trade data records is the United Nations Trade Data Elements Directory

(UNTDED)—ISO 7372, and the equivalent message syntax is the Electronic Data Interchange for Commerce and Trade (EDIFACT).

In a world where the trading communities have been restrained and diverted from maximising use of data networks by the delaying tactics of PTTs, the publication of technical data dictionaries is not enough to create the infrastructure or critical mass required for common acceptance of the media. It is one thing to say what to do, another to state how to do it, but at the end of the day a contractor is invariably sought who will actually do it, and for an acceptable price. In this regard ASTI has taken the issue of standards for data interchange several steps further—to the point of defining the input, output, handling, and the communications conventions, and providing the facilities and services for its members as required. The ASTI data structure and syntax standard is called TRADEMASTER which specifies: TRADEMASTER Data Elements (notation, directory, cross references to SAD and UNTDED); TRADEMASTER Database (record structure, record key); TRADEMASTER Message (EDIFACT data elements; user data segments; service segments; confirmation messages); TRADEMASTER Network (network access, network service protocol, network addressing).

A TRADEMASTER data file contains the data elements sufficient to produce documents necessary for the international movement of goods. By employing similar file structures under a database management language and a common message interchange system, any permutation of records can be extracted from the file and sent to a printer or another computer. The ASTI approach to system and network architecture has been to create a convention of using micro-computer workstations linked locally by local area networks to each other, to a central file server and to an external X.25 public data network.

ADVANTAGES OF THE ASTI APPROACH

The approach has two major advantages over central computer/slave terminal systems: it is relatively simple and fast to implement large numbers of communicating workstations - thus quickly generating the critical mass required for a return on equipment investment to be realised; the existing patterns and style of work of the shippers, forwarders, insurance brokers and other parties to the trade are maintained thus facilitating true implementation and acceptance of the system.

This latter point is crucial to the success of the whole enterprise and ASTI has therefore developed both a financial and a represen- tational structure for ensuring that education and training of its members is given the highest priority. There is no suggestion in the ASTI approach that trading will be automated, nor that the use of parallel communication channels will be obviated by the adoption of computer communication techniques for transferring and sharing shipping data. The benefits of data communications are marginal if correctly implemented and accepted by the users and of minor significance compared with the harm that can be done to a company by imposing a system which disrupts a successful pattern of doing business. From its inception ASTI maintained a stance of charging its members for membership and for all the services supplied. One of the simple lessons of the early days of telecommunications research was that attitudes to a product change when a price is attached and money changes hands. There was an instance in one of the Middle Eastern countries when the telephone company sent an attractive young blonde into the Souk to research the demand for electronic telex terminals. When the completed questionnaires were analysed, the warehouse was accord- ingly stocked and the next stage of securing the sales was attempted with less than complete success by the local engineers.

While the information coming back from a disgruntled freight forwarder demanding value for money may not at the time seem palatable, the value to system design is critical. By pursuing the policy of responding to what our customers told us over the last three and a half years, ASTI has established a membership in 15 countries. This now numbers hundreds and is steadily growing.

7

The Relationship Between EDI & Electronic Funds Transfer

Christopher Eaglen

INTRODUCTION

The number of electronic funds transfer transactions made between the millions of accounts held at the UK banks and building societies through the central automated clearing system at BACS Limited, has grown steadily over the past 20 years. In recent years this growth has continued as more originator organisations and personal as well as corporate recipients have recognised and taken advantage of the positive move towards electronic funds transfer (EFT), as society moves steadily away from cash and cheque transactions. They have realised there are financial benefits to be gained by changing from paper-based payments to EFT payments.

The large-scale system implementation for commercial computing, office automation, payroll service, direct debiting, data communication network and electronic data interchange (EDI) projects have led to a significant increase in the number of organisations who now have the technology in place to convert to EFT and to benefit from the BACS electronic funds transfer service. The technological advances in both large and small computer system applications have enabled the BACS service to be made available to the largest and smallest organisations alike. There are now over 140 software companies developing and marketing programmes for EFT applications and BACS interfacing. These programmes are available for most combinations of commercial computers and operating systems.

Corporate and public acceptance of the electronic funds transfer method for the direct credit payment of salaries, wages, pensions, benefit, purchase ledger and standing orders has firmly established and expanded the UK BACS service. There are now over 24,000 direct credit originators. Direct debiting for both regular household and routine corporate bills, for the automated collection of a whole payment or a budget instalment towards a regular bill, is now well established for collecting utility, insurance, rental, rates, loan, subscriptions and mortgage payments. This equally wide acceptance of direct debiting by both members of the public and the 3,400 direct debit originators, has reinforced the BACS service in the UK on a major scale.

In 1987 over one billion EFT transactions were processed by BACS, of which direct business-to-business corporate transactions accounted for just over two per cent. Of these over nine million were purchase ledger direct credit payments, and over five million were commercial billing direct debit collections. The annual growth rates in the numbers of EFT transactions for these two corporate applications were over 17 per cent and over 20 per cent, respectively. It is estimated that the remainder are regular corporate payments made for insurance and utility invoices.

It is in the two areas of purchase ledger direct credit payments and commercial billing direct debit collections that the relationship between EFT and EDI becomes significant for corporate organisations or the administrative entity.

HOW THE BACS EFT SERVICE WORKS

BACS Limited is one of the major EFT services operating throughout the UK. It facilitates electronic funds transfer between any two parties for a significant number of organisations which submit batches of EFT transactions for automated payment clearance. The service is simple to use, inexpensive, reliable and precise. Any organisation which is sponsored by one of the member banks can use the service to make and collect payment transactions between any two accounts, (bank, building society and giro), held anywhere in the UK. The principle involved is that a controlled payment is made electronically and automatically from one named account number to another named account number. This is done by merging and sorting the user information received by BACS Limited and passing it to the banks and building societies for application to their accounts. Funds are transferred by the following three stage electronic funds transfer operation: the preparation and submission of EFT transactions to BACS Limited by the originating company; either directly or via a commercial computer bureau service; the acceptance, checking, merging and sorting of the payments by BACS Limited into bank and building society order; the posting and updating of bank and building society accounts by the banks and building societies.

A representation of the BACS service is shown in Figure 7.1. Electronic payment files comprising sequences of EFT transactions are delivered to BACS Limited on magnetic input media, or by telecommunication connection to Bacstel. A number of different types of input media are accepted by the BACS service. These are: telecoms (PSTN—Public Switched Telephone Network, at various speeds, PSS—Packet Switch Stream, leased line, kilostream); magnetic tape (0.5", 9 track, industry standard); diskette (8" or 5.25", industry standard). Different input media types are used by the originator to meet the user's specific criteria for each payment application. Either single processing day or multi-processing day file processing is available. In the former case all the EFT transactions in a payment file are output by BACS on the same processing day, as for a payroll run. In the latter case a payment file containing a number of payments to be processed on several different payment days, up to a month ahead is processed in pre-dated stages. This enables batches of purchase ledger payments or individual payments to be post-dated to take account of credit periods or discounts and to be paid or collected on a pre-specified date.

Those organisations that do not have their own computer system can employ a bank or commercial computer service bureau. There are now five bank computer service bureaux and 40 major computer service bureaux who submit payment files to BACS Limited on behalf of their customers. Today 60 per cent of EFT users, accounting for 14 per cent of item volumes, send files of EFT transactions for direct credit payroll, purchase ledger payment and direct debit collection to BACS via a computer service bureau. The remaining 40 per cent of

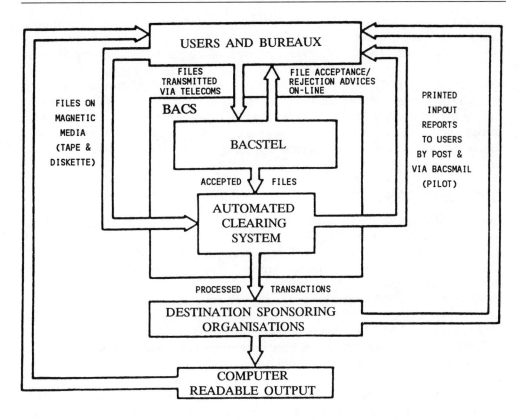

Figure 7.1 Schematic of the BACS EFT Electronic Data Interchange

EFT users, accounting for 86 per cent of item volumes processed, make their submissions to BACS directly. In some cases users of the service do make use of both direct and bureau submission methods. Each method being chosen for a particular type of EFT application. The originator's choice of input medium is made according to several criteria such as, geographical location, system availability, computer configuration, software development, telecommunications service, the time period available for preparation, submission and automated payment clearance, and the number of EFT transactions to be submitted in each batch of items.

The EFT transaction replaces the need for cheques, giros or cash. Each EFT payment transaction can carry an information cross-reference element with the payment. This is more than adequate for most credit and debit applications but may not provide, on its own, the total data content for some payment applications, when a combination of EFT and EDI techniques may be required. However, the BACS service does provide an optimum service where the reference data in Field 10 of the Standard Payment Record enables both computerised record identification and ledger entry matching to be achieved automatically.

Automated ledger reconciliation is now achievable using the bank statement magnetic tape service in conjunction with the BACS service. Those organisations that receive their banking details on magnetic tape from the bank, can read this data into their computer for transaction reconciliation. The computer will navigate the ledgers to match the EFT transaction data to one of the outstanding ledger payments. There are two methods of reconciliation where several invoice entries can be related to one payment. These require either the inclusion of an EDI reference within Field 10 of the EFT transaction, or a remittance advice link number to be contained in Field 10 of the EFT transaction and for this to be cross referenced in the EDI or E- Mail remittance advice sent across a separate EDI sevice. The vendor's computer can then reconcile the EFT payment with the separate invoice ledger entries listed on the remittance advice.

THE PROCESSING CYCLE

The EFT processing cycle is shown in Figure 7.2. This covers three working days. The deadline for receipt of data by BACS is 9 pm on Day 1. All BACS work is completed by 6 am on Day 2, by which time the data has been validated, merged and sorted into bank order, tapes despatched and telecommunications sessions completed to the computer centres of the destination banks and building societies. The originating user receives the important input report through the post, or via Bacsmail on the morning of Day 2. During that day the banks merge the BACS output with other data, and on Day 3 the payments are credited to suppliers' accounts and the corresponding contra record debited to the payer's account. The time from input to BACS to cleared funds at the destination banking account takes approximately 36 hours. When the submission is a multi-processing dayfile, BACS processes only the specific items on each of the specific dated days. Dates can be specified up to a month ahead. The key point to recognise is that although the processing cycle covers 3 bank working days, value is normally transferred on Account Entry Day, 9.30 am, at the opening of business. At that time, cleared funds are made available in the payee's account. The BACS service, in effect, deals with two types of EFT payment messages that have a fixed format. Single Processing Day EFT transactions are fixed format messages each containing 100 data characters and multi-processing day EFT transactions are fixed format messages each containing 106 data characters. The user provides the following five key elements of information for each transaction:

> the destination addressing information—bank or building society, branch, account number and name;

> the originating addressing information—bank or building society, branch, account number and name;

> the amount of the transaction and whether a debit or a credit item;

> the processing date—normally value is transferred between accounts the bank working day after processing day. This is called the Account Entry date and corresponds to the value transfer date;

> the Reference Data in Field 10. This is the EDI content of the EFT transaction standard record and can be used for computer or manual reconciliation or for an 18 character comment.

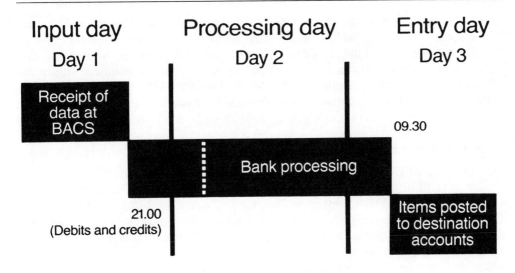

Figure 7.2 Schematic of the EFT processing cycle

APPLICATION OVERVIEW

In the early 1970s, the three most common applications for which the BACS service was used were standing order exchange, collection of insurance premiums by direct debit and salary payments to employees accounts by direct credit transfer.

In recent years, there has been a recognition that the BACS EFT Service can be applied to other types of direct credit transfer payment or direct debit collection applications with a saving in cost. In broad terms, the total cost to the user of making a batch payment through BACS can be less than a tenth of an equivalent paper based payment. The BACS service available in the UK currently offers commercial organisations economical and easy access to a reliable time-certain operation. The cost savings are significant (a factor of 10 is not unusual) and the benefits in cash-flow terms from efficient treasury management and reduced administration cost are significant for all scales of EFT use.

In the UK, it is estimated there are over 9,000 major public and private sector computer sites and there are over 150,000 micro-computers used in both commercial payroll and accounting roles. This large computer base incorporates many different types of hardware equipment, operating system software, application programmes and output media types. Over 8,500 computer systems are now operating, directly or indirectly, in an EFT role with magnetic media and over 2,000 with Bacstel telecommunications. There are a growing number of systems being used in both an EDI and EFT role as the need for further cost savings and office efficiency becomes recognised. EFT and EDI software now exists off-the-shelf for many types of applications.

For large dedicated accounting systems, bespoke applications programmes are required and these are either designed, developed and supplied by the systems programming organisations, or supplied by the specialist payroll and ledger development companies. This ready availability of application EFT and EDI software ensures that most EFT applications can be implemented within several weeks or months depending upon the size and complexity of the application. For standard payroll and purchase ledger applications where an off-the-shelf package can be used, the standard system can be procured, installed, tested and commissioned within one month.

THE EDI AND EFT PROCESSES

The EDI and EFT processes for data interchange can either operate independently in both time and application, or there can be some linkage through the use of a unique Field 10 reference link number embodied in both the EFT and EDI transactions. However, in a number of cases, Field 10 of the EFT transaction may be adequate for containing all the data for reconciliation of a transaction between two corporate organisations. For example, Field 10 may contain the supplier's invoice reference number. In this case the EFT route alone may carry sufficient information for the computerised reconciliation of ledgers. This is possible where certain database structures and bill coding methods can be applied across a principal payment group, or where the invoice payment reference data can be made specific and embodied into Field 10 of the EFT transaction. In some cases the remittance information could be exchanged across an E-Mail service by using a structured screen layout.

Figure 7.3 shows the schematic arrangement of the EDI and EFT routes and the EDI and BACS services. This includes commercial data interchange, electronic funds transfer, banking and bank statement or transaction details exchange, as well as computerised ledger reconcilation. An originator will use some, or all of these services depending upon the size of the payment application and the level of automation used for the accounting and banking functions. The originator may use the same type or different types of magnetic media and/or telecommunications data delivery methods for the EDI and EFT routes. Each media type will be chosen according to the hardware available, the number of transactions to be processed and the time criticality of the payment, or collection application.

BACS contra and standard record formats

The submission and file data structures comprise a header label, a contra record for each file, one or more files of EFT transactions (standard records) and an end-of-file trailer label. In the case of Bacstel submissions, there is the additional 'log-on' record and the 'end of submission' record. The computer system that originates the EFT submission EF files for BACS to process, formats the relevant data elements and EFT transactions into this structure. The data elements are keyed into each record, extracted from other program modules, or read from other input devices, such as swipe and slot card readers. The contra and standard record formats are described below

Contra record

Each file must be self balancing. Within each file the total value of credit contra records must be equal to the total value of credit records, which are debits to

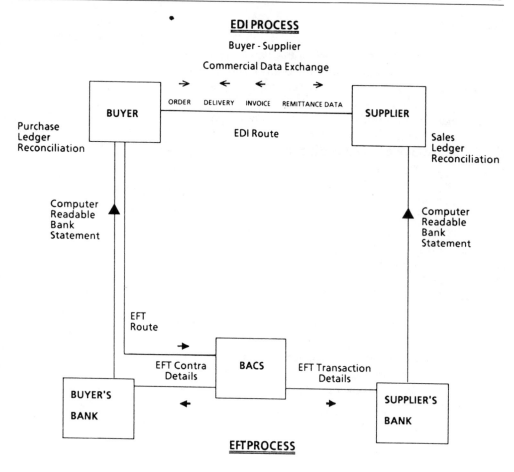

Figure 7.3 Schematic arrangement of EFT and EDI processes incorporating the EFT and EDI routes

the originator's account. Likewise the total value of debit contra records must equal the total value of the debit records. Contra records must be present on all files. Within a multi-processing day file there must be balancing contra records for each prcessing day for which data records are present on the file. The financial value of the contra record is entered on the originator's account, along with the originator's 18 character narrative in Field (i).

The format shown below identifies the allocation of the transaction fields for the credit and debit contra record.

Credit and debit contra record layout

The layout has both Fields (a) and (e) identical, and Fields (b) and (f) identical. There are 11 data fields in a single processing day contra-record and 12 fields in a multi-processing day contra-record. Field (l) carries the transaction processing date as Julian date.

Field	Use	Number of Characters
a	Sorting code number of the Bank branch at which the nominated account of the user is held and to which this record is to be directed.	6
b	Account number of the user's nominated account at the above bank branch.	8
c	Type of account code of the above account.	1
d	Transaction code.	2
e	Sorting code number of the bank branch at which the nominated account of the user is held and to which this record is to be directed.	6
f	Account number of the user's nominated account at the above bank branch.	8
g	Zero filled.	4
h	Amount in pence.	11
i	User's narrative	18
j	Contra reference.	18
k	Name of account to which this record is to be directed. **This additional field is for contra-records on multi-processing day files.**	18
l	Processing date of contra record.	6

Standard payment record

The standard payment record is used for the EFT credit or debit transaction details. Each transaction enables an individual payment to be made into a corporate or personal bank account or into a building society account. Field 1 carries the destination sorting code number and Field 2 carries the destination account number. There are two, 18 character data fields in the standard payment record used for reference purposes. These are Fields 9 and 10. Field 9 or Field 10 is printed on personal recipients' account statements. Field 9 contains the users name and Field 10 contains the reference information between two parties. Field 9 and Field 10 can be obtained on some personal and corporate collection accounts, or supplementary lists. Questions concerning the use of reference fields and the presentation of the reference data on specific account statements should be addressed to the bank or building society concerned as there are variations between statement formats. Some banks can issue a magnetic tape with bank statement details for recipient organisations that do carry Field 9 and 10 reference data elements for each account entry. Additionally, transactional details comprising Fields 9, 10 and 11 can be provided by some banks on magnetic tape. Both these tape based services can be used for computerised reconciliation purposes. Field 10 of the standard payment record can be used for specific cross referencing of transactions between parties and the data in the transaction may be used to transfer information electronically from the originator to the bank account and statement of an individual, or company. The Field can be used to carry purchase ledger and sales ledger references for either direct credits or direct debits.In order to enable automatic computer reconciliation to be completed, it is good practice to pass the recipients ledger, bill, or invoice number back to the recipient in Field 10. Each payment record relates to one transaction. The number of data characters per transaction are shown below.

Single processing day files (100 characters in length);
Multi-processing day files (106 characters in length, the first 100 characters being identical to the single processing day file format and the final six characters represent a future transaction processing Julian date).

Standard credit payment record

The standard credit payment record for Electronic Funds Transfer is structured as follows:

Field	Credit Records	Number of Characters
1	Destination sorting code number Sorting code number of bank branch to be credited	6
2	Destination account number Account number of account to be credited from the above bank, or building society branch account number	8
3	Type of account code of the above account	1
4	Transaction code	2
5	Originating sorting code number Sorting code number of bank branch at which user's nominated account is held	6
6	Originating account number Account number of the user's nominated account at the above bank branch	8
7	Zero filled or numeric reference	4
8	Amount in pence	11
9	User's name	18
10	Normally investors, roll, works, payroll, PL, or invoice reference number, or description	18
11	Destination account name Name of account to be credited **This additional field if for data records on multi-processing day files**	18
12	Processing date of data record	6

Standard debit payment record

The standard debit payment record for Electronic Funds Transfer is structured as follows:

Field	Debit Records	Number of Characters
1	Destination sorting code number Sorting code number of bank branch to be debited	6
2	Destination account number Account number of account to be debited from the above bank, or building society branch account number	8
3	Type of account code of the above account	1
4	Transaction code	2
5	Originating sorting code number Sorting code number of bank branch at which user's nominated account is held	6
6	Originating account number Account number of the user's nominated account at the above bank branch	8
7	Zero filled or numeric reference	4
8	Amount in pence	11
9	User's name	18
10	Invoice reference number or description for corporate customer billings	18
11	Destination account name Name of account to be debited **This additional field if for data records on multi-processing day files**	18
12	Processing date of data record	6

EXAMPLE OF EFT APPLICATIONS

The EFT payment method and the BACS service in particular are used extensively for both large and small-scale corporate and personal direct debit and direct credit applications. Several corporate EFT uses are described below.

Direct debits

There is no cheaper or more effective way to arrange for the payment of bills or invoices than to permit and authorise a supplier, who is a direct debit originator to direct debit your account. This is particularly true for regular payments to utilities and local authorities. In these cases the total costs of collection are borne by the originator. The internal reconciliation process in the originator's sales ledger(s) is fully automated, computersied and all details are resident on the originator's computer system. When the unpaid direct debits are returned to the originator on magnetic tape, by the originator's bank they can be read into the originator's computer system for final reconciliation and follow-up. This increases the level of automation and reduces the need for rekeying.

Some of the larger distribution organisations use the multi-processing day file method for automated commercial billing collection. This method enables the direct debit collection to be synchronised to coincide with the delivery of a consignment, or to be collected a specific number of days after delivery of the consignment. For the commercial billing application Field 10 can normally be used to pass the individual consignment reference number and associated data on to the recipient's banking account statement. The originator's data extraction and keyboard entry computer programs need to be sufficiently versatile to ensure that character by character entries can be made into Field 10. This enables each transaction to be uniquely coded for reconciliation purposes. In some cases, Field 10 can be used for more than one purpose, provided the total number of data characters does not exceed 18 per field.

Direct credits

When the originating organisation uses EFT, and the BACS service for purchase ledger payments to the supplier, the supplier's sales ledger reconciliation process can be made more efficient and effective by passing the unique reference data in Field 10 to the recipient's banking account statement. This reference data can include the supplier's invoice number in the pre-agreed field and data character positions the supplier has specified are to be used for computerised reconciliation.

Where the purchase ledger function is computerised it will generally list and record all the incoming invoices. The total indebtedness by due date and priority for payment will be listed. Generally, two sets of numbers will be held for each incoming invoice. These two sets will be the supplier's invoice number and the buyer's internal purchase ledger reference. Computerised reconciliation often requires the former to be returned with the payment. In the case of a cheque payment system, cheques may be drawn when payment becomes due and the total indebtedness is then broken down between debts incurred but not yet due and debts due for payment.

Thus, when a request for payment is received the amount due is either agreed, or the reason for a discrepancy is then posted without delay. However, with this approach the accounting record shows a misleading picture. It assumes that all the cheques made out were released, when in fact many days or weeks may pass before the last of these cheques are cashed. The cheque presentation delays are not always constant. Therefore, the actual value outstanding in respect of overdue invoices at any one time can only be established by adding together all the cheques not yet released, or by keeping a dynamic record of cheques still held. If required the EFT method can emulate the 'cheques in the drawer' system. By making use of the EFT and BACS service, organisations can obtain an improved, controlled, faster service for settling purchase ledger payments on specific dates. A purchase ledger system can be operated with a date analysis of invoices to produce the following: outstanding balances of invoices passed but not yet due for payment; invoices due but not yet passed; outstanding balances due, passed but not yet paid; balances paid. With the help of the above information, requests for payment can be dealt with effectively. If arrangements for payments are made with the supplier they can be told both the exact amount of the payment and also the exact date when payment was made through BACS into the supplier's account. The list in Figure 7.4 shows the purchase ledger payments that have been planned and the total amounts for the payments to be made on different dates. Therefore, the total financial commitment entered into is known. The last payment and the date of payment are indicated. Separate provision of this information by the computer system will enhance the originator's purchase ledger and sundry payments systems.

Paying a single invoice by a single EFT transaction

There are payment situations where each bill is paid by a single corresponding EFT transaction. The amount paid corresponds to a statement or single invoice value. In this case the supplier's invoice number can be carried in Field 10 of the EFT transaction. The supplier's invoice number becomes the Field 10 EDI-EFT invoice link. Then either the paper remittance advice or the single EDI,or E-Mail remittance advice will contain the same number as the EFT transaction. In Figure 7.5 for a single invoice transaction, the number is INVO 1234567880407Y. In those cases where the EFT Field 10 invoice link reference number is adequate for automated computer reconciliation, it may not be necessary to send a separate remittance advice as well.

This better practice of issuing a separate EFT transaction payment for each invoice can be further enhanced for sizeable invoiced amounts by including a separate EFT 'contra' entry against each payment. Using this method the buyer's bank statement carries an item by item entry for each invoice. This enables both the buyer's and supplier's bank statements to be matched item for item. This practice of using a single EFT 'contra' and a corresponding single EFT transaction for each invoice is better practice for larger valued payments because the reconciliation process for both parties is both precise and efficient. When questions do arise there is less time spent by both the supplier and buyer identifying and resolving payment discrepancies.

Paying a remittance advice for several invoices by a single EFT transaction

In that case where a single EFT transaction relates to the total value of a batch of supplier invoices, a Field 10 EDI-EFT remittance advice link number can be carried in the EFT transaction. This is shown as ABCD123456788040Y in Figure 7.5. This will be the same number as the same supplier's invoice numbers reference on the paper remittance advice or in the EDI remittance number (ABCD123456788040Y), within the separate EDI, or E-Mail remittance advice.

The supplier's computer system will input the EFT banking details and the EDI, or E-Mail details separately. It will link the data from the EFT and EDI, or E-Mail transaction files daily. It will automatically match each EFT entry with the corresponding remittance advice information and identify each invoice being paid. Then it will navigate the sales ledger(s), acknowledge each invoice paid and automtically complete final reconciliation of the individual invoices.

XYZ LTD

OUTSTANDING PURCHASE LEDGER BALANCES DUE FOR PAYMENT

RUN DATE 12/01/88
SERIAL NO. 46

BUYERS PL REF.	FIELD 10 - SUPPLIER INVOICE NUMBER	SUPPLIER NAME	BACS (B) CHEQUE (C)	LAST PAYMENT AMOUNT	DATE	PAY ON	AMOUNT DUE	DUE DATE	PAYMENT 20/1	ARRANGED FOR 27/1
XYZ1	4110 0190	J. Brown	B	2000	12/12		3000	30/11		
XYZ2	4104 0250	P Smith	B	500		1/12		600	30/10	600
XYZ3	4120 0330	M White	B							
XYZ4	4211 0425	J Little	B	700	10/01		800	30/11		
XYZ5	4236 0640	N Black	C	300	31/12		500	30/11	500	
XYZ6	4244 0735	N Gray	B	1000	15/12		1500	31/10		1500
XYZ7	4250 0810	T. Large	B	300	31/12		400	30/11		
XYZ8	4300 0907	G. Green	B	10000	20/12		20000	30/11		
						TOTAL	27000		1100	1500

DEDUCT PAYMENT TO BE MADE
20/01   1100 -
27/01   1500 -
TOTAL NOT RELEASED   24400

Figure 7.4 Illustration of purchase ledger payments that have been planned and the totla amounts for the payments to be made on different dates

SINGLE INVOICE TRANSACTIONS: EDI - FIELD 10 LINK

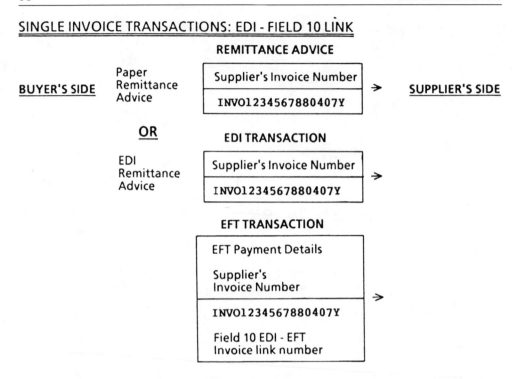

MULTIPLE INVOICE TRANSACTIONS: EDI - FIELD 10 LINK

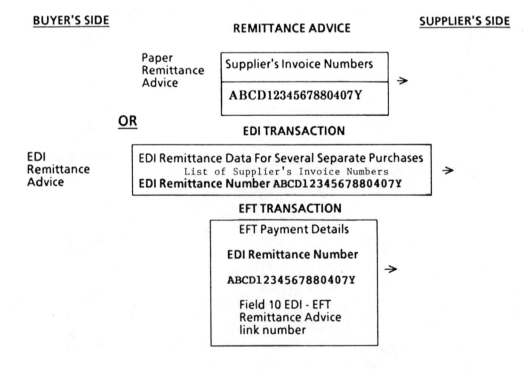

Figure 7.5 Comparison of single and multiple invoice transactions

Making regular multi-invoice payments with a single EFT transaction without a remittance advice

Instead of making an EFT payment for each invoice some large organisations prefer to pay a number of utility, or corporate invoices with one cheque, or a single uncoded EFT transaction. This can create problems with reconciliation when insufficient information is passed to the utility to identify each of the specific bills that are included in that particular multi-invoice payment. As an alternative to using remittance advices and to enable reconciliation to be automated in this situation, it is suggested that the following method could be established jointly by the invoice paying organisations and a utility, or corporate. This will enable the invoice reconciliation process to be fully computerised. When applied, this method should eliminate the need for most of the current manual reconciliation of regular multi-invoice payments This method can be used for direct credit EFT applications where multi-invoice payment and computer to computer ledger reconciliation are both prime requirements. An example of a method of coding Field 10 of an EFT transaction to enable multi-invoice payment reconciliation to be automated is described below.

A standard contra record layout for this method is shown in Figure 7.6 and a standard record layout is shown in Figure 7.7. These relate to an arbitrary example of an organisation and an electricity board. The method relies on the two parties pre-agreeing a sequence for the specific facilities. This sequence in turn is mapped onto a sequence of character positions in Field 10 of the standard record.

Example of an organisation paying electricity bills by EFT

This example happens to relate to electricity meters and electricity bills but the concept is applicable to other regular invoiced facilities. In each case the supplier and the payer agree which of the invoices will be grouped together and which facility will be sequenced to correspond to which particular EFT Field 10 character position. In the following example, the Field 10 element will comprise both a six digit reference number and a character code. Each character position of the code will represent one electricity meter and the corresponding electricity bill for that meter.

The payer: XYZ organisation agrees with the supplier: ABC Electricity Board to pay electricity bills in packets of 12 and requires some flexibility as to the precise date for each payment. The supplier, the ABC Electricity Board, allocate a number of multi-invoice tables to the payer XYZ organisation. Each multi-invoice table relates to (in this example) a packet of 12 electricity meters and the associated bills. The electricity meters may be located on one or several sites. A unique multi-payments reference number (MRN), in this case a six digit number 123456, will be allocated for each multi-invoice (MI) table.

The MRN will be held on the electicity board's database along with the payer's originating sorting code number and originating account number. This enables the ABC Electricity Board to identify who is making the payment, that is, the XYZ organisation and which specific electricity meters the specific payment applies to. The code occupies the seventh through to the eighteenth Field 10 character positions. One character position corresponds to one of the electricity bills. In this example the component character positions within this 12 digit Field 10 for each electricity meter are shown in the chart which follows.

Field	Description of Field & Content	Purpose	Length in Characters	BACS File/Record Acceptance Validation Checks	BACS Action if Record fails Validation Check
a	SORTING CODE NUMBER AT WHICH USER'S NOMINATED ACCOUNT IS MAINTAINED (same as Field e)	To identify the Nominated Account designated by the User to which this balancing Contra record is to be debited or credited	6	Must be a sorting code at which the User has a Nominated Account	AMEND RECORD by substituting in Fields a, b and c the equivalent details of the User's Nominated Account as identified by the contents of Fields e and f, (as amended to the Main Account if invalid)
b	ACCOUNT NUMBER OF USER'S NOMINATED ACCOUNT (same as Field f)		8	Must be the account number of one of the User's Nominated Accounts at the above sorting code	
c	TYPE OF ACCOUNT CODE OF THE ABOVE ACCOUNT		1	Must be the Type of Account Code of the above account	
d	TRANSACTION CODE	To identify the type of Contra record – whether a Credit Contra (debit record) or a Debit Contra (credit record)	2	If Field j is valid: a) Must be 17 (Credit Contra) and/or 99 (Debit Contra) b) The Nominated Account as identified by Fields a, b and c (or as amended if invalid) must be authorised to originate credit Data records if 17 and/or debit Data records if 99	REJECT FILE REJECT RECORD
e	SORTING CODE NUMBER AT WHICH USER'S NOMINATED ACCOUNT IS MAINTAINED (same as Field a)	As a double check on Fields a, b and c	6	a) If Fields a, b and c are not amended, must be the same as Fields a and b b) If Fields a, b and c are amended, must be the sorting code and account number of one of the User's Nominated Accounts	AMEND RECORD by substituting the contents of Fields a and b in Fields e and f AMEND RECORD by substituting the sorting code and account number of the User's Main Account
f	ACCOUNT NUMBER OF USER'S NOMINATED ACCOUNT AT THE ABOVE SORTING CODE (same as Field b)		8		
g	FREE FORMAT	Not used by BACS or the destination institutions	4	No check performed by BACS	–
h	AMOUNT (expressed in pence)	To identify the value of the Contra record	11R	Must be all numeric characters, **but must not be all zeros**	REJECT FILE
i	**ABC12345688040 7MAR**	To assist in the identification of the entry on the User's statement	18	No check performed by BACS	–
j	CONTRA IDENTIFICATION – 'CONTRA'	To identify the record as a Contra record	18	Must be 'CONTRA' folowed by 12 blank spaces	TREAT AS APPROPRIATE DATA RECORD AND VALIDATE ACCORDINGLY
k	ABBREVIATED ACCOUNT NAME OF THE USER'S NOMINATED ACCOUNT (as identified by Fields e and f)	To assist in identifying the Nominated Account designated by the User	18L	No check performed by BACS	–

Figure 7.6 Contra record layout (indicative example)

Field Number	Description of Field & Content	Purpose	Length in Characters	BACS File/Record Acceptance Validation Checks	BACS Action if Record fails Validation Check
1	DESTINATION SORTING CODE NUMBER		6	Sorting code must be currently registered in BACS masterfiles	RETURN RECORD to the User's originating account
2	DESTINATION ACCOUNT NUMBER	To identify the account to which the record is to be debited or credited	8	Must be eight numeric characters	AMEND RECORD by substituting eight zeros
3	DESTINATION TYPE OF ACCOUNT CODE		1	Must be a numeric character	AMEND RECORD by substituting zero
4	TRANSACTION CODE	To identify the type of record and whether a debit or a credit	2	a) Must be one of the permitted Transaction Codes (see Appendix B) b) Must have been designated by the User for the originating account c) Must be acceptable to the destination sorting code d) Must be in the range for Standard records (see Appendix B)	REJECT FILE REJECT RECORD REJECT RECORD TREAT AS APPROPRIATE DATA RECORD AND VALIDATE ACCORDINGLY
5	ORIGINATING SORTING CODE NUMBER	To identify the Nominated Account of the User from which the record originates	6	Must equal the sorting code and account number of oen of the User's Nominated Accounts (see Part I, Section 1.4)	AMEND RECORD by substituting the sorting code and account number of the User's Main Account
6	ORIGINATING ACCOUNT NUMBER		8		
7	FREE FORMAT	Not used by BACS or the destination Banks	4	No check performed by BACS	—
8	AMOUNT (expressed in pence)	To identify the value of the debit or credit	11R	Must be all numeric characters, **but must not be all zeros**	REJECT FILE
9	XYZ ORGANISATION	To identify the originator of the record	18L	No check performed by BACS	—
10	ABC12345688040407MAR	MRN and CODE	18	No check performed by BACS	—
11	DESTINATION ACCOUNT ABC ELECTRICITY BOARD	To identify the account to be debited or credited if the account number in Field 2 is not a valid account number at the sorting code in Field 1	18L	Must not be left blank if Field 2 is: a) blank spaces b) eight zeros c) amended by BACS validation to eight zeros	RETURN RECORD to the User's originating account

Figure 7.7 Standard record layout (indicative example)

Electricity Meter bill	BACS Record Character positions	Field 10 status and Character position	
1	71	7	P
2	72	8	P
3	73	9	P
4	74	10	P
5	75	11	P
6	76	12	I
7	77	13	I
8	78	14	I
9	79	15	N
10	80	16	N
11	81	17	I
12	82	18	I

When constructing the EFT transactions, the payer completes the reference information in the BACS record as follows:

Field 9 payer's name (XYZ organisation) from which the supplier can recognise the payer. (Fields 5 and 6 could also be used for this purpose).

Field 10: comprises the six digit MRN: 123456, that is, the MI Table reference, followed by the code for the individual invoice status of each of the electricity bills, that is, PPPPPIIINNII in this example.

The status of each invoice payment is as follows: P—paid already; O—outstanding invoice; I—included in this payment; N—not used.

Field 10 of the standard record in Figure 7.7 shows the MRN and a typical 12 digit sequence of payments contained in a multi-invoice payment EFT transaction through BACS. All the (I) characters denote the invoices paid in that particular BACS EFT transaction. Utility ABC's computer will take each character position of the code in turn from Field 10. It will identify each of the (I) (included in this payment) characters in turn and will obtain the invoiced amount for each facility from the ledger. It will add these individual amounts (I's) together for all the Field 10 characters in the code to produce the arithmetic invoice payment total. This will be compared with the Field 8 amount. On the agreement of the two total values the sales ledger entries will be marked off individually according to their status.

The utility's paper counterfoil invoices may carry the same utility and multipayments reference number. This number, for example ABC 123456, will be shown along with that invoice number, on each invoice counterfoil. If the payer still wishes to submit the paper counterfoil invoices by post, then it is suggested that the payer can print a separate covering remittance advice to assist with reconciliation. This will include the following: the utility and multi-payments reference number; the EFT payment into account entry date; each invoice number for a facility; each invoice amount; and the payment total for all individual invoices in this EFT transaction payment. This will correspond to the amount in Field 8 of the BACS standard record and to Field (h) of the contra-record, when a contra is made for each multi-payment.

If warranted, it is suggested that the paper counterfoil invoices could be processed through an OCR, or bar code slot reader coupled to a PC computer terminal. This PC could be programmed to read all the data from the slot reader and do the arithmetical summation of the individual invoice amounts. This would enable multi-invoice payment totalisation for automated reconciliation to be completed at the data entry station with minimal keyboard use, saving time and reducing errors.

This example method of handling multi-invoice payments will enable any two parties to reconcile lump sum multi-invoice payments with the separate batches of invoice entries against each of the utility's sales ledgers. If there are more than 12 regular payments to be made, another EFT transaction with a different MRN can be used to represent the additional packet of invoices.

CONCLUSIONS

This paper has highlighted some examples of the different payment techniques that can be used currently to enable organisations to achieve either semi-automated or fully-automated invoice payment and reconciliation. Originating organisations submit a wide range of sizes of EFT transaction files to BACS for EFT procesing. The file sizes submitted to BACS range from one item files to those multi-tape files totalling over one million items. Both regular and one-off payments are processed by BACS equally effectively. Three specific ledger payment applications using EFT and EDI methods are describbed in the paper:

When the unique payment identification for a single invoice is contained within Field 10 of an EFT transaction.

When a single EFT transaction is linked by a unique identifier in Field 10 to a separate EDI, E-Mail or paper remittance advice.

The remittance advice contains the same unique identifier, the list of invoices, dates and amount components relating to the payment and supporting information.

When a composite reference and code is generated to be contained in Field 10 of an EFT transaction. The code can represent a packet of regular invoices and their individual payment status. The receiving organisation computer can be programmed to decode the Field 10 reference on a character by character basis. This enables the status of each invoice in the packet to be qualified and those invoices paid within that EFT transaction to be reconciled against the ledger(s).

It is expected that future computer-based ledger programmes will include all the application features outlined in this paper to enable the full range of EDI, E-Mail and EFT facilities to be coordinated for enhanced purchase ledger, sales ledger, sundry and regular payment systems, management and administration. Future bespoke and standard software packages will include several different data entry routines to enable the originator of EFT transactions to select from a file or key-in the data to be contained in Field 10 of each different EFT transaction within a file.

8
UNICORN:
EDI in a Travel Reservation System

Anthony Allen

INTRODUCTION

UNICORN is the name given to describe the application standard designed for car ferry reservations and ticketing but equally applicable to other tourist, group and freight traffic travelling on ferries. As an acronym UNICORN stands for: United Nations Interactive (message) Concept Over Reservation Networks. It is aimed at an element of international trade which needs very limited documentation but the movement of which is forming an increasingly voluminous commodity—this element is called people. It is thus a different concept to the most readily accepted understanding of EDI. It is not really part of the trade cycle, because there is no paper passing between different bodies, nor is it a product, rather it is a service. There is a single user community, rather than a number of different self-centred groups. The aim of UNICORN is not to simplify the little paperwork that exists, but to apply the concepts of EDI to provide a common standard for processing transactions of an interactive enquiry nature.

Traditional EDI involves paperwork passing through a number of different bodies, including Customs. Interactive EDI is thus conceptually different, but the challenge has been to show that the rules still apply and the methodology is still valid. The only piece of paper required, at the moment, is the passenger's ticket. UNICORN lies within the framework defined in the UNECE EDIFACT standards and takes EDI into the arena of real time interactive use. Within the travel industry dialogues are held between the providers of services such as airlines, railways, ferry companies, hoteliers and car hire companies and the travel agents retained to sell those products to the public. The items for sale can be mixed into an *à la carte* programme to suit the individual or can be packaged together by a tour operator and sold as a total, usually discounted, deal. Because of commercial arrangements sales also take place between the service providers and between travel agents. Value added and data services providers also have active roles within the travel industry in order to carry the voluminous data traffic.

Until UNICORN was developed there were two methods of communicating data (short of using the telephone). Airlines and railways had developed their own message standards for internal communications but the travel agents had to link into the airline networks via special terminals using 'user hostile' messages. For other purposes in the UK videotex became the standard method of accessing service providers and the computer systems of tour operators. In continental Europe travel agents could use terminals for airline and railway reservations and for bookings with some tour operators. These are known as multi-access networks.

The main activities covered in UNICORN are the requests for and offers of ferry travel reservations and the associated activities of travel document production, pricing and the raising of the resultant financial account.

HOW UNICORN HAPPENED

In 1985 START, the travel agents' multi-access network in West Germany based in Frankfurt, informed ferry companies that it was interested in making connections for reservations and on-line price calculations. It was not concerned with defining the application level, but did require that the user's screen displays remained unchanged. Three ferry companies responded positively, Sealink, Townsend Thoresen (now P&O European Ferries) and North Sea Ferries. It seemed pointless for each ferry company to define a different interface when there was a prospect of cooperation thereby reducing costs at the West German end. It was resolved to try and overcome differences in computer systems and end-user screen displays by adopting a common interface if that were possible.

As with most service industries, the continual aim is to improve service to the customer. Sealink also visualised the need to communicate with other agents' computer systems in the future using as few different interface standards as possible. This would allow agents to standardise their own screens to suit their businesses and make the passing of data to the computer system independent of the final display. START was thus seen as the first of these common interfaces. History has proved this concept to be correct as global distribution systems being developed by the world's airlines also envisage connections being established with providers of non-airline services using standard interfaces.

The ferry companies held discussions and decided that messages similar to those used by the European railway administrations should be developed for both request and response messages. No account would be taken of the attributes of the terminal being driven or the computer hardware or tele-communications being used. The messages should be perfectly valid if passed on 'tablets of stone'. Unlike the railways, which had developed their own message structure, it was felt that the ferry companies' environment was such that generic standards would need to be used. Initial conversations with SITPRO suggested that EDI provided an appropriate message structure although it had been developed for batch transfer. A few paper exercises demonstrated that little change or addition was required for its use in the 'real-time' world other than to regularise the process of keeping conversing computer systems in step. At the same time casual conversations with the Automobile Association and the Caravan Club suggested that these organisations would also dearly like to get out of the pertaining viewdata environment for ferry bookings. Thus UNICORN was born, but at that time using UNTDI rather than the then unavailable and more recent EDIFACT standards.

THE PROBLEMS SOLVED BY UNICORN

It is as well here to mention that the travel industry has one of the most widely dispersed access-node requirements and, at present, the most common agent-access to service providers is by way of videotex (viewdata). There are two basic problems presented by this method of access.

Firstly, the number of computer systems to be accessed (about 25 in the UK) and their different screen presentations cause training problems to the users. Although limited standards exist in the presentation of frames, the end-user—in this case the travel agent—is totally dependent on the principal for dictating the screen format used.

Secondly, agents often strip data from final frames transmitted by service providers. This places limits on the ability of service providers to change or update displays, since agents will need to be told how to modify their programs to accept the revised data; this raises severe timing problems when a number of agents need to modify their systems. Principals have to accept long lead times for system changes and this generally causes friction.

The interface between the service provider and the client is currently the travel agent. This could well change in future years with the development of interactive telecommunication services—probably provided by cable TV networks or value added and data services providers. The travel industry was amongst the first to utilise videotex, initially by using Prestel for sell-and-record information but later utilising that standard as the basis for private viewdata systems. Access to these was by direct-dial to the service provider's nearest telephone number or by Prestel Gateway connections from a value added and data service. Videotext uses low-cost terminals and these are 'dumb', or at the most 'dim'. They merely display the information supplied by the host computer. What the more go-ahead travel agents needed was to computerise the back-office work associated with service providers' accounts and their own clients' booking files. Using a PC microcomputer it is possible to transfer data from a selected viewdata frame to disc storage for invoicing and account maintenance. This action however prevents the service providers changing their output displays as this would destroy the collection of the data by agents. Attempts have been made in the past to define data elements which could be transmitted to a PC after the final viewdata display. This does not solve the problem, for travel agents, of having to teach staff to use a large number of different videotext systems: the travel agent is not interested in dealing with their idiosyncrasies and would like to have the same inputs for all ferries or airlines or inclusive tours with the responses always looking the same. It is these requirements that UNICORN addresses by providing a common message standard for inter-computer system messages.

The possibility then, exists for interactive service providers such as, for example, cable television companies, to take these messages and for home consumption provide advertising value in order to promote the service providers' individual products. For the service provider this home consumption can be in English, or any other language, at the point of presentation. EDI allows that only the variable data be transmitted.

DESIGNING UNICORN

Figure 8.1 shows how the general configuration was envisaged with each participating ferry company writing one incoming request decoder and one response compiler. Each travel agent would need to write one request compiler and one incoming response decoder.

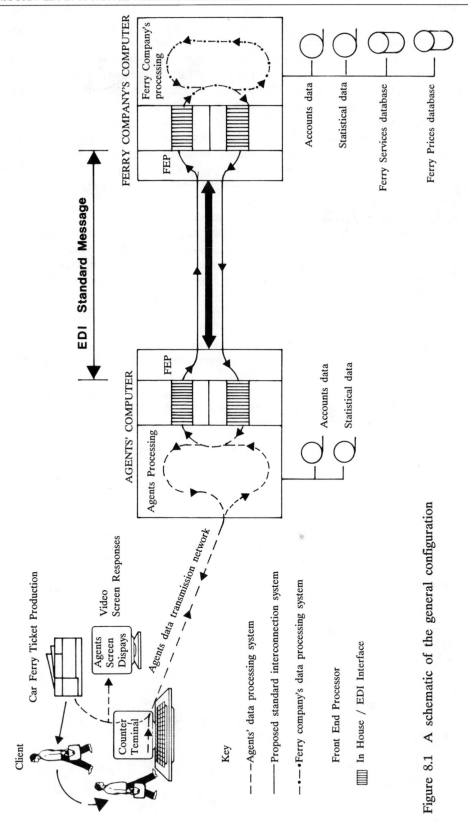

Figure 8.1 A schematic of the general configuration

The way in which agents' terminals are linked to the host reservation system may be visualised from Figure 8.1. As discussed earlier in this paper traditional methods of connection, including viewdata, mean that the agent terminal (at the far left of the diagram) is connected directly by the network to the host. Using EDI, that terminal is connected instead to the agent's computer. The agent's computer creates the UNICORN message, which is then passed through the Front End Processor (FEP)—which may be a real or a virtual machine—and the network to the host machine. The host FEP converts the UNICORN message and presents it to the reservation system as though it had come from a directly connected terminal, such as one sited in a Sealink reservation office. For Sealink, the greatest part of the investment in UNICORN was in defining and writing this conversion program.

Having agreed that EDI would be the adopted protocol, the ferry companies agreed basic messages remarkably quickly, in just four months. However much time was spent in devising how the conversations should be controlled. It was not permissible to allow just any message to be accepted and processed so it was decided that the missing factor was a general flowchart linked with a tabular description as to how the computer systems could be kept in step. A major headache was the organised starting of a transaction and the organised termination.

A final decision was taken to develop a series of 'state' tables. These tables are built to take into account all the messages likely to be sent or received; any break in this sequence will cause an error to be detected and the receiving system will then await retransmission or time-out. A garbled message in the right sequence will generate a retransmission request. Continued lack of success will cause the transaction to be abandoned and all files and states reset.

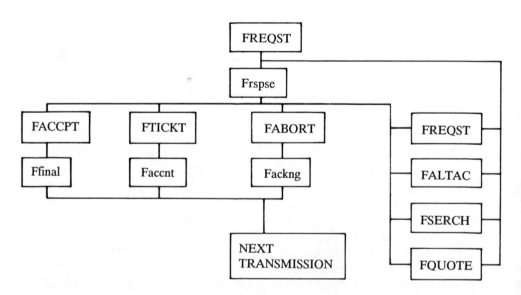

Figure 8.2 Flow chart showing the normal and allowable sequence of messages within UNICORN

The normal and allowable sequence of messages within UNICORN, are shown in Figure 8.2. Those messages shown in capital letters are those received by the host reservation system from the agency system, and those in lower case are the responses from the host. As can be seen from the example, there are only a very limited number of valid sequences (the example is only one of a number from the system) but does show the flow of messages that the host is able to accept; for example, following the right hand path, any number of 'Requests' can be made and, depending on the acceptability of the response to the travel agency user, another request can be made or the conversation can proceed to 'Accept', 'Abort' or the other designated options.

From Requesting System to Awarding System	Valid Old State(s)	New State	From Awarding System to Requesting System
FREQST successful	NULL. QA,QB	QB	Frspse
unsuccessful	NULL. QA.QB	QA	Frspse
FALTAC	QA,QB	As Old	Frspse
FSERCH	QA,QB	As Old	Frspse
FQUOTE	QB	QB	Frspse
FACCPT successful	QB	QC	Ffinal
unsuccessful	QB	QB	Frspse
FTICKT successful	QB	QC	Faccnt
unsuccessful	QB	QB	Frspse
FABORT	QA,QB	QC	Fackng
Change of CARF, if STAT = 1 or line drop	QC QA,QB	NULL	Close any open bookings

Figure 8.3 Message state table of a booking request conversation

Figure 8.3 demonstrates the way in which the host computer system 'Holds' the 'State' of the conversation, and shows how the state is updated as the conversation proceeds. The responses from the awarding system (the host) to the requesting system (the agent) match those in Figure 8.2. With the initial state being null the arrival of a message should present data to the application with the 'Message Header' segment containing two elements for continuity checking.

The third element within the segment, Common Access Reference (CARF), in UNICORN contains information as to the identity of the end user. As long as the value in CARF remains constant then the conversation is continued. Should the value change then the recipient has to take action to backout of any conversation and reset the state to null before processing. It was further decided that should the transaction value in CARF be changed or another message arriving with the status of the transfer (STAT) being set to 1 again then a new transaction had started. This would take care of circumstances when the transmitting terminal had changed although the circuit had not been disconnected. If STAT was reset to 1 but CARF remained the same value then the previous conversation had terminated but the terminal remained connected.

The fourth element within the segment—'STAT' Status of the transfer—is used as a progressive count starting at 1. In each successive transmission it is incremented by one and this effectively controls the checking of sequential transmissions. Should a message arrive with the value returned to 1 then the state is returned to null before processing. This may or may not be accompanied by a change of CARF.

As can be seen from the example of the state-tables in Figure 8.3, the instruction becomes quite clear: if change of CARF, STAT—1 or the communication circuit drops (necessitating backout of conversation anyway) then the state of the receiving system has to be placed back to null and any non-completed conversations backed out.

The United Nations Trade Data Elements Directory was used to describe as many of the elements as possible with the rest being agreed between the ferry companies as suitable. As the UNTDI message structure was devised for batch transfer it contains the overhead of a long transmission header (STX) and message header (MHD). There was a general desire to remove at least the STX segment but it was retained to provide commonality of message between real-time and batch when they may later pass over the same communications and also to provide identification for the standard CONTRL messages. No additions to the explanatory codes in segments MCR and MAC were found necessary as partial processing would be difficult in the interactive world.

Prior to implementation, advice was received from SITPRO that UNTDI would be modified to take in the requirement of the US to form a standard to be known as EDIFACT. From information provided it was estimated that an addition of five per cent would need to be made to the UNICORN development costs. It was therefore decided that UNICORN would be implemented from the outset using the EDIFACT specification. There proved to be no fundamental changes required to UNICORN user-defined segments beyond the concept of the nesting element (ITMA) becoming a sub-element of the segment description element. Message header and trailer segments however were all renamed and contained additional elements as summarised in Figure 8.4.

IMPLEMENTING UNICORN

The gestation period for the development of UNICORN is interesting as it demonstrates how quickly the fundamental principles can be specified but how long it then takes to reach a generally agreed final document. Work started in October 1985 and the initial issue of proposed messages was made in March 1986. This edition did not include much detail of message control beyond a Yes/No matrix of one message following another. The work associated with state-tables and flowcharts was added by June 1986 and the final TDI standard issued to major potential users in August 1986. No charge was made for this document as general acceptance within the industry was felt more important

TDI SEGMENT		EDIFACT SEGMENT	ADDITIONAL ELEMENTS
STX	became	UNB	AREQ (always set at value 1) AUTN (set to application name) TEST (set for test messages)
MHD	became	UNH	
MTR	became	UNT	MSRF (repeating UNB value)
END	became	UNZ	(NMST became CLCT) SNRF (repeating UNB value)

Figure 8.4 Summary of EDIFACT specifications

than covering production costs. The emergent EDIFACT standards were received from SITPRO in early December 1986 with a recommendation that UNICORN should move to the standard before too many connections were made. The four participants agreed to move to EDIFACT just before Christmas and the EDIFACT UNICORN document was issued generally in March 1987.

The time taken to write the software depends on the system supporting the interface. On Sealink the reservation system sits on an IBM computer 3080 running Airline Control System (ALCS) and is written in Assembler. The software took approximately one and three quarter man years of programming effort, with an estimated one and a half man years of user team time in specification and acceptance testing. It is estimated that each new end-to-end connection will cost about two man months, to iron-out problems of new users without previous experience. The software allows transmission under OSI using the X.25 protocol, and will run on either International Packet Switched Service (IPSS) or leased lines.

The choice of IPSS or leased line is based on cost and is an individual decision for the users, there is further advice on communications options in the section entitled *Implementing EDI*. As UNICORN sits at the Application level (as do all EDI messages) it is perfectly acceptable to use either option. The decision whether to use a leased line (at a fixed cost conveying all required volume of data) against PSS (at a cost comprising a leased line to the local exchange, with a connect time charge and a data volume charge) needs to be assessed. If data outstrips leased line capacity then two leased lines or total PSS may be cheaper.

Leased lines can rarely be justified other than on grounds of cost, although they do provide a slightly higher level of data quality, circuit guarantee, and perhaps a marginally faster transaction time.

Interpretation of an English language specification by the German team in START has caused problems and the initial production system in fact was achieved by the ferry companies with the Caravan Club in February 1988. Whereas Sealink uses an IBM system running ALCS, P&O European Ferries implemented UNICORN on their MODCOMP system running VAX 32 and North Sea Ferries on their IBM system running CICS/MVS. The Caravan Club integrated UNICORN into their foreign touring package running on their Prime computers. At present all communications are under X.25 but for START (running Siemens computers) P&O plan to pass messages along an existing leased line.

The emergence of the Caravan Club as a first agency system proved fortuitous—East Grinstead being closer than Frankfurt/Main. Testing of the first interfaces took only two months. Surprisingly the different ferry companies' computer systems provided few problems and software testing by the Caravan Club covered each area in parallel. The only serious problem for Sealink proved to be response time which on first release totalled one minute 25 seconds—hardly interactive. This was due to the programs being stored on disc and interrupts causing slow processing when in contention with other real-time activities. Movement to core has improved the performance to a four second response over X.25. In Sealink, X.28 is used for dial-up connection and X.32 for transmission via Packet Assembler and Disassemblers (PAD). Over leased line the breaking down of the message into packets can be avoided and even faster responses could be achieved.

LESSONS LEARNED

Although EDI and UNICORN dispense with display characteristics the state-table logic and error messages still require a basic selection process for selection of a screen mask and table set for element validity checking and display. In hindsight a segment containing the state of the transmitting system would assist the receiving system in providing the required checks of data and presentation to the user.

As an example, "Frspse" may be returned to an agent's system for a number of messages received (*viz* FRECAL, FRECLR, FREQST, FSERCH, FQUOTE, FCANCL). Although different systems may present data in different ways after checking element, segment and message validity, it is most likely that a number of different processes may be involved and screen masks selectable. The state check would allow primary element checking to be made more quickly and give the receiving system a prompt for final display.

Future systems may also find that more complicated state-tables can be developed to cope with 'errors', where data has been only partially processed and 'warnings' where data has been fully processed but additional information has been included to explain the response in code (for receiving system prompting) and language (for bug solving and possible straightforward screen presentation).

FUTURE ACTIVITY

Considerable interest in EDI is now being shown by the British travel industry. The Travel Industry Systems Standards Group have adopted EDI as being the method of communicating between computer systems. Such possible inter-connections are shown in Figure 8.5 which also shows the area covered by the present UNICORN protocol.

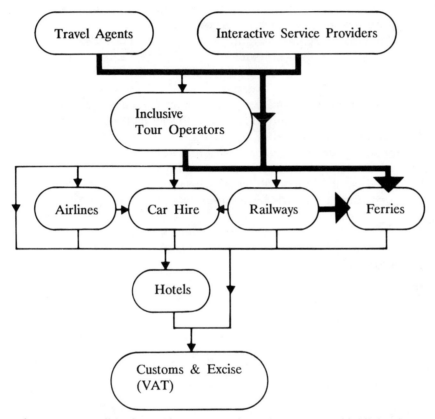

Figure 8.5 Possible future interconnections (UNICORN highlighted)

The advantage to users is that only one protocol, EDIFACT, needs to be developed by a host and by an agent to allow a full range of interconnectivity to be achieved. Any agent can contact any principal; any principal can be on-line to a customer. The motivation for this development will come from both the principals and agents who, in striving to develop the next generation of systems will look for ways to achieve greater connectivity at lower cost. Motivation will equally come from the network providers by creating the infrastructure for EDI messages to move across their networks, and from software suppliers by providing packages for agency chains to use. A principal needing to interface EDI into a reservation system must develop a unique requirement individually; all agency chains have similar needs and packages are already being deve-loped to meet them.

There are a number of advantages both for the industry and the general public. The industry will be able to rationalise its inter-system gateways; one car-hire organisation currently supports over 30 different connections. Sub-contractors will be able to offer better deals whereby reservations and pricing can be offered in real-time to front-end traders. This will enhance the ability to produce *à la carte* packages and short notice sales both of which are becoming the trend. Sealink are actively encouraging these developments to the level of issuing copies of the standard to interested parties at no cost, and advising those with a genuine interest on the steps necessary to effect implementation.

The general public will benefit from the developments because the screen displays produced by the standard messages can reflect national or regional language and presentation methods or allow trading groups to simplify training to a single standard for market sectors. There is no doubt that at some time in the future cable television will offer interactive services either directly or via the banks (for payment cover). Somebody is going to offer direct holiday sales (at discount) which will in the background actually result in various real-time reservations being obtained and presented as an *à la carte* holiday.

A system similar to the High Street supermarket/supplier system known as Tradanet is likely to be replicated for the travel industry. It is readily accepted that, in a similar way to Tradanet, a focus for standardisation is required for the travel industry. It is fundamental that all operators should talk to other users both about this and about the design of future messages, especially concerning those which are required and which may already exist elsewhere in the EDI community.

CONCLUSION

Conceptually there is little difference between a cabin on a ship and a hotel room or between a vehicle description for a ferry reservation and a car-hire request. UNICORN is only the first of many EDI projects which are expected within the travel industry. Sealink believes that it will become the future trend as more end-user travel agents become mechanised. There are logically many similarities with other EDI initiatives such as DISH, and Tradanet where the defined message structures could be adopted by the travel and tourist industry.

REFERENCES

The following documents were used or referenced during the development of UNICORN.

United Nations Economic and Social Council, Economic Commission for Europe, Trade Data Interchange Protocols (Ref TRADE/WP.4/R.359 GE.85-32342)

EDIFACT—Application Economic Commission for Europe, Trade Data Interchange Protocols (Ref TRADE/WP.4/R.359 GE.85-32342)

EDIFACT—Application Level Syntax Rules (ISO/TC 154—Ref ISO 9735) UNECE Trade Data Elements Directory GE.85-30171, incorporating ISO 7372

Trading Electronically

EDI has been growing long enough now for some patterns to be discerned. John Sanders, who is EDI Development Manager in the Trafalgar House Group, presents a review of some of these. A useful account is given of the early experience of EDICON—an association of companies seeking to build EDI links in the construction industry.

The law is an elaborate labyrynth of precedents which regulate what businesses may do. There are centuries of precedent for paper-based trading: there are very few precedents for electronic trading. How do businesses adapt existing law to using electronic documents? Bernard Wheble, who has had experience of international trade, presents a detailed exposition of the problem and some of the pragmatic solutions which businessmen can use.

Customs & Excise are uniquely placed both to observe and to influence the way business is done. Douglas Tweddle gives a review of progress in this important sector and a glimpse of the sort of developments we might see in the future.

9
EDI Development Groups

John Sanders

INTRODUCTION

Some individual trading companies have been tremendously successful in introducing EDI by the imposition on their organisation's trading partners of their own designed 'standards', whether they be syntax, message types or formats, or simply an in-house style. The competitive edge, or 'unfair advantage' gained by this type of system is shortlived. Most trading companies have, on at least one occasion, been presented with a *fait accompli* by a stronger trading partner. The relative strengths of the customer, or the supplier, are dependent on many issues and are, almost certainly, too complicated to be long lasting except, perhaps, where the final consumer is extremely weak.

An example of this 'weakness' is in the retail community where the ultimate customer (the individual reader), despite the laws of the land and our apparent choice, has little 'real' strength. The retail chains undoubtedly decide how one shops—would most people, for example, choose to stand in a check-out queue for as long as often occurs? The individual may have the power to select another shop, but is not able to dictate, and therefore receive as a consumer, the total level of quality, service and price often required. These same chains are able to press their suppliers in order that they receive the levels of service that they demand because they have great strength on their own. More often than not this pressure is manifested by an 'own standards' form of electronic trading, including EDI. The retail chains can do this in the knowledge that they are unlikely to be similarly 'attacked', and therefore disadvantaged, by their customers.

However, even in areas of domination an increasing number of organisations are discovering that this type of relationship, which does not bring the true potential benefits of EDI to the less dominant of the trading partners, is of only short term benefit even to the 'strong'. This is because, in most cases, the stronger partner is usually weak and, therefore, dependent in a different area of business. The threat therefore becomes that of weaker partners grouping together to become strong. Such a scenario is made more likely by the advances of electronic information systems such as EDI and it is fears such as these which have led to groups of both customers and directly competing suppliers becoming industry-wide EDI 'communities'. In most cases these communities have taken more time to set up and provide major benefits for their 'members' when compared with individual relationships but have ensured the longer lasting potential for the full realisation of the benefits of EDI. Even within such industry groupings there are several distinctly different types of community: closed user groups; value added and data services (VADS) user groups; hub (or honeypot) groups; EDI associations.

CLOSED USER GROUPS

The original style of EDI community was a closed grouping of like-minded, or closely associated companies. Most people will have dealt with this type of group which includes examples such as the airline reservation systems. Such groups generally do not utilise EDI for their main function, as they depend on direct on-line access to a host computer system, rather than the interchanging of information between independent computers. Such groups do, though, frequently have links from the main group into associated systems, for example for credit card authorisation.

A further example of closed user groups, which could be viewed as more typical EDI communities, are the container consortia that have brought together competitive, or complementary, deep sea cargo shipping lines in vessel or schedule sharing arrangements. These consortia have depended for their success, not just on the level of economically maintainable service but on the ability to transfer information between the partners both accurately, and on time.

The Atlantic Container Line (ACL) consortium has been in existence for more than 20 years operating cargo services from the UK, Scandinavia and mainland Europe to Canada and the US. From the first days ACL recognised that it would be impossible to harmonise the computer systems of totally independent partners such as the UK's Cunard Line, France's Compagnie Generale Maritime (CGM) and Sweden's Wallenius and Swedish America Lines. They therefore devised a system called 'Speed' that used fixed format messages to transfer the required information from one country, and its independent computer system, to another. These messages lacked the efficiency of 'flexible format' EDI but they played a major part in the success story of ACL. There are similar stories in the other consortia.

Over recent years a further type of closed user group has emerged based on ports in both the UK and elsewhere. They are similar to airline reservation systems in having their origins, and still the majority of their usage, based on non-EDI offerings. The Felixstowe-based system, FCP80, is a good example. Devised to provide a system for sending on-line requests for clearance to the Customs authority, it has grown to provide a vast amount of information to the port community, including that obtainable through EDI. Links have already been established, through the providers of networking services, to EDI specific communities. These links should ensure that their customers will be able to obtain an introduction to EDI in a relatively painless way. Whether or not this will be achieved, or whether port communities will hinder the development of true EDI is to be seen in the future, but there is no doubt that the potential for growth from such user groups is enormous.

Closed user groups normally develop their own standard messages, and in some cases their own syntax. This, whilst creating no problems if the user is only engaged in one such group, is very time-consuming and tends to generate confusion if the user, like most businesses these days, is trading in several industrial sectors. An example is provided by one of the largest computer manufacturers in the UK which has more transactions with their car hire and leasing company than they do with any electronics supplier—will they admit to being in the car hire sector? Most companies deal extensively with office equipment and stationery suppliers—would most companies feel they are in those industries? It is doubtful. However it is possible that the advantages of EDI could be more readily realised in peripheral areas such as these than in the perceived 'home business' sector.

One unmistakable advantage of closed user groups is the lack of requirement for any additional legal agreement to be specified for the EDI relationship. The trading agreement, or other joint operational contract, will normally cover the relationship in total, including those parts where electronic trading is utilised.

VALUE ADDED & DATA SERVICES USER GROUPS

There is little doubt that the emergence of value added and data services (VADS) has accelerated the growth of EDI and will have a major impact on the future direction. In an attempt to increase their profitability each of the more persistent VADS has set up at least one EDI user group in an industry sector. The effect of this is to pressurise the remaining members of that industry to feel that the only choice is 'join or be damned'.

A careful evaluation exercise has to be undertaken to decide whether the benefits of utilising the network's marketing and sales skills, to increase the number of electronic trading partners, are worth the risk of similar pressure from another sector, or whether the technical and capital investment would only be available if one joined the club. Of course, all is not doom and despair. The VADS suppliers have a tremendous amount of expertise built up over a number of years (both directly related to EDI, and gained from other Data Processing sources) and if correctly channelled many advantages are there for all to achieve.

Probably the most famous of all the VADS User Groups is Tradanet although, strictly speaking, it is more than just a simple user group. Tradanet is the service designed originally by ICL to cater for a need identified by members of the retail community within the Article Number Association. The ANA, with help from Tradanet, have designed their own messages and have used the original syntax approved by the UN for use within Europe (commonly known as UNTDI). From its naturally contained birth Tradanet has grown into one of the world's largest EDI communities, and is now used by several industries, not all of whom have aligned themselves with the ANA. It is now run and managed by INS (a joint venture between ICL and GE Information Services Ltd).

The exclusive contract negotiated by the ANA with Tradanet has ensured that this combined offering is rightfully known, and marketed, as a VADS User Group within the 'High Street' sector. The 'physical' network service is also used by groups that come into at least two of the other categories of EDI community—for example the hub activity of the B&Q Do-it-Yourself chain. Additionally, the DISH Pilot Project, whilst very much an EDI Association style of community, selected INS' Tradanet as its single VADS supplier for its trial of export deep sea messages and as such became, although temporarily, a VADS User Group.

Perhaps a truer example of a VADS User Group is provided by the SHIPNET project (which has been completed), set up by IBM in order that members of international trade and industry could evaluate the services provided by IBM's Business Network Services. SHIPNET did not attempt to enter into any major research and development activities of its own, as its prime objective was simply to evaluate the VADS. It used messages designed by the DISH member-ship. In an attempt to prevent any extension of the confusion caused between

DISH, SHIPNET and DISH's use of Tradanet, the members of SHIPNET decided at the end of their evaluation to reform as the IBM EDI Users' Group.

HUB/HONEYPOT GROUPS

Hub groups are a more acceptable form of the, 'you'll do it my way' pressure that epitomised the early days of EDI when all that mattered was the amount of muscle instigators could wield. Several of the VADS providers use hub (or 'honeypot') tactics to advance their own user bases more rapidly.

The providers normally start by convincing, or being convinced by, a major player in an industry, that he is the centre of the world as he knows it. The companies are normally the strategically important buying organisations which is why it is often possible to persuade the suppliers to that hub of the benefits of joining the wheel—or perhaps the disadvantages (no more orders) of not joining.

Most of the more recent examples of this approach have realised the advantages, to both sides in a trading relationship, of combining this hub approach with standards developed either by the industry as a whole, or by a wider representation of mixed industries. The B&Q Do-it-Yourself chain is a prime example of this type of exercise. They are currently in the process of enlarging their EDI activities to encompass all of their suppliers, using the message standards designed by the ANA with INS' Tradanet offering as the VADS.

Another similar activity is being jointly undertaken by British Coal and Istel utilising the Edict service. In Spring 1988 British Coal started to consider whether or not they should move away from their specific standards, a combination of work undertaken by other groups and their own, to those being developed within the EDIFACT structure. They have so far decided that they sensibly need to include the recognised standards in their future plans.

EDI ASSOCIATIONS

Probably the most important EDI community is that born by the coming together of different sectors within one industry to examine, discuss and develop EDI. Prime examples of this are:

The EDI Association for International Trade & Transport (EDIA) that was formed in September 1987 at the completion of the DISH Deep Sea Shipping Pilot Project and the SHIPNET evaluation of the IBM Value Added Network service;

The Organisation for Data Exchange by Teletransmission in Europe (ODETTE), the grouping of European motor manufacturers and suppliers, represented in the UK by the Society of Motor Manufacturers and Traders (SMMT);

The Conseil Européen des Fédérations de l'Industrie Chimique (CEFIC), a pan-European association of chemical manufacturers that are moving into EDI;

Electronic Data Interchange in Construction (EDICON), the
community for the UK construction industry in all its many guises.

The main strength of this type of EDI community is the ability to encourage
cooperation between the different disciplines within the industry to common
advantage. Benefit for the members is totally dependent on technical and
business cooperation, even with competitors. This does not, of course, remove
the competitive element from the supply of products or services. In fact
cooperation can, and often does, heighten knowledge of the quality of one's
product or service, and, particularly, the logistic importance of, for example,
correct delivery. Without doubt, EDI associations return the competitive emphasis from trading information about a product, back to the product itself.

Many suppliers have long since forgotten what they are really 'selling' and
have increasingly become merchants of information supply. EDI communities
allow this trend to be halted, for the benefit of each particular business, and of
society in general. Of course, some companies' traded product is information
itself. Even here, it must be remembered that the ability to provide information
attractively, and speedily, is of no use in itself if the information so passed is
incorrect.

EDI RELATIONSHIPS

What does become increasingly apparent, in any EDI relationship, is that in
sending information about products or services to our trading partners, we are
often oblivious to their real needs as receivers of this data. A good example of
this is the simple (?) invoice. The role of this document is, primarily, a request
for payment giving sufficient information for the receiver to know that the
charge is correct and who should be paid.

How often, when designing a new invoice print, do system designers talk to
the recipients? And, even less likely, how often do they listen? Within an EDI
grouping these discussions take place automatically. We rapidly discover that
about 25 per cent of any invoice is totally useless and meaningless to the
receiver. Examples such as 'sales representative's area code' are all too
commonly included on an invoice print, yet often it is difficult to check that an
invoice has been correctly made out because important pieces of information
are missing. Having spent many hours examining different invoices to see if they
can be catered for by existing EDI invoice standards, this author believes that
EDI communities will drastically alter, not just the content and use of electronic
invoicing, but the printed invoice (while that document remains in existence). In
many cases a competitive edge can still be given away to a direct competitor
within an EDI community if the lessons learnt by talking to one's trading partner
are not actioned. It is normally sufficient though, to obtain the edge over those
companies not sufficiently convinced of the potential of EDI to join a relevant
community.

It has been stated that those companies that 'wait and see' before committing
to any EDI project will gain most because they do not have to take the risks.
However, it is doubtful whether many important players will wait, partly due to
the natural fear, within organisations, that 'my competitor will get too far in front'
and partly due to the understanding within organisations that knowledge of

one's trading partners, and their requirements, is increased by membership of an EDI association.

It is normal for members of an EDI association to define the messages required within their own sector, or at least to have a major impact on international design groups. They do though, almost without exception, use whatever is available internationally, especially in the form of syntax and message standards. This is probably because the reason they joined is their belief in the common approach. In addition to the benefits mentioned above concerning a cooperative EDI Association there are several others, but there are also a number of disadvantages.

It is a normal requirement for any electronic trading partners to have an enforceable agreement to cover the scope, use and legal implications of their trading. In most cases these are drawn up by the association, using guidelines developed by the International Chamber of Commerce and approved by the United Nations. An association offers the opportunity for this agreement to be signed as a 'club' agreement. Such an arrangement means that in practice it is only necessary to check that any new trading partner has similarly signed, rather than having to draw up what could be one of the many agreements with each individual trading group.

As another example of the frequent warfare between suppliers and customers it could be easy to envisage the strength of the VADS suppliers placing unbearable pressure on their customers to become locked-in to one or more of their offerings, thus restricting both commercial and financial independence. An EDI association enables the customers to become strong in this area enabling joint deliberations with the VADS suppliers. Whether this 'clout' is used to ensure a better quality of service, to stabilise prices, or to encourage interconnection between the suppliers is, of course, a matter for the individual association, but without this form of grouping the struggle would be particularly one-sided.

Having explored the comparisons between the different types of EDI community above it is now salient to explain how one EDI association style community, EDICON, was set up. Such a description enables the reader to draw comparisons with his own industry, offering assistance in evaluation of how to set up a similar community.

EDICON—EDI IN THE UK CONSTRUCTION INDUSTRY

In spite of the UK construction industry being so large and such an important a part of the national economy (more than 230,000 organisations are engaged in construction activities), it has been relatively slow in applying not just the power of modern computing and communications but other technological advances for the improvement of its efficiency. Although there had been many initiatives in the computing and communications arena by individual companies and organisations, the lack of a central focal point for all parts of the industry meant that there was no national coordinated approach.

Towards the end of 1986 representatives of two of the UK's largest contracting companies, Trafalgar House and John Laing, met to discuss their knowledge of EDI and its possible application to the construction industry. Using the hospitality of one of the VADS suppliers, IBM, invitations were sent to a small group of companies within the industry to meet and further discuss the possibilities. The people concerned were representative of elements of the industry covering trading, design and contracting in addition to the information and computing services. The common thread was the pressing need for much more efficient communication between the separate parts of the industry, and between individual firms and organisations. It was decided that the example provided by other industries in forming an EDI association was the correct approach for the construction industry, and eight of the original attendees continued to meet to form the community. An early decision made was that the community should be registered as a company limited by guarantee to protect the interests of potential members. It was of paramount importance to the initiators that membership of EDICON be restricted to organisations that are an integral part of the construction process, with trading partners within the industry. This resolve will prevent peripheral organisations, or hardware or software suppliers from becoming dominant.

EDICON was to be organised in a pyramidal structure controlled by a council, elected by the membership at large, consisting of a chairman, secretary, treasurer, membership secretary and up to 10 other members. The first Council was not elected but was composed of representatives of the initial subscribing companies plus some 'missing' expertise from other member companies. An important facet of this Council was the mix of disciplines which came from within the industry, plus expertise in construction data processing, marketing and EDI. The strong feeling of wanting to succeed spurred the Council into a true cooperative spirit.

The development groups

The real work of EDICON was to be carried out by groups devoted to specific development or support tasks. The development groups broadly mirrored different activities within the industry, namely: invoices, orders and enquiries, bills of quantity, technical specification, product information, and computer aided design.

It was decided that the support groups should concentrate on activities common to all development areas. These were: industry coding, legal matters, and technical and EDI standards. Having formed the Association, its ruling body, and made ready the backbone of the working groups, invitations were sent to a restricted number of companies covering the whole industry, to attend the launch meeting at the end of March 1987. Again the hospitality of IBM was acepted, but without offering them any promises for the future.

The launch of EDICON

The number invited was carefully controlled, as much due to the uncertainty of what to do if either two or 200 turned up, as for any other reason. Written invitations were sent from a director of one of the founder member companies, each letter having been preceeded by a personal, verbal invitation. Out of the 40 organisations invited some 35 delegates from 28 companies attended. They were given presentations of EDI in general, its application to other industries, and the Council's outline plans for EDICON. Of the 28 attending companies 25 joined and became active participants.

The subscriptions were levelled at an amount (200) that should not have caused concern to any potential member, but money was the least of EDICON's needs. Of prime importance was the availability of staff and their expertise, from within member companies. This, along with accommodation and hospitality for the group meetings, was the immediate need. The early days of EDICON were not without trauma: even the most committed member sometimes found difficulty in continually releasing staff for working group meetings, and, more particularly, for 'homework'. Sensible planning of the workload, including the ability to appreciate a realistic speed of achievement, was essential. Publicity was deliberately kept low-key in the realisation that a rapidly expanding membership would be increasingly difficult to handle, until such time as organisational strength was built up. The exception to this was the need to ensure that no alternative EDI community for the construction industry was set up. Consequently, opportunities to speak to the media, or at conferences, were rarely declined when offered.

Contacts were established with the other VADS suppliers (INS, Istel and British Telecom) to complement the relationship with IBM. All these VADS operators were particularly encouraged to support activities through the Technical Support Group. The most important organisational decisions taken during those early days included establishing a working relationship with the EDI standards bodies in the UK, and with other EDI communities. Similar links were put in place with the international groupings, considered particularly important bearing in mind the emergence of the challenges of 1992. EDICON was able to utilise some of the experience gained by other EDI communities, notably those in shipping (EDIA and DISH) and the motor trade (ODETTE) by learning from their mistakes and successes, and in preventing any re-invented wheels. Of course, EDICON remains only too happy to return favours and will do so wherever possible.

The need to prove that EDI in the construction industry could work stimulated EDICON into putting most of its resources into establishing a first pilot project in which the benefits would be observed. The financial area, and particularly electronic invoicing, was chosen, primarily because it had been done before by other EDI communities, although never using an EDIFACT standard. EDICON chose to proceed with the first United Nations approved Standard Message—the EDIFACT invoice. In just over a year from the launch the first messages were being transmitted— a far from insignificant achievement. Progress over that year had also been made in all of the other development areas, proving the maxim that 'where there's a will there's a way'.

A book could easily be written, and may well be in the future, on the activities of EDICON alone, but it is hoped that this 'taster' gives some idea of the problems faced, and the solutions offered, in creating EDICON. Successful EDI communities are not magic: they are the result of dedication, hard work and, most of all, belief. In summary it is relevant to mention one final point. At the very first exploratory meeting one of the attendees stated that 'EDI may well be all right for some industries but it will never work in construction'. His reasons for dissention were given as the complexity of the industry, the huge number of participants and the total lack of relevant standards. Fortunately the author was able to show him a slide that had been used by the shipping industry to illustrate the resolution of similar problems in their area by utilising EDI. It was interesting to note that this shipping example had been 'stolen' in turn from the retail community where it was first used, thereby suggesting: 'No new problems—just a new industry. Long Live the EDI Revolution!'

NOTE
A list of EDI development groups in Europe, including information on how they have developed and membership information, is given in the section entitled *Further Information*

10
Creating Legal Relationships with Trading Partners

Bernard Wheble

INTRODUCTION

At a recent Customs Cooperation Council (CCC) symposium the statement was made that:

> International trade moves as much on information as on wheels, wings or water. Every transaction is held together as a documentary paper-chain.[1]

One speaker then demonstrated that paper-chain—some 50 documents stretching nearly an equivalent footage across the floor of the hall. The documents were varied, but they all had two features in common. Each acted as a 'paper' bearer of information, and each contributed to legal relationships affecting the trading partners.

Some were simple commercial documents—invoice, weight list, packing list and the like—spawned directly by the sales/purchase contract between seller and buyer. Others, stemming from the ancillary contracts necessary to achieve performance of the basic trading contract, were third party documents. Moving the goods from seller to buyer, for example, necessitates a separate contract with a carrier, a contract of carriage evidenced by an appropriate transport document. With air carriage it would be a simple document, an air waybill naming the consignee to whom the carrier will deliver the goods at destination. With carriage by sea it could be a more complex document, a negotiable marine bill of lading, with an intrinsic legal value in that physical possession of the document can give rights to the goods to which it relates. The trading parties may wish to be protected against the risk of loss of, or damage to, the goods in transit by a contract with an underwriter, evidenced by a certificate of insurance. The buyer may endeavour to protect himself against fraud by independent third party supervision of the goods, giving rise to a certificate of inspection, or, with certain types of goods, a certificate of analysis. The administrative requirements of Customs and other regulatory bodies may demand non-commercial type documents, such as a certificate of origin, or a phytosanitory certificate.

The commercial parties may arrange these ancillary contracts and obtain the relative documents themselves or they may prefer to employ intermediaries, such as freight forwarders, thereby inserting an additional link into the paper-chain. But whoever does the arranging, the:

> export documents between them contain about 200 different pieces of information, each a clearly defined source. So that

*every paper document is an assemblage of some sub-set of these
200 data items presented in some pre-defined format. And these
sub-sets interest—and have to be exchanged between—a variety
of sources: commercial, transport, insurance, banking and those
who are concerned with the mandatory requirements of
administrative law.*[2]

This means that part of the paper-chain, particularly documents of the type
detailed above, have to 'travel'—from the selling country to the buying one.
However goods moving on "wheels, wings or water" tend to outstrip the
documents. The modern need is therefore for an alternative and speedier
system for movement of the information, for electronic data interchange (EDI).

ELECTRONIC DATA INTERCHANGE

Electronic data interchange (EDI) has been defined in simple terms as:

*the replacement of the paper documents relative to an
administrative, commercial, transport or other business
transaction, by an electronic message structured to an agreed
standard and passed from one computer to another without
manual intervention.*[3]

In even simpler terms it has been suggested that:

*EDI is merely the same as documentation, ie a carriage and
passing on of information (data)—but without the paper.*[4]

Certainly, the paper documents, as "an assemblage of sub-sets of ... data
items presented in a defined format", would seem capable of shedding their
'paper' element, leaving the data to be "passed from one computer to another
without manual intervention" in the form of "an electronic message structured
to an agreed standard."

EDIFACT

For the above to hold true an "agreed standard" would be essential. An Italian
lawyer has suggested that:

*in an EDI world it would not make sense to manufacture a
computer which does not abide by the regulations which enable
it to converse with other computers.*[5]

Or, in the words of a leading EDI expert:

*a computer cannot receive messages without recognising and
understanding the rules which have governed the preparation of
the messages.*[6]

It therefore represents a major step towards the replacement of traditional
paper-based data interchange that:

*in November 1986, thanks to the work carried out over the past
decade in the United Nations in close cooperation with the*

*International Standards Organisation (ISO), a common language
called Electronic Data Interchange for Administration, Commerce
and Transport (EDIFACT) has been universally agreed. Specially
conceived for all forms of trade, this language is made up of a
comprehensive coded data register covering all words used in
trade by the various participating professions, and included in all
written traditional printed forms.*

*EDIFACT also provides a common syntax, as required by
computers, and will shortly offer packages including the most
frequently used coded messages and segments of messages to
facilitate the compilation of computer files.*[7]

Already less than two years later:

*EDIFACT standards have been welcomed and endorsed by many
governments and commercial organisations, including the
European Commission and US Customs.* [8]

This US Customs backing is particularly significant. A CCC spokesman has
pointed out that:

*Customs are, in effect, in a very strong position with regard to
standards. Being an arm of government they have the power to
specify which standards should be used in any communication
with their automated systems. They can, therefore, by adopting
internationally accepted standards themselves, be a powerful
influence on the rest of the trading community to follow suit.* [9]

Even with governmental backing, EDIFACT standards alone are not enough.
There must also be legal agreement as to the effect of exchanging information in
this new electronic language instead of in the form of established traditional
paper documents. Here, unfortunately, neither current statute law, nor case law,
offers much help. They are basically oriented towards paper-borne data, so that
the lawyer previously quoted finds it:

*really very difficult to apply the law which has been conceived,
measured and deliberated for trade based on paper to the new
technologies.* [10]

The result, according to a report of the United Nations Commission on
International Trade Law (UNCITRAL), is that:

*As the cost of ADP equipment has reduced, the cost advantages
arising out of its use have extended to an increasing number of
activities and users in all countries. One consequence has been
that legal rules based on pre-ADP paper-based means of
documenting international trade transactions are leading to legal
insecurity in some cases and in other cases are impeding the
efficient use of ADP where its use is otherwise economically
justified.* [11]

This, of course, has a bearing on the legal relationships between the trading
partners so thought has to be given to what are referred to as the 'legal

problems' of EDI—to distinguish them from the quite different type of problems associated with the software and the hardware.

THE LEGAL PROBLEMS OF EDI

In the area "impeding the efficient use of ADP when its use is otherwise economically justified" the problems are relatively easy to define. Research currently being initiated by the Commission of the European Communities (EC), for example, sees them as arising from:

> the legislative, case law or commercial practice requirements for
> written documents and/or manually signed documents and even
> the necessity to prepare, issue, send and maintain such
> documents in order to satisfy the need for evidence. [12]

This suggests problems with a mixed 'content', ie the requirements of the law or commercial usages, and the limitations of EDI.

National or international law may establish a mandatory demand for a specific document—the 'Original 3—for Shipper' air waybill of the Warsaw Convention on Carriage by Air, for example. Or the demand may arise under internationally accepted trade terms such as INCOTERMS, 1980 Revision, drafted by lawyers and commercial parties under the auspices of the International Chamber of Commerce (ICC)[13], the 'clean on board bill of lading' called for by the CIF term. Or it may stem from a standard form of contract used in a particular trade.

However a computer cannot transmit a 'document' as such: it can only transmit data. True, a computer can be programmed to produced a hard-copy print-out of the data in any prescribed 'documentary' format. But this could raise problems—of legal acceptability and of 'uniqueness'. Does such 'electronic document' satisfy the legal requirement for a 'document' - traditionally a paper one? Also, and of considerable commercial importance, is the print-out 'unique', or have more than one been made and handed to other parties, all possibly interested in using the print-out to obtain payment?

Again, as a legal requirement, or as a commercial usage for which there may even no longer be justification, there may be a demand for a 'manual' signature on the document. A bill of exchange provides a legal example:[14] a request for 'signed commercial invoices' is a commercial one. Once more the limitations of EDI become apparent. EDI cannot transmit a 'signature' as such, although it can authenticate the source of the data transmitted and the correctness of that data—possibly with more surety than a traditional paper document.

Yet again EDI reveals its shortcomings when the law, or commercial usage, demands a document with a special 'functional' characteristic, such as a negotiable bill of lading, where physical possession of the original document is as important as its data content. EDI can transmit the information, the data giving details of the contract of carriage and of the 'identified goods' to which that contract relates—and their apparent condition. It cannot, however, transmit the legal function of 'negotiability'.

These are comparatively simple problems, and in theory their solution should be easy—change the law and/or commercial practice. Accordingly, over the past decade there have been a series of major recommendations to governments and others from the Economic Commission for Europe (ECE),[15] the CCC and UNCITRAL,[16][17] for the replacement of manual signatures by electronic authorisation, the replacement of negotiable documents by non-negotiable ones, a reduction in the demand for mandatory documents, and the acceptance of computer records as evidence.

Unfortunately changes in the law, and in commercial usage, come slowly. In respect of air transport a proposed amendment to the Warsaw Convention for Carriage by Air was put forward 13 years ago providing that:

> *any other means which would preserve a record of the carriage*
> *to be performed may; with the consent of the consignor, be*
> *substituted for the delivery of an air waybill. If such other means*
> *is used, the carrier shall, if so requested by the consignor,*
> *deliver to the consignor a receipt for the cargo permitting*
> *identification of the consignment and access to the information*
> *contained in the record preserved by such other means.* [18]

The Protocol incorporating that proposal has not been ratified, and the paper air waybill is still a legal requirement. The United Nations Convention on the carriage of Goods by Sea (Hamburg, 1978) and the 1980 UNCTAD Convention on Multimodal Transport both provide for electronic signature, if not inconsistent with the law of the issuing country. Neither Convention has yet been ratified and become law and the 'Hamburg Rules' still retain the concept of a paper document [19].

In the commercial area INCOTERMS can be revised, standard contract terms can be changed, and non-negotiable sea waybills can replace negotiable bills of lading. INCOTERMS, it is true, are currently being up-dated and proposals have been put to the appropriate Working Party of the ICC for the inclusion of provisions that:

> *if so agreed between the buyer and seller, when the seller is*
> *required to carry out an activity for which documentary evidence*
> *is required—such as an invoice, insurance certificate, transport*
> *document, document required for administrative purposes or any*
> *other document required herein—the required document may be*
> *substituted by electronic data interchange (EDI) by or on behalf*
> *of a seller in a form agreed between the buyer and seller, taking*
> *note of the provisions of the International Chamber of Commerce*
> *UNCID (ICC publication 452—UNECE WP.4. R483) and EDIFACT*
> *(ISO standard 9735).*[20]

and that

> *reference throughout the text to 'transport document' should be*
> *followed by 'or electronic data interchange (EDI) message*
> *equivalent thereto'.* [21]

It remains to be seen whther these two proposals will be accepted. But commercial inertia—the 'we have always done it that way, so why should we change' frame of mind—is still proving an obstacle to changes in standard contracts and to all but a limited use of non-negotiable sea waybills.

Less easy to define is the 'legal insecurity' to which the UNCITRAL report also drew attention. Under established law, including rules of evidence, and commercial usages based on 'paper', the parties involved in trade know exactly where they stand. They can have what has sometimes been described as 'the comfort of security'. As the ECE pointed out over a decade ago:

> with paper-documentation there is a long-standing tradition that 'somehow, security is assured'—and, when the document is in negotiable form, there is some justification for this attitude, because of the special legal possibilities offered by physical possession of a 'piece of paper'—the negotiable bill of lading, for example.[22]

The ECE report further commented that:

> the development of collecting, processing and disseminating information by ADP methods demands a standard of security, but of a different kind. [23]

So new questions have to be asked—and satisfactory answers obtained. What, for instance, is the acceptability of 'computer-to-computer data' in evidence? Here the commercial standard may well be lower than that of the courts. Or, a problem currently troubling some European lawyers, when, and where, is a legally binding contract concluded if offer and acceptance are in the form of electronic data interchanges? Is it possible to obtain, or retain, legal and commercial security so that the 'paper' function can be continued in a paperless system and EDI be acceptable to the parties involved?

In so far as the evidential value of computer-to-computer data is concerned the UK Civil Evidence Act of 1968 gives the answer. This Act, which enables parties in civil proceedings to agree less stringent rules of evidence than in criminal proceedings: defines a computer as "any device for storing and processing information"[24]; provides for the admissibility as evidence of "a statement contained in a document produced by computer" [25]; subject to certain conditions regarding the operation of the computer "during a period" in which "the document containing the statement was produced by the computer" being satisfied [26]; and, the production of a certificate "identifying the document containing the statement", "describing the manner in which it was produced", "giving particulars of any device involved in the production of that document" and "purporting to be signed by a person occupying a responsible position in relation to the operation of the relevant device or the management of the relevant activities (whichever is appropriate)".[27]

Section 5(3) of the ACT, relating to the use of "a combination of computers" and "different computers acting in succession" would appear to extend these provisions to the use of value added and data services (VADS).

The more general question of 'commercial and legal security', of making EDI acceptable to the parties involved, is linked with other changes in the law. This has led to a suggestion of three possible courses of action:

> (a) to attempt to amend legislation by making politicians aware of the issues involved;

> (b) to go ahead without taking the legal world into consideration in the belief that, sooner or later, 'the real world conquers the legal world';

(c) to take a middle road being convinced of the validity of (b)
but seeking interpretations and settlements from the courts and
public administrations which make this clash less dramatic. [28]

The first alternative (a) would take time—and time is increasingly tending to be
of the essence where EDI is concerned. The second (b) is basically the view
expressed by a large commercial firm in the US as long ago as 1979, when it
suggested that:

the time is coming when we should be able to use VDU's with
staff having an input capacity to computer systems linking banks,
port authorities, Customs, forwarders, shipping companies and
airlines—and, if possible, the other end of the transaction[29]
adding *and the law must keep pace with this development.* [30]

Taking the middle road is more in keeping with ECE thinking that EDI:

is essentially first a technical problem, but later becomes one of
communication to and acceptance by the parties concerned, ie it
is a question of defining systems, describing and negotiating
relations between the actual users . . . . so that parties to an
international trade transaction come to know and accept them. [31]

In the context of negotiating relations between the actual users it has been
pointed out that:

so far as the legal problem is concerned, the ICC Articles
governing both documentary credits and collections are an
example of how, within limitations, it is possible to introduce a
measure of uniformity generally, with the acceptance of certain
responsibilities and liabilities, into an area where specific laws
governing particular types of transactions may not exist. [32]

THE UNCID SOLUTION

With the points outlined above in mind, and at the request of the ECE, the ICC,
working through a Joint Committee which included representatives of major
intergovernmental and non-governmental international organisations, has now
produced a set of Uniform Rules of Conduct for the Interchange of Trade Data
by Teletransmission, 'UNCID'.[33]

The work began in November 1985, and the end product, the Code, was
approved by both the ICC Executive Board and the ECE Trade Facilitation
Working Party in September 1987. The aim of the Joint Committee was to
produce rules which would, *inter alia*:

facilitate the use of EDI through a code of conduct accepted by
the parties engaged in such electronic interchange *(Article 1—*
'Objective' and Article 2—'Definition');

apply only to the interchange of trade data and not to the
substance of trade data messages transmitted *(Article 1, and*
Article 8—'Confirmation of Content');

incorporate the use of ISO and other internationally accepted standards to avoid confusion *(Article 2, Article 3—'Application'' and Article 4—'Interchange Standards');*

deal with questions of security *(Article 5—'Care' and Article 9—'Protection of Trade Data')* , verification and confirmation, and authentication of the communicating parties *(Article 6—'Messages and Transfers', Article 7—'Acknowledgment of a Transfer'' and Article 8)* , and logging and storage of data *(Article 10—'Storage of Data');*

*establish a focal point for interpretation that might enhance a harmonized international understanding and use of the code *(Article 11—'Interpretation').*

It was not intended that UNCID should be an end in itself. It was envisaged as a means to an end, a 'bridging operation' while the relevant international organisations identified the required adjustments to national and international law, brought them to the attention of the politicians and secured action. In the meantime UNCID also contributes to the achievement of these 'required adjustments'. Article 10, for instance, takes note of the evidential requirements of the UK Civil Evidence Act and Acts of a similar nature in other countries by its strict requirements that:

a complete trade data log is maintained of all transfers as they were sent and received, without any modification, that such data log should be stored unchanged at least for the period of time required by national law in the country of the party maintaining such trade data log and by specific rules for, the data referred to . . . . to be prepared as a correct record of the transfers sent and received.

In this connection it is worth noting a linking development in the technical field, that:

a new storage method in the form of unalterable data carriers is available, ie 'write once only' media storage . . . . offers a better security than paper documents. [34]

Private discussions suggest that Write Once, Read Multiple (WORM), with optical devices as the leading candidates, is likely to develop a specialist market for devices dedicated to demonstrating a user's audit trail with certainty. This would seem a development of considerable importance, since an early UNCITRAL study stressed that:

since paper is durable, paper-based documents and records can be expected to remain in existence for a longer period of time than is normally economically or legally necessary;

alterations of the document or other record can normally be detected. [35] *Whereas: telematics, in fact, has the disadvantage of being 'fleeting': the information appears and disappears from the screen, making it difficult to produce it as evidence of what has gone on between the parties.* [36]

UNCID Articles 7 and 8, dealing with 'Acknowledgment of a Transfer' and 'Confirmation of Content', although not in the sense of the legal concept of confirmation and acceptance of the substance of the data interchanged, can go some way towards answering the questions of 'time' and 'place'. As a speaker at the conference COMPAT 88 pointed out, this poses no problem from the technical transmission angle, because:

> EDIFACT users can request acknowledgment. The UNB
> Interchange Header segment contains an Acknowledgment
> Request indicator, allowing the sender A to check that B, the
> recipient, has received and identified the start and end of the EDI
> message. This check can, of course, be done after B had
> performed some more detailed content verification. The
> interchange agreement can spell out the degree of checking
> which A can rely on B having done when B sends back the
> acknowledgment.[37]

COMMUNICATION AGREEMENT (INTERCHANGE AGREEMENT)

The reference to 'interchange agreement' indicates the real application of UNCID. As a voluntary code of conduct it gains legal effect as a foundation on which a 'communication agreement' (data interchange agreement) is built—with such agreement standing as a contract between the parties. The nature of the 'communication agreement' will, naturally, be influenced by the users involved.

They may be members of the same discipline, exchanging standard messages of broadly uniform content within the terms of an in-house protocol. The banking world's Society for Worldwide Interbank Financial Telecommunications (SWIFT) provides an excellent example. It is a single discipline, closed-user system, with messages related to a comparatively narrow field of activities—electronic funds transfers, documentary credits and documentary collections. The messages are standardised and activities are governed by clearly defined rules and regulations incorporated into a 'users' manual'.

However, international trade demands interchange of data between different disciplines. The information contained in a traditional bill of lading, for instance, can be of interest to the commercial parties, banks, underwriters and Customs in addition to the issuing carrier. This multi-discipline interest and involvement means many players and complex relationships—and sometimes conflicting interests as more than one party may have a legitimate interest in the same data. The 'communication agreement' therefore becomes all the more important.

The UK Data Interchange for Shipping project (DISH) brought major carriers, exporters and forwarders together under SITPRO, with Customs as an observer and a limited bank participation. Its purpose was to prove the feasibility of exchanging data electronically, using booking, shipping instructions, freight account and transport contract (for example bills of lading and waybills) messages for deep sea cargo from the UK. It was felt that if the trials proved a success:

> an operational system could be developed for general
> implementation, ie to cover exports and imports from and to UK
> and Europe and between Europe and the rest of the world. [38]

DISH based its inter-party agreement, its communication agreement, on an early version of UNCID and, as its legal group later reported:

> *while a number of technical problems (largely communications and software related) had been identified during the trials, none appeared to have any legal connotations and the group could be satisfied that from a legal viewpoint the Interchange Agreement and User Manual had adequately covered the trial transactions.* [39]

Nevertheless, although the UNCID rules of conduct secure a common approach, the details and form of the communication agreement must be influenced by the size and type of the user groups, and vary accordingly. For this reason the ICC did not feel able to formulate a standard model. It appreciated that the agreement may be included in a protocol, or may form a separate document. Or it may contain additional rules, for example, rules bearing on the substance of the data interchanged, or on the underlying agreement, or on the professional approach.

The ICC did however consider it useful to outline certain elements that should be considered in addition to UNCID when formulating an agreement. Thus:

> *(a) there is always a risk that something may go wrong—who should be at risk? Should each party carry its own, or would it seem possible to link risk to insurance or to the network operator?*

> *(b) if damage is caused by a party failing to observe the rules, what should be the consequences? This is partly a question of limitation of liability. It also has a bearing on the situation of third parties.*

> *(c) should the rules on risk and liability be covered by rules on insurance?*

> *(d) should there be rules on timing, eg the time within which the receivers should process the data?*

> *(e) should there be rules on secrecy or other rules regarding the substance of the data exchanged?*

> *(f) should there be rules of a professional nature—such as the banking rules contained in SWIFT?*

> *(g) should there be rules on encryption or other security measures?*

> *(h) should there be rules on 'signature'?* [40]

It would also be important to have rules on applicable law and dispute resolution.

THE NEXT STEPS

The points (a) to (h) made above all help to structure a communicating agreement governing legal relationships with trading partners. What they do not do is to answer questions by one of those trading partners—'How and where do I start, to what user group do I belong, and who will be the other parties to the agreement?'

If it is true that "nothing does the job like a fresh point of view" the answers might come from a quick look into the crystal ball [41]. At the CCC symposium in February 1988 the Comptroller of the Australian Customs Service claimed that, "Customs is the keystone of the EDI arch", and in one way it is. As the CCC spokesman quoted earlier has also indicated:

> *the consequences of internationally accepted EDI standards*
> *should have a significant effect on Customs trade interfaces in the*
> *future. Instead of Customs-trade interfaces being confined to*
> *closed user groups it will be possible, through the use of the*
> *internationally accepted standards, for traders' automated*
> *systems to communicate with Customs systems in an 'open'*
> *environment.*[42]

The picture is less clear in the non-governmental area. The several commercial parties involved in a trade transaction have different interests that must be safe-guarded. In a paper-based data interchange environment banks can exert an influence in their 'paymaster' role—with documentary credits, for example. As long ago as 1977 the ECE was thinking that:

> *it would seem that modern banking techniques could make it*
> *logically—and possibly also legally—feasible to create what*
> *might be described as a documentless credit, ie to work the*
> *'conditional' bank undertaking of payment on the basis of EDI.*[43]

The present concept is of an instrument for effecting payment:

> *against stipulated documents, provided that the terms and*
> *conditions of the credit are complied with.*[44]

The suggested new concept would be along the lines of payment:

> *against submission by the beneficiary, or other parties acting on*
> *his behalf, by electronic data interchange, of stipulated*
> *authenticated data relative to stated goods, their carriage as*
> *stipulated and their control or ownership in transit, and change of*
> *control or ownership or release of the stated goods at*
> *destination, provided that the terms and conditions of the*
> *conditional bank undertaking are complied with.*[45]

It would take time to get international agreement on such a radical, though reasonable, change. But it is worth thought—a major think, in fact—on the part of the banks and their customers.

As an alternative, perhaps the value added networks could become the focal point for the communication agreement. Users could have a standardised communication agreement with a network, incorporating also a binding agreement between senders and receivers of messages routed through the network. This is, perhaps, an extension of the thesis presented by a speaker at COMPAT 88 who stated that:

> *both senders and receivers are bound by the interchange*
> *agreement that they have drawn up with each other and with the*

value added network supplier. The UNCID rules must be warmly welcomed as forming a useful solution for the drafting of such an agreement.[46]

This leads, however, to one final thought in respect to relationships with trading partners. An observation has been made that:

each time a new tool or system is produced, our more or less conscious attachment to tradition leads us to expect guarantees which were previously not only never fulfilled, but were not asked for.[47]

Paper-based data interchange has, in recent years, been be-devilled by fraud - the 'telling of a lie in writing'. No communication agreement will prevent fraud. A lie, false data, can also be fed into a computer, and, as the ICC has recently pointed out:

the speed of data transmission allows fraudulent transactions to be carried out within a very short time.[48]

The only sure way, therefore, of ensuring that the right goods really do move on "wheels, wings or water" is to take care in the selection of trading partners in addition to creating legal relationships with them.

REFERENCES

1 EDI—The Customs Connection: Brussels, February 1988.
2 B.S. Wheble, 'Trade Facilitation', Council on International Banking: New York, June 1986.
3 Simplification of International Trade Procedures Board (SITPRO): document (88) 06.
4 B.S. Wheble, 'Moving from paper documentary credits to paperless conditional payments', Electra 86: Hong Kong.
5 A.A. Martino, 'Paperless trade: legal and technical standardisation problems', COMPAT 88: The Hague, February 1988.
6 Etienne Dreyfous, 'And machine shall talk unto machine', ICC Export Directory International, 1988.
7 Ibid.
8 SITPRO: document (88) 07.
9 John P. Morrin, 'The effect of EDI on administrative problems'.
10 Supra—note 5.
11 UNCITRAL: document A/CN. 9/254, 8 May 1984.
12 EEC notice, 10 March 1988: 'The legal situation in the Member States relating to the use of trade electronic data interchange'.
13 The International Chamber of Commerce is a businessman's organisation, with a wide national and individual membership. It works through 'Commissions' of specialists from within its world-wide membership to present the business view-point to governments and international organisations, including the United Nations. It has also established a reputation for aiding international trading by drafting, and keeping up-dated, uniform rules of practice or conduct, eg 'Uniform Customs and Practice for Documentary Credits', which are voluntarily applied world-wide—and are recognised by the courts of many countries. INCOTERMS is one such ICC production, establishing a widely used standard set of rules for the interpretation of trade terms by buyers and sellers who seek clear definitions of their rights and obligations in international trade.

14   UK Bills of Exchange Act, 1882, section 3(1): "A bill of exchange is an unconditional order *in writing* , addressed by one person to another, *signed by the person giving it* ..." (emphasis added).

15   ECE document TRADE/WP.4/INF.61—Recommendation no.12.
      ECE document TRADE/WP.4/INF.62—Recommendation no.13.
      ECE document TRADE/WP.4/INF.63—Recommendation no.14.

16   ECE document TRADE/WP.4/R.330: 'CCC—draft resolution concerning the use of computer readable data as evidence in court proceedings.'

17   ECE document TRADE/WP.4/INF.97: UNCITRAL recommendations on legal value of computer records, subsequently endorsed by the General Assembly of the United Nations.

18   Montreal Protocol no.4, 1975, section III, Article 5.

19   Article 1.7: "A bill of lading means a document .... by which the carrier undertakes to *deliver the goods against surrender of the document"*. (emphasis added).

20   SITPRO: document PAD (88) 6.

21   Ibid.

22   ECE document TRADE/WP.4/GE.2/R.102, 10 November 1977.

23   Ibid.

24   Article 5(6).

25   Article 5(1) and 5(5c).

26   Article 5(2) and 5(5a and 5b).

27   Article 5(4).

28   Supra—note 5.

29   B.S. Wheble, 'Documentary credits', SWIFT Workshop, November 1985.

30   Ibid.

31   Supra—note 22.

32   Supra—note 29.

33   ICC publication no. 452: obtainable from ICC, UK, Centre Point, 103 New Oxford Street, London, WC1A 1QB, or ICC Publications SA, 28 Cours Albert Premier, 75008, Paris, France.

34   ECE document TRADE/WP.4/R.520,—15 December 1987.

35   UNCITRAL document A/CN. 9/265—21 February 1985.

36   Supra—note 5.

37   John E. Draper, 'Security, integrity and legality—barriers to EDI progress in Europe', COMPAT 88: The Hague, February 1988.

38   SITPRO: document PAD (86) 5.

39   DISH Task Group 3: minutes of meeting, 10 March 1987.

40   Supra—note 33.

41   International Federation of Forwarding Agents' Association (FIATA): Revue no. 1, 1987.

42   Supra—note 9.

43   Supra—note 22.

44   ICC Publication no. 400—'Uniform Customs and Practice for Documentary Credits', Article 2.

45   B.S. Wheble 'Electronic data interchange—the payment link', Electronic Banking: London, 1987.

46   Supra—note 37.

47   Supra—note 5.

48   ICC document 373/78, 23 March 1988.

11
EDI in International Trade: a Customs View

Douglas Tweddle

INTRODUCTION

Customs clearance of import and export freight involves the transfer of information about the goods—such as information concerning value, tariff classification, duty rates—from the importer or their agent to Customs and Excise. The development of electronic data interchange gives Customs the opportunity to facilitate the United Kingdom's international trade by helping to remove the vast quantities of paper documentation currently required and by improving the processing of information necessary to grant Customs' clearance to goods. The increasing use of EDI allows Customs to maintain efficient and effective controls whilst causing the least disruption to legitimate trade.

The main reasons for controls over imports and exports are: the collection of revenue which provides a significant proportion of Government income, for example over £10,000 million in Value Added Tax (VAT) per annum; the control of prohibited and restricted goods—that is dangerous drugs such as heroin, cocaine and cannabis, pornography, arms and ammunition and controls for plant and animal health; the production of accurate trade statistics, used for macro-economic purposes and which are often used by commerce as a valuable source of market intelligence.

The application of these controls involves information exchange on a massive scale. In 1987 there were nearly six million import freight consignments and nearly five million exports.

Traditionally, this information exchange has been based on the transfer of paper documents which give descriptions of the goods and of their status for Customs' purposes (claims to quotas, preferences to name but two examples). However, from the mid-1960s the increase in freight traffic (first at London's Heathrow Airport and, later, at the main maritime ports and inland customs clearance locations) led to increasing problems in the clearance of goods through Customs within acceptable timescales, and it became apparent that the traditional method of exchanging information on paper could not satisfy either Customs or the commercial requirements. Accordingly the Customs and Excise has, in conjunction with trade interest, introduced a series of computerised systems for processing Customs information in order to deal with the increasing workload more efficiently. The use of EDI techniques for the processing of import information has become essential to ensure a satisfactory customs clearance service for UK international trade.

This article outlines the historical development of EDI for clearing import freight and describes the main stages in the evolution of the present systems. This is followed by a brief survey of the potential and planned expansion of EDI facilities which Customs is likely to be involved in over the next few years and a description of those external developments that are expected to have a major influence. The survey includes an examination of the commerical, international and legal problems that must be overcome by Customs and the trade if EDI is to fulfil its potential.

PAST/CURRENT FREIGHT CONTROL SYSTEMS

Real-time systems

The London Airport Cargo EDP Scheme (LACES) was the world's first computerised Customs clearance system and was introduced at Heathrow Airport in 1971. It was a combined Customs clearance/cargo inventory control system developed jointly by Customs, the airlines and forwarding agents and was operated as a bureau service by the National Data Processing Service (NDPS)— part of British Telecom. LACES incorporated the direct trader input (DTI) method of entering information which allowed forwarding agents to input information directly into the Customs entry processing system which then validated the data, identified the goods against the cargo inventory system, performed the necessary accounting functions, selected a proportion of consignments for examination and automatically gave notification of clearance. The DTI system was supported by paper documents which had to be produced to Customs within a specified period. LACES enabled goods to be entered to Customs much more quickly than under previous manual procedures, leading to the large majority of imports being cleared within an hour once the supporting documents had been presented and the inventory details checked to confirm that the goods had actually arrived. The Air Way Bill was very significant in the development of LACES since it provided a readily available and worldwide accepted Unique Consignment Reference Number. The inventory control facility based on a common cargo reference allowed cargo manifests to be 'written off' electronically to enable the full benefits of automation to be achieved.

The success of LACES led to the introduction of the Customs Project Team (CPT) system in the surface area where the increased complexity introduced by the implementation of European Community legislation had led to delays in clearances and less effective controls on goods. The CPT systems was developed and operated by Customs as an in-house project and was installed in 13 major maritime ports in 1978. The direct trader input method of entry was not used and paper declarations were presented to Customs by the forwarding agent in the traditional manner and then input into the computer system by Customs data processing personnel. The obstacles in the way of implementing a direct trader input system at that time included the disparity between the requirements of the various types of maritime trade, for example roll on/roll off (Ro-Ro), deep sea and short sea, and the logistical problems in dealing with a very large number of forwarding agents, shipping lines, and port authorities all with different, and often competing, interests in the international movement of freight. In the late-1970s, when it became necessary to consider the replacement of the LACES and CPT systems, changes in the needs of Customs and the trade users led to the separation of the Customs entry processing arrangements from the commercial inventory control system. The Departmental Entry Processing

System (DEPS) was introduced in 1981 as a replacement for the Customs aspects of LACES and CPT system. DEPS retained the direct trader input method of declaration for air traffic and the Customs input procedures for maritime trade.

The commercial inventory control side of LACES was superseded by Air Cargo Processing for the 1980s (ACP 80) covering freight movements at London Heathrow, Gatwick and Manchester Airports. The system incorporated a facility for the capture of export information, provided on-line computer links with the independent cargo tracking systems that many of the world's major airlines had installed by that time, and offered a 'bureau' inventory control system for those airlines which had not developed such systems.

In the early 1980s the increase in maritime traffic due to containerisation of deep sea traffic and a massive growth in Ro-Ro led to problems similar to those experienced at Heathrow in the 1960s. It often took longer to clear cargo at Customs that to transport to or from another country. The manual commerical customs clearance procedure could not cope with the volume of trade. The only solution was for individual ports or groups of ports to introduce their own direct trader input systems. These systems have been developed and operated by Port Communities consisting of port operators, forwarding agents and shipping lines. Though each Port Community is an independent trade development all have a common interface with the Customs entry processing system (DEPS).

The port community at Felixstowe was the first to introduce direct trader input facilities in 1985 and the system, called Felixstowe Cargo Processing for the 1980s (FCP 80) proved so effective in terms of quicker clearances and more effective commercial control over the movement of goods that other ports were soon encouraged to follow. The number of ports and inland locations with direct trader input facilities has grown rapidly and by the end of 1988 nearly 60 locations will be linked to DEPS via six port community systems based at Dover, Felixstowe, Southampton, London Port, Northampton and London Airports. In total over 1500 different companies are connected to DEPS for customs clearance purposes and over 1100 firms are using intelligent computer to computer links.

In addition to developing DTI facilities the major port communities, including Felixstowe and Dover, have introduced sophisticated Port Information systems which include inventory control tracking facilities and links to other networks. Most other port communities have long-term plans for the development of similar systems tailored to meet the specific requirements of their ports.

The DEPS system has recently undergone a major redevelopment to cater for the significant changes to international freight procedures introduced on 1 January 1988. This involved a level of standardisation and harmonisation of customs procedures which has important implications for the development of EDI. The Harmonised System for the classification of goods which has now been agreed to by over 90 countries should mean that ultimately the whole world, both Government and the trade, should be using the same basic method of classifying goods. The Single Administrative Document (SAD) replaced over 100 national import, export and transit documents throughout Western Europe and is likely to form the basis for a world customs declaration. The standardisation of data elements and codes brought about by the SAD and the Harmonised System will greatly facilitate the international use of EDI. The updated version of DEPS continues to be developed and operated by British Telecom Applied Technology (BTAT) the successor company to NDPS.

Batch systems—period entries

In addition to the real-time entry processing systems, Customs and Excise also operates a batch facility known as Period Entry. This was the first EDI system for Customs clearance using independently recognised standards and currently uses the Trade Data Interchange (TDI) system developed by Simplification of Trade Procedures (SITPRO). The facility is available to larger traders with regular traffic and is currently used by about 130 companies, mostly multi-nationals, accounting for approximately 10 per cent of total UK imports by value.

Goods are cleared on an initial simplified declaration while full statistical and accounting information is submitted by the importer monthly to Customs in batch either on magnetic tape or by direct data transfer. Period Entry traders received an occasional visit by their local Excise Officer to resolve any queries and for checks to be made on the accuracy and completeness of the periodic returns. This system is available for both imports and exports, though the export facility is not greatly used and Customs intend to hold discussions with potential export users to see what can be done to make it more attractive.

The advantage of Period Entry to the importer or exporter lies in the simpler and quicker clearance procedures. The rapid and more certain customs clearance has allowed Period Entry traders to make substantial savings by reducing their stock levels and by lowering customs clearance costs. The main advantage for Customs lies in the receipt of information in electronic form direct from the commercial system used by the trader.

Because of its association with a relatively small number of very large commerical organisations the Period Entry system is seen by Customs as a prime candidate for an eventual move towards the use of a commercial value added and data services (VADS) and also for a migration to the Electronic Data Interchange for Administration Commerce and Trade (EDIFACT) standard.

FUTURE FREIGHT CONTROL SYSTEMS

Customs have been developing a successor to DEPS called Customs Handling of Import and Export Freight (CHIEF) which will extend the facilities provided and take advantage of recent developments in computer technology, such as programming languages and advanced database techniques. The Government has decided that negotiation should take place with BTAT with the aim of agreeing a contract for the development and operation of CHIEF.

The initial phase of CHIEF will be implemented in the early 1990s and will basically replicate the existing DEPS facilities, although it is proposed to extend DTI facilities to cover as many imports and exports as practicable. Subsequent developments of CHIEF will see the introduction of a comprehensive export system which it is intended will cater for inputs from individual exporters, using VADS, as well as from Customs agents linked to the Port Communities. Additional facilities that are planned for CHIEF include links with the Department of Trade for writing off licences electronically, the facility to process bulk import data on a store-and-forward basis, links to the European Commission in Brussels for a real-time quota control, and automated CAP facilities.

CHIEF will take customs freight processing into the next century and will be designed to be sufficiently flexible to cope with both planned charges and future developments in international trade. Significant developments are expected to arise from: the increased use of EDI by firms involved in international trade; further harmonisation and standardisation of European Community customs systems and procedures; the move to the European Community Internal Market by 1992; the use of EDIFACT standards for data interchange.

TRADE EDI DEVELOPMENTS

Commercial organisations are expected by Customs to explore ways of maximising their investment in direct trader input and port information/inventory control systems. Developments already under consideration include an extension of the port community network services such as those proposed in the recent BTAT/ Maritime Cargo Processing initiative and the Dover Community's recent export proposals.

Current UK trade trials along the line of the Data Interchange for Shipping (DISH) and the network-based community of IBM users are expected to be extended to included data interchange trials with Customs. Initial discussions are in progress on the possibilities of an EDI trial between UK Customs and trade and their counterparts in France and other Member States. It is thought probable that the European Commission will propose similar Member State pilot trials in order to test the post-1992 Internal Market system.

An EDI trial is currently taking place in the international sphere involving both the European Commission and the US Customs authorities and three UK and US based multinational companies. If this is successful it is likely to be extended to included more commerical organisations in other Member States as well as, at a later stage, covering exports from the US to the European Community. As the United Kingdom is a leader in the use of computers for customs clearance, HM Customs and Excise expect to be fully involved in these trials. Initial discussions are taking place for an export trial involving the receipt of Period Entry export data via VADS. This could be extended to a full-scale pilot trial involving interested VADS users at a later stage.

CADDIA/CD Project initiatives

The requirements made by the European Community, Cooperation in the Automation of Data and Documentation for Imports/Exports and Agriculture (CADDIA) Initiative and the Coordinated Development of Computerised Administrative Procedures Project (CD Project) are expected to be a major force for the increased use of EDI by EC administrations and commerce.

The Commission is expected to make proposals under the CD Project in the near future for the migration of Customs systems to the EDIFACT international standard. Changes will also be necessary for intra-community and third country freight controls with the advent of the Internal Market in 1992.

Internal market

Lord Cockfield's proposals for the Internal Market include the replacement of frontier controls to make the European Community an area 'without internal frontiers for the free movement of passengers and goods'. A number of important issues remain to be resolved by Member States' Governments before the shape of the Customs controls post-1992 can begin to be identified with any degree of certainty. These include the approximation of VAT rates, the harmonisation of the rates of Excise duties, the prohibited and restricted goods and goods subject to plant and animal health controls.

Although the nature of these controls post-1992 is as yet unclear it is widely recognised that the development of EDI facilities by Member State Customs, commercial organisations and the European Commission will be an important factor if information is still to be collected for fiscal, control and statistical reasons and the planned removal of intra-Community frontier controls is to occur. The CD Project is seen by the European Community as having as major role to play in ensuring that the necessary Community-wide EDI infrastructure is in place.

The reduction or elimination of physical, technical and financial barriers within the European Community will undoubtedly lead to a significant boost in intra-community trade and will add to the rapid growth of EDI between the United Kingdom and the rest of Europe.

STANDARDISATION

UK Customs and the European Commission consider the development, under the auspices of the United Nations, of EDIFACT as the internationally agreed standard for messages to be central to the production of Customs and trade EDI messages, and believe that it must be strongly supported.

The Single Administrative Document standardised the data requirements for customs clearance throughout Western Europe. In the longer term it is possible that a worldwide standard Customs clearance message could be produced based on the SAD. It has also allowed the European Community and the EFTA countries to examine the development of standard electronic messages using the EDIFACT standard and based on the SAD data elements. The production of the various formats (for example a stand-alone message, or an invoice-embedded message to name but two) for such a SAD standard message is now actively under discussion in Brussels under the auspices of the CD Project.

The development of international standard Customs/trade messages is also being discussed by the Customs Cooperation Council (CCC) ADP Sub-Committee and the UK EDI Association. The CCC ADP Sub-Committee has recently come to an agreement with the International Air Transport Authority (IATA) on the production of standard Customs/airline messages for the report and release of aircraft cargo via automated systems. This success has led to negotiations with the organisations involved in the maritime area for a similar agreement for sea carriers.

Customs and Excise is represented on the Council of the UK EDI Association and is also actively involved in the Customs and Other Governmental Issue (COGS) working group and the Message Design Coordination group. The message development work of the CD Project, the CCC ADP Sub-Committee and the UK EDI Association will be submitted to the Customs Message Development Group of the EDIFACT Board for formal approval as United Nations standard messages. UK Customs is participating fully in the standardis-ation activities of all these bodies. The development of the Harmonised System and the European Integrated Tariff (TARIC) has allowed goods subject to Community regimes, for example preferences and quotas, to be uniquely identified and will thus facilitate the production of the standard messages for data purposes that are envisaged under the CD Project.

LEGAL ISSUES.

The ultimate aim of Customs is to move towards full electronic data interchange of import and export data in which there will be no requirement for supporting paper declarations. There is currently an export facility in the DEPS system which is fully paperless and it is planned that all the export declaration on the CHIEF system will eventually be made by electronic messages unsupported by paper documents. While this would also be feasible for imports there are a number of legal complications which will have to be resolved before it can become a reality.

The first of these concerns the delivery of legally acceptable documentation to Customs by means of electronic data transmission. The problem arises with the authentication of these messages as the law currently requires signed documents in order to provide evidence of identification. Arrangements will, therefore, need to be made to provide for some other acceptable evidence of identification which can be accommodated on an EDI system.

The admissibility of evidence of computer readable data in both civil and criminal proceedings may also cause problems. Under the system of common law decisions are reached by the court on the basis of the precedent of previous cases; at the moment insufficient cases have been brought before the courts involving electronic data evidence for such precedents to have been set. The legal position on the status of such evidence is, therefore, still in some respects unclear.

Another potential problem lies in the checks that Customs need to make on the electronic messages received. To be effective it is necessary that the Customs' control on messages received via EDI should include the powers of access to the traders' records, computer systems, and traders' premises. This is to ensure that the message has not been tampered with either in the database itself or in transmission. In the UK this problem has been covered by the Customs and Excise Management Act 1979, - though again the same problem arises over precedent; there have been insufficient cases in the courts so far to provide a clear expression of the legal position. There have already been cases in the Period Entry sphere where difficulties have arisen over the authentication of an electronic message or in the checking of a database held on a computer outside the United Kingdom. Those particular cases have now been resolved satisfactorily, but they provide an indication of the problems that must be solved by Customs Administrations and the trade as EDI is increasingly used as the main vehicle for the transmission of international trade information.

These legal issues will need to be resolved by legislation and by Community and international agreements before the current requirement for a paper document to accompany an import declaration made on EDI can be discontinued. However, once legal difficulties surrounding official declaration are sorted out the spotlight will fall on the need to eliminate paper documents.

CONCLUSION

Over the past 20 years the achievements of UK Customs and trade organisations in the development of electronic data exchange in the freight control area have been substantial and have provided considerable benefits to both Customs and firms involved with international trade. The increasing use of EDI by European Customs Administrations and trade and the forthcoming production of the EDIFACT standard now provide the opportunity to break away from the limitations of the existing 'closed' computer systems.

The successful development of open systems for data exchange will require the close cooperation of Customs administrations and the trade within the United Kingdom and in the rest of the European Community. What is envisaged is a gradual migration towards increased automation in cooperation with the trade and not a sudden 'big bang' involving a complete break with the present systems. This means that any investment made by traders in computer systems for Customs purposes should be safeguarded and not be under threat from sudden changes in Customs' requirements.

UK Customs will continue to play an active role in the work of the UK EDI Association as well as continuing to work with the current longer-standing Customs/trade consultative arrangements.

Considerable barriers need to be overcome before the EDI infrastructure is sufficiently in place within Europe to enable the international movement of freight to benefit fully from the use of EDI. Nevertheless, UK Customs sees EDI as the only way of ensuring that Customs administrations can exercise their controls while placing the minimum burden on trade. When electronic trade is the routine method of passing information to Customs, importers and exporters who insist on continuing with outdated manual procedures may find that the Customs clearance service they receive does not satisfy their commercial requirements.

Implementing EDI

David Jackson's particular concern is helping organisations with training in preparation for EDI. He spells out how important full corporate support is to a successful implementation. In his words, "functionally led EDI implementations run the risk of excluding potential users and thereby failing to maximise benefits."

The wide range of communications services available for data interchange can appear daunting. There are the public networks—for telephony or data transmission. The data networks come in a variety of forms—some offer packet switching, others offer a messaging service. Some applications may justify leasing a circuit. Large businesses often find it beneficial to lease multiple circuits and manage them as a private network. Edmund Lee, with the BT Public Data Network, gives an account of the options.

Systems Designers (whose civil business is now part of Scicon Limited) have built some very useful software products for EDI. David Palmer and his group there have worked with may companies, introducing them to EDI. In his paper he draws upon this experience to give simple, straightforward advice, particularly for the smaller company approaching its first EDI project.

Keith Blacker coordinates EDI developments in Lucas Industries. He takes a wide-ranging view of the needs to be met by an EDI project. The sometimes-provocative questions which he raises will help staff in a larger organisation to run a successful project. Perhaps just as importantly, his advice should help in selling the approach at all levels in the business.

12
Preparing the Organisation for EDI

David Jackson

The significance of EDI for business has already been amply demonstrated. It heralds the transition from intra to inter-company information systems and has the potential to influence strongly a company's competitive position. It seems obvious therefore that the decision to adopt EDI and its subsequent implementation must be carefully planned. This planning must be done on a corporate basis; functionally led EDI implementation runs the risk of excluding potential users and thereby failing to maximise the benefits.

Whilst it is impossible to describe a planning framework that applies equally to all organisations, this chapter will highlight the major points that should be covered when planning and implementing EDI. The importance of planning the introduction of EDI cannot be over emphasised: the end result will more than repay the time and effort consumed.

TRAINING

It is appropriate that the first step in EDI planning is one of education as it is undoubtedly a key to success. Education avoids the danger of making the same mistakes as predecessors, speeds the planning and implementation cycle and helps maximise the success of the project. In addition to simple understanding, education and training in EDI performs two other tasks. Firstly, training is an excellent vehicle for communicating corporate attitudes about EDI and demonstrating the support that senior management is giving the project. Secondly, it helps prepare people for the changes that are coming. If people understand what is happening and why, the resistance to change is likely to be lower. Training for EDI falls into three areas: general awareness, users, information systems staff.

Awareness

The starting point is the recognition within the organisation that EDI is worthy of detailed consideration: and here is the first important message. Those organisations who implement EDI out of choice, rather than being forced into it by trading partners, will find the planning and implementation process easier. They will have more control over such things as the timescale and the carrier system used; the end result of which will be a more comprehensive, corporate EDI project. Building awareness must be done properly, fail here and the project will go no further. The only way to really interest people is to sell them benefits—which implies that different messages have to be given to different groups. Senior managers should be told of the potential for locking-in customers, of improving service and (of course) of the cost benefits. Information systems managers will need to be aware of the potential for reducing workloads and improving data accuracy. The case for EDI will be strengthened if the message contains examples of competitor companies (or companies in similar sectors) that have benefited from EDI.

User and information systems training is necessary because unless these groups have a firm understanding of the concept, operation and applications of EDI, they will be unable to contribute fully and effectively to the project. It is unlikely that this training will be available within most companies and therefore some external source must be used.

There are three major sources of training to consider. EDI suppliers will provide training as part of the package offered. The content of the training will favour the services they offer and is probably therefore not ideal. Consultants are acquiring expertise in EDI (they, too, recognise its importance) and will build training into EDI projects. There are also a small number of independent consultants who offer EDI training. Independent training organisations offer courses on both the business and information system aspects of EDI. When considering the need for training, it is important to set out the objectives to be fulfilled and identify the course that most closely meets those needs. It is also wise to send a team of people to the same training programme—with representatives from each of the main groups. This ensures that team members are not working from different viewpoints, thereby minimising the potential for conflict.

Training is also important when dealing with trading partners. If they fully understand EDI then it is likely that they will more readily move in the same direction. At the appropriate stage in the project, training that brings together both partners can bring particular benefits as they become acquainted with each other's problems and viewpoints.

The EDI project team

As already indicated, EDI has to be considered on a corporate basis and it is therefore important that the planning reflects this. Whilst the initial awareness building may be carried out by an individual, the more detailed planning and implementation has to be a team effort. For the purpose of discussion, the term 'project team' will be used. In most cases this will be a group of functional specialists working part-time, although at a later stage, large EDI projects may require a full-time team.

Project membership

The art of setting up any project team is to balance the need for representation from all the interested parties against the need to keep the team to a manageable size. The author's preference, based on the premise that the effectiveness of a committee or working group is in inverse proportion to the number of members, is for small teams supplemented by co-opted members when specialist inputs are required. Membership of the team should initially be drawn from the major users and information systems providers.

The users should be represented by staff who are responsible for managing the interface bridged by the data flow with some representation from senior management who can take the wider, corporate view. Participation from outside bodies should be avoided until the company is in a position to explain coherently its approach and needs for EDI. Once the scope of the project is established however, the early involvement of major trading partners is essential. Remember, EDI needs at least 'two to tango'. Early involvement will allow them to develop their EDI strategy in parallel, further reducing the lead-time to full implementation.

Team members should be selected on the basis of their ability and willingness to contribute rather than simply their current position. One willing volunteer is worth ten pressed men! If these individuals do not fully understand EDI, then they should be the first to undergo training; remember, they will become the EDI champions—spreading the good word about EDI.

Project leadership

Like membership, leadership of the project team should also be flexible. In its early stages, the emphasis of the project is on the need for and the business implications of EDI and the team should therefore be led by the users. As the project moves into implementation, two closely related, but essentially separate streams of activity evolve: hardware and software implementation and co-ordination with trading partners.

These two tasks require different teams, but their activities must be co-ordinated by the full project team; leaders of these sub-groups should also be members of the project team. The only link now missing in the chain is the top link; to whom does the project team report? The strategic importance of EDI has been amply explained in previous chapters. Equally important is the recognition that EDI is an interface with trading partners, many of whom may be customers. For these reasons, it seems obvious that the project team should report to a board level function, if not the board itself. This has the added advantage of reinforcing the support the project has from top management.

ASSESSING THE NEED

Information is an essential prerequisite for any EDI project, indeed it determines whether an EDI project is needed! A considerable amount of data is necessary, without which the project team will be unable to work. Remembering that EDI is the transfer of structured data, the obvious place to start is with existing data flows (both incoming and outgoing)—much of which will be form-based. For each 'form' (or other structured data set), the following information is needed: origin—who and how; recipient—number and type; frequency of issue/receipt; purpose.

The author suggests that this survey is not limited to known applications of EDI, but attempts to cover the whole range of data flows. This will allow companies to begin discussions with trading partners (be they commercial organisations, governmental agencies or even other operations within the same company) about the possibility of establishing an EDI link to replace the current transmission medium. Someone has to be the first to suggest a new application; there is no reason why that should not be you.

Having collected the data it is important that redundant, duplicate or unnecessary data flows are eliminated. It would be a foolish error to use EDI to efficiently transmit data that has little or no use. Ranking the information in different ways will help to identify the major areas of potential EDI application. Suggested ranking criteria include volume of transactions, value of transactions, frequency of transactions, criticality of transactions, and number of trading partners per transaction type.

Even at this early stage, it is important to keep one eye on the future. For example, if the purchasing department is about to rationalise its supply base, the number of orders/invoices will dramatically fall. These plans must be built into the projections for data traffic volumes. The information collected at this stage will guide the membership of the project team, identify the costs and benefits of the project, and help in negotiations with network suppliers.

In addition to the need to collect information internally, this initial period should be used to gather information about the EDI services and activities in appropriate industry sectors. (See section on *Further Information.*) The analysis of needs is one of the inputs to the cost/benefit calculations. It is important to calculate both the set-up and on-going costs associated with EDI. Set-up costs include: additional hardware, amendments to software, EDI service joining fee, and consultancy and training costs.

On-going costs include: EDI service fees (annual membership, logon, data transmission and storage charges); hardware rental; PTT network charges (over and above EDI network charges). Wherever possible, a value should also be put on the benefits accruing from EDI, for example: reduced postal charges, reduced stationery costs, staff savings (document handling, data entry and correction and supervision).

Benefits relating to improvements in the organisation's operations can also be quantified. These benefits may, for example, be reduced inventories, better cash flow management, the effect of building in switching costs or improved responsiveness to customer needs. Whilst these figures are only estimates, they will give some guide. A valuable spin-off from this activity is the thought process that goes into identifying the possible benefits as it requires a thorough examination of EDI and its impact on operations.

The costs and benefits will of course vary according to the ratio of EDI to paper-based transactions. This must also be considered when analysing the figures as the level of cost and benefits will be incremental. In particular, the benefits associated with removing the paper-based system will only be fully realised when all transactions are effected under EDI. At some point, a decision has to be taken on the next step. In the vast majority of cases, this will be a decision about how to implement EDI. This involves selecting suppliers, pilot projects, negotiating with trading parties and amending existing computer systems.

SELECTING SUPPLIERS

Selecting an EDI service is a crucial activity in the EDI implementation process. A wrong decision will result in unnecessary changes at a later date. The first choice is between joining a public service such as Edict or Tradanet, or an appropriate closed user group (CUG) such as the CEFIC project for the chemical industry. This choice is not available for most EDI users as the closed user group projects cover a relatively small number of users. It is the author's opinion that closed user group (CUG) projects will eventually join with public services. As more applications for EDI develop (and they will), then members of closed user groups (which are usually industry specific) will find themselves having to operate through two or more services. In the short term however, CUG's may offer the best service where the analysis suggests that EDI traffic is restricted to members of this group.

If trading partners operate in a variety of industries or if no CUG exists for the industry, then a number of third party suppliers exist. The user base will be the major factor in service selection. The number of users is one factor, but as important is the profile of these users in terms of the industry sectors covered. Large numbers of subscribers in one industry sector will attract other subscribers in the same sector thereby increasing the number of trading partners that can be accessed.

The level of service offered is important. Not all the facilities offered by a service will be of equal significance so the profile that most closely matches required needs should be identified. Some of the main factors which should be explored are network coverage (national and international), data formats supported, format translation, message status reporting, audit reports, data recovery, data storage, archiving, design and implementation support, security and user friendliness.

It is advisable to give potential suppliers the data that has been collected and a brief outline of how it is envisaged that EDI will be used, with a request for a detailed presentation of how their service could meet these stipulated EDI needs. Suppliers should be quizzed carefully on their present and proposed services, the action they are taking towards service interconnectivity, pricing (request examples of set-up and on-going costs based on the data supplied) and the support they will offer in implementation and dealing with trading partners. It is also advisable to insist on seeing their latest list of subscribers. It is as well to remember that the criteria for selection are subscribers, service and price; and in that order. At this point in the project, it should be possible to put together a detailed implementation proposal for senior management approval. This plan should contain: a description of the planned applications; the effects on staff and major changes to operating policies; a detailed statement of costs (both set-up and operating); the benefits of using EDI (both cost and intangible benefits); a detailed time-phased implementation plan; and a statement of possible future developments. When approved, this plan becomes the project plan which acts as the guide for the project manager and the basis of measuring the time and financial progress of this project.

Integrating EDI into systems

EDI is a powerful tool for improving the communications between trading partners. The full benefits, however, only accrue if EDI is viewed as an integral part of a complete system rather than just a communications peripheral. This means that existing procedures are reviewed and amended to take account of the EDI environment. Viewed in its simplest form, EDI is merely a front-end to existing systems and as such requires only minor changes to implement.

A bridge needs to be built between the existing processing system and the EDI network. This involves action in two areas—message formats and communication protocols. Proprietary software to translate existing message structures into a format acceptable to the EDI network can be purchased for most types of equipment and it is therefore an unnecessary use of resources to develop a custom package. The exception to this is where existing systems are to be substantially redesigned in order to take full advantage of EDI. For example, it may be advantageous to change the procedures for the receipt and processing of incoming data by using the opportunity provided by EDI to establish less bureaucratic trading processes with trading partners. Validation procedures and initial actions on data should also change to reflect the greater data accuracy achieve by utilising EDI.

In addition to computer procedure changes, related procedures should also be reviewed. If invoices can be matched against valid orders and receipt notes, why bother with further invoice checking? Indeed why not automatically generate payment (via Bankers Automated Clearing System on-line, another example of EDI)? Only by questioning the purpose of each part of the transaction processing cycle can the full benefits of EDI be achieved. Those who argue the need for insurance through parallel manual procedures should determine the costs of providing that insurance and the likelihood of it being needed. The aim should be to automate the fixed administrative tasks and free resources for more complex tasks that require the judgmental and analytic skills which people alone possess.

PILOT PROJECTS

The successful transition towards EDI implementation can be considerably eased by the use of a pilot project, the objectives of which are: to prove the benefits of EDI; to prove the operation of the interface between existing systems and the EDI link for both incoming and outgoing data; test the operation of the EDI clearing house and/or the carrier network; and refine the operating cycle.

The lessons learned with a pilot project will minimise the problems of full scale implementation. As a learning exercise, the pilot project should be used as an opportunity to produce a guide for future additions to the network. Selecting the pilot project partners must be done with care. It is essential to have a small (therefore manageable) number of partners that represent (as far as possible) the profile of the overall trading base. It should include high volume, high complexity partnerships and at least one example of each transaction. The period of the trial should encompass at least one complete operating cycle of the partners involved to allow problems at any stage to become evident.

The major purpose of a pilot project is to prove the concept and assess the accuracy of earlier cost/benefit statements. As always, the costs are easy to assess. The decision to proceed to full implementation requires that the pilot project has been successful—both in operating and financial terms. The author finds it difficult to envisage failure of the pilot on operating terms as there already exists sufficient experience in most of the major trading transactions.

NEGOTIATING WITH TRADING PARTNERS

Only when a critical mass of trading partners are using EDI will the real financial and operating benefits be seen. The greater the percentage of partners using

EDI, the more possible it will be to scale down the 'paper based' operation (an important point to remember when assessing the cost/benefits of the project). There are basically two approaches to enlarging the EDI fraternity—persuasion or coercion. The latter is only available to organisations who have some leverage over their trading partners; for example, Austin Rover have included the use of EDI in their conditions of purchase, effectively requiring their suppliers to use EDI—or risk losing Austin Rover's business. This approach carries the risk of losing a valued trading partner who may not want to move towards EDI at the present time.

Persuasion is perhaps the most favoured method. It involves educating partners of the advantages—for both partners—of using EDI. The mutual benefits have to be explained and illustrated. Pilot project partners can be very valuable here in helping sell the message. Nothing convinces as effectively as someone who has first-hand experience. Another effective tool is to prepare a cost/benefit statement for a small number of trading partners based on the volumes of transactions in your trading relationship. Any positive benefit from just one relationship can be sold as an enormous potential benefit over all their trading relationships. EDI service suppliers should be involved in this selling exercise. They are the experts and should field questions about the operation, security and cost of the service.

Whether this process is done on a one-to-one basis, or via a special meeting of trading partners depends on three main factors: the number of partners involved, the need to maintain confidentiality about who you trade with and your ability to bring a number of trading partners together at one time.

Full implementation

Full implementation is in many respects a misnomer. There are always going to be new trading partners to convert, new application areas to consider—or preferably—to develop (someone has to take the lead) and a continual evolution of communication and message standards. Having set out on the EDI route, it is important to 'stay with the pack'. Benefits will go to those who continually evaluate their current and proposed use of EDI and push the barriers to further applications further back. Industry and professional groupings are already active in this field and only by becoming involved in their activities can influence be exerted. Do not be put off by considering that this is only for the big companies. To borrow an analogy from the Japanese, a series of constant drips of water will wear a hole in a stone more effectively than one large torrent.

SUMMARY

The key to successful implementation is in planning and preparation. Only by carefully considering the need, method of operation, the scale and period of implementation and carrying out a comprehensive cost/benefit analysis will the right decision be made. This is not to suggest that the planning period should be too lengthy; one to six months (depending on the scale of the proposed use of EDI) should be long enough. The real need is to implement EDI effectively and quickly so that the organisation can take advantage of the considerable benefits which EDI can deliver.

13
Selecting Communications Services for EDI

Edmund Lee

INTRODUCTION

Other articles in this *Handbook* have dealt with the technical and commercial considerations for selecting and setting up application systems to support EDI. This chapter examines EDI communications options in the context of the underlying and broader issues of organisations' corporate and inter-company data communications requirements. Whilst initial experimentation with EDI may be treated by organisations as stand-alone developments, sooner or later they will be embracing EDI and this will mean integrating the EDI functions both in the corporate network and in external networking implementations. The drive towards doing this is to realise greater advantages through more complete integration of EDI.

Conventional definitions of EDI involve the concept of documents (or files) being exchanged between two or more trading entities in support of quicker and less costly methods of procurement, supply and payment for products or services bought or sold. These definitions tend to exclude intra-company exchange, whether inland or international; within an organisation this is a vast area of interaction and processing which currently dwarfs external exchange. Corporate techniques for exchanging and processing information must be taken into account when planning external EDI.

Not only is the motivation to adopt EDI coming from established communities trading electronically with standard syntax and formats, but pressure on suppliers is also coming from large companies and customers setting up individual trading relationships. It is in such cases that the implications of EDI on the supplier's organisation and network plans must be most carefully assessed. With regard to communications the three main issues that need to be considered are; firstly, whether other large consumers and customers may also demand EDI links which require different implementation, secondly, to what extent the EDI requirements affect the main plans of the network, and thirdly, which communications services to select.

ORGANISATION

A starting point for determining the most suitable communications services is to decide where in the organisation the EDI application will be operated and who the end-user will be. Invoice keying, order entry, just-in-time purchase, stock updating, delivery, Customs and Excise notification, and BACS transfers may occur in different departments staffed by different users. The scale of the EDI requirement (that is to say whether there are to be many user departments, whether the EDI will depend on existing processes within the organisation, the size of the EDI application) will determine whether the application is developed as a part of the organisation's existing processing and networking facilities, or developed in isolation. Large, frequently run and organisationally dependant applications will require a high degree of integration and use of existing systems. At the other end of the scale a stand-alone PC for one end-user department which is not reliant on any real-time or batch data connection from within the company could suffice.

SELECTING THE COMMUNICATIONS STRUCTURE

Four scenarios are examined to indicate the data communications options a company might adopt when introducing EDI. These are referred to as Integrated-External and Integrated-Internal (where applications require connection to the main processes of the company in order for EDI to function) and Partitioned-External and Partitioned-Internal. These partitioned scenarios are situations where the EDI requirement applies to one end-user department for document exchange outside the company and, in the Partitioned-Internal case, a pair of offices in the company for an isolated application internally. The possible generic communications structures are shown below.

Integrated-Internal network structure

The corporate network is already in place. The existing network would, typically, be based on a centralised star network configuration possibly with multiplexing, or a peer-to-peer communications service based on a switched network configuration. Examples of these configurations are SNA networks and X.25 packet switching networks. The structure assumes the need for automatic gathering and distribution of information from and to a central CPU and departmental processors, and some manual input and control. The EDI application may require overlaying onto a back-up system too.

Integrated-External network structure

As with the internal structure, a corporate network is in place. External communications are also set up, perhaps bilaterally on private circuits or via PSS. The need for scheduling processing of documents will dictate the use of a store-and-collect facility which will typically be an external mailbox system such as Telecom Gold. Integrated structures should consider all permanent external applications (EDI among them) so as to achieve economies of scale. A managed data network with X.25 interfaces, which offers the switching of calls securely to and from the company to more than one destination, provides this sort of external network connection.

Where access to more than one customer or supplier for different EDI services becomes necessary, as is likely, this form of external network connection will become increasingly attractive as gateways between the EDI VADS operators appear.

Partitioned-Internal network structure

This situation is a point-to-point requirement, typically PC to mainframe. The cheapest way of setting this up is by using the PSTN as an adjunct to the mainframe's network ports, or a LAN where this exists. If volumes are high or security considerations rule out the PSTN, a private circuit connection to the corporate network will be required.

Partitioned-External network structure

This is a simple configuration requiring no connection to the corporate network. The EDI application is likely to be developed on a PC and external communications will probably be via the PSTN to the EDI clearing house or correspondent. The most suitable network solution and most appropriate protocols will be different for each of these scenarios.

PROTOCOLS

The main types of protocol and their suitability for an EDI communications service are considered first. Protocols in this instance refers to the station-to-station procedure for handling the correct transmission of data across a link, and the data stream. The main protocols relevant to EDI are given below.

3780 & 2780

These are block-mode protocols used for one way at a time (half duplex) exchange of data in batch. Commonly referred to as Remote Job Entry (RJE) they are used between processes—PC to mainframe, departmental mini system to mainframe.

Partitioned network structures will find this method most suitable as it offers a widely available means of transmitting files error-corrected over the PSTN. The characteristics of the files are likely to be low volumes of data generated in a stand-alone PC. Most communications hardware suppliers support these protocols. They have been established for many years and they originate from the early IBM Data Processing environment.

3270 & 3770

Whereas 2780/3780 is the *de facto* batch protocol from the BSC environment, 3270 is the *de facto* screen display data stream. It is nearly always associated with SNA/SDLC. SDLC is the link level transport mechanism, usually point-to-point cluster controller to FEP, supporting and protecting the integrity of the 3270 data stream across the link. 3370 is used for batch work in the SNA environment. For large applications where SNA is the principal corporate communications standard of the organisation and the network structure fits the integrated network scenarios, 3270 and 3770 SDLC are appropriate.

In addition to the conventional point-to-point, multidrop and 37X5 environments, 3270/3770 SNA is run over packet switching networks. The MultiStream SPAD service uses PSS to do this; data streams are carried transparently.

VT100, TTY & CO3

In very many processes, documents are exchanged interactively by an operator or admin clerk filling in forms on a workstation attached locally or remotely to a host system. In addition to 3270, CO3 and Screen VT100 apply. CO3 is similar to 3270/SDLC in concept and exists in the ICL environment. VT100 is a character-interrupt protocol and is usually restricted to terminals which are directly attached to a DEC host system.

X.25

The X.25 protocol is the standard method of interfacing to packet networks. It is made up of three levels: the physical or line level where the control of the electrical interface is defined (V.24, V.35 and X.21bis); the link level which, with HDLC, ensures that data is transported across a link with integrity and under the control of both ends of the link; and the packet level where data is split into packets, where calls have addresses associated and are dynamically multi-plexed such that many calls to many addresses can be transported simul-taneously on a single link.

X.25 defines the interface between inter-linked equipment. This equipment is usually host or terminal controller and packet network switch; but it can be point-to-point host-to-host or terminal-to-host. Most of the protocol relates to the interface between the equipment which is directly interconnected. Some aspects, though, relate to end-to-end handling such as the flow control of data and the signalling of addresses, closed user group membership, and reverse charging. The manner in which data is handled in a network between hosts or terminal equipment is not merely a function of the X.25 protocol but the design of the network itself. The facilities (for example closed user groups, reverse charging), the performance of the network, routing and its resilience, are all determined by the network and the way it uses packet switching techniques.

X.25 is suitable for the integrated network structure scenarios where cor-porate communications are based on X.25. Partitioned network structures can also opt for X.25 because the protocol is firmly supported by PC comms card manufacturers as well as all the main DP and OA equipment manufacturers.

NETWORKS

More significant than the protocol is the network which is to be selected for EDI. This is because the selection can involve investment decisions which are far more important, particularly for the integrated network structures. In selecting the appropriate type of networking for EDI, the breadth of applications which the network is required to carry needs to be considered. EDI is only going to be one of many applications in an organisation. It is one type of messaging application; the generic messaging application is electronic mail and this is a likely requirement of the organisation. Other generic applications could include interactive information retrieval, internal on-line transaction processing and file transfer.

Separating the functions

For network communications within a company (the partitioned or integrated-internal network scenarios), the company organisation is likely to be flexible enough to schedule document interchange between departments. The existing communications structure and methods should be capable of bearing the EDI application.

In the case of external document interchange, particularly the integrated-external user who is going to integrate this within his company, the selection of the communications service ought to rest on how well the EDI bearer service fits the company's communications equipment and can mesh with, or provide a gateway to this network. An EDI bearer service to which existing equipment can be connected, for example X.25, saves investment in new peripheral equipment and possibly avoids the need to check with another equipment vendor.

The capabilities of the EDI application and the bearer network should be considered individually when deciding which EDI solution to adopt. The function which EDI clearing-house operators provide, and the network needed to connect the application, answer different problems. The EDI application is a processing problem, one of conversion, storage, collection, and auditing. The network is an infrastructure problem, the bearer of a wide variety of applications, economic wide area access as and where needed, routing, resilience, multiplexing, switching, and data stream and protocol conversion.

Network management

Resilience, performance and quality are features required from any network which bears corporate applications. In seeking connections to external applications and systems, whether offered by a third party or a trading partner, the same degree of quality is required. The scale and complexity of management of a network are significantly greater than for a stand-alone system if high quality standards are to be achieved and maintained. For those who construct their own corporate networks or provide managed data networks, such as BT with the Public Data Network, the investment in management is recognised as being stringent for every application. The specification of management includes high quality of service, minimal performance delays, high grade of service, ease of reconfiguration, the ability to handle change, and wide geographical coverage. To take an example the Public Data Network, with PSS as its core, provides very high network availability. All network links are backed-up and routes replicated; switch hardware has hot standby redundancy, and the network automatic-

	Build Your Own		Public Data Network	
	Start Up	Recurring	Start Up	Recurring
Year 1	108	102	20	89
Year 2	-	107	-	89
Year 3	-	107	-	89

All figures are in £,000s

Figure 13.1 Full cost comparison of network implementation options

ally reroutes sessions without breaking them should elements in the network path fail during a session. These availability characteristics are demanded by time-critical and interactive applications and EDI traffic benefits from this.

A good network management and maintenance operation is essential to sustain a high quality of service. This applies to any data network which has to be capable of providing the communications infrastructure for a company's internal and external networking needs. This is the area which requires the most expense in skills. The costs of doing this outweigh the capital investment of the equipment in the network, and intercompany services, just as much as corporate networks, require this level of commitment. The EDI system operator should where possible take advantage of this level of investment because the financial structure of the system business will not carry the wide area network investment and running costs on its own.

The other significant issue in deciding whether the EDI clearing house operator has the appropriate network solution for the company who wants to integrate external EDI within his company (the integrated-external scenario), is the extent of geographic coverage provided. Whilst any one supplier-customer trading relationship may only need a few sites interconnected, there may be many hundreds of such relationships with numbers growing rapidly. The sum of these relationships will require national coverage both with direct connections and dial-up access. The cost structure to support this will dwarf the EDI application investment—consequently the management focus of such applications operators should be understood by the potential user. Most EDI operators regard the delivery network as a utility and where this utility has been developed to support EDI processors, the design is characterised by coping with batch sessions with a narrow traffic profile. This limits the use of the network for anything else, for example building or augmenting a corporate network to share applications other than EDI.

The managed network

With the functions of system and network separated there are three implementation options available for the network. These can be either to extend an existing private network ('build your own'), to adopt a managed data network solution or, thirdly, to use a managed data network to complement the 'build your own' network.

One of the main determining factors will be cost. It is often actually cheaper to use a managed data network solution (the Public Data Network) than for the company to build the network for itself. This is especially so when all related costs are included; that is to say, all equipment including network management tools, skilled staff resource, and all leased items such as private circuits.. The comparison for a 22-site network spread nationally is shown in Figure 13.1.

Costs of using the Public Data Network comprise connection charge and quarterly rental for each dataline (direct connection) from the customer's equipment interface (V.24, V.35, X.21bis). PSS has charges for use; 4·5p for 10kbytes of batch data and 14p for 10kbytes in a typical interactive X.25 session. As use increases lower rates apply. The MultiStream SNA/SDLC and BSC services have only time-of-connection charges. A list and a visual representation of the main Public Data Network services is shown in Figure 13.2.

Figure 13.2 Public Data Network Services

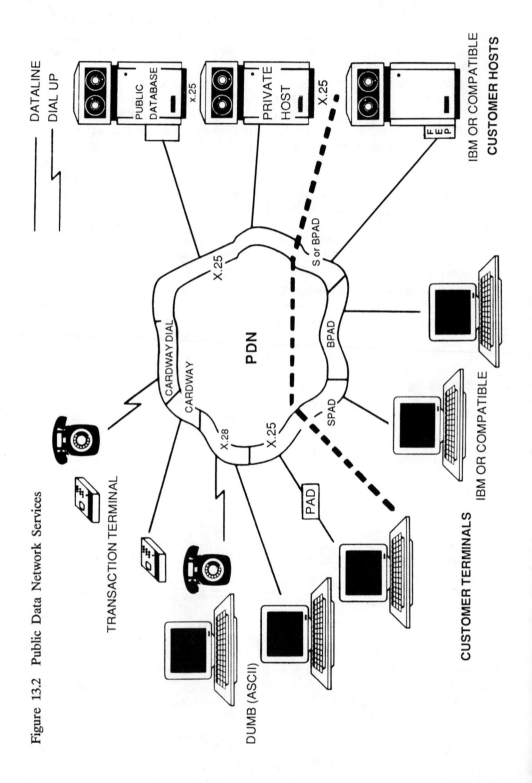

NOTES
The Public Data Network comprises:

PSS X.25 Dataline - enables computer equipment and terminals from over 80 different manufacturers using the international X.25 datacomms standard to communicate.

PSS X.28 Dial-up - for the connection of a very wide range of simple terminals, automated devices and microcomputers to communicate with hosts connected to the PDN. They use the public telephone network to make the connection to the nearest access point.

PSS X.28 Dataline - as for X.28 Dial-up but with a permanent physical connection between the terminal and the network, offering the advantages of dedicated access and rapid call set up.

MultiStream Synchronous Services - these enable IBM and IBM-compatible equipment to take advantage of the high resilience of the PDN, giving terminal systems low-cost, dedicated access to SNA and BSC mini-computers and mainframes. The two services available are:

SPAD - offers upport for SDLC/SNA communications.

BPAD - allows 3270 BSC terminals to switch and connect to multiple host computers.

MultiStream EPAD - provides full end-to-end error-protection between the users' equipment by ensuring that the dial-up link between the user and the PDN is protected.

MultiStream VPAD - allows terminals to use the PDN to access videotex hosts.

Cardway - a service which enables authorisation terminals in retail premises to communicate with the major credit and charge card host computers to verify transaction. Direct linkage to the network provides a rapid response.

Cardway Dial - this system uses the public telephone network as the access method to the PDN for Cardway transactions.

IPSS - access to over 100 packet switched networks in more than 70 countries is available through BT's International Packet Switching Service.

Both PSS and MultiStream have 100 per cent coverage and a very wide user base across all sectors of industry and commerce. They are important vehicles for EDI with many applications. Their ubiquity makes them suitable for inter-business communication, typically connecting customer and supplier, as well as for the corporate network.

Alternative communication methods

PSTN and private circuits are common alternative ways of linking trading partners. The choice of PSTN will depend on the length of time to be spent transmitting data files, the distance between the partners, and the cost of equipping FEP ports and auto-answer modems on the recipient's host system. PSTN is the simplest way to get going for the partitioned-external user who has no existing wide area network implementation and who is not attempting to integrate the EDI with internal systems.

For large, frequently transmitted files, and where there is a need for more privacy than the PSTN provides, a range of analogue and KiloStream private circuit services are available from BT.

CONCLUSION

At first sight a wide range of communications options exist for EDI. The choice can be made by considering the network structure, the extent to which EDI is to be adopted, and by considering the EDI application as a separate function from the network. In this way a robust network can be planned and implemented which is flexible to meet growth and future applications requirements. Getting the company network structure right is the main communications issue. EDI bearer services may be suitable but the most likely answer will be for the company to build the network itself or lease a managed data network such as the Public Data Network.

14
The Enabling Factors for EDI

David Palmer

INTRODUCTION

This paper aims to give guidelines to the successful implementation of EDI particularly in small companies, to point out the common pitfalls that could trap the unwary and to show that the implementation can be a straightforward and painless procedure. The techniques suggested are aimed at assisting those companies who need to implement EDI quickly, but those companies which are looking at EDI implementation in the longer term should take heed of the advice as they will face very similar problems. No matter what the size and type of organisation, the enabling factors are the same.

One factor which often causes difficulties in EDI implementations is that the timescales imposed can be very short. There are often two reasons for this. Firstly, in companies that have decided to use EDI to help achieve their business goals, it has often taken a great deal of time and effort to persuade senior management to make the investment. This is because it can be difficult to do a cost/benefit analysis which presents a good case for EDI. Once senior management have seen the light, however, they expect EDI to be in place the next day. After all, they have often been told how easy it all is. Secondly, EDI is often driven by large companies who envisage large potential gains from implementation. Such companies achieve their objectives by persuading their suppliers to participate. These suppliers are often small companies with much to lose and the invitation to join in usually takes the form of, 'an offer you can't refuse'.

In both of the scenarios given above it now falls on some hapless individual to 'go away and do it'. The author and many of his colleagues have talked to scores of individuals such as these.

COMMITMENT

SD-Scicon has seen more EDI implementations falter through lack of commitment than for any other single reason. In most cases this does not mean a lack of willingness to proceed, on the contrary there is often almost a sense of desperation to go ahead. What is lacking is the commitment of adequate time and resources. Implementing EDI is a straightforward process, but there is a lot to arrange and do. To start using EDI successfully everything has to be in place at the same time. In order to achieve successful implementation a realisation of the true human resources necessary is important, for example just to investigate the alternatives and control the dependencies can be a full time job.

EDI is seen, however, as an unusual project. It encompasses all areas of computing from applications to communications. The person most likely to be assigned to it, therefore, is the all-rounder who can tackle any project on any machine in any language. Such a person may seem initially to be the ideal candidate. Unfortunately this person's qualifications almost certainly mean he or she is the payroll support person, or is the only person in the organisation who can really get to grips with that ancient order processing system, written by a software house which went bust just before they documented it. Or in a company without its own computer resources, the assignee will be some equally talented individual who is the only person who can really understand export document-ation to Albania. It is paramount that such pitfalls are considered when selecting the person to be responsible for EDI as there is much more to do than is apparent at the outset.

Whoever is responsible for EDI must have EDI as his or her number one priority. Committing manpower in this way has to come from the top. At an ODETTE seminar on implementing EDI, at which I spoke,the audience was a mixture of people who were about to start implementation, were part way through, or had completed it. When I gave my sermon on commitment, the latter two groups could be readily identified by the furiously nodding heads. At a recent conference I was approached by an individual from a large company I had visited some months before. He confirmed my suspicions by stating, "You were right. I still have my other job to do and we have made very little progress". EDI implementation is a demanding project which requires the full time involvement of one or more people. The project must be properly planned and adequately resourced. Remember that there are other companies involved who are depending on your company to achieve its objectives.

Having touched briefly on the subject of commitment it would be salient to discuss some of the practical issues involved in implementation.

COMMUNICATIONS METHODS

There are currently two communicatons options for practising EDI. These are value added and data services (VADS), and direct communications via public or private networks.

The choice of method in most cases will be dictated by the major trading partner(s), although increasingly the very large companies who have been using EDI for some time are offering a choice. Without getting embroiled in the VADS versus direct links debate, which is discussed in greater depth elsewhere in this book, the basic characteristics of the two options are outlined below.

Value added and data services (VADS)

A value added and data service supplier provides a variety of services, but most revolve around the most significant service to EDI, which is to provide a store-and-forward facility. What this means is that the sender of the data sends it to the VADS, the VADS splits the received data by recipient, rather like a postal sorting office, and then stores the data so that the recipient can pull it off the VADS at a convenient time. To give a typical example, a supermarket chain may send all its fresh food orders to all its suppliers daily and will tell its suppliers that the orders will be on the network by two o'clock in the morning. The suppliers can then decide what time they will take the data off to suit their organisation, taking into account the time it takes to process the orders, assemble the goods and ship them. Not forgetting to allow time for problems, of course.

The VADS vary in the extra value they add, but they may allow the data to be extracted by document type, for example all orders, by trading partner or by date. The great advantage of the VADS is that the recipient can control the receipt of the data. The major disadvantage is that this facility costs money.

Direct links

Direct links may be divided into two types: via a private network or via a public network.

Private networks are obviously more limited in scope as they allow communications only with the network owner. There are a number of such networks operational and they do bring major cost benefits to the operators. For the companies on the other end, however, there is the potential danger of ending up with a room full of terminals, each connected to a different private network.

Public networks can potentially reach all over the world, depending on the arrangements between the various telephone companies in the countries. This is a popular option in Continental Europe. Costs are much lower than for a VADS, being limited to the cost of the connect time (the phone call) and the subscription to the public service. The major disadvantage is that the recipient has to be in a state to receive the data, just as a phone call can only be made if the called party's phone is working and not engaged. While multiple calls can be handled to an extent, this is largely limited by technology. Whether this manifests itself as a real problem in practice only time will tell.

In future, public networks will offer store-and-forward services using X.400 and several VADS are committed to providing X.400 connectivity. This may become the standard method of communication for EDI, but several key technical issues must be resolved first. Paul Dawkins' paper, chapter 5, gives an introduction to X.400. Nick Pope, in chapter 20, treats the use of X.400 to support EDI in some detail.

COMMUNICATIONS PROTOCOLS

Whichever communications method is chosen,a communications protocol has to be used to send or receive data. There are many possibilities. For some reason the thought of using a communications protocol strikes fear into the hearts of many people, including computer professionals. In practical terms there is no need to know any more about them than is known about the communications protocol used every time a telephone is lifted.

If direct links have been chosen, the protocol may well be dictated by the trading partner(s). If a VADS is being used there may be a wider choice, but the choice will depend on the type of computer used and the protocols supported by the VADS. The most common methods of communication are Asynchronous, Binary Synchronous (2780/3780), SDLC and X.25. All have their merits and drawbacks. Briefly asynchronous protocols are cheap to implement but are the slowest (that is, the most expensive in call charges) in operation. 2780/3780 is quite cheap to implement on most computers and is generally reliable. The main

problem is that these protocols are *de-facto* standards and some implementations are more standard than others so some companies have had difficulty in
getting the communications working. SDLC is generally a trouble-free route, but
tends to be limited to IBM environments. X.25 is, on the face of it, the best
protocol. It offers built in error correction and is an international standard. It is
not widely used for EDI in the UK, however. Cost and implementation difficulties
appear to be the main reasons, though this may change with increased usage. If,
after discussion with the direct trading partner or the VADS supplier, the user
is left with a choice as to the type of computer hardware to choose, the following
factors will help in making the decision:

> Do you already have communicatons hardware and software
> installed? If you have and it is suitable then use it.

> Alternatively, it may be advisable to investigate what would be
> best for the future.

> Cost—the cost of communicatons software and hardware can vary
> considerably between different types of computer. Also, the
> speed at which data can be sent affects the cost of transmission:
> the slower the protocol, the longer the phone call.

> Do you intend to use multiple networks? If so, you should try to
> choose a protocol which will be suitable for all of them. The
> delivery lead-time for communications hardware and connection
> to the appropriate network varies considerably and may be
> incompatible with your trading partner's needs in some cases.

In practice, if a VADS has been chosen it would be prudent to accept the
supplier's advice. If direct links have been chosen it is very likely that the
options are limited as has been discussed above.

THE PHYSICAL LINK

The physical link can either be direct, using a leased line, or dial-up, using an
ordinary telephone line. The choice should be dependent on the volume of EDI
traffic, the frequency of use and possibly the time of day that messages are to be
transmitted or received. This choice, therefore, basically boils down to running
costs.

Dial-up is suited to low levels of EDI traffic. The normal speed of transmission
on dial-up lines is 1200 bits per second (1200 bps) for asynchronous traffic and
2400 bits per second (2400 bps) for sychronous traffic. In lay terms this means
that a normal telephone exchange has to cope with the transmissions and they
are relatively slow. This in turn means that the phone calls used for transmission
last longer and ultimately cost more. The more traffic there is, the longer the
phone calls last and the more they cost. Normal call tariffs apply, so peak time
calls will cost more than off peak or overnight use.

The alternative is to use a leased line or X.25 access line, which is effectively
a dedicated piece of wire between the trading parties. Charges for leased lines
are on an annual basis regardless of the amount of traffic or the time of day they
are being used.

An analysis of the expected volume of EDI traffic and the communications methods employed should be carried out to assess whether a dial-up or a leased line should used. Before moving on it is worth making two important points concerning the physical link. Firstly, it is not usually advisable to use a telephone connected to an internal switchboard. This often results in an unreliable connection. It is preferable to use a line direct to the telephone exchange (a separate telephone number), so time should be allowed (in the project timetable) for installation of this dedicated line. Secondly, leased lines are not installed overnight, in some areas it can take months. Again sufficient time should be allowed for installation.

COMMUNICATIONS HARDWARE

At this point the 'EDI implementor' should have a piece of wire coming into their place of business and some hardware and software on their computer to pass the data to the wire. The next requirement is a piece of electronic equipment to control the actual telephone call. This is the modem and it is available in a wide variety of different types. There are V21, V22, V24 modems and combinations thereof; there are also manual or auto-dial options on most modems.

In truth there are two basic types of modem—asynchronous and synchronous. The choice is further simplified by the fact that there are only a handful of modem manufacturers. The rest of the suppliers 'badge engineer' the equipment. The problem is however that amongst this array of products, some will work to the user's requirements and some, unfortunately, will not. In order to facilitate the correct choice two parties should be consulted before the final decision is reached. The first is the network provider. This is either the VADS supplier if one is being used or the telephone company if not. Both will have lists of tested modems that they know will work in the user's chosen environment. The second party to be consulted is the supplier of the communications software. This source of information is particularly important if auto-dial has been chosen. For example, 3780 is a supposedly standard communications protocol, but one of the VANs operators has identified at least 23 variants. The communications software drives the modem and therefore the two must be exactly compatible. If the software supplier states that the software will drive modem X and modem Y only, it is imperative that the statement is believed. If I have one *cri de coeur* it is not to buy modem Z because the supplier says, 'it's just the same.' It might be, but probably is not.

One small item which causes a disproportionate amount of trouble is the modem cable. It is important to be very precise in specifying the requirements for the modem-to-computer cable, particularly if an autodial model is being used. Incorrect cabling is a common source of problems, particularly with PC installations.

TRANSLATION SOFTWARE

EDI messages are structured according to international standards. The two most common in Europe are UNTDI and Electronic Data Interchange for Administration Commerce & Transport (EDIFACT). These standards are discussed in far greater detail elsewhere in this *Handbook* but, to paraphrase, these standards define a syntax and a 'grammar'. EDI messages are then designed using these rules. In-house data on the user's own computer must be extracted and translated into the appropriate message format using these rules and *vice versa*. This requires some computer software which has to be bought, as a package, or written in-house.

The existing packages, of which the best known is SITPRO's Interbridge (further information in Appendix B), are fairly complex pieces of software which require to be set up for the particular message variants that each EDI practitioner is using. Given that most newcomers to EDI are starting-out to send or receive one message to or from one trading partner, the option of writing software specific to those requirements can look attractive. Particularly if the standard being used is UNTDI, writing software for one message is not a major problem. However, the messages are under continual development, more and more companies are adopting EDI and any company putting EDI capability into place should look to the future.

To give a specific example, the author visited a company recently which was going into EDI because one of their customers in the retail trade had, 'asked them nicely' to join in. A short discussion established that all their major retail customers were active in EDI (UNTDI standards, 16 messages developed), all the manufacturing customers were active in EDI (EDIFACT standards, 3 messages developed), many of their raw material suppliers were starting an EDI pilot (EDIFACT standard, 4 different messages) and they exported 70 per cent of their goods, bringing them firmly into the transportation initiatives (EDIFACT standard, 6 different messages). That company is not at all unusual in business terms but could, by taking part in established international initiatives, use 29 different EDI messages using both TDI and EDIFACT standards. They saw this as an opportunity to capitalise on the investment they were making to satisfy the requirements of one major customer. General purpose translation software was a must for them, as it will be for most businesses in the long term. General purpose translation software takes a different order of magnitude to develop. Developing software specific to one situation is almost certainly a waste of effort in the long term.

MESSAGE HANDLING

By now the reader should have a good appreciation of a number of the components necessary to exchange data electronically. To use another analogy, we have the equivalents of the Post Office, the paper, the envelopes, the stamps and the language that the documents are to be written in has been selected. The next component to be discussed is the message handling functions of EDI which, to use the postal analogy, equate to the activities of the post room by the office juniors, secretaries and filing clerks.

Firstly, there is some software required to interact with the network. This gives commands to the network to instruct it as to what the user wishes to do and also handles the network responses. VADS suppliers have the required software available off-the-shelf for the more common computers and operating systems. The commands and responses themselves vary enormously from network to network but they all handle in some way the dialogue between the user's computer and the network. A typical exchange would be the computer's equivalent of the following conversation:

Hello

Hello

Here is my data, are you ready?

Yes

OK, catch

Got it

Have you any data for me?

Yes

Send it please

OK, catch

Got it

Goodbye

Goodbye

The above has demonstrated how it is now possible to get data in and out of the system but, in a situation where multiple message types and different standards are being used, the translation software has to be told what it has to handle. The best approach to this problem is to set up profiles for each trading partner which records details such as which standards are being used, which messages are being exchanged, what days the partners wish to exchange them on, what time the exchange should take place, what the trading partners' network address is and so on. It is also necessary to record details of the network such as: what telephone numbers to use; the passwords; the days of the weeks and times of day the service is available; details of the physical link—(modem type, line speed). In this way the user defines all the interfaces to the outside world.

All this passing of data to and fro has to be controlled on the user's system and recorded. At the very least it is necessary to keep a record of what data has been sent and received. This is important because under normal circumstances most users will not want to send or receive the same data twice. Controlling the sending of data is quite easy, requiring a status indicator against each message showing the data as unsent, sent or perhaps held (to be sent but not during the next session). On incoming data, each message has a unique reference which can be checked against the electronic records thereby ensuring that it is not a retransmission. Obviously, under some circumstances, it will be necessary to resend data or receive it a second time, so there is a need for a mechanism to override the controls that are in place.

The whole point of EDI is to get rid of paper. This means that in a true EDI environment, there is no permanent paper record of what messages have been sent or received. It may be difficult or even impossible to recreate the data so it is vital that backup copies of all messages are held on magnetic media. If the user is in a large machine environment, it may be that they can hold the send-and-receive messages on their database and take advantage of the backup and restore facilities. If not, it is extremely important that all messages are carefully and regularly backed up. Particular attention should be paid to this point if a micro is being used for EDI as in the experience of the author micro users are not used to operating a rigid and regular backup schedule.

Finally, some documents (currently only invoices in the UK) require extra controls for legal purposes. For invoices, HM Customs and Excise require the creation of extra paper records of EDI transactions for VAT audit purposes. A description of the requirements outlined by HM Customs & Excise is given in chapter 24.

EXISTING APPLICATIONS

The requirements for interfacing to existing applications vary enormously from company to company. Each company will have to do its own investigation, but some key issues that are common across all companies are indicated below.

Where does the data come from and go to?

Do not make the assumption that all the data to be sent is held on the computer application that currently generates the paper. Likewise, do not assume that all the data being received can be stored on the existing application. Many people find this statement very puzzling at first. To take an example, that of the company's invoice. Most of the data to be sent electronically is on that form, but some of it is pre-printed on the paper. Items such as the company name and address, VAT registration number and payment terms are often pre-printed. It is therefore important to undertake careful data analysis, comparing the data on the EDI message and the paper form it is replacing.

What extra information needs to be held?

Again, this will vary according to the application. As an example, if data are being sent, an indicator will be required on something like the customer or supplier file. At the very least, this will identify which trading partners have to have their data placed on the EDI extract file and not have the paper generated. It may also be necessary to cross-reference the trading partner profile to identify what message is to be generated and which network is to be used. Even if all the trading partners are using the same standards, for example TRADACOMS, they may be using different versions of the message (TRADACOMS Invoice Version 1, TRADACOMS Invoice Version 2).

Can I interface with my existing applications at all?

The answer to this question is, of course, yes, but it may be more difficult than at first thought. A situation often found is when companies are receiving data, for example orders. Most companies have been moving steadily over the years towards on-line systems and it is not uncommon for these systems to have no batch interface. EDI is a batch application. There may be no existing way of getting the data into a user's application short of printing it and re-keying it on-line. This rather negates the whole point of EDI. A batch interface may have to be designed and written. Is there anyone these days who knows how to design and write batch applications?

COMPUTER CONNECTION STRATEGIES

The whole subject of implementing EDI can produce some quite heated debates, but the subject of computer connection strategies has produced some wonderful confrontations. To put it in perspective, there are two ways of going about an EDI connection. Firstly there is a direct connection from the network to the main computer housing the user's applications. Secondly, a front end processor can be used for the connection. This is typically a PC. The vast majority of companies really want to use the direct connection but a significant number are using a front-end processor (almost all a PC). The arguments in favour of the front-end processor are cost, speed, ease and strategy.

As far as cost is concerned, PC software is cheap. Communications hardware is cheaper on a PC. It is usually cheaper to connect to a network using a PC. The author is aware of one company that found it cheaper to buy a PC, communications hardware and all the software than just to buy the 3780 communications software for their minicomputer. Concerning speed, PC solutions are generally available off-the-shelf. Some necessary software and hardware may not be immediately available, or not available at all, in some mini and mainframe environments. Development loads may mean that the DP department or the third-party software supplier may not be able to do the development work in the timescales required. Ease is due to the availability of proven software and hardware. Some computers are notoriously difficult to persuade to talk to networks. It may be that a front-end processor is the only viable option.

Often a strategic argument is advanced—some companies have decided that they do not want their EDI systems to be on their main computers. The reason usually given is that this approach offers better control over the process of communicating with the outside world and gives a greater degree of flexibility for the future.

From the points made above it would appear that the front-end processor approach offers significant advantages. There are a number of drawbacks however, which in some cases have relegated this approach to a stopgap measure. The two significant drawbacks are performance and interconnectivity. Performance is characterised by its effect on the cost of EDI transmissions which are in turn heavily dependent on the length of the connect time. The slower the processor, the greater the cost. Also, for serious volumes of EDI traffic a front end processor may just not be fast enough to cope with the workloads.

To adopt the front-end processor approach means that data must be passed between the two computers, causing problems of interconnectivity. This in itself may be difficult and some people use magnetic media, although software is available which can achieve this on most common computers. If the computer vendors cannot provide the software, there are proprietary products available and the public domain software 'Kermit' is in common use. Even when the inter-connection is possible, it causes problems and again may have severe performance limitations.

Basically, using a front-end processor, typically a PC, is a cheap and quick way to get going but may not be the correct option. As a purely personal point of view, the author believes that the front-end processor approach will become widely used in the future, but using minis with good communications facilities in place of the PC. This will depend on the availability of message handling software for these machines, although such software is likely to become available as X.400 store-and-forward services develop. It should be pointed out, however that many respected figures in the world of EDI disagree strongly with this point of view.

SUMMARY

At the outset of this paper it was stated that the implementation of EDI can be a straightforward and painless procedure. I have spent much of this paper describing how complicated it is. There is no discrepancy here. To use another analogy, the internal combustion engine is a fairly complex device. Given the mechanical components, a good manual, the right facilities, the right tools and sufficient time, most people could assemble one. There are a lot of parts, but given a broad understanding of the principles of operation it is really no more difficult than a child's construction set. So it is with EDI. The components exist and they can be put together.

When my group first became involved with EDI two and a half years ago, we could see a vision of the future with EDI transforming business practices. We see the vision being turned into reality. If you are already committed to using EDI, it is hoped that this paper has alleviated some of your fears. If you still do not think EDI is relevant to you, I hope you stay in business, but the competition from those who are using EDI will get tougher.

15
How to Build Effective EDI Links

Keith Blacker

The preceeding articles should now have made the reader aware of the benefits of EDI, of the issues that have to be addressed and of the technical factors that have to be explored. But how does the potential implementor start to prepare and plan their first project? This paper brings together the ideas already explained in previous papers and develops them in the sequence suggested for project implementation. The objective is to provide EDI links which are commercially and technically effective.

There are six stages to the project which can be readily identified:

* developing the business strategy;

* planning the technical mechanism for EDI;

* choosing the project partners;

* planning the interchange project commercially;

* planning and undertaking the interchange project technically;

* following through when in production.

DEVELOPING THE BUSINESS STRATEGY

Many of the early EDI projects took a long time to get under way. There were technical issues but the projects often lacked commercial drive because one or the other party had not sorted out the strategic implications of EDI and did not have a policy to support such bi-lateral conversations. In some examples, EDI was an 'ego trip' for the information systems department as it was a very attractive new field of work. In other cases it was part of a personal campaign within a functional department such as sales, purchasing or finance. Such enthusiasm should have been directed within the business to create a company strategy on which trading discussion could start.

As the first project is planned a commercial strategy is required within which the role of EDI is defined. This needs to detail whether EDI is a peripheral support to the business or whether it is a major component of some new business outreach. The question, why do you want EDI? also needs to be answered. A number of possible answers exist. It can be a means of moving the existing paper documents more quickly and concisely. It can be used to integrate the information systems between your company and those with whom you trade, thus improving the service you offer. EDI can be used to generate new types of business or eliminate whole functions which become redundant. If some of the trading links become electronic, what will the impact be on your trading partners? They will use the first or second project to learn. Looking beyond that, what will the impact be on the ongoing operation? Will your sort of EDI integrate within that organisation and enable it to establish links with other enterprises with which it trades? Increasingly the talk is of trading partnerships and yet some of the early EDI projects made the mistake of putting partners in a straight-jacket for the future.

Are you going to start with customers, suppliers or the service providers (for example transport, banks, and insurance)? If the first link is with customers, are they twisting your arm or are you taking a lead and augmenting your service? If your first link is with suppliers, are you wishing to automate your paperwork process, or is EDI but one component of a supplier development programme? As the customer you could just instruct them that this how you intend to work and leave them to cope with that approach within their operations. But if EDI is part of a plan to improve the supply mechanisms, the resulting communication should be to the advantage of both parties. If your first link is with a service provider, is it to satisfy his wish for cleaner, cheaper information or is it to give you a more effective service at lower cost? When you have formulated your strategy it needs to be agreed within the company at the appropriate level, otherwise the project will not get the support it needs. If wholehearted support is not forthcoming, then at least get agreement for a trial, thereby enabling some practical testing to be carried out.

PLANNING THE TECHNICAL MECHANISM FOR EDI

Your company has now decided to use EDI. It is necessary to do some technical homework to decide how you are to communicate with other companies. You must decide which applications will be affected and define the interfaces that will be required. You must choose the message standards and communications protocols you will employ.

If you are responding to a trading partner who offers a personal computer based solution with a pre-determined configuration and packaged software, then the answers are easy to define, if that solution is acceptable to you. If you are integrating your applications environment with that of your trading partner you need to review the whole subject in more detail.

In your enthusiasm to get on with the first EDI application it is difficult to think about the needs of the second and third application. Planning an EDI architecture now will simplify those later projects, otherwise you may find yourself with a cat's cradle. The simplest way to build the first EDI application is to attach all the mechanics directly to the application software: thus the software for generating and decoding the syntax, to control the communications and to manage the release timing could all be integrated with the application itself. For independent single application machines such an approach may work well. If at a later stage the application has to support more than one message standard, or the computer environment has other resident applications that will employ EDI in the future, then you should set up a common service module as a gateway to the outside world. Such a module might provide the communications protocols to the various networks, the syntax coding/decoding software and, if suitably designed, offer a common data and control interface to the various applications. Investment in such a gateway has proved of immense value to some companies and is the envy of others who now face the addition of new applications without one.

While preparing an approach to the EDI interface of your application it is worthwhile defining a general interface method that will work with subsequent projects—particularly if you are unable to develop a common gateway module at this stage. Your first application may be a new one that will link only with partners using EDI: that is fortunate and can be custom designed for the purpose. Most applications systems have EDI added to them, alongside the existing methods of data entry and data presentation. In these circumstances, when sending data you probably need a filter mechanism to divert some data away from the print queue and towards the EDI utility. The filter could be hard-coded for the EDI destinations, but more sensibly you need to extend the application database to indicate the output transmission route for each company. When receiving data you must decide whether the data validation should be common with other data entry methods or whether the validation can be limited because the format standard provides some form of validation in its own right. The validated data from the EDI route can then be merged with that entered locally.

There is a significant issue in the use of codes such as supplier codes and part numbers. This is discussed more fully in the section on planning the project commercially.

Having defined where EDI fits into your commercial strategy, it is often straightforward to define the initial messages that you will send or receive: for example invoices, orders or bank giro credits. The first message is usually easy to choose; the second is easy if it was considered when deciding on the first: the third is less obvious. Take the invoicing environment for example. Receiving EDI invoices saves a great deal of work for customers but has limited benefit to the supplier. The customer avoids the cost and delay of entering the data and avoids tracking and rectifying the keying errors. The supplier only avoids the cost of printing, stuffing and postage. Returning remittance advices is of great benefit to the supplier.

Returning invoice query messages is beneficial to both parties in quickly resolving queries on received invoices. Thus message choice and the sequence of implementation is closely linked to your understanding of the effect of EDI on your operation and on that of your partner.

The choice of message standard gives rise to more argument and discontent with EDI than almost any other factor. While national, international and sectoral standards are maturing and while the experience in implementing EDI with more than one standard is limited, the choice may have a very serious impact on trading partners. If a key customer asks you to link to him with a particular standard the decision is effectively made for you. If you are linking to suppliers the choice should depend on which standard most of them can understand and support. If you review your range of suppliers, customers and service providers, they will be in a host of different industrial sectors. Message standards tend to be divided on a national or industry basis, thus you must choose the standard that can be supported by the majority of companies that you are targeting. As a general guide it is wise (if you have the freedom) to choose a standard which is stable, but which has the highest compliance with international message design standards. Migrating from one standard to another is costly in development resources and in the effort needed to coordinate the parties. Future headaches can be avoided by choosing a standard that has the prospect of remaining current for a long time.

As the use of EDI becomes more widespread, standards must be harmonised. Failure to do so will force many companies to support a number of standards as they communicate with the whole range of customers and suppliers. For now you probably need to include in your planning the use of more than one standard.

The choice of communication network poses almost as big a dilemma as choosing the message standard. While the Value Added Data Services (VADS) remain separate the choice must be conditioned by the range of companies with whom you wish to communicate. When networks interconnect the choice will become more straightforward: you will then be able to link to the one of your choice even if your customers and suppliers are linked to other networks. For now, however, if you are the first in that community to implement EDI then choose the network which suits you best. The other community members can be asked to subscribe to the chosen network. If some of your target partners already use EDI with one particular network then this is clearly the one to choose. If however they are using more than one network you will need to join more than one to reach everyone. As the use of EDI grows this situation is becoming more commonplace.

Finally you could choose the network that is convenient to you or the majority of your partners and persuade the others to join, but here you need to be very conscious of the effect on those partners. VADS subscription rates are very expensive for smaller companies who are asked to join more than one network. Furthermore the setting-up of more than one link to different VADS or different direct links can be complex and costly until international communications standards become widely accepted and adopted. So make a choice which will keep the network simple if possible, but be very conscious of the implications for your partners. Once the networks have interconnected and communications protocols have been standardised the selection will reduce to finding the one which is most commercially appropriate for you.

CHOOSING THE PROJECT PARTNERS

First and foremost the choice must be dictated by your commercial strategy and the business tactical plan. You have already decided whether your entry into EDI will be with a customer, supplier or service provider. Within that chosen group you should select the company that is important to you commercially, because you wish to retain or build-up that business or because you respect its influence in the marketplace.

Such a selection procedure needs to be tempered by two factors. Firstly you need to have a healthy relationship with the other party. The technique may be new to you or your experience limited. The project may have technical difficulties or it may prove challenging to reach agreement on the various data interpretations. If your relationship is basically good, it will withstand the strain of any difficulties encountered while you are learning. If the opening relationship is strained the chance of implementing an effective exchange mechanism and gaining a proper understanding of the issues are greatly impaired. A first EDI project in these circumstances should be avoided because the commercial relationship itself is at risk and the experience is likely to limit the enthusiasm for further similar projects.

The second factor in selecting the partner is to find a company which has done it before, preferably with the same message type and standard. The partner will then have experience of the issues involved, will have previously made the sort of decisions that you are about to encounter and moreover will have working software. New software at both ends of a new communications link can be quite difficult to commission. Experience has shown that a project with both partners learning takes about four times as long as one where the technique is new to only one of them. If you are undertaking a trial to identify the real benefits of EDI the results will emerge more quickly if you are working with an experienced partner.

PLANNING THE INTERCHANGE PROJECT COMMERCIALLY

So far it is you who have studied the issues and made the decisions internally. You need to repeat much of the same process with your trading partners and come to joint decisions. For many companies which have been involved in early EDI projects these questions, discussions and decisions arose through the development and implementation of the project. Projects are accelerated considerably if the core questions are brought to the front and decisions taken early. These decisions range through: the scope of the information to be exchanged; the standard to be used; the data communications route; defining the operational timetable; negotiating the interchange agreement; setting up the project management mechanism.

Many of the issues around selecting the message, the message standard and the communications route were discussed in the previous section of this paper. These same issues need debating and resolving with your partner, but this time it is necessary to detail the scope of the information more fully. Will the proposed EDI traffic encompass all the business between you, or just for one location, one division, one product range or one service? Has the sender a means of separating that class of traffic from the remaining business? Are the supplier codes, customer codes, part numbers and addresses sufficiently unique not only to select the agreed data at source but also for correct processing on receipt? EDI is the migration to *automatic* integration between you and the other partner. Very often, when documents are received manually, *people* will correct data inaccuracies or interpret data before it is entered into the receiving company's computer. These manual interventions must be teased out before EDI can begin. The commercial people alone can sort this out.

The presentation of codes needs to be agreed. Take part numbers for example: the two parties need to agree or understand whose part number will be used and the precise representation of that number. Will the ''-'' and ''/'' that appear in the catalogue be included in the transmission? What about those blanks that are inserted when writing the numbers by hand? How will you keep both companies updated when new part numbers are created or one number is superseded by another? The construction of every coded data element must be discussed and agreed and any new working practices for creating these numbers introduced *before* EDI transmission is started.

Because EDI offers a faster transmission route than postal services (or even fax if the data has to be manually entered into a computer on receipt) you need to examine the operating timetable for generating, transmitting and receiving the data. Important benefits can result from examining the dates and times when the data is created relative to the times when the receiving process is run. If an order transmission is received at three in the afternoon instead of five in the evening, it might mean that orders could be processed for despatch that afternoon rather than the next day. If stock usage transactions are received by six in the morning rather than eight in the morning, vehicle deliveries and manufacturing production could be planned for that day rather than a day later. The timetable needs to examine the whole cycle from the original source of the data, through its transmission to the tasks where it is finally used, to identify where adjustments can be made which will give worthwhile service improvements.

Next comes the interchange agreement. Some of the EDI trials have used formal interchange agreements throughout. Others have avoided any form of agreement and have relied on goodwill between the participants. Some industries have well-defined and agreed terms of trade which are fairly confused but trade successfully continues none the less. In the absence of a suitable body of legislation and case law, the companies taking part in an EDI project need to take a view on the role of an Interchange Agreement. Some form of agreement is required on working practices, how to avoid problems and how to resolve disputes. Whether this is a signed agreement or a verbal understanding depends very much on the relationship between the companies, the normal practice for the industry and the nature of the information being exchanged. It is advisable, however, for the partners to use guidelines such as the International Chamber of Commerce Uniform Rules of Conduct for Interchange of Trade Data by Teletransmission (UNCID Guidelines) as the basis for discussion to ensure that sensible working practices are devised and agreed. This aspect of the trading relationship is treated by Bernard Wheble in chapter 10. It may be necessary or legally prudent to embody the decisions reached into a formal signed agreement as outlined by John Sanders in chapter 9. An EDI project has at least two characteristics which distinguish it from an internal information technology/management services project. The first is that there is no single manager for the project as a whole because there are two parties each with project management responsibility. The other distinguishing feature is the vital role of the commercial manager from each company. An EDI project is between two partners. This in turn gives rise to two separate development methods and standards which are coordinated together rather than having a homogeneous project team which reports to a single client. Project managers are usually systems people reporting to a client manager or business team. In an EDI project the project manager for one partner's development may well be a systems person but the overall project management between the companies must fall to the commercial principals in the two businesses. They should manage the overall project, reach the various understandings required (albeit with technical support) and arrange for the various interpretations of data to be resolved. Their involvement should be very full. Three levels of interface management need to be established at the beginning, these are: who are the commercial principals in the two companies? Who are the two systems people who will liaise technically? Who are the operating personnel who will confer when day-to-day issues arise after the link has gone into production? If you are involved with VATable documents such as invoices and credit notes both parties will need to advise their local Customs and Excise offices. Customs and Excise require at least one month's notice to audit your completed system; it is wise to advise them as soon as you agree to exchange such documents as this helps them to be able to help you. Further information concerning the requirements are explained in chapter 24.

If all these factors have been discussed and agreed commercially you are in good shape to continue the project technically.

TECHNICAL PLANNING OF THE INTERCHANGE PROJECT

With the commercial interchange issues decided or being resolved there are four stages in the technical implementation: agreeing the precise meaning of data; setting the detailed operational timetable; integrating the two applications; testing the transmissions.

The message standard will define each data element and segment in the message, define whether each element is mandatory or conditional and define the precise representation of each element. Between the two companies you need to decide which conditional data elements you need or intend to use. If you are exchanging only one message type then the names and addresses, order details and so on may need to be fairly full. If you are using a set of messages spanning ordering, delivery and invoicing the information may be detailed only once in the sequence thus minimising the data to be transmitted and processed.

Your commercial colleagues will have agreed the broad timetable for end-to-end transmission. The two technical coordinators must now establish the precise operating timetable to fulfill those objectives: when complete original data is available; through any processing at the senders end; through data extract and syntax building; through the transmission route including any clearing centre; through syntax removal and on to the receiving application. Each has to be estimated and planned to ensure that the overall objectives can be met.

If the timetable for transmission is fairly loose you can use normal manual controls to schedule and execute the various computing and transmission components. If, however, the timetable is tight or you plan to provide a fully automatic operation then part of the technical planning must include the design of various triggers. At one end the data creation must automatically initiate the processes through to auto-dialling the network or clearing centre. The receiving end must be able to continuously 'listen' for incoming calls, or regularly trawl the clearing centre for mailbox data or have a timetable for collecting data from the clearing centre. On receiving data the syntax removal and subsequent application need to be 'chained together'. While the trigger mechanisms are unique to each end you need to ensure that each partner understands the other's approach and can check that it all hangs together.

The need for access security controls must be reviewed. Depending on what information is to be exchanged you will have a greater or lesser need to authenticate the sender and to authorise the contents of the transmission. You will need to devise controls which are appropriate to the risk and which can be supported by the standard, by the network and by the other party. Each company will decide the audit controls needed at its respective end. It may be necessary to decide overall audit controls, particularly where financial transactions are involved.

You are now ready to detail the mechanics: to decide the computers to use at each end (probably already defined in practice); sign the contracts with the network; understand the type of communication line to be ordered and the modem required; define (with the network) the communication software to be used and how to instal it; choose the source of the syntax software and learn about its installation and testing; plan the technical project to instal it all, test the components individually and then test them together.

When complete you are ready to start testing with your partner. You will very quickly see how thorough the commercial planning has been. This list may look daunting but is necessary the first time through. If you have assembled and tested the components carefully this will stand you in good stead for both this and subsequent links.

Finally as in any good information systems project, you will produce documentation. Documenting the implementation within each organisation will be taken for granted. One party, however, will need to take responsibility for documenting the specific interpretations of the message data elements, the code representations and the integrated timetable. These items are certain to be revised at some time in the future when the recorded decisions will prove essential.

FOLLOWING THROUGH INTO PRODUCTION

When you have completed the implementation and moved into production, that is sending live data, there are several more things to consider: when to stop the paper flow; tracking down and resolving problems; reviewing the opportunity for simplification; message change control.

The decision to cancel the existing paper documents often seems difficult to make. This is the crunch point when you are stopping the old method of working and have to rely on the new. While testing has to be thorough and may require some parallel running, a well-defined cutover to the new method is essential otherwise there is a danger that the old practices and delays that you are seeking to eliminate will continue. So agree a short sharp testing period and then cease the paper chain. If problems occur their resolution will be faster if you do not go back to paper but persevere in clearing the issues quickly. Problems and difficulties may well arise during production operation. There are already agreed people in place to diagnose and resolve the operational issues should they occur. There are two broad approaches to resolving such problems: one is to 'find a way around the problem' and the other is to fix it at source. 'Finding a way around' may be quicker but leads to a variety of secondary procedures which you have just spent time trying to eliminate and is the reason (for example) why one company's paper invoice layout has become different from others. If you spend time understanding how the problem has occurred and fix it at source then the simplification that you have worked for can be maintained. By finding proper solutions you will avoid a mix of temporary bypasses and additional work in the future.

When in production you will be able to see how well this new trading relationship works. After a few months you should formally sit down with your trading partner and look at the effect of the change. You may well find tasks that you are still doing are rendered obsolete because the electronic transmission is so much more precise and consistent than the original documents received by post that were manually interpreted. You should also review audit procedures to check that they are working adequately. This review gives you the opportunity to simplify the whole trade process and hence reduce its costs while probably improving its effectiveness.

You will have implemented a message standard at one particular version or revision. At this time EDI messages are under continuous development and are changing in a mix of small and large steps. It will be necessary for two companies and sometimes whole trading communities to upgrade from one message version to another. Many companies are reluctant to make these changes: they are quite content with their use of the older version and sometimes the newer versions offer no advantage to them. However as message standards change to address the needs of wider trading communities and to harmonise the work of different industrial sectors, common understandings about message upgrading will have to be decided. Otherwise there will be as many versions of messages as there are trading relationships thus undermining the very reason for 'standards'. In your partnership and trading community you need to agree formal procedures and timescales for the introduction of new message standard versions.

If you have achieved all this successfully you will quickly effect significant improvements to your business. As you progress you will be preparing your company for trade in the next decade.

Value Added and Data Services

Several major service providers have written about their businesses in this section.

EDI is a young industry and it is perhaps a compliment that IBM are already involved. Many a pundit wondered how IBM would counter the competitive threats of first the mini, then the micro. We have seen IBM achieve large market shares in both markets. Their interest in EDI shows that they are not about to allow any erosion of their market share in DP through this development.

ICL carved a very distinctive place for themselves through the Tradanet initiative. A good account of this from a standards viewpoint appears in Tom McGuffog's earlier article. The network services are now run by International Network Services the joint venture between ICL and GE Information Services. John Jenkins gives us chapter and verse to demonstrate how substantial their user-base is today. He also introduces a ten-part model which INS like to use in describing the service which they market to meet their customers' EDI requirements.

Istel, once the internal systems house for the British Leyland group, recently made the interesting transition to independence following a management buy-out. Phil Coathup describes how Istel have been able to help the rapid growth of trading communities over the last three years, not merely in their original market sector but also in distribution, health, travel and finance. They are now one of Europe's largest EDI service providers.

16
The IBM EDI Service

Ray Smithers

WHAT DO WE MEAN BY EDI?

The term Electronic Data Interchange (EDI) has been in use now for several years to describe a wide range of implementations, from personal messaging to distributed intelligence applications. For the purposes of this paper EDI is assumed to mean:

> *The transfer of formatted data between computer applications,*
> *running on different machines and using agreed standards, to*
> *describe and format the data contained in the messages.*

The significant words here are computer applications and formatted data. Application to application communication implies that there is no manual intervention required to complete the transfer or to decide how the data is to be processed when it is received. Formatted data is taken to be data which is in a pre-arranged format and can be processed directly by the receiving application. It does not necessarily imply the use of any international standard, such as EDIFACT, although those standards are playing an increasingly important role in facilitating the development of EDI.

Our definition of EDI could, of course, apply to data transfer within a company, an activity which is already well developed but which still results in the use of paper for external communication. It is in the arena of extending electronic trading between enterprises that the techniques described in this paper are likely to make their greatest contribution.

IBM'S ENTRY INTO THE EDI MARKET PLACE

The base mailbox service underpinning the IBM EDI service is Information Exchange which was developed by IIN, the IBM network services provider in the United States, and was introduced into the UK shortly after the announcement of Business Network Services in 1986. Later that year IBM United Kingdom began negotiations with more than 30 companies in the shipping and export trade community which led to a six month pilot of document exchange over the IBM network using standards emerging from the DISH committee. The experience gained in this pilot led to a number of conclusions about the nature of the products required to support an EDI service and on the way they should be brought to a marketplace so varied in terms of size of enterprise, types of equipment and applications in use, and of experience of data processing. These conclusions form the major part of this article.

IBM is now contracted as the preferred supplier for EDI in the London insurance market (LIMNET), and for the European reinsurance market (RINET) and is engaged as one of the three suppliers conducting pilots with the construction industry (EDICON). In addition to these industry community activities, the IBM EDI service is in use in the banking, retail, insurance, manufacturing and retail environments.

THE MANAGED NETWORK SERVICE

The IBM Managed Network Service was the subject of an article in *The VANS Handbook* (Editors: Chang & Hitchcock, Online Publications, London 1987) and has been featured in a number of publications. For the purposes of this article suffice it to say that in the United Kingdom it is an SNA network of 'meshed' design with access nodes close to all highly populated and industrialised areas of the country and offering a wide range of connectivity and OSI support.

An important function of the network in the EDI environment is its ability to convey a wide range of services—EDI, electronic mail, interactive sessions, bulk data transfer—through a single connection. All the services offered by BNS are run on the single Managed Network Service. Furthermore, through its gateway into the IBM International Network Service, access to the services offered is available throughout Europe, in North America and in the Far East.

INHIBITORS OF EDI

Our experience in the pilot we conducted with the trade and transport community enabled us to identify a number of inhibitors to the implementation of EDI and led to new ideas and changes to overcome them. The main inhibitors appeared to be the agreement of common standards and building an EDI interface into new or existing computer applications. Other inhibitors to EDI implementation occur because EDI is essentially a batch process since data will arrive from the mailbox batched by message type. The problem is that many applications today rely on interactive data entry. Getting into EDI, therefore, requires new application modules to be built which can create and receive batch input to interface with existing application data bases. People will undoubtedly require some retraining to work in a 'paperless' EDI environment. However, the service must be designed and implemented with ease of use in mind from the start, with the ability to use existing, well-known applications as far as possible. The legal aspects of EDI, particularly the requirements for audit trails, need to be carefully considered and 'interchange agreements' established between trading partners as to how messages, like orders, are to be treated. Costs of implementation must, naturally, bear a favourable relationship to the benefits anticipated.

The IBM EDI services and products can address some of these issues and with the introduction of the Edilink products our ability to extend the areas in which we can provide support is considerably improved. The IBM EDI services certainly help in the area of building EDI interfaces by providing more of the function related to the handling of EDI data on the customer's machine. The support provided in the services for handling UNGTDI, ANSI X.12 and EDIFACT formatted documents, as well as unformatted data, means that, whatever formatting or data standards are adopted, the customer can expect that our products and services will be capable of handling them. The EDI services are capable of providing secure means of transferring data which have the means of providing good audit trails and with Edilink this function is extended. Edilink and the Network Interface products can influence the cost of implementation by providing software and services which reduce the amount of effort each individual customer will have to put into developing EDI solutions.

COMPONENTS OF THE IBM EDI SERVICE

IBM Information Exchange—a store-and-forward mailbox system

The IBM network can be used to handle direct transfer of data between computers but the use of a store-and-forward mailbox service can have several advantages in the EDI environment, these are outlined below. All the messages, addressed to each trading partner, can be sent together in a single transmission to the mailbox. The store-and-forward service then puts each message into the required mailbox for collection by the recipient. This means that there is no need to make lots of separate connections to each trading partner's computer. In addition all of the messages from each trading partner can be placed in a single mailbox and can be received in one transmission.

The processes of sending and receiving can be carried out when, and as often, as it suits the business requirement and is not dependent on time zones or when each partner's machine is ready and available to make transactions. Further each computer only needs to be able to communicate with its own mailbox and does not have to communicate with a variety of other computers using different methods and protocols.

The store-and-forward mailbox service which IBM offers for EDI, and which runs on the IBM network, is called Information Exchange. In Figure 16.1, which displays in simplified form the whole EDI process, this part of the service is shown in the bottom two layers.

Each user's computer communicates directly with Information Exchange but only indirectly, through independent mailboxes within Information Exchange, with other users. By these means it is possible to provide communications between trading partners with very different computer systems.

EDI components on the user system

As may be seen from Figure 16.1 there are a number of functions to be performed before an EDI message can be transmitted into the network—and to be performed in reverse order when received. There are three major 'logical' components which are outlined below.

The business application

This provides the end user interface and allows the input, verification and manipulation of data. This application is, of course, specific to a particular situation and, at its most rudimentary level, could be a simple data entry capability.

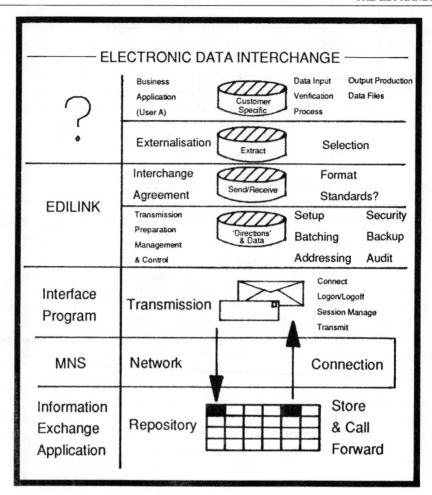

Figure 16.1   A simplified representation of the EDI process

The message handling function

This takes, as input, files of data output from the application stage and 'packages' and formats them to the standards agreed with the recipients. This function is provided by a combination of purpose-built software and Interbridge routines. Similar function is required to handle 'in-bound' messages.

The network interface function

This handles the connection and transmission of data to the network and manages the generation of appropriate commands to send and receive messages to and from Information Exchange. For PCs and IBM host machines running under the MVS Operating System this function is provided by the standard Information Exchange products, PC/IE and MVS/IE respectively. For other IBM, and non-IBM machines it can be provided using a Remote Job Entry transmission to the Batch Data Interchange (BDI) service, running on the network as part of the IBM Information Exchange service.

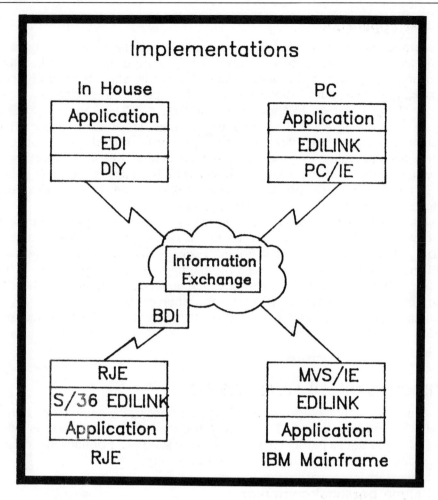

Figure 16.2 The options available for using the Information Exchange Service

Figure 16.2 displays the options available, including an 'in-house' solution where, assuming software and hardware compatibility across the service, the various EDI components may be developed by the customers to use the Information Exchange service. Any complete EDI solution requires all the functions described above, plus a management and control layer which oversees the progress of data through the various processes.

The EDI enabling function—Edilink

To enhance the function of the network interface products there is a requirement for an EDI enabling package. This provides the ability to translate user data into messages formatted to UNGTDI or EDIFACT standards. The Interbridge product from SITPRO provides this function and is already in use with many customers. It must, however, do more than just translation. It must provide all of the other control and audit functions including validation of data, batching and addressing. This function is provided by the Edilink product.

The user application

The user application is the source of the data used to create the EDI messages and will also process the received messages. This application could be part of the existing mainframe applications, which handle the whole business function, or a package from an outside software house designed for a specific job. As one example of many, for an exporter this could be a PC package called SPEX, which is available from SITPRO and is designed to produce export documentation. The output from this package is primarily printed documents but it also has the capability to produce a file containing the data which would otherwise be printed. It is this file which would be used as the source of data for the EDI functions. There are many other packages and in-house developed systems which can be made to work in this way.

The integration of these applications into EDI is, however, dependent upon the availability of the two layers of function below it in Figure 16.1. This function is generic and its availability, in the Edilink package and the network interfaces, should greatly speed up the process of adapting existing applications to EDI, and that of delivering new ones. These 'common' functions of message handling should not have to be written by every application developer. Edilink provides well-defined and open interfaces so that any user application can access its functions.

CATEGORIES OF EDI APPLICATIONS

There are three broad categories of EDI applications which could use Edilink as part of their implementation. These categories are described here as: stand-alone EDI workstations particularly on PC; integrating EDI functions into existing applications; providing EDI functions in package applications.

Stand-alone personal computer

As the name suggests a stand-alone application should be capable of operating without reference to any other application, or data. An EDI 'workstation' package should be designed specifically to create and receive standard data messages in the agreed industry formats. It should have enough function to process these messages and hold any standard data for their creation but it is not a replacement for any business applications which might be available on any other machine. The sorts of use such an application might have are indicated below.

A primary application is for the small organisations who will be encouraged into EDI either to gain competitive edge or because of customer or supplier pressure to do business in this way. This kind of company may well still be running manual business systems without any computer support. The workstation approach is also relevant for large companies wishing to start in EDI at a departmental level, or wishing to find a low cost, low effort, way of getting into EDI for evaluation purposes. Large companies may also have another interest in standalone workstations. Any company which has already identified the benefits of electronic trading for itself, and wishes to offer a product for their customers or suppliers to use, may well want to offer a simple, but customer-tailored stand-alone system.

For EDI to be viable in these ways the need is for a low cost entry system which does not need the support of a computer department and can be operated by the existing clerical staff. The system should be complete and delivered if possible as a single package. PC Edilink would require the addition of data entry and receive functions which are specific to the types of messages being transmitted. The Interbridge software, used for format conversion in Edilink, is table driven; this means that as new messages are agreed or amended the only effect on the workstation is an update to the tables. (Further information concerning Interbridge is given in Appendix B.)

The table could also have an important role to play in the operation of data input. The Interbridge tables are the single source of data for the construction of a message. They are used as input to the data validation module of Edilink and could be used as input to drive generalised data input screens since they contain all the information necessary to say what fields must be present to make up a message. Whenever a new message type is put into the Interbridge tables, it could automatically be possible to start using it by presenting a generalised data entry screen with the necessary validation. We would expect that stand-alone workstations will be offered by software houses, working in conjunction with IBM, and using Edilink as a base.

This type of stand-alone implementation can only be a step towards full EDI. Until the data can be integrated into the business applications the full benefits cannot be achieved.

Existing applications

Companies with existing business applications and wishing to add EDI capability require both network interface and message handling software with a defined interface into the existing applications. It is important for EDI to be implemented in such a way that it is treated as an extension of the existing system. All of the existing business functions which build and use the data in the corporate data bases should be left unaltered. EDI should simply use the existing data bases and not create new ones.

Data which is required to build the standard EDI messages should be extracted from the existing data bases and put into an interface file to be passed to Edilink for formatting and transmission. The layout of this interface file can be specific to the individual application but must be reflected in the Interbridge tables.

Data received into the machine is de-formatted before being passed to the existing applications and used to update the system data bases. Before being used to update the company system it will probably need to be validated and 'checked in' by someone. Bear in mind, however, that they will not be keying in the data but just ensuring that it is correct.

A stand-alone PC could be used in this way as an intelligent front end to such an application. The data to create the interface file on the PC would be extracted from the main business application and passed to the PC for processing and transmission.

The package application

In this enviroment the Edilink functions and network interface software could be used in a similar way to any other existing application. However IBM would prefer to encourage and work with the software vendor to develop a standard EDI interface which would allow the user to buy a complete package from his vendor with 'built in' EDI function, training and support.

DELIVERY OF THE IBM EDI SERVICE

As may be inferred from the above, IBM is encouraging software vendors to develop applications and modify existing applications, which will work with the other elements described to enable customers to join the IBM EDI service with the minimum cost and disruption to their businesses. To this end an IBM Business Network Services Agent programme has been developed to mobilise the skills and experience of the software vendors in particular industry environments.

The role of these Agents will be to develop and install user applications, to modify existing applications to provide the necessary interface to the IBM products described and to market, on our behalf, the Edilink and Network Interface products and the use of the IBM EDI Service. They will be responsible for the successful installation of the software products on the customer site and the necessary training of the customer's staff. We hope to have more than 20 software vendors registered as Agents in this programme by the end of 1988 and can already count System Designers Ltd, ESL and The Software Connection among those signed up.

This pragmatic approach to the implementation of EDI represents, we believe, an opportunity for our customers, large and small, to take advantage of what some are calling the 'EDI revolution' with the maximum speed and the minimum of effort. It is, finally, worth noting that we in IBM are taking our own medicine. IBM plants have aggressive objectives to start EDI with their suppliers and we plan to pilot electronic billing of our customers later this year—all using the products described in this article.

17
The INS EDI Service

John Jenkins

International Network Services (INS) is now into its second year of operations, bringing 'paperless trading' to trade, commerce and industry around the world. Changing the way business is carried out is hard work but, armed with the many and varied benefits EDI can offer all kinds of organisations, significant headway has been made. Attitudes to EDI have changed in line with growing awareness.

THE INS SERVICES

When INS was formed at the beginning of 1987 EDI was seen all too often as a picture of the future and, in many cases, a lot about 'hype'. This is no longer the case.

Our various EDI services operate across many, diverse market sectors—Tradanet for national trade, Brokernet in the insurance industry, Motornet for the motor industry and Tradanet International for international trade. We have established a number of case studies of companies up and down the supply chain where considerable business benefit is being demon- strated through the use of paperless trading. One major retailer, for example, now sends over 10,000 orders a month to 100 suppliers, saving in excess of £500,000 a year in telephone calls alone as well as reducing stock holding by 10 per cent. If an order is satisfied in a timely and accurate manner the supplier will get paid for the goods six weeks earlier, a good example of the mutual benefits of EDI. So EDI has become a reality. Increasingly, both large and small companies are dependent on EDI for the transfer of vital business information between themselves and their trading partners. Indeed, their business pros- perity now relies on the continuous availability of the EDI service and the integrity of the data being exchanged. Since orders and deliveries will be processed more quickly, these companies are taking advantage of more efficient communications to hold lower stocks and enjoy the competitive edge that this offers.

While this increased use of EDI clearly brings commercial benefit to providers of value added and data services (VADS) such as INS, it also puts a heavy burden of responsibility on our shoulders—one which we fully under- stand and accept. It is imperative that all VADS suppliers provide a very high quality of service to meet this growing dependence.

Now attention is turning to the implementation of EDI not only within an individual organisation, but throughout a trading community. The successful implementation of EDI covers a wide spectrum of activities and procedures, both on a managerial and a technical level—from providing a secure tele-communications connection, to creating meaningful business messages and influencing trading communities as a whole to adopt EDI. For any organisation contemplating the adoption of EDI within its trading community it is important to understand the elements that make up a complete EDI service. Each of these elements form an integral part of a *whole* solution; while each component is vital to the service, it is the whole that is the key to successful EDI.

THE BASIC COMPONENTS

Initially there is the backbone of the service—the network itself. In choosing an EDI service there are three key criteria to be met by the physical network.

First of all, the network must be truly nationwide and resilient to ensure uninterrupted service. The network used by INS is based on the X.25 packet switching protocol and supports a triangulated topography to ensure that alternative paths are available in case of failure. It provides local call access to 95 per cent of the business population of the UK. Secondly, it must ensure maximum connectivity for different types of computer to communicate using their own different protocols. Finally, the network should also have international links, which will be covered in more detail later in this paper. The network used by INS supports the wide variety of protocols used by different manufacturers' computers including SNA, 3780, CO3 by a process of protocol conversion. This allows proprietary protocols to be converted to and from a common protocol, X.25, which is used to transfer data around the network. Our 'any-to-any' interfacing policy is made possible through the use of special purpose Network Protocol Processors (NPPs). Built by AT&T specifically for this task, the NPPs operate at one million instructions per second (mips) and support both synchronous and asynchronous protocols.

MESSAGES STANDARDS

The key to the communication of meaningful business information such as invoices, orders, delivery instructions and a host of others with trading partners, is to agree a standard to define both the messages and the electronic envelope. These are used to structure data being exchanged into a form which can be understood readily and processed by the recipient's computer.

In the UK and Europe there are three commonly-used standards for EDI messages: TRADACOMS with the largest single message standard community in the world; ODETTE used mainly in the motor industry; EDIFACT, the develop-ing message standard for international trade.

All these support both the electronic envelope and the message itself. The use of accepted standards really is essential for cost-effective EDI. Without agreed data standards a company would receive data in a different format from each of its trading partners. The data would then have to undergo a series of conversion processes, one for each trading partner, before the information received could be interpreted and processed by its computer system. The importance of the message standards for EDI cannot be over-stated, since they provide the all-important business meaning to the data exchanged by trading partners. After all, why exchange data if it cannot be understood? The development of EDI in the UK leads the rest of Europe, if not the rest of the world. Much of the credit for this must go to the Article Number Association for their development and support of the TRADACOMS standards. Adopted by many different market sectors, TRADACOMS are currently the most widely adopted standards in the UK. However EDI is not only about data exchange within the UK. Many organisations' business hinges on trading across country borders. In the last year, the EDI world has witnessed the emergence of a new standard specifically designed to meet international trading requirements. Known as EDI for Administration, Commerce and Transport (EDIFACT), this new standard has been ratified as an ISO standard (ISO 9735) at the syntax and structure level, with invoice and order messages already approved in draft form. The coming months will see many new EDIFACT messages develop quickly.

We at INS are committed to EDIFACT—indeed, we were the first EDI supplier to announce support for EDIFACT. At the same time, however, we recognise the very significant TRADACOMS community, particularly within UK trade and industry. As a service supplier, we believe our role is to work closely with the various standard-making bodies, such as United Nations Joint EDI Committee (UNJEDI), ODETTE and the ANA, to enable us to understand and react quickly to developments in the important area of message standards.

THE HEART OF THE SERVICE

If the network is the backbone of the EDI service, the envelopes and messages must be the life-giving blood flowing around the body and the store-and-forward service, can only be described as the heart. Messages destined for trading partners are pumped into this central part of the EDI system and then transmitted on for collection. More specifically, electronic envelopes containing trading messages are transmitted from the sender's computer system at a convenient time to him to his personal postbox within the service. The service then distributes these envelopes to the various recipients' mailboxes, held on the service, where they are ready for collection by each recipient's computer system at the most convenient time for him.

It is this store-and-forward approach which enables the exchange of commercial documents to fit in to each organisation's trading pattern, work schedule and even time zone. Until now, most public attention has been focused on the elements of a service discussed so far. These form the basis of any EDI service - indeed the offerings from the various EDI service providers in these areas are functionally similar. Now, however, as EDI is accepted as a new business practice, the emphasis is changing and it is other aspects of the service that are growing in importance. It is these elements that will differentiate between competitive services and determine relative market shares.

DIFFERENTIATING BETWEEN SERVICES

So what are these important differentiators then? First to be considered is the functionality the service offers the user.

This can be considered in eight parts:

Full password control over access to the service and the user's postbox and mailbox to provide security.

Checking of trading relationships, or 'mutual exchange authorisation', ensures a user will never receive data from unexpected trading partners nor receive any unexpected message formats from authorised trading partners.

Message integrity checking, both within the message itself and within the electronic envelope, means any faults in the user's data formatting system can be detected, preventing incorrect data being accepted by the service.

Extensive audit trails confirm that messages have arrived at the postbox, been forwarded to the relevant mailboxes and collected by the recipients. The INS service offers full audit trails in four key areas—the "Session" (the connection time at which messages are transmitted and received), the postbox, the mailbox and trading relationships.

Multi-criteria file selection allows users to select and extract specific files at their convenience to fit in with their business processing cycles, for example order and invoice processing systems.

User file control is a further function offered to give the user full control over the deletion of all files in his mailbox.

Magnetic media handling option enables users who do not have the facility to transmit and receive data directly via telecommunications to do so using magnetic media, such as tape or floppy diskette.

Extensive security processes are incorporated in the service to ensure that highly sensitive trading information is kept safe and secure.

'Enabling services' is a further important service differentiator and concerns the interface between a user's application and the EDI service. Clearly it is important to minimise the time and effort required to get users implemented on to their chosen service so that they can start exploiting the benefit to be gained from EDI.

To ease the task of connecting a user's application to the EDI service we offer a number of products and services, which fall into three areas: interface systems; standards translation software; and industry specific systems. Known as Trada-Start products, INS' interface systems have been designed to provide the new user to the service with an easy and cost-effective implementation path. There are a number of such products available covering a range of machines, from large mainframes down to the IBM PC compatible. We have been working closely with the software industry to rapidly increase the number of 'off the shelf' packages to offer our users.

In the area of standards translation, we recommend the use of the Interbridge package originally developed by SITPRO which is available from approved distributors, such as SD-Scicon.

Finally, we have developed industry specific solutions for particular trading communities—like our Equator workstation for the Data Interchange for Shipping (DISH) community. This is an example of how a service provider seeks to meet the needs of the marketplace by providing a total solution—application software and, where necessary, hardware too, delivered as a 'shrink-wrapped' package, complete with customised training.

As part of our strategy to provide users with the easiest possible implementation path we place great emphasis on user support. This comprises implementation packages containing different levels of documentation, software, testing services and consultancy. Also included are formal training courses at the start of the implementation process to make new users aware of the activities required before they reach 'live' status on the service.

Once beyond the implementation stage, it is vital that customers continue to receive support to help them get the best from their use of EDI. Since the services are available round the clock, 24 hours a day, 365 days a year, to meet the demands of the trading community, so too is our Service Desk, which operates all day, every day, including Christmas.

MAXIMISING THE BENEFITS

For an individual organisation to fully exploit the benefits it derives from using EDI, it must maximise its trading community, both in terms of the number of partners with which it trades and the number of documents types exchanged. Accordingly, the provision of a high degree of support at the community level is another vital element in successful EDI. This support involves understanding the requirements of different trading communities and working closely with them to encourage the use of EDI in their respective industries. In this capacity we have actively supported EDI-specific seminars organised either by individual customers who are leading their communities into EDI, and with trade associations who are recommending the use of EDI within their particular industry.

A good example of this is the conference held in November 1987 by the two major electronic component trade associations in the UK—Electronic Components Industry Federation (ECIF) and Association of Franchised Distributors of Electronic Components (AFDEC). The conference, attended by over 80 leading electronic component companies, heard spokesmen from the industry explaining the advantages and the implications of implementing EDI.

The final component of the INS EDI service relates to gateways between the EDI and other services—electronic mail, viewdata, access to central databases and links to equivalent international EDI services, for example. Such gateways are a significant addition to the portfolio of a service supplier. At INS we believe our customers should be able to satisfy all their business requirements through one supplier.

The first, and perhaps the most important, requirement of this kind, particularly for multi-national organisations, is for worldwide communications, the ability to use EDI on a truly international scale. This requirement is increasingly developing, for if it is costly to move paper-based commercial information within a country, then it is many times more expensive on an international scale. The service suppliers must provide the solution. The business requirement is for local access and service around the world, where and when it is required. This market need is well illustrated by the initiative of CEFIC, representing the European chemical industry. CEFIC is currently piloting the Tradanet International service which links our EDI services with the largest EDI service in the world—EDI Express operated by G E Information Services. The Tradanet International service will be used by all types of organisations with international requirements to communicate with their trading partners worldwide. Suppliers unable to provide a true international service, with full functionality and local 'on the ground' support must collaborate to do so.

A further trend is towards the interlinking of competitive networks, as certain industries already involved in EDI realise that gateways between services would enable them to further increase the benefits of using EDI within their organisations. INS is already working with Istel to link our respective EDI services for the motor industry. This is in response to a request from the industry trade association, the Society of Motor Manufacturers and Traders (SMMT), to interlink networks to facilitate the expansion of EDI within the motor industry. INS will continue to foster these relationships for markets which depend on interlinking to exploit EDI fully.

The offerings we can make constitute an extremely strong portfolio of products and services designed to allow the rapid adoption of EDI throughout whole trading communities. We are working closely with standards bodies and major EDI users to ensure that our services continue to satisfy the market need.

EDI—THE FUTURE

So, where to now for EDI? Profitable trading requires fast communications direct to where action is going to be taken. EDI is the electronic bridge for achieving just that—the enabler of fast and accurate business communications. In its turn this is the key to effective logistics—an important and often neglected point. EDI does not just reduce the paper mountain; it offers us new ways of working—new methods, new practices and new processes. This is where the future benefits of EDI will unfold.

With an increasing emphasis on the control of logistics and 'just-in-time' processes using EDI, we envisage that an organisation's supplier community may well shrink. Companies will tend to trade with fewer suppliers, working more closely with each one and focussing on issues such as the quality processes within the supplier's organisation. Those who cannot meet these demands for quality will no longer supply their market. Thus we see trading communities of the future forming closer business relationships with those (fortunate) suppliers who are prepared to concentrate on efficiency and quality. EDI will be an essential part of this new business process.

If EDI is to play such an important role, the burden on the EDI service providers will only increase. The demand will be not only for a totally reliable service, available all day, every day, but for total EDI solutions as described above. INS will continue to grow its total portfolio of services to meet these demands in order to maintain our leading position in this exciting and rapidly developing market.

18

EDI Services from Istel

Phil Coathup

BACKGROUND

'BL sets up electronic mail service for data'

This was the headline in the *Financial Times* of 11 July 1985 which announced to the world that Istel had launched the Edict service. At the time we were pleased with the attention we received—both from prospective customers and competitors alike. With the benefit of hindsight it is easy to see what an understatement this press coverage really was—both for Istel and electronic data interchange.

Shortly after this announcement, Istel moved into private hands via a management-led buyout. Istel is now one of the UK's largest software and service companies, with 1450 staff and a turnover in 1987 of just over £70m. The company offers a unique range of computer and communication integration skills to a number of focused markets—engineering and manufacturing, distribution, finance, health and the leisure sectors.

It would be true to say that many people in the commercial world—including Istel personnel—underestimated the effects of electronic data interchange on the business community. Three years ago, although there were references to strategic benefits, the emphasis was on issues such as the raw cost of transmitting documents and the interaction of the VAT man to electronic invoicing. Now these are rarely mentioned. Instead, factors such as improved logistics, just-in-time distribution, and the exploitation of the opportunity brought about by the single European market in 1992 are the main issues. The rate of introduction of EDI has also taken us by surprise.

From the viewpoint of the service provider, this dynamism has probably been the most challenging aspect of delivering EDI. Electronic data interchange is not only a new use of (admittedly old) technology, but it also requires the introduction of a new business philosophy. This means that there has been no pre-defined view of the basic elements of an EDI service, and even less perception of the overall costs.

For a harassed purchasing director attempting to justify the investment required for the introduction of EDI to his Board, times were, and still are, hard. For an even more harassed director of EDI services in a VADS company attempting to satisfy both his prospective customer and make an honest wage from the business, times have been even harder.

Three years on, it is still unclear what a full EDI service should provide and at what price. Perhaps it will be a sign of a mature market when true value for money can be judged. Despite these difficulties, the UK has really bitten the EDI bullet in a big way. Through careful investment in both technology and marketing the UK has acquired a very strong reputation throughout the world for rapid progress on the implementation of EDI. Istel has played an integral part in this success story. This paper describes the unique features of the Edict service, highlights some of the important issues facing the EDI industry, and indicates how Istel will be addressing them.

SERVICE HISTORY AND EVOLUTION

Since the launch of Edict at the Wembley Conference Centre in June 1985, many companies have entered the EDI marketplace. However, it is significant that Edict is the only successful EDI service that continues to be delivered by the same company. We would argue that this is a direct result of the experience and planning that went into the specification of the original service. The requirement for Edict originated from the automotive manufacturing sector within the UK. This industry was facing a number of issues. Amongst others: a requirement to increase productivity to remain competitive; the introduction of just-in-time (JIT) manufacturing and distribution; increasing amounts of paper brought about by JIT methods and single line invoicing; a need to rationalise the supplier base; and a move towards global sourcing.

Against this market-specific background, a number of factors were also seen as important in the development of the Edict service. At launch, by definition the service would only have a few customers, thus reducing the utility of the network to prospective customers. Considerable effort was required to attract a critical mass of users. This was best achieved by building natural trading communities following the trading links in the economy. EDI services were destined to become business utilities, just like the telephone, telex and facsimile are today. To do this they could not be constrained by artificial boundaries around markets or trade sectors. The establishment of artificial monopolies by governments or trade associations by endorsing single services was not in the long-term benefit of the industry as a whole. EDI services must evolve with customer requirements. However, because these were ill-defined, product development needed to be closely related to likely customer *use* of the service.

The customer base of the Edict service therefore evolved in a 'natural way', by following the trading links in the economy. Firstly, with the backing of Austin Rover and later with ODETTE endorsement, the service was promoted to the automotive manufacturing community. A trading community of suppliers to the automotive sector was established very quickly. However, due to the overlap between industries, a much wider range of companies were attracted to the service—from aerospace, through mining to chemicals. This initially successful engineering and manufacturing sector now accounts for approximately 70 per cent of Edict customers and here the service truly has a critical mass of customers.

Edict can now immediately offer 20 to 30 trading partners to almost any company operating in the engineering and manufacturing sector. This is a tremendous incentive for any company wishing to get involved in EDI. Sectors whose suppliers traded on the periphery of the engineering and manufacturing industry also began to realise the benefits of electronic trading. Thus certain

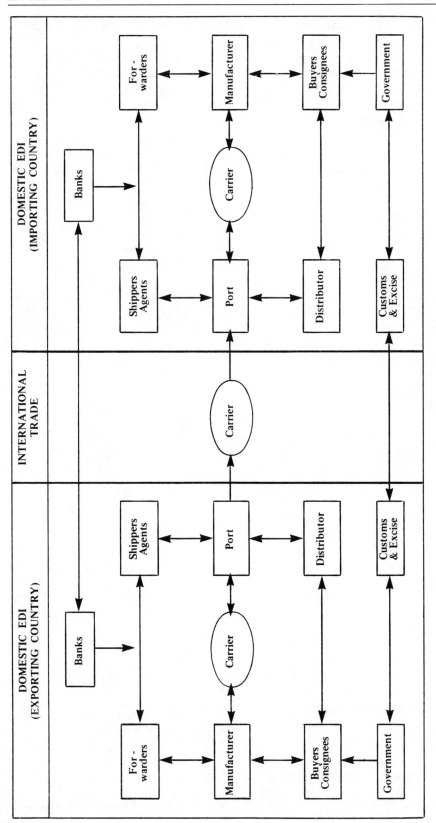

NB. Although this appears to be a closed system, at some stage the goods are delivered to the end user.

Figure 18.1 Diagrammatic structure of international trade

sectors of the retail industry and the health sector were attracted to the Edict service.

All these organisations were using the service to exchange commercial documents—trade data interchange—where the types of documents being exchanged are purchase orders, delivery schedules and invoices, and the link is normally between a manufacturer and supplier. Having improved the link back to their suppliers, manufacturers then began to improve the links with their own customers, dealers, distributors and agents. This often involved the exchange of commercial transactions but included other vital information such as price updates and warranty claims, etc, and the necessary details to update databases. Here Edict was being used as a means of transferring files of information in a controlled and auditable manner.

The whole area of file transfer has grown significantly over the years. For instance, in the leisure sector Edict is being used to transfer files of holiday details between tour operators and travel agents. In the finance sector, Edict is being used to transfer files containing credit agreements in order to reduce fraud in the High Street.

In 1988 Edict is now a multi-sector EDI service with customers in engineering, manufacturing, distribution, health, travel and the finance sectors. This growth has resulted from Istel's flexible approach to reacting to customer demand and following the natural trading links within the economy. This approach will be an important factor both for the development of EDI and for companies wishing to exploit the benefits of electronic trading. As shown on Figure 18.1, trade and international trade is a multi-sector, multi-organisation operation. An EDI service must be able to satisfy the diverse requirements of a wide range of customers in order to become an truly universal business utility.

This has lead the Edict service to be extremely flexible in terms of data formats. In theory the service has the capability of handling *any* standard document layout—UNGTDI, TRADACOMS, ODETTE, ANSI X.12, VDA, EDIFACT—and in fact the service is handling live data in many of these formats. However, where the added value format translation capabilities of the Edict service are required, business and technical decisions need to be taken in order to ensure that the result is of use to both ends of the trading relationship.

To summarise: Edict is a fully functional EDI service provided by Istel, offering store-and-forward capabilities for the excahnge of commercial and technical documents in a standard format. The service has considerable flexibility, and even has the capability of translating between standard data layouts. The main core of customers exist in the engineering and manufacturing industries, but the service also has customers in distribution, health, travel and finance. The strength that Istel has accumulated in the past three years has been in rapidly developing EDI trading communities, so that the benefits can be quickly evaluated. Istel views Edict as a key enabling technology—as a means to an end, not as an end in itself. Through its market specialists Istel has the unique capability of embedding Edict into applications so that the full benefits of electronic trading are realised.

ACCESS TO THE EDICT SERVICE

Before the physical means of access to the service are defined it may be worthwhile to establish the minimum requirements at the user site These are:

a trading partner—perhaps obvious, but there must be at least one company able and willing to exchange the agreed data in the agreed format.

a computer—this can be anything that can hold a data file and communicate via a telephone line. This could be anything from the humble home computer to the mightiest of mainframes. In fact, 30 per cent of the computers attached to Edict are PCs.

a model—this allows the digital computer to communicate via an analogue telephone line.

a telephone—a minimum requirement

software—this is of two types: communications software to control the files sent to and received from the service; application software to manipulate the files before transmission and after receipt.

We have found that most companies will have many of these items already—for instance, the telephone and the PC. However, we have also noted that there will be an infinite variety of customer preference in this area. For instance, there are over 40 different manufacturers' computers connected to the Edict service. Although one third are PCs, this does mean that two thirds are mini or mainframe computers.

Added to this must be the myriad of software suppliers providing application and utility software for these machines. Over the years Istel has developed relationships with a number of software suppliers, who are now well versed in the intricacies of EDI and Edict. From time to time these are featured in the *Edict Interchange Newsletter* distributed quarterly to users and prospects. We would be interested to hear from other software houses wishing to become involved in EDI.

Istel does have a range of software tools that can aid users coming onto the Edict service. These can be anything from the humblest receive-and-print module to a full-blown application interface. However, these are offered as options and not pre-requisites for coming onto the service. Full project management of the implementation onto the service is always available.

There are basically two means of accessing Edict. These apply no matter where in the world the customer is located: dial-up—where the Public Switched Telephone Network (PSTN) is used to link the computer to the Istel network, offering low cost, fairly low speed access; leased line—where a permanent high-speed connection is established between the customer's computer and the Istel network. There are a variety of ways of physically driving the connection between the customer's computer and the Edict service. These are best discussed at the time of implementation.

The Istel network is connected to a number of networks both in the UK and throughout the world. Edict already has customers in the United States, Japan, Western and Eastern Europe. Customers access the service through a variety of networks, using a variety of access methods. Istel has devoted considerable resources to the whole area of international EDI. The international network poses very little problem—there are now many companies that can provide very adequate international networks. The major difficulty is to provide high quality EDI support on an international basis. Throughout 1988 and 1989 Istel will be announcing means of providing such support to enable companies to take full advantage of the benefits of global EDI.

FUTURE DEVELOPMENTS

EDI has experienced incredible growth over the past three years and has a dynamism that is perhaps unique. There are several issues that will have to be faced over the next few years, both for Istel and the EDI world in general. Some of these are summarised below.

Format translation

This has been an integral feature of the Edict service since it was launched. It has been both the most used and the most misunderstood facility. Many standards-making bodies have accused us of working against them by offering to translate document formats. In fact, this facility has done much to aid the introduction of data standards by allowing companies to migrate to a universal standard in a controlled manner, rather than having to re-write applications when a new standard version is introduced. In this respect the translator will do much to aid the introduction of EDIFACT. The second area of misunderstanding has centred around what the translator can actually do—or more accurately, what it can not do. It is not a means of covering up bad business practise. It cannot, beyond certain limits, invent data that does not exist.

Interlinking of services

This must happen in order for EDI to become a true business utility. The creation of closed networks and artificial monopolies cannot be good for anyone in the long term. Istel has always expressed commitment to interlinking customers and potential customers should stress the importance of interlinking to all service providers.

EDIFACT

Istel's position on standard data layouts is clear—they are Edict's lifeblood: they ensure that EDI, and therefore Edict, grows and develops. Istel is therefore fully committed to the widespread introduction of the EDIFACT standards. We have even seconded staff to SITPRO to aid their pioneering work in the introduction of such standards. As stated earlier, the Edict translator will aid in the introduction of the standards by allowing companies to migrate to them over time. Edict is already handling EDIFACT syntax messages, and as soon as they are stable and a customer requirement is logged, will begin to handle full EDIFACT messages. We have to realise that there are a great many companies already using the national TRADACOMS and ODETTE standards. The investment of these companies in EDI must be protected.

X.400

Much has been written about the effect that X.400 is likely to have on EDI. Both operate in the field of messaging and offer tremendous potential. Istel will almost certainly offer X.400 gateways in order to add functionality to its messaging and file transfer facilities. However, it must be stated that at the moment X.400 and EDI—certainly when expressed as EDIFACT—*are* incompatible. We have met many companies that claim to be doing both, but in reality they are modifying the facilities of one in order to achieve the other, for example addressing. The work of Vanguard in highlighting the incompatibilities needs to be supported and continued so that X.400 can become a true vehicle for EDI.

CONCLUSIONS

In this paper, the scope of facilities available from the Edict service have been described. We have not given a detailed technical description of access protocols, security procedures and archiving features. EDI is not a technology but a business philosophy. It is having a tremendous effect on the nature of the relationship between trading partners. It will assume an even more important role as 1992 and the single European market approach. Certainly in the UK EDI has reached a state of maturity such that the technology and networks are taken for granted. What is now really important is how the electronic trading is integrated to the trade cycle. Istel and Edict can play a unique role in this integration.

Major Trends—Charting the Future

In the final part of this book we have collected three papers which, in very different ways, look at the future.

Earlier in 1988 the DTI, through its Vanguard project, placed several studies concerning EDI with major consultancies. We are grateful to the DTI that they have permitted two of these consultants to write on the same topics here.

EDI is bringing to the fore issues of compatibility between computers and between networks. It would be natural that computers exchange data as readily as any two phones can establish a call. However, the computer industry is dogged by proprietary standards which make this hard to achieve—a dream rather than a reality. Alison Bidgood, with Coopers & Lybrand, takes a cool, disinterested look at the situation: what it is that users want and how the market is likely to develop.

The X.400 series of recommendations concern messaging between computer systems. They have been developed through the cooperation of public tele-communications operators worldwide. The essentials of this important series of standards were set out in Paul Dawkins' article. There is a close apparent fit between the needs of EDI and the service offered by X.400. Nick Pope, of Logica, writes on this topic in more detail, drawing out the various technical options which are possible. Many observers feel that electronic messaging, using X.400 to give wide interworking, is going to be an important business. If a successful fusion with EDI can be achieved, then it would benefit users considerably.

Gil Patrick, the founder of Patrick Consulting Associates, has been very involved with the EDI scene in the UK and is well qualified to take a strategic view of the trends which are in operation. I feel that his attractive prose sometimes makes palatable some very hard-hitting obervations. It will make sense for all of us to take to heart the lessons he draws out which close the editorial portion of this book.

19
VADS Interworking: a Cloud on the EDI Horizon

Alison Bidgood

VADS Framework

The UK Government clearly signalled its belief in competition in the tele-communications industry with the licensing of Mercury Communications as a competitor to British Telecom in providing public network services. This formed the cornerstone of the subsequent VADS licences in 1982 and 1987. Both were formulated on the principle of creating a framework for open competition and minimising official interference with the development of the VADS market. This opened the way to any number of companies developing VADS services, and several hundred registered as VADS suppliers under the terms of the original licence. At one time, the number of registrations was taken to be one and the same as the number of active suppliers, until it became clear that many companies had registered as a precautionary measure. The important point in the present context is that more than one company set about putting together a proprietary network for VADS services, and today there are at least half a dozen companies selling a variety of VADS services over their networks to third parties. Even more important, these networks are physically separate at the moment. Unlike the national telecommunications networks, one network's customers cannot normally send messages to another network's customers.

OPTIMISTIC START

To understand the significance of the lack of communication between networks, it helps to look briefly at the way in which VADS have developed in the UK over the last few years, and above all the take-off of EDI. Here there are two distinct sets of circumstances—those in which the VADS suppliers find themselves, and the way in which their customers are coming to see VADS services.

In the early 1980s, there was a rash of bullish forecasts predicting meteoric growth in the VADS market. For a number of very understandable reasons (with 20:20 hindsight) these forecasts have proved too optimistic—or at least the associated timescales were too short. In practice, it has taken longer for users to get from pilot to implementation than originally thought. Against this back-ground, VADS suppliers were making the high, up-front investments needed to put networks and all the associated hardware, software and management structures in place—and probably based many of their business plans on the forecasts that failed to materialise.

At the same time, over in the user camp, the early adopters were beginning to experience the practical benefits of VADS, and in particular those associated with EDI. Here it is interesting to note that the conventional advantages—the much talked-about cost savings associated with reducing paperwork errors and stock levels—fade in importance as companies make progress down the EDI track. Cost reduction and efficiency continue to play a part, but as they gain EDI experience, users begin to understand the strategic significance of the way in which electronic trading is changing their business relationships. In turn, this has given rise to a band of 'EDI Crusaders'—users who have seen the light and are sallying forth to spread the word to the EDI blind, lame and deaf.

Switch back again to the VADS suppliers, who are struggling to build up revenues through signing up new subscribers to their networks, and through stimulating traffic levels from existing subscribers. One of the most cost-effective ways of gaining new customers is to target communities of interest, both in the sense of trading clusters and individual industry sectors. If you can sign up a company like Marks & Spencer, you almost automatically gain most of their suppliers as customers; if you can become the *de facto* EDI network for an industry sector, new users come to you as the only practical choice. This approach on the part of the VADS suppliers was reinforced by the marketing fashion of one-stop shopping, which is another way of saying that the more you can bundle goods and services together, the less likely customers are to shop round your competitors.

The success of this strategy on the supplier's part has been patchy. In some sectors, one EDI network has emerged as the industry standard, in others the major companies in the sector are split between rival suppliers. Additionally, greenfield sectors are disappearing. As EDI proliferates, competition between suppliers to conquer key accounts and industry sectors intensifies. As with most head-on competition, in theory suppliers should differentiate themselves in terms of quality, but the temptation is to take the short cut and compete on price. As supermarkets have found in the past, price wars have no long-term winners.

SEPARATE TABLES

EDI users are finding out the truth of the saying 'it takes two to tango'—in other words EDI is useless unless it can be used to communicate with trading partners. At the same time, it is becoming increasingly clear that in many cases, the dancing partners are joining parties sitting at separate tables. Currently two principal groups are most affected: companies in industry sectors where several VADS suppliers are active, and companies that do business across a number of industry sectors. These can be both diversified multinationals or smaller companies with a broad customer base.

These companies are being faced with a stark choice; either they subscribe to a number of EDI networks or else they run the risk of losing business. And this is a real threat. As major EDI users are emerging from pilot stages and moving towards implementation throughout their businesses, they are increasingly insisting that their suppliers trade on the same system, irrespective of whether they are ICI or Joe Bloggs & Sons.

At this point it is useful to ask why subscribing to more than one EDI network is seen as unacceptable. For the smaller company the answer is obviously cost. Multiple EDI networks mean multiple joining fees and subscription charges without any great cost savings to compensate. The view of the large company is more complex and seems to be rooted to some extent in a philosophical approach to networks and suppliers rather than the practical issues. Certainly cost is much less of a consideration for large companies, particularly in terms of fees and subscriptions. Some have already spent heavily on writing in-house software to integrate access to several suppliers. The arguments against users developing their own solutions to multiple EDI networks come under a number of headings, encapsulated in the following statements:

> *Why should we, the users and customers, be put to the time and trouble of finding solutions, when the suppliers can solve the problems for us?*

> *In any case, it offends all logic that public EDI networks—which all do the same job—should not be able to pass messages to each other.*

> *The whole point of networks is universal access—nobody would use the postal system if you could only send letters to half the population.*

> *Even if the cost of multiple subscriptions is insignificant, there are hidden costs to bear in terms of management time and overall efficiency.*

> *As a major company, we must ensure that our smaller suppliers are not disadvantaged through having to move to electronic trading.*

Not unnaturally, the most vocal users are those who are caught in the conflict between rival EDI networks. However, even those who are relatively comfortable with the *status quo* are beginning to realise that sooner or later they too will come up against the same problems. In addition, many are beginning to think about the longer term implications of being locked into one VADS supplier, and the pain involved in revising internal systems and procedures to fit in with a different supplier.

BATTLE LINES

EDI users and interested trade associations are banding together to put pressure on VADS suppliers to connect up their networks. Simultaneously, users' demands go beyond mere physical connection. There is general agreement that EDI suppliers would have to be in a position to deliver a lot else besides just installing gateways. In particular, users need to be assured that inter-connected EDI networks would offer end-to-end quality in terms of security, reliability and audit trails. After that, they want to see levels of service remain high, and not descend to the lowest common denominator.

In recognition of these factors, the term 'interworking' has been selected to describe user needs, rather than 'interconnection.' Interworking implies the necessity of commercial as well as technical cooperation between EDI suppliers to provide the level of service that users are looking for. VADS suppliers have been aware of the growing demand for interworking for some time, but until recently have postponed facing the issue squarely. Most probably some have been hoping that interworking was a flavour of the month topic which would disappear with time, as undoubtedly it brings with it a number of unpalatable commercial decisions and actions. First and foremost, interworking will mean that the VADS suppliers will have to cooperate with each other in a way that no commercial organisation would care to do with its their competitors. Not only will technical standards and protocols need to be normalised, but more sensitive details such as tariff and cost structures will have to be shared with rivals. Perhaps even more crucially, up to now the VADS suppliers have essentially been marketing the capabilities of their networks, which after all represent the bulk of their investment to date. In an interworked environment, this corner-stone is removed, and the suppliers will have to switch to selling true added value.

IS INTERWORKING INEVITABLE?

The short answer is almost certainly yes. Demand from users for interworking is not going to go away; in fact just the opposite. As new user groups are formed to start looking at VADS and EDI, they are learning from their predecessors and stipulating that suppliers give undertakings on interworking before being selected. In parallel, cross industry user groups such as the EDI Association are being set up, with interworking as an issue high on their agendas. A further consideration is the total size of the UK market. Even with a much wider use of EDI than at the present time, it is questionable whether half a dozen separate networks are sustainable in the long run; the cake is simply not big enough.

Added to this is a contention that is difficult to prove but intuitively correct, namely that companies unsophisticated in their use of information technology see the necessity of choosing a network as a major barrier to starting off on the EDI road. The dilemma has been compared with the situation which faced companies in the 1960s and 1970s when selecting computer systems—fine if you chose the eventual winner, but you could incur frighteningly high exit costs if you got it wrong. With EDI, many potential users could be taking a wait-and-see approach in case the market shakes out and they are left backing a loser.

In the short term, the demand is undoubtedly for interworking between EDI applications on separate networks, and moves on the part of suppliers in this area would go a long way towards dissipating the growing criticism from some parts of the user community. EDI is emerging as the giant of the VADS family, and as such is overshadowing the other members such as E-Mail and databases. As a result, it is considerably less clear whether there will be a demand in the future for extended interworking between a range of applications, or whether EDI is the only area where interworking is needed.

Looking at the problem from another point of view, we should ask ourselves what is likely to happen if the EDI networks do not develop the means to pass data to each other. Crystal ball gazing is a dangerous sport, but there are some preliminary indications of the way in which things may go to use as a basis. One possibility is that if major users come to the conclusion that the VADS suppliers are not going to provide the type of service they require for whatever reason, they will migrate from third party networks and start to install their own links with major trading partners. In many ways the framework for such a development is already being created with the move by numerous companies to reduce the number of suppliers. In such a scenario, the EDI suppliers would be left with the lower volume business, which would probably prove to be uneconomic and thus impact on the viability of their companies. The inevitable consequence would be that EDI would become a rich man's sport, with smaller and poorer companies becoming second class citizens.

IS INTERWORKING UNIQUE TO THE UK?

Looking round the world, interworking is likely to be an issue in a number of countries, and eventually on an international scale as EDI networks expand. However, the UK is unique in the way in which VADS have developed, and the speed with which interworking has become a burning issue. The United States and Japan provide interesting contrasts; both countries have the same EDI infrastructure of competing and separate networks, but in neither is there much evidence at the moment of demand for interworking. In the US this is probably due to the simple fact that user communities are much larger than in the UK so that companies have to get further down the EDI track before bumping up against significant restrictions on who they can trade with electronically. On the other hand, EDI in Japan is still too embryonic for interworking to have surfaced as an issue yet. There is also a greater focus there on international rather than domestic trade.

Some other countries have learnt by the UK experience and taken account of interworking when planning the legal framework for VADS networks. Both Singapore and Hong Kong propose to licence a single network operator, believing that multiple systems that are not interworked inhibit the value of EDI to the economy as a whole. In France, prospective VADS suppliers must undertake to interwork their networks.

CONCLUSIONS

In many senses, the sun is shining on the EDI world. Many users are beginning to reap the tangible rewards of an initial act of faith followed by several years of dedicated work. A growing number of both users, potential users and key influencers no longer need convincing of the real benefits that EDI can bring to individual companies and the economy as a whole. Increasingly companies within communities of interest are cooperating with each other to produce practical solutions to EDI implementation. Even with the task of developing and agreeing standards—an area traditionally fraught with disagreements—a start-ling amount of progress has been achieved through goodwill, enthusiasm and sheer hard work. Interworking is apparently the biggest cloud in the sky, and looks set to grow into a thunderstorm.

It is in everybody's interest to find a solution. Users clearly stand to benefit from greater access to other users, and by avoiding being tied into a single, isolated network. Suppliers have the least incentive in the short term, but the longer term could bring compensations from higher numbers of users and

20

Meeting EDI User Requirements with X.400 Now and in the Future

Nick Pope

BACKGROUND

In 1984 the International Telecommunications Consultative Committee (CCITT) produced the X.400 Recommendations for Message Handling Systems. As described in Paul Dawkins' article, 'Open communications standards: their role in EDI,' these provide the basis for a store-and-forward service for the transfer and handling of messages around the world. X.400 is one of several CCITT and ISO (International Standards Organisation) standards for Open Systems Interconnection (OSI).

As the user base of EDI increases the need for open communication to be applied to EDI becomes more urgent. A recent study for the Information Technology Users Standards Association undertaken in the UK by the National Computing Centre identified EDI as a major application for X.400.

Although they are both concerned with application level aspects of communications, standards for EDI and X.400 have developed independently. Until recently there has been little or no coordination between these activities. Recognising this, Vanguard, a joint Government and Industry initiative on value added and data services, commissioned Logica to carry out a study into EDI and X.400. The objective of this study was to prepare a statement of requirement for further standardisation for input into EDI and X.400 standards activities. The study investigated the relationship between EDI and X.400 and the requirements of existing and prospective EDI users for the handling of EDI messages.

In Paul Dawkins' paper the use of X.400 for EDI was introduced. This paper goes into more detail about the technical relationship between EDI and X.400 and considers the capabilities of X.400 to meet the requirements for EDI messaging. It outlines two approaches to using existing X.400 Recommendations to support EDI and suggests a future extension to X.400 defining an end-to-end protocol specifically directed at EDI.

X.400 OVERVIEW

The X.400 Recommendations define two main protocol systems (see Figure 20.1). One, the Message Transfer System (MTS), provides the basic messaging service for transferring and distributing messages from an originator to one or more recipients. The other, the Interpersonal Messaging System (IPMS), is an end-to-end protocol which operates over the Message Transfer System specifying a common structure for messaging between people. The MTS protocols may be related to an envelope which carries information independent of its form or structure. The IPMS protocols define the layout of a particular type of content with fields for information commonly needed in person-to-person communication, for example the subject covered by the message. In the future other end-to-end message content protocols may be defined for applications other than person-to-person messaging, for example computer-to-computer EDI.

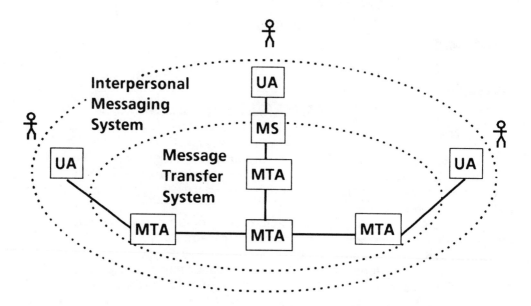

Figure 20.1   X.400 basic structure

The services defined in the 1984 X.400 Recommendations are provided by two main components, the Message Transfer Agent (MTA) and the User Agent (UA). UAs provide the user interface into X.400 and support the end-to-end IPMS services. MTAs provide the services of the Message Transfer System, storing and forwarding messages from the originator's User Agent to the recipient's User Agent.

In 1988 CCITT will be issuing revised X.400 Recommendations to provide compatibility with other OSI protocols and to add additional facilities. Any system supporting X.400 '88 will be backwards compatible with X.400 '84 components. These revised Recommendations have been agreed technically and should be fully ratified by CCITT towards the end of 1988.

One of the major additions to X.400 in the 1988 Recommendations is the Message Store. This optional component, which lies between a UA and its MTA, accepts messages from the MTA on behalf of the User Agent, and stores the messages for selective retrieval by the User Agent. In X.400 '84 a user can only receive messages in the order in which they are sent to him. The X.400 '88 Message Store allows a user to select and retrieve individual messages based on particular attributes. For example, the user can select and retrieve a message on a specified subject from a particular originator. The Message Store can use attributes relating to both the MTS protocols and the IPMS protocols.

IPMS AND EDIFACT

There are close parallels between the X.400 IPMS protocols and EDI basic syntax standards such as the EDIFACT Application Layer Syntax (ISO 9735). They are both end-to-end protocols defining a common structure for a set of electronic documents to be transferred together. One is directed at person-to-person communications while the other is directed at computer-to-computer communications.

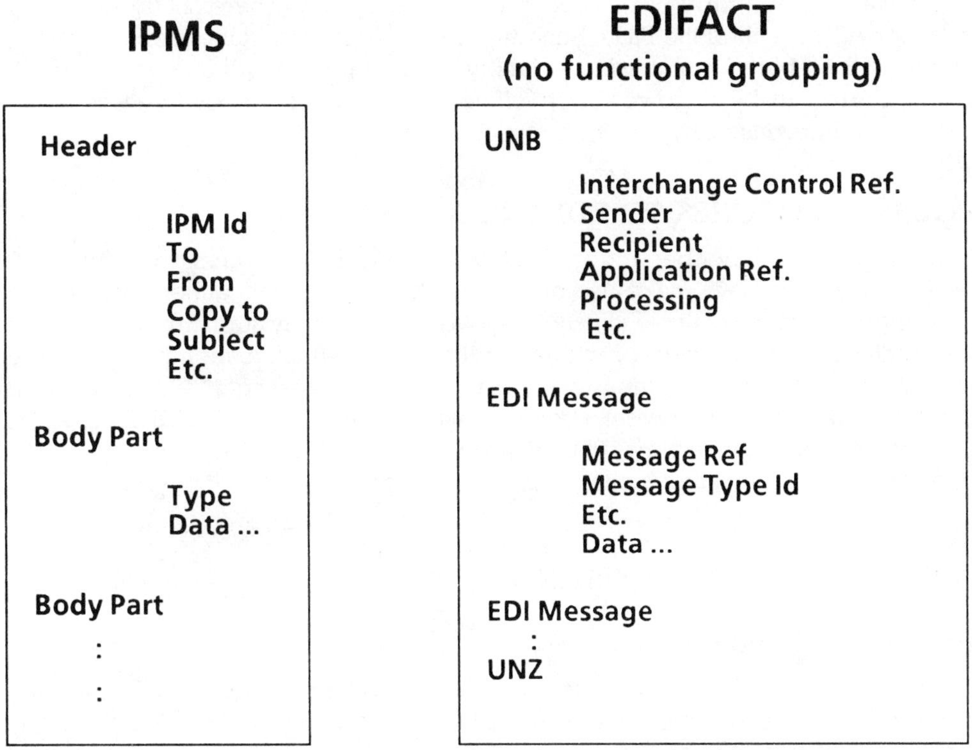

IPMS

EDIFACT
(no functional grouping)

```
┌─────────────────────────┐    ┌─────────────────────────────┐
│  Header                  │    │  UNB                        │
│                          │    │        Interchange Control  │
│        IPM Id            │    │        Ref.                 │
│        To               │    │        Sender               │
│        From             │    │        Recipient            │
│        Copy to          │    │        Application Ref.     │
│        Subject          │    │        Processing           │
│        Etc.             │    │          Etc.               │
│                          │    │                             │
│  Body Part               │    │  EDI Message                │
│                          │    │                             │
│        Type             │    │        Message Ref          │
│        Data ...         │    │        Message Type Id      │
│                          │    │        Etc.                 │
│  Body Part               │    │        Data ...             │
│    :                     │    │                             │
│                          │    │  EDI Message                │
│    :                     │    │    :                        │
│                          │    │  UNZ                        │
└─────────────────────────┘    └─────────────────────────────┘
```

Figure 20.2   Structure of basic unit of transfer for IPMS and EDIFACT

As shown in figure 20.2 the structure of the EDIFACT unit of transfer (called an EDI Interchange) and an IPMS unit of transfer (called an X.400 Message Content) are similar. Both have a heading with fields giving general attributes of the information being transferred. Many of these fields have similar meanings. For example, the IPMS header contains the fields *Message Identifier, To, From* and *Subject* which can be compared with the EDIFACT header fields *Interchange Control Reference, Interchange Sender, Interchange Recipient* and *Application Reference*. Furthermore, an EDI Interchange brings together a number of EDI Messages to be transferred together in the same way as an IPMS Content brings together a number of X.400 Body Parts (although, unlike EDIFACT, IPMS does not provide functional grouping).

There is also a similarity between the EDI acknowledgement Service Messages currently being defined for EDIFACT and the IPMS Receipt/Non Receipt Notifications. Both provide a means for a recipient to indicate to the originator that data has been transferred successfully, although the exact meaning is slightly different. The EDI Acknowledgement indicates that the internal structure of an EDI Message has been checked, whereas the IPMS Notification only relates to receipt without any implication of acceptance.

The main difference between the IPMS and EDIFACT (and most other standards for EDI, such as ANSI X.12, UN/TDI) is in the syntax and encoding of information. EDIFACT is a concrete syntax based on character strings with delimiters between fields. Each field has a defined maximum length. Whereas X.400 is based on an abstract syntax notation called ASN.1. ASN.1 separates the specification of the form of protocols from its encoding. The existing encoding rules for ASN.1, called the Basic Encoding Rules, represent data items as a string of octets (8 bit bytes) comprising a data type identifier, length and value. ASN.1 is considered to be a powerful specification tool for protocols with complex structures and is used by all OSI application protocols.

FOUR APPROACHES TO EDI AND X.400

Four approaches have been identified to carrying EDI Interchanges with X.400 (see Figure 20.3). Two make use of existing X.400 protocols either carrying an EDI Interchange directly within an Message Transfer System Envelope as an Externally Defined Content or within the IPMS Body which is then placed inside the MTS Envelope. The other two are based on extending X.400 to define a computer-to-computer content protocol (which I will call the EDI Messaging System—EDIMS) similar to IPMS. The EDIMS would either carry an EDI Interchange in an existing syntax transparently or encoded using ASN.1.

APPROACHES USING EXISTING X.400

EDI in MTS Envelope (P0)

The content of an X.400 Message Transfer System Envelope, which normally carries the IPMS protocols, carries an EDI Interchange as an 'Externally Defined Protocol' instead. The form and structure of the EDI Interchange is transparent to any component of an X.400 based messaging system. With this approach the EDI syntax protocol does not impinge on X.400. Addressing information is all that is needed for the X.400 MTS to correctly deliver the Interchange.

The main disadvantage with this approach is that the Message Store, as it is based on the use of ASN.1, cannot easily recognise the internal fields of the EDI Interchange. Thus, EDI Interchanges cannot be retrieved selectively from the message store using anything other than general X.400 attributes (eg originator, time of submission). For example, an Interchange containing orders could not be selected by using the EDI Message Type Identifier held in the Interchange Header, as this information would be unrecognisable by the Message Store.

In the United States the ANSI X.12 committee for EDI communications has proposed this approach as an interim solution to carrying EDI over X.400. It is yet to be seen how widely this approach will be adopted.

EDI in IPMS Body Part (P2)

An EDI Interchange is carried within the Body of the IPMS Content protocol. Where there is a correspondence between them, the EDI Interchange header

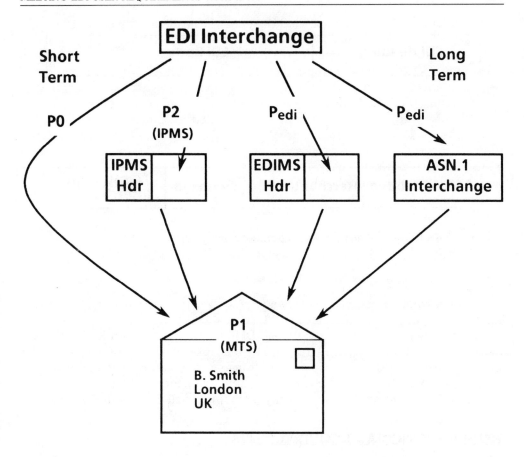

Figure 20.3   Four approaches to EDI and X.400

(UNB) fields can be copied into the IPMS header fields. Thus this information can be used by an X.400 Message Store to enable particular interchanges to be retrieved selectively. This approach may be considered technically less elegant than the previous one and there may be some redundancy in the information carried. However, the greater flexibility and the ability to use the '88 X.400 Message Store to its full potential overrides any disadvantage.

At the time of the Vanguard study this approach had been adopted by two European PTTs (France and Holland) and by Conseil Européen des Fédérations de l'Industrie Chimique (CEFIC) as the basis of an experimental service.

FUTURE APPROACHES USING X.400 EDIMS (PEDI)

A protocol could be defined to support computer-to-computer messaging as an alternative to the X.400 IPMS protocol which is designed to support person-to-person messaging. Such a protocol might be similar to the basic EDIFACT Interchange structure but would be defined in terms to fit in with the X.400 architecture and in particular use the same abstract syntax, ASN.1.

It is suggested that this EDI Messaging System (EDIMS) protocol could carry EDI Messages in one of two ways (see figure 20.4). Firstly it could carry them by

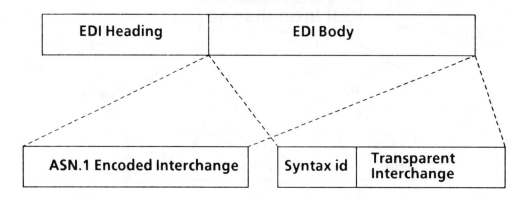

Figure 20.4   EDIMS structure with alternative body types

placing the whole of the EDI Interchange, encoded in an existing syntax such as EDIFACT, after an EDIMS header. The EDIMS header would contain any information needed to select individual EDI Interchanges from an X.400 Message Store, such as might be copied from the UNB header of an EDIFACT header. The EDI Interchange itself would be carried transparently and remain untouched by the X.400 system. Secondly it could carry them by encoding the EDI Interchange itself in ASN.1 up to, but not necessarily including, each individual EDI Message.

USER FUNCTIONAL REQUIREMENTS

In considering the use of X.400 for EDI it is necessary to look at the functional requirements of users in handling EDI Messages. As part of the Vanguard study into the use of X.400 for EDI, 12 interviews were held with users and suppliers of networking services for EDI on the requirements for handling EDI messages. The aim of these interviews was to find out their views on the relative importance of the facilities already provided by X.400 and to identify other facilities might be usefully provided in any future extensions to X.400.

As a result of these interviews 28 particular facilities were identified as being of importance for a significant proportion of EDI users. It should be noted that these facilities relate only to the type of facilities that could be provided by a store and forward service such as X.400. There are application areas, such as interactive EDI, which were considered to be outside the scope of the study.

The requirements identified can be broadly classified in seven areas as described below.

Transfer

By far the most important requirement of users is that messages are reliably transferred between computer systems without loss or corruption of data. X.400 provides facilities to ensure reliable transfer of messages between long term data storage (for example disc). Lower level mechanisms detect and recover from data errors. Therefore, barring destruction of the discs holding messages in transfer, it is virtually impossible to lose or receive corrupted data.

Storage and selective retrieval

Many users indicated that often there was a need to be able to select individual interchanges for processing independent of the order in which they were sent. There were two main reasons given for this. Firstly, many users wanted to retrieve interchanges containing EDI Messages of the same type together so that they can be processed in one 'run'. For example, all orders might be retrieved to be run through a batch order process. Secondly, occasionally users needed to select a particular high priority EDI Message for processing ahead of others, eg an urgent order for goods.

The X.400 Message Store, as defined in the 1988 Recommendations, supports storage and selective retrieval. However, as mentioned earlier, the message store cannot be fully utilised if an EDI Interchange encoded in an existing syntax is carried directly in an MTS envelope (approach P0 above).

Interworking

As the use of EDI spreads the importance of interworking between different user communities and their networks increases. Currently, user communities are being established around several different networks or VADS. A user who wishes to operate within two communities who are on different VADS normally has to have two network connections. In addition, major corporations, which have their own internal networks, have a similar requirement for interworking with other external networks.

There are two aspects of X.400 which aid interworking between separately managed networks. Firstly, being an open protocol which is becoming widely established, X.400 provides a common reference for the services to be provided in handling messages in different networks. Secondly, X.400 from the outset recognised the concept of interconnecting separately managed public and private networks. In X.400 terminology these are called Administration Management Domains and Private Management Domains. X.400 defines protocols in terms of interconnecting Management Domains.

Security and audit

Since in many cases the correct operation of a company's business may depend on information received through EDI, security is considered very important to many users of EDI. Currently, one of their greatest concerns is with resolving legal disputes. Hence the greatest emphasis is on audit. Most users trust network operators to provide the necessary internal network security and to restrict any communications to those between specified trading partners. However, as the size and interconnection of networks increases, consideration may need to be given to ways of further protecting EDI messages which do not depend on the internal security of the networks being used.

Such protection, independent of the network provider, can be achieved by the use of encryption and other cryptographic techniques, as already used in the banking community. The 1988 X.400 Recommendations include optional services for security which use advanced cryptographic techniques, not only to provide confidentiality but also to digitally sign a message so that the identity of the originator can be proven subsequently. Currently, X.400 does not fully define a common standard for auditing, although hooks have been left for the addition of auditing facilities by implementors. It is likely that future extensions to X.400 will define a standard means for remotely accessing audit information.

Acknowledgment

It is clear that some form of acknowledgement of successful receipt (or failure) of an Interchange is required. It is unclear, however, exactly when acknowledgements should be sent or what they should indicate. This partly reflects the uncertainty of the exact point when it can be said that the recipient (or his communications agent) becomes legally responsible for an interchange. In the case of the recipient having a message store within the network (or VADS) which holds messages on his behalf, three possible points for acknowledgments have been identified (see Figure 20.5): acknowledgment by the message store on delivery of an Interchange to the store; acknowledgment by the message store on retrieval of an Interchange from the store; and acknowledgement by the recipient having checked the Interchange and accepted it for further processing.

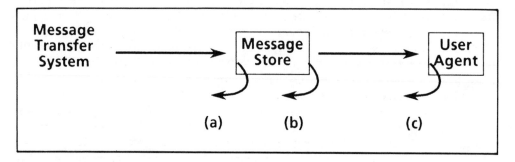

Figure 20.5   Possible points for acknowledgement

It should be noted that this level of acknowledgement would not indicate that the content of the EDI Messages within an Interchange has been successfully complied with, for instance where an order cannot be fulfilled due to lack of stock.

Further complications are added if functional groups of Messages from within an Interchange are retrieved from the Message Store. X.400 provides two levels of acknowledgement. One, provided by the Message Transfer System, can be used to indicate whether an Interchange has been successfully delivered to a Message Store. The other, provided by the Interpersonal Messaging System, can be sent either by the Message Store or the final recipient on retrieval.

Administration

There are several parameters relating to users connected to an X.400 system which need to be maintained. For example, the X.400 system has to be informed of changes to a user's network address or name as used to identify originator or recipient of messages (called the ORName in X.400). This information could be passed off-line to the network administrator for the information to be fed directly into the X.400 message switches (that is MTAs). However, by defining special administrative protocols, X.400 enables the user to update this information without the intervention of the network provider.

In certain situations, where the user does not wish to concern himself with administering the details of the operation of his X.400 interface, and the network provider is not aware of his particular requirements, a third party administrator may be called in. This third party administrator could act on behalf of a group of users well known to him. It has been suggested that such facilities might be added to X.400, although no such additions are currently being considered.

Other facilities

X.400 provides several other facilities which can be of use to certain EDI users. For example, X.400 systems have the ability to copy the same Interchange to several recipients. It has been suggested that this facility could be useful in distributing information such as price lists to a group of customers. Also, X.400 allows the user to indicate the urgency of messages so that urgent information may be forwarded ahead of lower priority messages.

Performance

There are two aspects of the performance of X.400 which might be considered to limit the applicability of X.400 to EDI: speed of delivery and maximum size of messages that may be transferred in one unit.

Firstly, being a store-and-forward service which potentially covers the whole world, the providers of X.400 services are unable to guarantee a fast delivery time. Existing agreements by the public telecommunications authorities recommend that X.400 based services transfer messages within the following times for three levels of priority: urgent (45 Minutes), normal (4 Hours), non-urgent (24 Hours).

These figures give the worst-case performance and it is expected that deliveries within a few minutes can easily be achieved in most situations. It should be noted, however, that X.400 would not normally be expected to give the near-instantaneous response expected for on-line interactive systems.

Secondly, again due to X.400 being a store-and-forward service, there is a limit on the largest message that can be transferred by X.400 systems in one go. The X.400 Message Transfer Agents must hold messages in backing store during transfer and there is inevitably a limit to the size of this backing store. Thus the maximum message size is limited. Currently, most X.400 systems will only carry messages up to 2 Megabytes long. As technology improves this upper limit is likely to increase. However, it is inevitable that given some limit on the size of a message there will be users that require to transfer information which is larger.

In the majority of cases it is not considered that these limitations will significantly limit the use of X.400 for EDI. Where communities have a particular need for higher performance then an X.400 service may be specifically configured to meet their needs. An alternative approach, where high performance interconnection is required without any message switching, is to directly interconnect two user systems (see Figure 20.6). In this case the X.400 MTA to MTA transfer protocol can be used directly between the user systems bypassing any intermediate MTAs. With this second approach the only performance limitations are within the user's own computer systems.

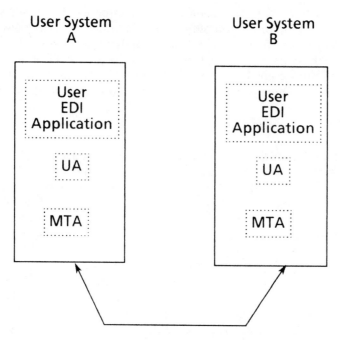

Figure 20.6 Direct interconnect configuration for optimum performance but no message switching

SHORT TERM ISSUES

Any community of EDI users considering X.400 needs to address several issues to ensure that it is used in a consistent manner and that future links with other communities are as straightforward as possible.

Firstly, a decision has to be made as to which of the approaches to carrying EDI in X.400, as identified earlier in this article, is most relevant. EDI Interchanges are to be carried either directly within the MIS envelope (the P0 approach), or use is made of the IPMS protocols to carry an EDI Interchange within a IPMS Body Part as if it were a person-to-person message (the P2 approach). The approach chosen depends not only on the functional requirements but also on the approach taken by other communities.

Secondly, the details of how X.400 parameters are to be used for the specific requirements of EDI must be agreed. The specification of this type of detail is commonly called a profile. As already mentioned in an earlier article there are several groups working on profiles both in Europe and America (eg TOP for technical and office environments, GOSIP for systems procured by the government). Some work on a profile for EDI over X.400 has been done in the USA by ANSI X.12 (the American National Standards Institute committee which deals with national EDI standards). The ANSI profile only considers the P0 approach; no thought has been given to making use of the IPMS facilities. In the UK the GOSIP EDI task force is developing an EDI X.400 profile which covers both approaches. However, as yet there is no general initiative to define a profile for general use across Europe.

The profile for the P0 approach is fairly straightforward as no use is made of any of the application specific parts of X.400. The profile for the P2 approach needs to define how use can be made of two aspects of the IPMS protocol. Firstly, the details of mapping from EDI header fields to IPMS header fields need to be defined where there is a close relationship between the two (for example EDI Application Reference to X.400 Subject). Secondly, the exact usage of IPMS Notifications (ie acknowledgements) needs to be defined. The profile should define exactly where and when an acknowledgement should be sent, as discussed earlier.

With the use of a protocol such as X.400, which provides universal connectivity and can be used to interconnect several networks, particular attention has to be paid to security. The 1988 Recommendations for X.400 define a comprehensive set of features for security in message handling which is considered to more than adequately meet the security needs of EDI.

Currently, there is no universal addressing scheme for EDI. Each community allocates its own addresses. This causes no problems until members of one community wish to interact with members of another. Then there is a chance that the same address may be allocated to two different companies. As the interconnectivity between EDI communities increases so the likelihood of addresses clashing increases. X.400 being an open protocol which facilitates interconnectivity makes this problem more pressing.

X.400 itself does not have any problem with addressing. It has a hierarchical scheme for allocation of globally unique addresses. EDI Interchanges, however, have their own fields for addressing which are of limited length. If there is no scheme for uniquely allocating addresses which go in the EDI header field, full use cannot be made of the global connectivity which X.400 provides. This issue can only be fully resolved internationally by a body, such as the EDIFACT board, defining an addressing scheme for EDI.

LONG TERM ISSUES

In the long term EDI would be best supported by X.400 if there was an alternative to the existing Interpersonal Messaging System end-to-end protocol directed at computer-to-computer messaging. As already mentioned earlier such an EDI Messaging System (EDIMS) might be similar to the EDIFACT basic structure but would be defined in terms which would fit in with the X.400 architecture. This however requires the extension of existing X.400 protocols, or the definition of a new protocol by CCITT or ISO.

Already CCITT have a 'question' on how X.400 might be used to carry EDI. This will form the basis for starting work on a new CCITT Recommendation. CCITT normally works in a cycle of four year study periods. This means that, unless special accelerated procedures are followed, a CCITT Recommendation for an EDIMS is not likely to be published until 1992.

ISO have been working in parallel with CCITT to produce a standard called Message Oriented Text Interchange System (MOTIS) which is technically identical to X.400 1988. It is likely that ISO will also define an EDIMS for MOTIS. ISO do not work to such a rigid timescale as CCITT. Thus it is possible that an ISO standard for an EDIMS might be produced before 1992.

CONCLUSIONS

By far the biggest advantage of using X.400 is its potential for universal connectivity. Already X.400 services have been established in most Western European countries as well as in North America and Japan. Also, all the major computer manufacturers support or have made commitments to support X.400. Potentially X.400 can provide the same connectivity as has been achieved by the telephone service.

X.400 provides a very close match with the functional requirements for handling EDI messages, as identified by the Vanguard EDI and X.400 study. The X.400 1984 Recommendations met about 50 per cent of the requirements and with the 1988 extensions approximately 70 per cent of the requirements are met. In the long term, with the definition of an end-to-end EDI Messaging System protocol for X.400, there is the potential for meeting all the user requirements. This can be compared with the facilities that can be provided by the ODETTE file transfer protocol which has been used by some EDI communities as an interim to the provision of OSI standards. ODETTE FTP meets just under 50 per cent of the requirements identified.

The limitations in the performance of X.400, in speed of delivery and maximum message size, are not considered to be of concern to the majority of EDI users. Where there is a very large amount of data to be carried, or a quick response is required between two companies, then a direct network connection can be set up between them and the X.400 MTA to MTA transfer protocol used for the reliable transfer of messages. It should be recognised, however, that there will be areas of EDI which are not suited to X.400, in particular interactive EDI. This requires a near instantaneous response and most of the facilities of X.400 would give an unnecessary overhead.

With the removal of the trade barriers across Europe in 1992, X.400 defines the type of open communications service which can be quickly set up to meet the needs of efficient trading across Europe. Already some groups are setting up experimental services using X.400 to carry EDI. It is hoped that X.400 will soon be used to its full potential, providing a broad communications base to help trading communities effectively meet the challenge of the next decade.

NOTE

Copies of Logica's Report to Vanguard on EDI and X.400 can be obtained from: HMSO at the address given in Appendix D.

21

The Challenges of EDI Decision Making

Gil Patrick

EDI will probably have a greater impact on the way we do business than any other factor. It will be tempting in this paper to treat EDI too simplistically. The demands of business ensure that time is spent on operational matters, and it is easy to regard EDI as something which simply gets rid of paper and generally speeds up information flows. However, over the next 10 years or so, EDI will probably have a greater impact on the way business is carried out than any other factor.

This paper is primarily concerned with the strategic implications of EDI. It considers the special characteristics of EDI, and the demands it will place upon the user. It goes on to look at the opportunities presented, and the threats posed, by EDI, and concludes by suggesting how individual companies should react. As seems appropriate, this strategic approach views EDI in its broadest sense. The term EDI is taken to describe all types of electronic communication of information involving computers, whether between people or between computers, or between computers and people, but excludes voice communications.

PROBLEMS ASSOCIATED WITH EDI

EDI will bring with it some of the same problems as computers. While it is certainly revolutionary, in a sense it is not new. EDI is conceptually a natural continuation of the revolution which was started by the invention of the computer. There are two aspects of the computer revolution which are particularly relevant to EDI. The first is that one of the main reasons why there is not a microcomputer on everyone's desk, is that most people spend most of their time communicating information rather than processing it. The second is that the way information is processed has changed out of all recognition in the last 20 years.

It is fascinating to note that the delivery mechanism for all this processed information has hardly changed at all.

Transaction data is moved from one computer to another through the mail, directories are compiled on wordprocessors and then delivered to users as bound volumes, and internal memos continue to keep many a mailroom busy. The retention of these traditional delivery mechanisms has, no doubt, softened the blow of computerisation, but these old reliables are about to be removed by EDI, and there will be nothing of the past to soften its blow.

As a component of the same revolution, EDI will bring with it some of the same problems as computers. To start with computers are complex and potential users need to invest time and effort to understand them. EDI adds a dimension to this complexity because it links computers together. Because of this and because the most effective way to develop an understanding of this technology is to use it, most first time users do not fully understand what they are buying, or what impact it will have. This is not a criticism of industry, it is a simple fact of life, and characteristic of computers and EDI.

Lacking an understanding of the technology, many first-time users buy as an act of faith. They have faith in a salesman, or in a friend who has made a recommendation, or in their own ability to solve problems as they arise. Unfortunately this faith is often misplaced because the salesman or recommender, while understanding the technology, does not understand the user's business requirement. It has been said that the ignorance of businessmen about computers is only exceeded by the ignorance of computer people about business. Again this is not a criticism of anyone, it is simply a recognition of the fact that technology specialists cannot be expected to have a sound understanding of a business. The problem is further compounded by the frenetic rate of change in the field of information technology. Understanding information technology today is no guarantee that it will be understood tomorrow.

COOPERATION OF TRADING PARTNERS

Given these similarities with computers, and the fact that many of us have fought our way through the traumas of computerisation, it might be tempting to think that EDI implementation would be all down hill. However, EDI has a few problems all of its own. No reference has to be made to competitors or trading partners when companies computerise their operations. Indeed there is every reason not to inform others of these developments since they can be decisive in obtaining competitive edge. This is not the case with EDI. EDI can only be used with the cooperation of trading partners. Indeed to make sense of EDI usually requires many different organisations, often with conflicting interests, to work together in a community.

With enough employees generating enough internal communications traffic, organisations of all sizes can and do use internal electronic mail systems. Most people however, even in the largest organisations, communicate externally nearly as much as internally, and therefore the full potential of electronic mail systems cannot be achieved until there is coverage comparable to the telephone network. This poses problems to users and suppliers alike. They would like to use the technology to competitive advantage, but cooperation with competitors is needed to exploit the technology. A new type of delicate balancing strategy is required.

The need for cooperation is even more extreme in the case of on-line database systems. These suffer from a vicious circle. On the one hand, potential information users are prepared to use systems if the system has enough up-to-date information to offer 'one stop shopping'. On the other hand, information providers are prepared to supply the information and maintain it, only if there are sufficient users.

There is nothing delicate or balancing about the type of strategy required in this case. Without some sort of decisive move, requiring or involving high degrees of cooperation, such systems may never reach the critical mass needed to start making money. In fact to 'almost' succeed with such systems can be much more expensive than to fail miserably and quickly. Instead, bold decisions are required, similar to those made by the French with the introduction of Minitel, but which carry a great deal of risk. In France about three million telephone subscribers have received terminals from the PTT free of charge. The terminals provide on-line access to the telephone directory and to information about a whole range of products and services. The general idea is that having created a very large number of instant information users, the vicious circle described above will be avoided.

The problems associated with EDI in its purest form, those of exchanging structured data directly between computers, offer a different set of strategic planning problems. Individual companies, usually large ones with huge purchasing power, can and do create EDI communities with their suppliers. The traffic is sufficient, without the participation of competitors, to justify the system, and the exclusion of competitors can create a major competitive edge.

Two problems seem to arise from these individual company initiatives. The first is that competitors tend to team up against the one who made the first move; and the second is that competitors in an industry tend to have common suppliers, who are faced with major problems if their customers each require them to use a different system. Again, EDI presents each of the participants with major strategic alternatives. For those who are in a position to initiate systems, for competitive advantage, will the advantage gained be worth the risk of exclusion from a future community? For those subjected to such initiatives, do they just do what they are told, or are there ways they can protect themselves from unreasonable demands?

EDI COMMUNITIES—THE LONGER-TERM TREND

Whatever short term moves are made, it seems likely that the longer-term trend will be towards communities of companies which trade with one another, within industry sectors, which will adopt standards and agree to cooperate on a technical level. It is also likely that these communities will become international and will gradually merge with one another, at least to a degree. To complete the analysis of the special characteristics of EDI therefore, it is salient to study how these communities might form and develop.

At one extreme EDI communities are created within existing organisations, and the process is quite straightforward, because someone has the authority to make it happen. At the other extreme the people involved belong to different organisations, independent of one another and, indeed, often with conflicting interest, and no single organisation or person has any real power or authority over the others.

While acknowledging the possible undesirable results of the exercise of power by an organisation in the EDI area, the fact is that the greater the amount of power that can be exercised, the quicker and easier it is to create an EDI community. For example, just as individual companies can choose to use an electronic mail system and impose it on their employees, so a very powerful customer can 'persuade' its suppliers to trade with it electronically.

Where no-one has the power to dominate, communities have to grow organically, and although the results of this process may well be much more balanced and healthy from the point of view of the community as a whole, the process is usually slow and tortuous. Many negotiations have to take place, involving large numbers of people, often over long periods of time. Difficulties are compounded by the initiatives of individual organisations which can be divergent and involve substantial investments.

Many of the EDI communities which have been created to date are of the former type, and are dominated by one or a few powerful companies. In a relatively free market economy such as ours however, EDI developments in the future will depend on organic growth. Many if not most companies will therefore be faced with a considerable strategic dilemma. Someone has to take a lead and a company that chooses to lead may find itself having to commit resources excessively to that role. On the other hand, if it does not take the lead, it is possible no-one else will either, in which case the benefits of EDI may be missed.

These then are the key characteristics of EDI and the strategic issues they raise in business decision-making. With these points in mind it would be useful to move on to the impact EDI will have on businesses, the extent of which will explain why the strategic decisions relating to EDI, although difficult, will be extremely important.

THE IMPACT OF EDI

The role of electronic mail

One of the least obvious, but most beneficial, changes which will take place with EDI implementation will be the substitution of a proportion of our telephone traffic with electronic mail. This assertion is usually met by the objection that most businesses depend on personal relationships and that electronic mail weakens or even destroys such relationships. In addition much of the evidence seems to contradict this assertion. Voice telecommunications are growing rapidly. The use of telephones on trains, in cars, taxis, even on buses is commonplace, and indeed the constant use of the telephone almost seems to be a required characteristic of the modern thrusting businessman.

Despite the evidence, and the objection, the substitution will happen because, in certain circumstances, electronic mail is a much more efficient means of personal communication. It is well known from experience that a large proportion of the telephone calls placed do not reach their destinations, and this is not usually the fault of the telephone systems. Often successful connection depends on the person required being at their desk, at the exact time the call is placed and not being occupied doing something else, which cannot be interrupted. Therefore, a great deal of time and effort is wasted on unsuccessful calls. In addition to this many of the successful connections do cause disruption, because irrationally, many people who would not allow someone to interrupt a meeting in person, are prepared to answer the telephone during a meeting. Others who are more rational, or more fortunate, use their secretaries to block the telephone. Indeed it seems that the main function of some secretaries is to take their bosses off-line.

The opportunities to improve personal productivities through the use of electronic mail are therefore abundant. If the communication is merely transmission of factual information, or in any circumstances where an immediate response is not required, electronic mail probably makes more sense than use of a telephone. The message can be prepared, transmitted, received and dealt with at the convenience of the sender and recipient respectively. A spectacular example of this is provided by the Interflora system. Until recently florists dictated literally thousands of messages over the telephone to other florists every day. In March 1985 Interflora, which is an association of florists, installed specially developed terminals in 50 selected florist's businesses. The terminals allowed orders to be sent between florists by electronic mail, with screen layouts prompting for necessary information but leaving plenty of scope for unstructured information. By early 1988 the number of terminals deployed, all free of charge, had reached 2650, or 95 per cent of the UK Interflora membership. As a result most of the messages now go by a form of electronic mail, leaving the florists to do the job they are trained to do, and leaving the shop owner with markedly reduced telephone bills. Incidently the number of terminals returned by dissatisfied users to date, is one.

Obtaining the personal productivity benefits from electronic mail depends heavily on individuals choosing the appropriate communications medium for whatever they want to achieve. While electronic mail is more appropriate than voice in some circumstances the opposite can also be true. Indeed choosing the right blend of media is the secret of success. Given the right blend, people are able to spend more time communicating and less time trying to communicate. It is fair to say that without the right blend, the opposite can be true. It is rumoured that a very senior executive of one company, which had recently installed an electronic mail system, sent out a rather dramatic message to all users. The essence of the message was, "I found 500 messages in my mail box and I have deleted them all. If anyone has sent an important message recently would they please repeat it."

THE ROLE OF ON-LINE DATABASES

Turning now to on-line database services; some of the problems associated with starting up such services have been described above. Despite these problems and the evidence that many services have taken a long time to build up, and others are in difficulties, they will become the normal way of obtaining certain types of information within the next 10 to 20 years. This assertion is based on the inefficiencies built in to existing information sources, which could be overcome by EDI.

A vast body of information is provided for consumption by large numbers of people through the medium of printed matter: directories, guides, data sheets and magazines; railway, food, hotel, travel and consumer guides; telephone directories, nautical almanacs and so on. Interestingly they have some important characteristics in common: they are almost all out of date; in many of them only a small fraction of the information is wrong; users often do not need most of the information they contain.

Of course they could all be replaced with new publications, but since most take months, or even years to produce, it is doubtful that there is such a thing as an up-to-date printed directory. In addition, in many cases the rate of usage does not justify the investment. In practice guides and directories are usually only replaced at a point when the level of inaccuracy is so great that they cease to have any real value or cannot be supported by telephone enquiries. In theory it would make much more sense from everyone's point of view to obtain most of this type of information directly from on-line database systems. The level of inaccuracy on such systems can be kept at a much lower theoretical level than on printed ones, and the process of up-dating is much more simple. In addition, instead of purchasing entire databases, as with guides and directories, users can pick and choose what they require. Another major benefit is that given better information, users have to make far fewer supplementary telephone calls, and suppliers can provide a far lower level of telephone service. In fact the only major disadvantage currently is the need to distribute pictures of products, hotels and resorts. Where these are needed a supplementary paper based service is required; this may not be the case in the future.

In order to turn this theory into practice, achieving a huge improvement in information dissemination, and thereby effecting a significant change in the working lives of information users and suppliers alike, it is necessary to persuade people to use on-line systems. Access has to be a feasible proposition for large numbers of people. Searching for information has to be very simple, and the cost has to be supportable in the marketplace. The real challenge however, is not so much persuading people to use on-line systems, it is to persuade them not to use the traditional ones.

The main barrier, in fact, to the development of on-line systems is the near impossibility of parallel running. Each method of providing information is expensive and running both at the same time for any length of time is economically unacceptable. In addition the availability of the paper system at the same time as the on-line systems makes it very difficult for the latter to take-off. People are reluctant to change methods and learn new skills. Parallel running lets them off the hook.

Access progressively ceases to be a problem because if very large bodies of information are accessible on-line, and traditional methods are no longer needed, it becomes much easier to justify the capital cost of access. This is aided by the decreasing capital cost of access with time. After the initial capital cost of setting up, the running cost of such systems should be substantially less than printing, publishing and telephone support methods. Using on-line systems one person can provide information to an unlimited number of people at the same time; the same person using a telephone can only provide information to one other person at a time. It also seems reasonable to assume that distribution of information electronically should be less costly than printing and distributing pieces of paper, particularly when computer systems are now the usual source of printed materials.

Given the reasonable assumption that on-line systems will be much more efficient and cost effective than paper systems, the issue should concentrate on when rather than if they become the norm. It is also reasonable to speculate that since parallel running is near impossible, the transition from paper systems to electronic ones will happen over a fairly short period of time.

The changes necessary over the next 10 to 20 years will be both radical and rapid. Much more time will be spent creating and using information and much less time will be spent obtaining and providing information. Since the whole process of decision making is related to obtaining and analysing information, no one should underestimate the impact these changes will have on their lives.

CHANGING ROLES

With the implementation of EDI people will spend less time creating and storing documents and more time checking and controlling data as it passes through the system

Millions of orders and invoices are processed every day on highly sophisticated computers, and are then printed out on pieces of paper to be mailed to other companies, who then take the information from these pieces of paper and key it into their computers. Few would argue with the assertion that it would make more sense for these computers to talk to each other directly, electronically. Indeed hundreds of companies are already trading with one another electronically, using EDI services, and their numbers are growing rapidly.

The advantages of eliminating the enormous task of processing paper, which electronic trading yields, are easy to understand. The implications for the way transactions are processed are less obvious. For example, orders and invoices are currently created and processed with electronic trading, however, there is no need for orders and invoices. Instead practitioners are concerned with the processes of ordering and invoicing, which are parts of the same process. Purchasers enter, and transmit to suppliers, data which specifies what they wish to purchase, at what price and under what conditions. Suppliers modify the same data and transmit it back to purchasers to indicate what has been shipped and what is owed. The same data can then be used to instruct banks to transfer funds electronically and complete the transaction. The participation of people in this process will change from being largely concerned with creating and storing documents, as well as checking and controlling the data, to one of mainly checking and controlling data as it passes through the process. All trading organisations will need to change; in addition others such as Customs & Excise, the Inland Revenue, and the accountancy firms will be forced to rethink their businesses.

The discussion has concentrated on the impact of EDI in terms of electronic mail, on-line database systems and electronic trading, but they are all part of the same concept. If a supplier has provided information through an on-line system, then he should be in a position to receive purchase data through the same system and thus start the transaction process. This suggests that there is every reason to integrate on-line systems with electronic trading. Since transactions are hardly ever completely straightforward further integration with electronic mail makes sense. This electronic integration will be supported by the telephone, which the user will have more time to use.

EDI—ENABLING BETTER BUSINESS PRACTICE

There is a common theme running through this paper, concentrating on the impact all of this will have. Business is essentially about creating, developing and fostering human, financial and physical resources which will develop the right products and services of the right quality, at the right price, in the right place at the right time. All other activities are subsidiary to these, and this includes functions such as accounting, stock control and administration, which seem to occupy excessive amounts of management time and effort today. EDI will allow us to concentrate on the things that matter and thus be better at them.

In summary, EDI will have a major impact on the way we do business. It will provide great opportunities to some companies to improve their entire business process, from the design and creation of new products and services, through the manufacture and distribution of these products, to the support and assistance provided to customers. Since it relates to information it will be particularly important because information is increasingly a component of products and services, in the form of user instructions. EDI will also provide huge opportunities for the 'information' industries. It should be noted however that an opportunity for one company may be viewed as a threat to another. As there will be winners there will also be losers, and companies will determine which of these they are by how well they take the difficult strategic decisions relating to EDI. There are a number of lessons to be learnt and these are now outlined.

THE LESSONS TO BE LEARNT

Invest in EDI education and training

Surely the first, and probably most important, lesson is to invest in knowledge about EDI. Whatever business one is in, whatever situation is prevailing, and irrespective of what decisions are or should be made, it is essential to acquire a sound understanding of EDI and its implications. Every organisation, with the support of the chief executive, should initiate a programme of education which involves a wide cross-section of their people. Probably the best approach is to appoint a particular person to lead the effort. That person should develop a detailed knowledge of EDI and should be responsible for ensuring that key people in the organisation, including the chief executive, have a sound understanding of the implications for them.

The education programme should consist of: taking relevant publications such as those listed in the bibliography in Appendix D; holding internal seminars and events. Companies should also be aware of what the value added and data services (VADS) suppliers have on offer. Of particular importance, organisations should make sure they are aware of EDI developments in their own industry, both at home and abroad.

Participate in the creation of EDI communities

Having prepared themselves to make EDI decisions through education, organisations need to adopt a strategy in regard to their involvement in one or more EDI communities. Perhaps the first major decision is whether or not to involve competitors in EDI initiatives. If it is possible to form an EDI community with trading partners only, then a significant competitive advantage could be gained. However, there are a number of problems associated with this approach. Firstly, it may be difficult to persuade trading partners to join a single company initiative, and therefore a great deal of effort could be used up with little result. Secondly, if competitors respond by forming an industry EDI community, the original company would find itself isolated.

The creation of communities encompassing whole industries seems inevitable in the medium term, so it would seem sensible for individual companies to join with their competitors and trading partners in the development of such communities, unless there is a very strong case indeed for individual company initiatives. If other companies are not willing to participate in such developments then individual companies should undertake their own EDI initiatives. The worst case is to do nothing. In practice many companies have set up internal on-line database systems, designed to provide information for various people including their own sales staff, agents, dealers and customers. Their success in persuading these people to use the systems has been very variable, and it might be tempting to regard some of these projects as failures. However most of the companies concerned have benefited enormously from these projects. They have gained first hand experience of such systems, they have established procedures for providing the required information and keeping it up-to-date, and most importantly they are in a very strong position to take a leadership role in the eventual formation of industry systems.

Provision of necessary skills

A third major lesson to learn is to invest in skills training when introducing any new system which requires people to change the way they do business. Most database systems require some basic training, and some require quite advanced training to master search techniques. In the case of electronic mail, the requirement for training is even greater, not so much in using electronic mail systems but in organising one's communications to strike the right balance between electronic mail and telephone. If electronic mail is implemented with little explanation, the users may tend not to use it because they are unaware of the benefits. On the other hand if the benefits of electronic mail are oversold, the system may be overused, resulting in unnecessary communications and unnecessary copying of messages, thus clogging up everyones' mailboxes. Either of these extreme situations could be avoided by appropriate training and discipline, and this could make the difference between success and failure.

The role of Government

A fourth important lesson is that there are important roles for Government to play in EDI. Because it purchases in enormous volumes for areas such as education, health and defence, Government is in an excellent position to obtain the benefits of EDI, and to provide leadership by example to the private sector. In addition, because of its independent position Government is uniquely positioned to act as a catalyst in the development of EDI communities. Indeed this is a role which the UK Government has been playing very successfully over the last year or so via the Department of Trade & Industry (DTI) through the Vanguard initiative.

To summarise, EDI will impose on all of us very important strategic decisions. To respond to this challenge we all need to acquire a sound understanding of EDI and its implications. Finally, we need to start making decisions and taking action now. This is real life, not the dress rehearsal.

Further Information

This section has been included to provide information on all of the major EDI developments that are taking place in Europe. The editors felt that no evaluatory editorial would be necessary although readers are advised to use the contact information provided should further information be required.

In addition, this section includes UK Customs & Excise's requirements for users in the UK exchanging invoice and accounting information. These are merely introductory notes: users are therefore adviced to liaise closely with Customs & Excise when considering the 'live' implementation of EDI.

22
Review of EDI Developments in Europe

David Hitchcock

This review was prepared in cooperation with Blenheim Euromatica SA and does not claim to cover all the developments now crowding on to the European EDI stage, but it offers a convenient summary of important, well-defined activities.

Political EDI initiatives such as TEDIS (EEC) are also discussed in this review. EDI is applied in a growing number of sectors: automotive; pharmaceutical; retail/distribution; aerospace; defence; all transport modes; chemicals; tourism; construction; reservations; banking/finance; insur- ance; Government, Customs, Chambers of Commerce; electronics.

Most of recorded Electronic Trade/Business Data Interchange (ETDI/EBDI) growth, in Europe, is in automotive and retail/distribution at about 100 per cent per annum and more. Other sectors are slower coming. The overall growth pattern is at about 40 per cent per annum. Following this review, in Chapter 23, is a classification of the developments discussed.

ACP 90

Air Cargo Processing in the Nineties

This UK airport Customs clearance system, replacing ACP 80 at Heathrow, Manchester and Gatwick, is the latest in a series of cooperative airline/ agents/Customs schemes, going back to the pioneering London Airport Cargo EDP Scheme (LACES), commissioned in 1971.

Like all modern airport EDI systems, ACP 90 reflects increasing sophistication in cargo clearance practices, resulting in reduction of Customs dwell-time from up to two weeks before LACES to a few hours today. ACP 90 serves airline shed operators (both with and without their own in-house systems), freight agents, UK Customs and Excise, agent consolidation centres and airlines' own in-house cargo tracking systems. Users have access to the system for inventory control, and facilities are provided to allow agents and freight forwarders to log on to airlines' own in-house systems, for space reservation and interrogations. ACP 90 has 440 users both on and off airport over a wide geographical area, with about 1000 terminals connected directly to the system via both public and private BT circuits and the SITA network. Users include 13 airlines via in-house computer systems in Europe, North America and the Far East, more than 400 agents, and

HM Customs. ACP 90 is linked to the Departmental Entry Processing System (DEPS) which is run by Customs for Customs purposes. Further information concerning ACP 90 may be obtained from: John Arnold, HM Customs & Excise, Customs Directorate, Dorset House, Stamford Street, London SE1 9PS. Telephone: 01 928 0533.

ALFA

This cooperative, Customs/airline/agents, airport system was commissioned at Frankfurt in 1978 and, by 1984, had been extended to Stuttgart and Munich. It allows traders to transmit cargo and import declarations data directly from their own in-house systems to the ALFA computers.

It is planned to extend ALFA, eventually, to all other German airports. German Customs are studying the feasibility of using the system to effect clearance before arrival. This would be limited initially to large shippers, with approved status and systems security and to the rapidly growing flow of express airfreight shipments. Further information concerning ALFA may be obtained from: H Braun, Manager Cargo Handling Affairs, Deutsche Lufthansa AG, Von-Gablenz-Strasse 2-6, D-5060 Koln 21, West Germany. Telephone: 010 49 221 8261. Telex: 8873531.

ANA

Article Number Association

The Article Number Association is governed by a Council, elected by the membership. Policy decisions are made by quarterly Council meetings and are based upon recommendations and reports from various Committees with specialised expert areas of interest.

The ANA Secretariat is operated by the Secretary General, an Executive Staff and Administrative Assistants, and services the Committees and Council by providing information, acting as the link between the membership and the Committees and implementing the Association's policies. The ANA Council and Committees consist of the following: Council, Finance and General Purposes Sub-Committee, Technical Working Party, Working Party on Trading Data Communications, Publicity & PR Sub-Committee Working Party on Access to Sales Data. In the context of EDI, the Working Party on Trading Data Communications is particularly significant as it has developed standards for both paper and electronic communications. It is currently under the chairmanship of Tom McGuffog of Rowntree Mackintosh, an author in this book.

The group's pioneering work on structuring communications passing between manufacturers, wholesalers and retailers such as orders, invoices and price information into a form which can be communicated electronically has found widespread acceptance. The Working Party is continuing to develop and refine the standards so the efficiencies of the inter-computer communications can be realised by a wide range of companies and over several message types. Tradanet a national network for the electronic communication of TRADACOMS messages has also been established by ANA in conjunction with ICL.

In parallel with the electronic data interchange standards the Working Party progresses the standardisation of paper documentation and the ways in which documentation is used.

Further information concerning TRADACOMS is available in the section of the book entitled Standards for EDI, and for Tradanet in Appendix A. Additional information may be obtained from: Nigel Fenton, The Secretary, Article Number Association (UK) Ltd, 6 Catherine Street, London WC2B 5JJ. Telephone: 01 836 2460. Fax: 01 836 0580. Telex: 299388

ASTI

L'Association de Services Transports Informatiques

Over the last three years significant changes have been taking place in the world of freight transportation and electronic communications. These have included the introduction of low cost 'compatible' computers, the Single Administrative Document (SAD) - which reduced over 100 Customs documents in the EEC to one - the provision of public electronic message services connected to the public packet switched data networks, and the growing awareness of Electronic Data Interchange (EDI).

During this period ASTI has been serving the needs of its members by carrying out a programme of education and training in the nature and use of EDI technology, and at the same time carefully analysing the needs and wants of its members in terms of EDI for freight transport.

ASTI is an independent, Swiss based international association of companies and individuals which was formed to facilitate the interchange of trade data through data networks. The organisation has been in existence for over three years and has a growing community of members in Europe, North America and the Far East. It is particularly strong in the freight forwarding sector, and has many companies exchanging consignment information on a daily basis between the Far East, Europe and other parts of the globe. Membership costs £250 per annum per organisation. ASTI serves three main purposes:

> to provide usable common formats for the interchange of trade
> data, in harmony with the institutional standards being developed
> by SITPRO and the various national and international standards
> bodies.

> to facilitate the interchange of this data through the widest
> possible variety of equipment and data networks, including the
> telex network, by managing the contracts with the
> communications carriers around the world, and providing data
> standards to participating software houses and systems designers.

> to educate and train members in the application and practical
> implementation of EDI technology and systems.

The Results Of Research

One result of these three years of research and development was seen at the Worldfreight 3 banquet held in London during October 1987 when the Director General of the Institute of Freight Forwarders handed a rather special SAD to

HRH the Princess Royal. It was for a Save The Children Fund consignment and was the first transmission of an electronic SAD anywhere in the world.

This particular SAD had been produced using ASTI-Freightnet software which was then electronically transmitted to HM Customs & Excise via two networks under ASTI control. The details on the SAD had been originally transmitted to ASTI via the telex network into an electronic mailbox controlled by British Telecom (BT). The information was then recorded from the network into the database supporting the application used to generate the SAD, checked for accuracy and then printed out whilst at the same time a file transmitted the details back via a local telephone call into BT's public data network and transferred through two different mailbox services to HM Customs & Excise.

During the four days of the exhibition the ASTI-Freightnet system was demonstrated on six different stands including HM Customs, BT, GTE Telemail, the Institute of Freight Forwarders, ICC Systems and Integer Micro Systems. A variety of mini and micro computers were used to exchange SADs and freight information data files. The micro software was developed by Freight Informatic Systems Ltd, a software house dedicated to developing systems and software for ASTI members. All the data files used standard data elements wherever possible. At the same event ASTI announced that the communications costs for exchanging standard data files were fixed at £100 per month for unlimited usage. This last point did provoke some astonishment. The above events go some way to illustrate the approach ASTI has adopted in bringing the practical benefits of EDI technology to as wide an audience as possible. ASTI has over 150 members and they include Brantford Seacargo Ltd, Moonbridge Shippers Ltd, P & O CL, Seascope Insurance Ltd, Canadian National Railways, Baxter Hoare Ltd—who were also members of the DISH pilot group - MCP plc, Schenkers Ltd, Great Universal Stores plc, The Institute of Freight Forwarders and the John Lewis Group.

A vast majority of ASTI members employ the network services for the transmission of consignment data. During the period ASTI has been in existence it has attempted both to educate and to ensure that members can pass information between themselves as easily and as cost effectively as possible. At the same time it has kept a close eye on the standardisation processes taking place in the EDI arena and when solid standards are developed it will ensure that members are both aware of and utilise those standards. It is with this in mind that Trademaster was developed.

The role of Trademaster

Trademaster is essentially a file definition that covers all of the data elements possible in a consignment. In addition the data elements used are those found in the United Nations Trade Data Elements Directory (UNTDED) and the SAD. Each record also carries the appropriate tags and segment identifiers used in EDIFACT. It is therefore possible for recipients to construct any messages that are eventually agreed by the various EDIFACT working groups from the Trademaster file, whilst at the same time providing a functional data transfer mechanism for users now. This last point is most important as many of ASTI's members have no time to wait for the working groups to conclude their deliberations, and as new messages emerge or element definitions are en-hanced it can advise all members using Trademaster immediately. Each

Trademaster file carries a unique identifier which relates to ASTI mailboxes providing identification and security but at the same time does not preclude that file being passed on to other correspondents in the chain. Members who use Trademaster files enjoy fixed price tariffs negotiated on their behalf by ASTI, and thus benefit from greatly reduced communications costs. All applications software which is developed to work in harmony with ASTI networks utilise the Trademaster.

Some operations presently carried out by ASTI members via the networks include consignment tracking, customer order transfer, manifest construction and transfer, invoice transfer and inter-office job file transfer. The consignment tracking activity involves the transfer of the latest position report of a consignment from the transport controller to the customer and any other parties involved who also need the information. This activity is being carried out by a number of companies but the most interesting involves one organisation which coordinates the data flow at a central location in the Far East by consolidating the information from a number of branch offices in six other countries and then transfers it to the UK for dissemination across Europe. In every case public packet switched data circuits are used and the resulting files are handled by very powerful public electronic mail systems all under the management of ASTI. The equipment used is primarily micro computers but the mail switches themselves can support almost any type of terminal or computer system. The software for this application was, like the SAD, developed by Freight Informatic Systems Ltd.

Also in the freight forwarding sector some ASTI members receive bookings transmitted from the customer's mailbox into the forwarders mailbox which is downloaded into the agent's computer, processed and grouped together into a manifest which is transmitted, again via the mailbox system, to the corresponding agent at destination. One particular user has taken this philosophy one stage further and as soon as goods are received in the warehouse complex in Milan, the Milan computer system is updated and a corresponding message is transferred to another system in the London office. This ensures that each end of the transport chain has a picture of the cargo available for shipment at any time.

The collection of Customs Duty and VAT is a major component in the role played by the customs clearance agent in the UK. This money is supposed to be collected immediately from the importer by the agent when the goods arrive, however the nature of the transportation industry and the short transit times in Europe ensure that this is seldom the case. It is possible for an agent to enjoy a facility which allows for the deferment of the sums due until the following month to allow time to collect the appropriate funds. The agent must provide guarantees to HM Customs and because of the very substantial sums involved this is often well beyond their means. It was with this in mind that an 'off-shore' mutual insurance company was established which guarantees deferment facilities for members of it so long as the company knows in the shortest possible time the total of it's liabilities by members. Therefore each working day transaction files including payments and invoices are passed via ASTI to the mutual based in the Channel Isles. The transfer is automatic and the programs for transferring the data were developed specifically for this application. It is fair to say that without this facility many of those companies involved in the scheme would be unable to trade at the volume which they are doing now.

The Educational Requirement

All of the systems and services available to members have been developed in consultation with the eventual users and therefore ASTI understands how vital the educational element is in the adoption of EDI. The transition from the traditional manner of doing business to EDI in the shipping sector requires patience and an intimate understanding of the inner workings of the industry. All of the key members of ASTI have backgrounds in the shipping industry and can therefore explain in familiar terminology the benefits and advantages of doing business in this way. This day to day involvement ensures that any new opportunities that present themselves are immediately recognised and can therefore be exploited. Brantford Seacargo and the Michael Gibbons Group (controlled by Powell Duffryn Shipping Services) are just two members who regularly hold internal seminars with ASTI for management and staff explaining the issues at some length. This fosters a favourable attitude amongst employees who would probably feel threatened by EDI developments and hamper their introduction.

In many cases the shipping departments of most companies do not feature very heavily in the corporate automation strategy but they do tend to have a PC. This is what has been seen as the key by ASTI members because with a relatively small investment in a modem and some communications software the shipping department concerned can communicate with its agents and carriers in a manner which is both more flexible and reliable than existing methods. The partnership which exists between ASTI, its members and their customers means that in the three years since its inception every member can say that they have benefited in some way from the association.

ASTI tends not to catch the headlines for its developments and successes in the EDI field but three years of continued growth, a growing international user community and the introduction of exciting new applications for members hold great promise for the future.

Further information concerning ASTI may be obtained from:

L'Association de Services Transports Informatiques, 36 Rue de Lausanne, 1700 Fribourg, Switzerland.

United Kingdom: Ken Lyon, Director, Transport Informatic Services Ltd, 11 Cedric Chambers, Northwick Close, London, NW8. Dialcom 76:SVT1002. Telephone: 01 289 7717.

Trevor Horton, Director, Freight Informatic Systems Ltd, Samson House, Arterial Road, Basildon, Essex SS15 6DR. Dialcom 76:SVT1143. Telephone: 0268 540745.

Bill Williams, Phil Draper, Directors, ICC Systems Ltd, 29 Main Road, Romford, Essex. Dialcom 76:SVT1235. Telephone: 0708 730360.

Membership Fees

Corporate subscription: £250 per annum.

Network mailboxes: £100 per month per mailbox.

Micro software: monthly rental or outright purchase depending on application.

BACS

Bankers' Automated Clearing Services Limited

BACS Limited provides the reliable and secure national batch Electronic Funds Transfer Service for Automated Payment Clearance of Electronic Funds Transfer transactions in the UK. This service enables standing orders, direct credits and direct debits to be processed for the public and private sector corporate originators. Originators submit files of EFT transactions to BACS Limited, directly, on magnetic media, or by telecommunications, or via a bank, commercial, or private computer bureau. BACS Limited checks, merges and sorts these files of EFT transactions for each of the member banks and building societies. The actual debiting and crediting of the specific corporate and personal banking accounts then takes place at the banks and building societies.

Overview Of The Service

BACS Limited is owned by the British Clearing Banks and two building societies. It has operated two major integrated electronic funds transfer centres for 20 years. BACS Limited operates, maintains and upgrades the dual-site BACS EFT facilities. Each computer site hosts a number of large mainframe computer systems, non-stop fault tolerant multi-processors, mini-computer systems, branch telecommunications and network management systems, magnetic tape and diskette reading equipment, as well as operator control terminal units. BACS Limited is the largest dedicated automated payment clearance facility for Electronic Funds Transfer in the UK. In volume terms, it is one of the world's largest Automated Payment Clearing Houses. During 1987, over one billion electronic funds transfer (EFT) transactions were processed through the computer systems at Edgware.

Each originating organisation is allocated one or more unique user numbers. Currently, over 40,000 user numbers are registered with BACS Limited to enable originators to process the EFT submissions, files and daily transactions. The organisations send magnetic tapes and diskettes by post, courier, or datapost to the reception centres in the City of London and Edgware. For time critical and minimum delay electronic funds payment the Bacstel telecommunications data capture service is used by originators for over 10,000 user numbers. Over eight per cent of the data input to BACS, over 10 million transactions a month, are submitted via the Bacstel synchronous telecommunications network. The Bacstel service has over 2,000 and point connections and connects over 19,000 user numbers directly or via bureaux, to the BACS system by telecommunications.

BACS Limited outputs a number of advices and reports for each user number submission to meet all the technical, security and confirmation requirements. These advices and reports are used to enable the operations and user personnel to reconcile and to check the content of each submission. One of these reports, the Input report is made available overnight to users, by post and to a limited extent, by electronic mail, via the British Telecom Dialcom UK E-Mail services. This electronic Input report service is called Bacsmail and it enables the user to have access to their Input report data by 09.00 hrs on processing day, day two of the BACS processing cycle.

More corporate organisations are now implementing the EFT method for purchase ledger and commercial billing applications. It is estimated that, there is a potential of at least 200 million corporate transactions to be converted out of paper cheques into EFT transactions per annum. Organisations have specific and often unique payment and collection requirements. They have become innovative in their use of the BACS service. BACS provides the large-scale EFT processing and data capture systems through which the user's information is checked, merged, sorted and streamed.

Currently, there are 10 major direct crediting applications and 21 major direct debiting applications in everyday use throughout the UK. Of the 342 million EFT direct credit transactions processed last year, nine million were direct credit purchase ledger payments. Of the 465 million EFT direct debit transactions processed, over five million were direct debit commercial billing collections. The potential volume for corporate to corporate EFT transactions in the UK is estimated to be over 200 million per annum. This represents one third of all UK non-cash trade payments between businesses. It is in this area that EFT and EDI methods can be combined to further reduce the paper dependency and reduce costs for the user and the recipient.

Major EFT applications

Direct Credit Payments

Charity transfers; child benefits; credit card refunds; expenses; interest payments; monthly salaries; pensions; purchase ledger and sundry payments; saving contributions; weekly wages.

Direct Debit Collections

Budget account payments; credit card retailer settlements; commercial billings; hire purchase payments; household rates; life insurance premiums; loan payments; non-life insurance premiums; membership fees; mortgage repayments; national insurance contributions (self-employed); rates; rents; savings contributions; subscriptions; TV licences; TV rental payments; utility bills (gas, electricity, water, telecommunications).

The following are Members of BACS Limited: Abbey National Building Society; Bank of England; Bank of Scotland; Barclays Bank plc; Clydesdale Bank plc; Cooperative Bank plc; Coutts & Co; Girobank plc; Halifax Building Society; Lloyds Bank plc; Midland Bank plc; National Westminster Bank plc; The Royal Bank of Scotland plc; TSB England & Wales plc; Yorkshire Bank plc.

Bacstel overview

Over eight per cent of BACS EFT transactions are input via the Bacstel Service. Some of the features of Bacstel are described below. Bacstels telecommunications data capture service enables originators to connect directly to the BACS computer centres, for submission of EFT transaction automated payments. In general, any user who can conform to the widely popular BSC (2780/3780) or X.25 protocols and print the advices received back down the line can submit data through the Bacstel service. User connections via the Public Switched Telephone Network (PSTN), leased lines, Kilostream or Packet Switch Stream (PSS) are currently available.

The specific advantages of using telecommunications compared with using magnetic media are: it is fast and independent of distance; it eliminates the need for data to be transported; reporting back is instant—on completing a transmission the sender receives back from BACS a file acceptance advice, or if a rejection error has occurred, a file rejection advice.

Definitions

Record: a collection of related items of data treated as a unit of information. A record corresponds to an EFT credit or debit transaction.

Block: a group of continuous characters recorded on and read from a storage medium as a unit.

File: a major collection of data, consisting or records originating from one user.

Volume: a single complete transmission unit, that is a Bacstel transmission.

Transmission format: the file format used by BACS for transmission for Bacstel telecommunications is based upon that used for magnetic tape.

Transmission duration: transmission durations for various line speeds and numbers of EFT transaction items for Bacstel submission are dependent on transmission block size, line quality and length of record.

Typically the durations are shown in the table below:

Number of EFT Items	Duration of Transmission to BACSTEL		
	2400 bps mins	4800 bps mins	9600 bps mins
500	5	3	2
1000	10	5	3
1500	15	8	4
2000	20	10	5
4000	40	21	10
10000	100	50	25

Files submitted by telecommunications users are subject to the security checks that are applied to all BACS input. Access is controlled through the use of passwords, and submissions via telecommunications will not be accepted unless preceded by a logon message containing a valid password.

Transmission Protocols

The protocols used for connection to Bacstel are shown below.

TYPE NUMBER	CONNECTION TYPE	SPEED (bps)	CCITT RECOMMENDATION
1	PSTN	2400	V.26 bis +
2	PSTN	4800	V.27 ter
3	Leased	2400	V.26 bis +
4	Leased	4800	V.27 bis
5	Leased	9600	V.29
6	Kilostream	2400	X.21 bis
7	Kilostream	4800	X.21 bis
8	Kilostream	9600	X.21 bis
9	PSS	*	X.25 +

At BACS the PSS connection is at 9600 bps, but users may connect to PSS at other speeds supported by British Telecom. An EPAD connection to PSS is under trial.

Both V.26/X.25 are used for the EDI and EFT applications interfaces. Types 1-8 are the Binary Synchronous Communications (BSC) link level and 2780/3780 message control. For connection type 9, the 3-level protocol known as CCITT recommendation X.25 is used. Line code is EBCDIC, and ISO-7 (in transparent mode) is also allowed for data. For connection types 1-8, the minimum block length allowed is 80 characters and the maximum block length is 2048 characters. For connection type 9, the usual packet size is 128 octets (characters) but packets of up to 1024 octets may be transmitted.

Two types of service are available for telecommunications users they are: scheduled service and on demand service.

Further information concerning BACS may be obtained from: Derek Balmforth, Head of Business Development, BACS Limited, Unit 17, Humphrys Road, Luton, Beds LU5 4TB. Telephone: 0582 600161. Fax: 0582 608086. Head Office: De Havilland Road, Edgware, Middlesex HA8 5QA. Telephone: 01 952 2333.

BEDIS

Booktrade Electronic Data Interchange Standards Committee

There are at least six standards in widespread use in the book trade in the UK. In order to facilitate agreement on common message standards The MARC Users' Group set up BEDIS. It was recognised that its members should represent library cooperatives, public and institutional libraries, library suppliers, system suppliers and the ANA.

Considerations

BEDIS recognised that there were a number of existing standards, deeply entrenched, and with many existing users. Some of them were unlikely to change. The Working Party recognised that it needed to use both pragmatism, and common sense: some of the factors which contributed to the final recommendations are outlined below.

> W H Smith book turnover represents 20 per cent of the total
> turnover of the UK retail booktrade. W H Smith's use of

Teleordering provides its financial underpinning. WHS has made it clear that it wishes to use the main British commercial standard for electronic transmission of orders and invoices, which is TRADACOMS.

Some 40 per cent of order lines from the retail booktrade are now carried by Teleordering. Booksellers and, indeed, publishers on the Teleordering network would not welcome changes that cost them either time or money.

The American BISAC standards have been formally adopted, for instance, in Australia. Several Australian libraries already send orders to export suppliers in the UK, in the BISAC format. The needs of those customers must be taken into account.

The library world has used the UK MARC format standard for bibliographic record structure and as a format for data transmission for over 20 years.

Whitaker files have an average of 1,000 alterations a day made to them as a result of the application of electronically transmitted instructions from publishers.

Publishers have made it clear that they wish to cooperate with their customers, but want more information on what their customers are likely to be doing.

A number of librarians have made it clear that they wish to be able to join Teleordering. However, the Teleordering format is too restrictive for the needs of the library world. Several library suppliers who supply systems able to communicate only with them, and which tend to create a situation in which it is possible to deal only with that supplier, have made it clear that they recognise that this is not a long term solution.

Local government agencies ordering books, Boots, Menzies and other large organisations, use now or propose to adopt the TRADACOMS standards for order transmission, invoice transmission and receipt.

Positive Factors

BEDIS established early on that it had a number of factors working in its favour: these are outlined below.

Teleordering made it clear that it was prepared to change its standard for order gathering from booksellers and transmission to publishers, to whatever was more beneficial to those customers. Whitaker made it clear that it would adopt any agreed industry standard for price and status advice.

The Executive Secretary of TRADACOMS made it clear that if the TRADACOMS standard was not suited to all of the requirements of the book world, then whatever changes were necessary to make it applicable to the book world would be made.

The UKMARC format has a very wide user base (although not among publishers); UK librarians have many millions of pounds invested in systems dependant upon it.

Constraints

The Committee identified the following as factors which complicated its work.

The area of work verges on the technical, and available expertise is thin on the ground.

TRADACOMS exists, and is the chosen standard of a number of the most important companies and organisations in the book trade. The Committee therefore could not look at the BISAC standards, for instance, and recommend the exclusive adoption of BISAC.

Conversely, BISAC exists, is in use in North America, and has been adopted in Australia. Many UK booksellers and library suppliers have a substantial amount of export business and their customers may be expected to use BISAC. Therefore the Committee was not in a position to recommend an augmented TRADACOMS standard and to ignore BISAC.

Very early on the Committee recognised therefore that a number of organisations in Britain were going to have to learn to live with two standards; and that the Committee must make sure that it tried to point the way towards the easiest possible translation, where translation is necessary, between BISAC and TRADACOMS.

Terms Of Reference Of Working Parties

BEDIS decided to split its work, so far as was possible, into interest areas. For instance, publishers are beginning to appreciate the importance of holding bibliographic records in their computers, and being able to communicate these to outside parties. Therefore the first Working Party reported on 'The Applicability of MARC to Publishers'.

The second Working Party was asked, to some extent, to state the obvious: the advantages to a bookshop or library supplier of holding details of inventory in an industry standard form, and if that standard should be MARC based. The third Working Party was asked to report on the 'Applicability of TRADACOMS to librarians, library suppliers and library booksellers for order transmission and receipt, and invoice transmission and receipt'. The fourth Working Party was very much oriented toward checking that Teleordering could use the TRADACOMS standard for order receipt from booksellers, and invoice transmission to booksellers, without it upsetting existing users.

The members of the Working Parties were chosen for their 'bottom line' interest in the areas being dealt with. The full briefs of the Working Parties can be found in the BEDIS Discussion Paper.

Management Summary

The work of the BEDIS Committee was not intended to be exhaustive and should be seen as a first step in the process of examining the requirement and establishment of standards for the electronic transmission of data within the book trade. In the absence of any widely used or recognised world standards, it has concentrated on the UK marketplace, whilst recognising important developments elsewhere. Conveniently, and for sound practical reasons, 'the data' can be subdivided into two categories—bibliographic and commercial. The Committee's preliminary findings can be summarised as follows.

Bibliographic data

The most widely used standard for storage and transmission of bibliographic data in the UK (and overseas) is MARC. Currently this is amongst the library/library supply community. It is recommended that MARC be adopted as the standard for all parts of the book trade.

There is a strong case for publishers to use computers to hold bibliographic details of their books. Whilst publishers need not hold information in MARC format, it should be capable of being transmitted in MARC or MARC compatible format, to enable widest possible dissemination. If necessary MARC standards should be adapted to accommodate publishers' requirements.

Commercial data

Order transmission

The Teleordering standard is the most widely used. Teleordering can accept orders in TRADACOMS format and convert to Teleordering format for publishers. Neither Teleordering nor TRADACOMS standards can currently accommodate library orders. It is recommended that TRADACOMS be adapted to cater for library orders and that this become the standard. The new TRADACOMS standard should also be able to accommodate chasers.

Invoices—statements

TRADACOMS should be adopted as the standard for publishers' invoices and statements. TRADACOMS should be adopted to cater for invoices and statements sent to libraries.

Product description

The most widely used format in the book trade is MARC. TRADACOMS should adopt the MARC standard for book trade product description.

Status messages

There is a need to achieve uniformity of status messages, for example ip, op, rp, rpnd.

Other Considerations

Some overseas customers/suppliers of UK booksellers and library suppliers use the BISAC standard for orders, invoices and product description. It is unrealistic to expect other countries to adopt TRADACOMS standards and, therefore, conversion between the two will be necessary. A guide for converting orders from BISAC to TRADACOMS, and *vice* versa, should be prepared.

In adapting its standard to accommodate specific book trade requirements TRADACOMS (the ANA) should, where possible, follow BISAC standards. This will facilitate subsequent conversion from one standard to another.

Summary

This summary has been taken from BEDIS Committee Discussion paper published in April 1988 on behalf of the MARC User's Group by J Whitaker & Sons Ltd. Further information concerning BEDIS and copies of the discussion paper may be obtained from: David Whitaker, Chairman BEDIS, J Whitaker & Sons Ltd, 12 Dyott Street, London WC1A 1DF. Telephone: 01 836 8911.

BROKERNET

Further information concerning Brokernet may be found in Appendix A.

BTAT

British Telecom Applied Technology

BT Applied Technology is the commercial computing services division of British Telecom and provides a wide range of computer-based services and products to government and industry. BTAT is currently the largest provider of cargo and customs management computer systems in the world.

Recently, the company secured major contracts for the provision of ACP90, a cargo community scheme for Heathrow, Gatwick and Manchester airports, and for DEPS (M)—the development and supply of the modified Departmental Entry Processing System to HM Customs, which provides for all Direct Trader Input (DTI). During the last 12 months it has also successfully developed and implemented major systems for the Port of London (PACE) and for Lufthansa German Airlines (Spacelink).

British Telecom has offered services for international trade since 1970 when, in conjunction with HM Customs and Heathrow Airport Traders, it designed, installed and managed LACES—the world's first automated cargo community system. The company is also making a major investment in the development of new services for its users in conjunction with its partners in international trade facilitation including Telecom Gold, ASTI-Freightnet and MCP (proprietors of FCP80, the maritime cargo control system based at Port of Felixstowe).

Future facilities will include the provision of national port inter-system messaging; low cost direct trader input interfaces for UK users and low cost international messaging and document interchange services. Further information on all the individual initiatives mentioned above is available elsewhere within this section. Further information concerning BTAT may be obtained from:

Robert Halhead, BTAT, 60-68 St Thomas Street, London SE1 3QU. Telephone: 01 407 3456. Telex: 268589. Fax: 01 403 5531.

CARGONAUT

This is an advanced cargo-clearance network designed for Schiphol Airport. It is unusual for such cooperative schemes in that the airport authority is a 'senior partner' along with Customs, airlines and agents.

The system, still under development, will act as a high-speed switch for conveying data among all sections of the air cargo community. The scheme provides for interfacing with the Dutch Customs SAGITTA clearance system and its inventory addition, DOSYS. Extension to include export processing is planned for 1989. Further information may be obtained from: S F Zimmerman, Managing Director, Cargonaut Gebouw 72, 1117 AA Schiphol Oost, Netherlands. Telephone: 010 31 20 517 3160.

CCC

Customs Cooperation Council

The CCC is a worldwide organisation of Customs administrations (104 members, among them are the members of the EEC). One of its main aims is the harmonisation and simplification of Customs formalities with a view to facilitating international trade. In this regard the CCC is interested in EDI and the role it can play in helping to achieve such aims. The CCC fully supports international standardisation efforts in the field of EDI and indeed is playing a part in helping to develop standard electronic messages for exchange between the automated systems of Customs and other trade partici- pants. The Council's ADP Sub-Committee is charged with this task and other tasks relating to Customs ADP applications. Further information concerning the Customs Cooperation Council may be obtained from: G D Gotschlich, Director Customs Technique Directorate, Customs Cooperation Council, rue de l'Industrie 26-38, B-1040 Brussels, Belgium. Telephone: 010 322 513 9900. Telex: 61597. Fax: 010 322 514 3372.

CD

EEC Coordinated Development of Computerised Administrative Procedures

This European Community project will coordinate the development of computerised administrative procedures. Undertaken within the overall framework of the Cooperation in Automation of Data and Documentation for Imports/Exports and Agriculture (CADDIA) programme, the CD project will, eventually, computerise all export and import Customs clearance in intra-Community and external transactions trading.

The project also proposes to inter-link Member States' national Customs services and to facilitate interfacing between Customs' systems and those of the business community. This initiative reinforces the move towards the true frontierless Europe by 1992.

CEFIC

Conseil Européen des Fédérations de l'Industrie Chimique

The European chemical industry with a market size of over 170 billion per annum has a pivotal position in European and World trade and has trading relationships with virtually every sector of business and industry. International EDI is of vital strategic importance to the chemical industry. Accordingly an EDI project has been set up under the auspices of the European Council of the Chemical Manufacturer Federations (CEFIC) and with the support of the European community (CEC-DG XIII).

ICI—a world class company—is fully committed to the project, both in the UK with ICI Chemicals and Polymers Ltd and through ICI Europa representing its European subsidiaries. Other Companies taking part include AKZO (Netherlands), Atochem (France), Bayer (Germany), Ciba-Geigy (Switzerland), DSM (Netherlands), Enichem (Italy), ERT (Spain), Hoechst (Germany), Montedison (Italy), Rhone-Poulenc (France), Shell (UK/Netherlands) and the European subsidiaries of the US companies, Dow, Du Pont, Exxon and Monsanto. The project commenced in January 1987, following preparatory work in the previous year. Initially there were working parties concentrating on the Systems and Telecoms, Messages, and Legal aspects of the trial under the overall direction of a Steering Committee. A separate working party is managing the administration of the trial and liaison with network and software suppliers. The project is committed to the use of EDIFACT standards for data messages. Initially the EDIFACT order, invoice and general message will be used. Special EDIFACT messages of particular significance to the chemical industry (eg quality data message) have been developed.

Major telecoms requirements were for the availability of a range of connection options including support for X.400, the ODETTE File Transfer (OFTP) (and X.25), as well as traditional protocols such as bisynchronous (2780/3780), and asynchronous.

The trial started in April 1988 and will last for six months using the EDI Service/Network provided by GE Information Services Ltd. Initially the trial is between the original steering committee member chemical companies only, but after the evaluation of the trial in October 1988 the objective is to set up a production service linking to other chemical companies and later to all customers, suppliers, customs, transportation, ports, banks.

A user manual has been prepared and it is proposed to make it available to interested parties. CEFIC will coordinate a list of companies wishing to join at the end of the trial. Companies are invited to contact CEFIC for further information: Rutger A A Hopster, CEFIC, 250 Avenue Louise, Box 71, B-1050 Brussels, Belgium. Telephone: 010 322 640 2095. Telex: 62444. Fax: 010 322 640 1981.

CHAMBERNET EUROPE

This is an EDI 'back-up' project sponsored by Chamber of Commerce organisations from six European countries. Based on an earlier EEC Commissionfunded programme for 'Multilingual Product Description and Coding (MPD)', CHAMBERNET will provide an automated multilingual list of product descriptions in main Community languages. Further information concerning CHAMBERNET may be obtained from: W Telkamp, Managing Director, Holland Export System, Watermolenlaan 1, 3447 GT Woerden, Netherlands. Telephone: 010 31 3407 3301.

COST 306

Cooperation in Scientific and Technical Research

COST is an EEC/EFTA programme to initiate and promote European collaboration in a number of high-technology sectors. COST 306 is a project specifically directed to research- ing and analysing information flows in international transport. The aim is a data-exchange concept which would eliminate traditional paperwork problems and facilitate the uninterrupted movement of vehicles and freight. Project participants include Austria, Belgium, Denmark, Finland, France, the Federal Republic of Germany, Italy, The Netherlands, Norway, Sweden, Switzerland, and the United Kingdom. The COST 306 Demonstration Manual includes recom- mended data representation and technical standards, together with guidance on liability issues, and economic and organisational aspects of telecommunication implementation. Further information is available from Henk van Maaren, Wilheminasingel 28, 3135 JR Vlaardingen, The Netherlands. Telephone: 010 3110 4346756. Telex: 20010 PMS NL attn. CETIMA VLD.

DAKOSY

This data-communication system was established in Hamburg, in July 1983, to dovetail a number of systems already in operation and to provide a special, combined service for port users.

Expansion of the system's capabilities, including the use of standard forms for certain types of trading operations is being planned. The feasibility of including the Free Port's administration in the system is also being tested.

Two other systems, TALDOS and CONDICOS, designed for the specific needs of tallymen and container operations have been grafted on to DAKOSY. Further information concerning DAKOSY is available from Peter Burkert, Dakosy GmbH, Cremon 9, 2000 Hamburg 11, West Germany. Telephone: 010 49 2241 142671. Fax: 010 49 2241 142889.

danNET

danNet is a Danish VADS supplier formed by IBM Denmark and KTAS (The Copenhagen Telephone Company—the largest operating telephone company in Denmark). The share capital is 100 million Dkr. The purpose of danNet is to provide VADS to the Danish business community. Among the services provided are: protocol conversion; access to information databases; electronic mail; file transfer; EDI.

danNet is heavily involved in introducing EDI for the Danish business community. This involvement has resulted in the development of a number of pilot projects in a variety of different areas.

Pilot Projects

Approximately 10 pilot projects are in different stages of planning and implementation. These projects cover most of the important sectors in the business community (insurance, assurance, banking, retail and construction). The projects are planned to run in the second half of 1988 and are expected to become truly operational services by the beginning of 1989.

Basic EDI developments

To support these pilot projects danNet is developing basic EDI services for both mainframes and PCs.

The mainframe solution includes an EDI-server, which based on an 'EDIFACT-file', is able to distribute single documents to recipients. In addition services such as logging, status reporting and the like will be included in the service. Access to the EDI server is obtained by using the dan/Link service, which via usual IBM and Digital protocols connects users to danNet.

In order that users are able to start EDI projects as simply as possible danNet has also developed an 'EDI workstation' based on IBM compatible PCs. The PC may be hooked up to danNet by means of both asynchronous and synchronous protocols. This solution is an important contributory factor in the pilot projects and for small businesses.

The next step in the development process of danNet will be the development of EDI services on top of OSI services, that is, X.400 and FTAM. Further information concerning danNet may be obtained from: Bent Baek Jensen, R&D Manager, danNet, Blokken 9, DK-3460, Birkerod, Denmark. Telephone: 010 45 282 1600. Fax: 010 45 282 1644.

DEDIST

Data Element Distribution in Trade

This project is preparing guidelines for the representation of trade data in inter-Nordic and other international ETDI communications. Initiated by Finland DEDIST now includes support from Denmark, Norway and Sweden. Further information concerning DEDIST may be obtained from: Funnar Sunblad, SWEPRO, Box 450, 40127 Goteborg, Sweden. Telephone: 010 46 31 637277. Fax: 010 46 31 802681.

DEPS

Departmental Entry Processing System

This Customs system, managed by British Telecom Applied Technology (BTAT), an entry for which can be found earlier in this section, provides Direct Trader Input (DTI) facilities to reduce cargo-clearance times and improve the quality of information flows from carriers and agents.

DEPS is linked to both ACP 90 (Heathrow, Manchester and Gatwick airports) and FCP 80, operated by Maritime Cargo Processing (MCP) at Felixstowe and 10 other UK ports. DEPS checks import entry declarations, calculates duties and taxes and selects goods and documentation for Customs examination. It provides comprehensive accounting information and collects UK trade statistics. DEPS runs 24 hours a day, 365 days a year with greater than 99.5 per cent system availability. The system runs on IBM plug-compatible NAS 8033.

UK Customs are now developing the next generation of cargo clearance ETDI systems, starting with Customs Handling of Import and Export Freight (CHIEF). Its enhancements will include the real-time allocation of claims against EEC quotas, possible interlinking—in accord with CADDIA—to other, initially French, Customs, and interfacing with the Department of Trade and Industry to 'tally off' clearance against import licences. Further information concerning DEPS may be obtained from: Robert Halhead, BTAT, 60-68 St Thomas Street, London SE1 3QU. Telephone: 01 407 3456. Telex: 268589. Fax: 01 403 5531.

DISH

Data Interchange for Shipping

This UK project now also known under the generic title of EDIA (Electronic Data Interchange Association) links four exporters, five shipping lines and a forwarder to develop an ETDI system which would allow exporters/importers to exchange data with shipping lines, trailer and Roll-on/Roll-off operators, airlines and freight forwarders. DISH has developed a set of unified messages including bookings, schedule changes, shipping instructions, accounts and contracts. It is now expanding internationally through the formation of a joint working team with INTIS, DEDIST and SEAGHA. Further information may be found under the entry for The EDI Association (EDIA).

DOCIMEL

The purpose of this project is to develop computer links between railways, their customers and Customs. It aims to reduce needs for data-acquisition, eliminate, if possible, physical despatch of documents, and improve the quality of the rail transport service.

Each consignment generates a computer file, beginning with input data from the shipper and working through necessary additional information, along the line of physical transit, towards preparation of relevant detailed accounts.

Contents of any file could be printed locally for a particular need or customer. The system is planned to meet the requirements outlined below.

It should permit automatic exchange of data, not only between railways, but also with customers and Customs. It should also take account of the complex relations between partners based on data-requirements for the tasks entrusted to each of the parties. Its use of EDI should not affect the functions of the CIM consignment note, especially the rights it confers on shippers and the consignee. Further, it should improve railway services through automation of operations during the contract of carriage and provision, to the user, of better information and control of the goods during the transport operation.

The system will, in the longer term, simplify processing and transmission of large-scale data-flows in such operations as transport, planning, regulation and monitoring, financial estimating, billing, accounting and proceeds distribution, and management statistics, logistics and market information. DOCIMEL will use EDIFACT for message construction.

EAN

International Article Numbering Association

This international body groups many national Article Number Associations. It develops and promotes the uniform, international EAN product identification system, and ensures observance of related operating specifications and procedures. In all, 75,000 companies have joined one of the national article number organisations, and so participate in the EAN system. Most EAN organisations have been commissioned by their members to develop a standard communication system, including telecommunication facilities, allowing purchase orders, delivery and confirmations invoices, product descriptions and other information to be sent automatically to trading partners' EDP systems.

EAN has formed a working party to look at the international implications of all these national activities. This has agreed that a common interface between different systems should be based on EDIFACT and that individual article number associations should be encouraged to adopt EDIFACT whenever possible, particularly for international trade purposes.

The United Kingdom's Article Number Association, however, has already developed its own highly regarded Tradanet retail and distribution system on the basis of TRADACOM ETDI standards, and forecasts that some 4,000 UK companies will be using TRADACOMS by 1990. TRADACOMS messages are based on a rigid, very efficient format, which is particularly suited to domestic trading. These advantages are unlikely to inhibit any but a few current TRADACOMS users from migrating to EDIFACT in the foreseeable future. The most promising path to reconciliation is through a suitable TRADACOMS/EDIFACT translation facility. Further information concerning EDIFACT and TRADACOMS standards may be found in the papers concerned with message standards.

EDIA

The EDI Association

The EDI Association was formed on 15 September 1987. Its objectives are: to provide a forum for the UK's international trade and transport participants to develop common positions, policies or plans to ensure that EDI users' practical requirements are met; to promote the use of EDI in the international trade and transport area in the UK so that users get the maximum commercial advantage from its implementation; to support the implementation of EDI applications international trade and transport; to foster the progress of EDI in international trade and transport.

The Association brings together prospective and actual EDI users. It already has over 160 members. In order to achieve its objectives it has set up six 'interest' sections which are actively developing messages and other user requirements. These sections cover: Deep Sea Transport; Short Sea and Surface

Transport; Air Transport; Banking and Financial Services; Insurance; Customs and other Governmental Issues.

• The new EDIFACT version of the Data Interchange for Shipping (DISH) Project International Transport Order Message Scenario is now being maintained by the Association. The scenario covers booking, shipping instructions, transport contracts, and freight invoicing Technical Support Groups covering message design coordination, communications/software and legal issues have also been formed.

The senior officers of the Association are:

President:	Sir Angus Fraser, KCB TD
Chairman:	Mr M Voss, Guiness Exports
Vice Chairman:	Mr A J Metcalf, Philips Electronics
Hon. Secretary:	Mr R Dale, SITPRO
Hon. Treasurer:	Mr R Wainright-Lee, Barclays Bank
Hon. Membership Secretary:	Mr R Holmes, Cunard-Brocklebank

There are four classes of membership which will each attract different levels of annual subscription and joining fee. The classes and fees, to which VAT should be added, are as follows:

Class of Member	Annual Subscription	Joining Fee
EDI Users, Potential Users & EDI Consultants	£200	£100
Software Houses	£400	£200
Trade Associations	£100	£50
Value Added Networks	£800	£400

Fuller details of the way in which the Sections and specialist groups operate, the responsibilities of the Council and the election of Council members are set out in the Bye-Laws and the Articles of Association which are available from: Mr R Holmes, Hon. Membership Secretary, Cunard Ellerman Ltd, Lancaster House, Mercury Court, Tithebarn Street, Liverpool L2 2QP.

EDICON

EDI in Construction Limited

This is a UK initiative to develop a common ETDI project to serve construction companies and associated interests.

The market opportunity is considerable. The industry covers some 100,000 companies and a high proportion are likely to use EDI at some future date. Current projections put the figure of users at about 5,000 by 1990.

Despite this opulent domestic catchment area, EDICON is unlikely to remain purely national. While comparatively few UK construction firms exploit overseas markets, cross-frontier contracting is much more common in Continental Europe. Swiss companies seem particularly interested in EDICON. Further information concerning EDICON may be found in the paper entitled 'European EDI Development Groups' and from: John Sanders, The Chairman, EDICON, 51 Adelaide Road, St Denys, Southampton SO2 1HU. Telephone: 0703 552809.

EDICT

Further information concerning Edict may be found in Appendix A.

EDIFICE

EDI Forum for Companies Interested in Computing Electronics

This is a specialised forum, seeking to promote the use of ETDI by companies in the European electronics and computer industries, and is, like ODETTE and CEFIC, a major transnational ETDI/EBDI effort. Like them, too, EDIFICE is being supported by the EEC Commission, through the provision of meeting and secretarial facilities. Further information concerning EDIFICE is available from: Eric Hugenholtz, Manager Trade & Customs, Philips BV, Postbus 218, 56100 MD Eindhoven, The Netherlands. Telephone: 010 3140 756903. Fax: 010 3140 755186.

ERTIS

European Road Transport Information Services

The main purpose of ERTIS is to increase the efficiency of transborder road transportation services. ERTIS aims to improve transportation efficiency by using and/or developing advanced information transfer technology. ERTIS comes under the aegis of the EUREKA project and participants include: Belgian Road Haulage Federation; Danish Road Haulage Federation; Norwegian Truck Owners' Association; Datafreight (UK). Further information concerning ERTIS may be obtained from: EUREKA, Department of Trade & Industry, Ashdown House, 123 Victoria Street, London SW1E 6RB. Telephone: 01 212 0249. Telex: 8813148. Fax: 01 828 3258.

FCP 80

Felixstowe Cargo Processing 80

The dramatic change in trade patterns which followed British entry into the EEC, produced considerable congestion at ports immediately adjacent to main Community markets. Felixstowe was particularly affected. Means had to be found to meet and manage constantly increasing cargo flows, with closer and closer delivery schedules.

The FCP80 system, introduced in 1983, has reduced clearance times from days to hours through its direct entry links to Customs. Today, the FCP 80 and port inventory system, run by Maritime Cargo Processing (MCP), is used in 10 other major British ports and already serves over 400 customers.

Familiar systems are being used in other UK ports, including London, (PACE) and Dover, and by the Associated British Ports group, including Southampton. Further information concerning FCP 80 may be found under the title of Maritime Cargo Processing (MCP) in this information section and also from: John Hammond, Chief Executive MCP, Unit 1 Orwell House, Ferry Lane, Felixstowe, Suffolk IP11 8QL. Telephone: 0394 674422. Fax: 0394 673363.

GBA

Gemeentelijke Bevolkings Administratie

GBA is a Dutch government project to automate all city hall demographic administration. This X.400 based service administers tax, pension and military service across the nation. 'Open' network architecture (including PC interfaces) and the security of the system are key features. Further information concerning GBA may be obtained from: Philip de Roos, GE Information Services BC, Kabelweg 37, 1014 BA Amsterdam, The Netherlands. Telephone: 010 31 208 46825.

IBM INFORMATION EXCHANGE SERVICE

Further information concerning IBM information Exchange Service may be found in Appendix A.

INTIS

International Transport Information System

INTIS was set up in 1985 to create and operate a communications network and information structure in Rotterdam. INTIS' activities are directed at supporting the information flows in the transport process by means of electronic data interchange (EDI).

INTIS offers the following services: standardised messages; network facilities; tools; consultancy.

INTIS offers an open, international network for the transport sector, intended for the exchange of standardised messages on the basis of EDI. In order to make it easy to initiate EDI, INTIS has developed software for the personal computer.

INTIS: Standardised Messages

The standardised electronic messages used by INTIS are being developed in close cooperation with those directly involved with them in the world of transport. Users include shippers, transporters, freight forwarders, liner agents, carriers, container terminals and customs authorities. They stipulate their requirements and INTIS then adapts them to the international norms for electronic data interchange. In this respect EDIFACT is a central concept. All messages which INTIS develops for use in the field of transportation are based on EDIFACT.

INTIS is working closely with similar English, Belgian and Scandinavian organisations. One of the most obvious benefits of this international liaison is the development of the International Transport Order (ITO), a widely applicable order. This ITO is a part of the International Transport Messages Scenario (ITMS) which streamlines communication between shippers and forwarders on the one hand and transporters and carrier agents on the other. This scenario is unique in that it may be used for all modes of transport: deep sea, shortsea, inland waterway, rail, road and air. The message standards are developed stage by stage, until ultimately the entire chain of transport, from shipper to consignee, will be standardised.

The INTIS network

The INTIS Network is a Message Handling System for the exchange of standardised messages. The system is open to every organisation in the transport chain. Users of the network may choose one of the following options for linking up with the network: a personal computer as a stand-alone terminal; a personal computer linked on the one hand as a terminal to the INTIS Network and on the other hand to the in-house computer system; direct linking of the in-house computer system to the INTIS Network.

INTIS has developed several software packages for personal computers. With these, Intisface packages, electronic messages can be composed, sent, received and stored. Intisface is available for the shipping instruction, the Single Administrative Document and also for container handling messages between liner agent and container terminal. New packages are being developed. The Intisface software can be linked to the in-house information system. In that way in-house information systems do not have to be adapted before starting with EDI.

Connection to the INS and GE Information Services networks

In addition to its international and intermodal aspects, INTIS has a third major characteristic, its wide coverage. EDI in transport is international, therefore INTIS has created links with the existing computer networks of IBM, General Electric and the Dutch Telecommunications Authorities (PTT). Thanks to such links it is now possible for companies in different countries to exchange information using EDI. This in turn means that companies who can utilise the IBM and General Electric networks in their own countries are now able to exchange information with the Port of Rotterdam using EDI. Further information concerning INTIS may be obtained from: J C Otten, General Manager, INTIS BV, Marconistraat 16, 3029 AK Rotterdam, The Netherlands. Telephone: 010 31 10 4254255. Telex: 26080. Fax: 010 31 10 4256414.

KOMPASS

An integrated information and documentation system, established in the port of Bremen in 1981, KOMPASS is being regularly improved and updated. This real-time, two-way communication system, structures, processes and monitors data-flows in individual management, administrative and operational units. The system also links them to one another and to the relevant services of the Bremen Port authority. Other ancillary communication systems, such as LOTSE, DAVIS and CCL have been developed for specific port activities: maritime trade, export operations, container management. Further information concerning KOMPASS may be obtained from: Werner Lampe, DBH Datenbank Bremische Hafen, Bremen, West Germany. Telephone: 010 41 421 3090247. Fax: 010 41 421 3090257.

LOG

Logistik & Kommunikation

LOG, like COST 306, is a transport sector project, but operates at the national level within the Federal Republic of Germany. It aims to assist data interchange and the linking of different data processing systems by overcoming three common problems: differences in the structure of messages for exchange; differences in hardware; differences in data communication concepts.

The LOG solution, which centres on the use of front end processor (FEP) techniques, supports the EDIFACT standard. Further information concerning LOG may be obtained from: F Bumba, Logistik & Kommunikation GmbH, Fothaer Strasse 18, 4030 Ratingen 1, West Germany. Telephone: 010 49 2102 475005. Fax: 010 49 2102 499406.

MCP

Maritime Cargo Processing

Maritime Cargo Processing was formed in June 1985 to manage, market, sell, develop and enhance the integrated Port Information System known as Felixstowe Cargo Processing in the 80s (FCP80).

Background

FCP80 was born out of a need to reduce clearance times for cargo arriving at the rapidly expanding port of Felixstowe. By 1980 further growth was being threatened by the fact that the paperwork required to facilitate the movement of cargo through the port was creating a bottleneck in the Custom House, which resulted in clearances taking between three and six days. The local Port Users' Association approached Government at the highest level, which resulted in a visit to Felixstowe by the Treasury Minister. He advised the Association that no additional manpower would be made available and that it should look into the possibility of introducing Direct Trade Input (DTI) of Customs import entries at the port. Although no such system was in operation in the UK maritime ports, London Airport had been using DTI successfully for a number of years, first with LACES and latterly with ACP80.

The Port Users' Association immediately grasped the business significance of the techniques and a working party was formed, consisting of wharfingers, the Port Authority, the forwarders/customers brokers, the shipping lines or agents, HM Customs and the transport and trucking companies. It soon became evident that the airport system would not be suitable for the maritime environment and the working party resolved to develop their own system, FCP80. The system was introduced in two phases.

Phase I

Direct Trader Input—was effected in January 1984. It was concerned solely with providing local forwarders/Customs brokers access to the central Customs computer, Departmental Entry Processing System (DEPS). This alone had a dramatic effect on clearance times, reducing the average from three days to six hours. The main reason for this reduction stems from the fact that, because the agent communicates directly with DEPS, any errors on the import declaration are returned for correction prior to the paper entry being produced, enabling forwarders to present local Customs with entries free from validation errors. This, in turn, allowed Customs in the Entry Processing Unit to concentrate on specific and 'real' checks.

Phase II

Inventory control commenced for imports in early 1985. It concerns the creation and maintenance of a central file relating to every vessel, every item of import cargo and every item of export cargo. This data is available to all users of the system, subject to their access rights. The inventory system comprises a computer file for each vessel due to call and arriving at the port. It shows the date and time of estimated arrival and also the actual date and time of arrival and departure.

There is also a computer file and manifest information from each port of loading and there is a facility whereby equipment control information passes automatically to the Ship's Agent, a facility for Customs entries to be compared automatically against information on the manifest file, a facility to 'write off' the cargo, a facility for commercial and Customs release authority to pass automatically to the wharfinger, a facility to control removal and reception of cargo and a facility to maintain security of confidential information.

The inventory control aspects go as far as possible in the use of manifest information by asking for certain elements to be entered in a particular format. This had to be an interim answer until standards were available; MCP could not wait, but all known possibilities were taken into account through involvement with SITPRO, ISO and other standards bodies.

Phase II introduction had the effect of reducing the average clearance times still further to two hours. It also removed the need for ships agents to distribute copies of paper manifests (and amendments thereto) and for Customs to issue paper release notes, since all this was achieved through FCP80's inventory using the files and facilities mentioned above. These clearance times were achieved and maintained during a period of dramatic growth in entry through-put at Felixstowe, from 240,000 at the commencement of Phase I to 480,000 in 1987.

FCP80 proved to be commercially successful and is now in operation in 12 locations, including nine ports, two Inland Clearance Depots and an airport.

The Future

Although technically in advance of any other UK Port Information System, FCP80 is still under development. Apart from ambitions of increasing subscribers within the UK Freight Industry and then to UK industry in general, MCP seek to complete the link to their overseas trading partners. This is where problems still exist, for though the answer is simple until now it has been almost impossible to achieve.

Traders, from seller to purchaser, despatch to delivery, payment to receipt of funds, need the means to transmit and receive data. They need to use existing equipment, gain access to international networks and transmit to their client's existing equipment. Unfortunately the range of equipment is vast, there are many international means of data transmission and there are many local, national and commercially interested sectors. These include the hardware supplier, network operators and the service providers. In short, electronic data interchange (EDI) is the current challenge. From the above observations it is clear that implementation depends on acceptance of internationally agreed standards. Such standards are emerging and are fortunately being driven forward by the trader to serve his needs and are now generating the means to send and accept data from and deliver it to a variety of manufacturer's equipment. The major hardware manufacturers have acknowledged that Open System Interconnection (OSI) is desirable and inevitable. It will not happen overnight, but it is happening. MCP can look forward to the day when its system can capture data in an internationally agreed format in the area of invoicing, payment, bills of lading, letters of credit, etc where many commonly used documents are being reshaped into EDI format. The UK is seen to be ahead in the development of EDI use and MCP is playing an active part through membership of The EDI Association.

The Company is also making full use of developments as they occur. Software was commissioned and installed in February 1988 which allows our 500 subscribers to access services such as Transpotel, Boxmart and EXIS via the IBM and GE Information Services networks. In June 1988 final testing took place of software which enables subscribers to use the Transpotel EDI system for transfer of SADs and Invoices, both nationally and internationally. EDIFACT standards of message formatting will be used as they become available and participation in the EDI Association's activities is seen as important in this respect. Enormous advantages accrue to MCP subscribers; they do not need to invest in communications equipment and a great deal of software, since most of this is taken care of centrally. It also means that they need only one terminal, with access to all facilities being made through their FCP80 equipment, using a menu to select the required service. Tests on an X.25 link took place in early 1988 and it is hoped that this will be in place by the time this publication goes to press.

It is MCP's intention to make the system as flexible as possible, so that subscribers can continue to benefit from all developments in the VADS/EDI area, irrespective of the network on which they are based, without the need to become involved in technical detail, save perhaps installing some minimal end-user software.

MCP has always regarded its FCP80 System as the standard by which other port information systems are judged. It is hoped that, through cooperation, collaboration and coordination, within the framework of competition, MCP will also be among the front-runners as an EDI service provider. The sites currently served by FCP80 include: Felixstowe, Harwich, Great Yarmouth, Lowestoft, Chatham, Sheerness, Teesport, Bellport (Newport), Sutton International Freight Terminal (Nottingham), Southend Airport, Lenham ICD. There are currently over 350 users. Further information concerning MCP may be obtained from: N J Hammond, Chief Executive, Maritime Cargo Processing plc, Suite 1, Orwell House, Ferry Lane, Felixstowe, Suffolk IP11 8QL. Telephone: 0394 674422. Fax: 0394 673363.

MOTORNET

Further information concerning Motonet may be found in Appendix A.

ODETTE

Organisation for Data Exchange by Teletransmission in Europe

Introduction

In the summer of 1983, the four major vehicle manufacturers in the UK approached their trade association, the Society of Motor Manufacturers & Traders (SMMT) to support activities in forming a Committee. The objective of the Committee was to investigate and recommend procedures for transmission of commercial information directly between suppliers and manufacturers' computers.

In the course of the investigations, contact was made with the German Automotive trade associations, the VDA, who had been working on the concept for some time and had a procedure operating within Germany, between vehicle manufacturers and some of their main suppliers. Agreement was reached, in principle, that discussions on a European basis would be desirable and the UK made similar approaches to France, talking with Renault and Peugeot, and Italy talking to FIAT.

There was mutual agreement to joint discussions and a date was fixed for March 1984 where all four countries met together at the EEC in Brussels to decide how to organise the way forward. Belgium and Holland indicated their interest in the subject and were also invited. At this meeting it was agreed that a Committee should be formed to investigate, develop and coordinate standards for teletransmission of information within the automotive industry. At subsequent meetings it was agreed that five Working Groups should be set up to commence detailed work on data elements, formats, syntax, communications and a pilot project.

A 'Memorandum of Understanding' by all parties involved was drawn-up. This document states the intentions of the group and signature indicates the intention of each country to participate whole-heartedly in the work of the project. Signatories also agreed to subscribe to central funds which are used to offset administration costs and some travel and subsistence for officers of the Committee.

It was agreed that the position of Secretary should be a permanent post for the life of the ODETTE Project and the SMMT agreed to loan Mr Shepherd as from January 1985.

The efforts of the Working Groups were consolidated into the publication of the first set of standard formats (messages) in 1985. In subsequent years it was agreed that the development of further formats and the start of implementation into the working environment would take place.

In the context of the auto-industry and the relations between constructors and suppliers, the aims of ODETTE: *are* to define the rules (standards) which will permit the communication between constructors' and suppliers' computers; *are not* (at least currently) to design and install the software and hardware necessary to implement these standards (such tasks being the responsibility of each

ODETTE member). ODETTE can therefore be viewed as a standard and not a system.

General Organisation

The objective of the ODETTE project is stated in the Memorandum of Understanding which all participating countries sign:

> *To act as the coordinating Committee to assist with the implementation and use of European standards to enable the teletransmission of data between suppliers and manufacturers to standardise the documents which are currently used (in both content and structure), to establish a common syntax, to suggest transmission systems, to experiment with the products thus defined and provide a framework for use by the Participants.*

> *To act as a forum for the discussion of other activities that would benefit from a joint European approach aimed at improving overall efficiency.*

The Committee is drawn currently from Belgium, France, Germany, Italy, The Netherlands, Spain, Sweden and the United Kingdom, predominantly from members of the automotive industries, with Austria, Denmark, Eire, Finland, Luxembourg, Greece, Switzerland and the USA receiving regular information through correspondence.

Countries participating in the Committee are referred to as parties and the recommendation is that each party may send a delegation of up to three representatives to the main meeting. It is further recommended that the three delegates should ideally be organised as spokesmen supported by a representative of the vehicle manufacturers and a representative of component suppliers. In addition to the official delegation parties may also have observers in attendance. Other interested organisations such as the European Commission, Customs and Industry organisations such as CLCA, CLEPA and the national Trade Facilitation Representatives are also welcome to attend as observers by prior agreement.

It is expected that delegates to the Main Committee undertake the responsibility of representing their country's views at meetings and of communicating the working of ODETTE to their countries. This responsibility is discharged via the support of national groups organised either through trade associations or through special bodies set up specifically. The national organisations are expected to be able to draw on wide experience, expertise and range of interests. It is not necessary for the national organisations to be registered with ODETTE and all reporting is expected to be achieved via the delegation to the Main Committee.

From the parties a Chairman and Vice Chairman are elected for a duration of one year supported by a permanent Secretary. This group is known as the Executive and is responsible for planning the overall strategy of the project, controlling the administration, coordinating the efforts of the participants and for generally promoting interest in and enthusiasm for the ODETTE Project.

To support the strategies of the Executive, Working Groups are formed to undertake specific areas of development. At the moment these comprise:

Group 1: To identify data elements required, element sizes, element terminology and to compile directories.

Group 2: To identify the elements to be combined for a particular transaction, to assess the status of each element and to structure the elements into a message format for transmission.

Group 3: To provide the syntax rules to be used in the designing of messages.

Group 4: To provide recommendations on the methods to be employed for the physical transmission of information.

GROUP 5: To coordinate practical tests so as to confirm the validity of the work of the Groups and to report on the results regularly.

Group 6: To investigate and report on potential legal problems linked to the electronic transmission of trade data.

Group 7: To provide recommendations on codification aspects of messages.

Group 8: To investigate and make recommendations on syntax software and where necessary undertake contractual negotiations.

A central budget has been agreed to cover the costs of staff and travel for the Secretariat and the travel costs of the Executive and Group Leaders. At the moment the Commission is providing meeting rooms and translation facilities for the main Plenary Sessions, most other meetings are organised through group leaders. Costs of these meetings together with staff time and costs are absorbed by the individual companies. The central budget is charged on a share basis with France, Germany, Italy, Spain, Sweden and the UK contributing two shares of the total each; Belgium and The Netherlands one share each. To reduce the number of currency exchanges the costs of the Secretariat are paid in two instalments, January and June, with all other costs being balanced against contributions within each country, any adjustments necessary being made in June and December by actual cash transfers.

No provision has been made in the central budget for any consultancy or software sub-contracting although it is recognised that it may be necessary to obtain external support. Should it be necessary, each national delegation will be expected to obtain the required additional funds from its own country after the matter has been debated and a unanimous vote obtained in the main Plenary Session of the Committee.

This initiative was launched before EDIFACT received international recognition although ODETTE now intends to migrate to that standard over a number of years from their current Trade Data Interchange (TDI) protocol.

Points of contact should be made via the Leader of the delegation in each country, a member of the Executive or Group Leader, or direct to the Secretary if this is thought more appropriate. These lines of communication may be used to obtain information on the work or to make submissions to the Main Committee or Working Groups. Further information concerning ODETTE may be obtained from: Alan Shepherd, The Secretary, ODETTE, C/O SMMT, Forbes House,

Halkin Street, London SW1X 7DS. Telephone: 01 235 7000. Telex: 21628. Fax: 01 235 7112.

PACE

Ports Automated Cargo Environment

PACE provides the geographically widespread London Port community with access to the Direct Trader Input facilities of DEPS. It also provides other local facilities, such as electronic mail and the generation and routeing of key output prints. This entails message switching and computer protocol conversion, which allows the London Port community to transfer information automatically throughout the community, for example, the notification to terminal operators and wharfingers of Customs clearance.

London Port is currently enjoying a renaissance. Moving some 50 million tonnes of freight this year and growing at more than five per cent per annum, London handles more than two and a half times as much freight as its nearest UK rival and PACE is becoming essential to the continued growth and success of the Port community. PACE is the most flexible of all DTI systems, offering a choice of three different computer communications protocols, which makes linking up as easy as possible. The community of freight agents, shippings agents, shipping lines, terminal operators, wharfingers, HM Customs and Excise officers and others, are spread out over a 30 mile radius of London and will generate in excess of 210,000 import entries during the systems' first full year.

PACE runs on a dualled ITL Momentum 10000 configuration and offers a choice of four physical access options (kilostream, private circuit, multipoint and dial-up) and CO3 and 3270 synchronous and the VT100 asynchronous protocols. There are more than 25 different types of end-user equipment currently linked to PACE, from Amstrads and Apples through IBM, Olivetti and ICL PCs, up to DEC mini-computers, with the vast majority running intelligent software. Further information concerning PACE may be obtained from: Robert Halhead, BTAT, 60-68 St Thomas Street, London SE1 3QU. Telephone: 01 407 3455. Telex: 268589. Fax: 01 403 5531.

PERIOD ENTRY USER ASSOCIATION

The Period Entry User Association was formed in 1984. Its major objectives are to promote Period Entry systems of Customs clearance (import and export), provide a national point of reference to Period Entry users, provide a forum for discussion between both members, and HM Customs & Excise, thereby influencing the future direction of the Period Entry system and import/export formalities in general.

The Association has not been directly involved in the development of EDI systems or formats but its members are already actively using EDI to provide data to HM Customs & Excise in a number of forms, many having their own in-house EDI systems. The Association is, therefore, involved with the practical use of EDI and for this reason take an active interest in system developments.

The Association is a unique organisation providing the opportunity for people actually involved in the day to day import/export process to converse directly with Customs Officers involved in the policy making process, on a regular basis. This position has enabled changes to be made far more effectively than might otherwise have been possible. Further information concerning The Period Entry User Association may be obtained via the registered office at the following address: The Period Entry User Association, 18 Beech Glen, Crowthorne Road, Bracknell, Berkshire RG12 3QL.

PHARMNET

Further information concerning Pharmnet may be found in Appendix A.

RINET

Reinsurance and Insurance Network

The purpose of RINET is to place the insurance industry in the strongest possible position for developments in financial services worldwide, by improving the efficiency and speed of communication between insurers, brokers and re-insurers. Development of RINET has occured because: new opportunities are being made available through information technology; networking is success-fully developing between industries; international networking is inevitable in the insurance and reinsurance markets.

The Objective Of RINET

The objective is to build towards one common network with one message standard for the whole industry. This should necessitate only one interface and one conversion between the network and the in-house functions of the individual users. The benefits of such an approach lead to: increased speed of business processing; improved accuracy; improved efficiency due to standardised message exchange and direct 'desk-to-desk' communication between business partners; cost reduction through lower transaction and administration costs; access to external information services.

The current market position is that: network services are commercially available; no commonly accepted message standard exists; many companies will welcome technical assistance to exploit network services.

RINET will provide the following: a data network that interconnects different EDP-systems between individual users; software that will enable companies to join the network; standards for accounting messages to be exchanged through the network; assistance in implementation; a foundation for the eventual development of additional functions such as standardised offer and acceptance procedures, transfer of funds and accumulation of statistics. RINET will be developed by using a value added and data service supplier to provide: file transfer functions for standardised reinsurance accounting messages; a mailbox function for free format messages; access to financial databases; other services as required.

In addition PC software will be provided to member companies allowing easy and quick linking to the network. Functions of this software will include: data communication; interconnection to in-house mainframe; calculations of the individual outgoing accounts based on the total figures; conversion between in-house and RINET codes; editing and listing facility.

It is highly likely however that many companies will find it convenient to develop their own software for their mainframe computer to link directly into the network.

Message Standards

RINET will adopt internationally accepted principles (EDIFACT) supported by UN, EEC, ISO and national standards organisations. Additionally RINET will: allow flexibility in the amount of data provided; provide the ability to convert between RINET and in-house standards; and as a first step develop standards for non-life treaty accounting messages.

Implementation will start in 1989 following a test phase in 1988 and will concentrate on Europe as a first step, then other markets through an expansion of RINET or through interconnection to similar networks. With this in mind it is proposed to establish: a company with full infrastructure and its own staff that provides all the services; a 'societe cooperative' with headquarters in Brussels working on a non-pofit basis for the insurance industry. All European insurance, reinsurance companies and brokers will be invited to become RINET members from the start with RINET being entirely financed and controlled by members. Initially ownership will be equal to each member company, however, in the long-term ownership will be in proportion to usage. Management of RINET will reside with: a board composed of representatives of national markets; a Management Committee; and a General Manager.

Financial Arrangements

Each member will initially be required to subscribe share capital of BF 200,000 and guarantee RINET a loan of BF 2,000,000. Members may guarantee larger amounts as loans. From amongst the founding members substantial loan commitments have been made. The pricing structure of RINET will be based on; volume-related user charges plus annual subscription; receiving companies will pay the costs for 'standardised' messages the sender will pay for 'free format' messages.

The following companies were founders of RINET: The Mercantile & General Reinsurance Company plc; Munich Reinsurance Company; Nacional Reaseguros SA; Nederlands Reassurantie Groep NV; Skandia International Insurance Corporation; Societe Commerciale de Reassurance; Swiss Reinsurance Company; Unione Italiana de Riassicurazione SpA. Further information concerning RINET may be obtained from: Xavier Dereppe, General Manager, RINET SC, Boulevard de la Woluwe 660 Bte 3, B-1200 Brussels, Belgium. Telephone: 010 322 761 6211. Fax: 010 322 770 1673.

SADBEL

This is a computerised clearance system operating at Customs posts in Brussels, Antwerp and Zaventem. A declarant inputs consignment details to the Customs computer which then returns a validated declaration to his computer/printer.

The system will be extended, progressively, to the 15 or so main Belgian

Customs posts, by 1989. The other 75 offices are being equipped with microcomputers to validate import declarations and process accounts.

Similar Customs systems are being launched in almost all European countries. SOFI in France, SAGITTA in The Netherlands, DEPS in the UK.

SEAGHA

Systems Electronic and Adapted Data Interchange in the Port of Antwerp

SEAGHA is a cooperative company, open to all, founded with the objective of setting up, managing and operating a data transmission system. SEAGHA was founded by the 'Antwerpse Gemeenschap voor de Haven' (Antwerp Port Community—AGHA), on 28 October 1986, as a cooperative company by the six professional associations listed below. For operational reasons these six associations are divided in to three groups. One group is concerned with goods handling—The Professional Association of Antwerp Master Stevedores and Port Operators and The Association of Cargo-Handling Enterprises; another group is concerned with forwarding activities—Association of Shipping Agents for Industry and Antwerp Freight Forwarders Association; the third group is concerned with shipping—Antwerp Shipping Federation and Belgian Ship-owner's Association.

The foundation of SEAGHA and the decision to set up a data transmission system, were the result of an inquiry carried out by the Studiecentrum voor de Expansie van Antwerpen (Studycentre for the Expansion of Antwerp—SEA) which inquired into the need of a computerised port information system. This inquiry took place among the member companies of the aforementioned professional associations. SEAGHA's Board of Directors has nine members, with each group being represented by three Directors. There is also an Executive Committee with three members (1 representative for each group) in addition to SEAGHA's General Manager and AGHA's Secretary-General.

This SEAGHA-organisation is charged with the task of setting up and development of the SEAGHA-system. The nominal capital of the cooperative is unlimited. The starting capital amounts to BF seven million, contributed by the six professional associations being part of AGHA, plus the Chamber of Commerce and Industry of Antwerp. To be able to use the SEAGHA-system, the potential subscriber must first become a cooperative member, and must also comply with a number of contractual obligations.

At present, individual companies are able to associate after having received the approval of the professional association of which they are a member. To this end they have to subscribe for at least one share (current value amounts to BF 125,000) and for a maximum of 10 shares. Companies providing other services can become a member through the agency of the professional associations concerned with the three groups.

Since SEAGHA is an open company and, as will be seen below, an open system as well, other companies which are non-members but are involved either nationally or internationally in port or transport operations will be allowed to participate in SEAGHA at a later stage, once immediate requirements have been met. This however, will be on condition that they comply with the contractual terms set out in the code of internal order.

From this it is apparent that there are two sorts of users: directly involved users (cooperative members)—companies which are members of one of the professional associations; indirectly involved users (contractors)—firms or authorities which are not members of one of the professional associations but which can be further classified by location, that is, the Antwerp region or elsewhere, in Belgium or abroad.

The SEAGHA system

SEAGHA is a system which provides its users, either computerised or not, the means (programs, equipment and support included) to convert data on documents into structured data sets in accordance with internationally recommended standards and to transmit these structured sets as electronic messages to one or more addressees of their choice. The system required to achieve this, consists of several components: SEAGHA-Support; SEAGHA-Bridge; SEAGHA-Net; SEAGHA clearing; the SEAGHA manual.

SEAGHA-Support

Organisation

The general manager supervises the whole team and concept. He is supported by staff functions including secretarial service and strategy and planning functions. A traditional administrative service attends to the bookkeeping, finance, personnel, legal problems and purchase.

Customer support

This department is divided into a sales service, responsible for public relations and sales and an after-sales service which is responsible for customer follow-up and help-desk.

Program development

From the very start, SEAGHA made it clear that it would be responsible for the analysis and the development of the software.

Documentation and training

To be able to use the SEAGHA-system, users will receive the necessary documentation and training. A permanent service will be responsible for the training of the users in order to familiarise them with the software and hardware.

Installation and implementation

The installation and the implementation of the hardware, consisting of the systems and the network, is prepared and supported by the SEAGHA organisation on the user's premises.

Exploitation and maintenance

The product support department is responsible for the well-functioning of the hardware installations and the upkeeping of the system. The analysis and development of the software will be constantly improved and updates will be delivered to the customers.

An EDI-department assesses the evolution of the standardisation of data elements throughout the world. By means of EDI, commercial transactions will be realised between different user systems: these systems will communicate at a higher speed and at a higher grade of security than was possible up to now. Electronic messages are set up in cooperation with on the one hand the working groups active in the Antwerp Port Community and on the other hand with the national, European or other working groups, members of the user-communities. Running across this formal organisation is the project organisation which is developed as the project involved, demands. The SEAGHA organisation will be staffed in relation to the progress of the project as a whole.

SEAGHA-Bridge

As SEAGHA allows users, who have already computerised, to participate in the SEAGHA system, while retaining both their own in-house system, programs and data structures, and the fact that these systems may differ in make, operating system and programming language, it is necessary to adopt a common language in order to make communication possible. This communication between computers is made possible by an interface which is similar to a bridge, SEAGHA-Bridge.

Translation to a common language

As for the common language, it has been decided to opt for international standards for the electronic data interchange of commercial data. These standards are adopted by the United Nations and the International Standards Organisation (ISO). These standards also specify how the data should be structured. The SEAGHA-Bridge interface provides software which translates the in-house data structure to these international standards and in the opposite direction.

Input Handler and Output Handler

For non-computerised companies, modules are to be provided for data entry and storage. To utilise this facility the user of the SEAGHA-system firstly has to give, by means of the input handler, a manual input concerning the content of the message. This happens by means of an input program and input screens (Master Document Generator). The electronic messages will be transformed by the output handler again into readable standard documents which will be printed. Existing data can be modified. These stored data can then be used to construct universal standard messages, which can, if wanted, be returned to the network, thus closing the ring.

In this way, SEAGHA ensures that, thanks to the SEAGHA-system, non-computerised companies can nevertheless participate in the electronic data interchange. In addition to this, modules are available to all users, regardless of whether they are computerised or otherwise, for printing out the stored data or for editing them as the user may require. The user, if he wants, can then use this module to convert electronic messages or other stored data into conventional messages.

Formatting and deformatting

The first step is to collect the required data from the in-house computer, and format and structure them in accordance with the international standards. They are then packaged, still in accordance with international standards into universal standard messages and the message thus created is passed to the network for transmission to a predetermined addressee. In the opposite direction, software in the module captures a universal standard message from the network, unpacks it and formats the remaining data to conform to the in-house data structure and transfers it to the in-house computer system.

Front end processor

All these functions can be monitored easily by using an orderly, user-friendly menu-driven interface. This interface, SEAGHA-Bridge, is being developed by SEAGHA for installation and application on a front end processor. This offers technical advantages such as improved definition of responsibilities, relieving the in-house computer and providing a physical barrier between the in-house computer and the network. The front end processor can moreover serve as a stand-alone system. If there is no internal computer system, this offers a convenient solution for non-computerised users who nevertheless want to participate in SEAGHA. On the other hand a stand-alone system, installed on remote locations, can offer a convenient extension of the in-house system.

Users, who want to apply the SEAGHA-Bridge functions on their in-house system must attend to the development of the necessary software themselves, however, they must conform to the specifications required by SEAGHA. To summarise there are three possibilities for the use of SEAGHA-Bridge: the non-computerised firm, uses SEAGHA-Bridge as an EDI stand-alone system; the user disposing of an in-house system, places in front of this a front end processor which has to carry out all the specific tasks of SEAGHA-Bridge; the computerised user applies the SEAGHA-Bridge functions on his in-house system.

SEAGHA-Net

The third component of the system is SEAGHA-Net. This is a network consisting of two components, each of which is a subsystem. The first subsystem is formed by the public telephone (PTT) or the DCS-network, or a combination of both, and the necessary modems for connecting users to the node described below. In principle the network is a star-network which may consist of common telephone lines of the public switched net, leased lines and lines belonging to the PTT's DCS network (X.25 protocol), which may be leased or otherwise.

SEAGHA-Clearing

SEAGHA-Clearing forms a second sub-system, and is a message despatching centre which also serves as the node and traffic controller.

Security control

SEAGHA guarantees the confidentiality of the contents of the messages by applying special techniques. A strict logic security is applied to both users and message traffic. SEAGHA sees to it that the traffic and the type of messages between users can not be checked by other users. Strangers will not have access to the system.

Electronic mailbox function

The electronic mailbox function in fact allows users to drop messages in various 'mailboxes' belonging to a number of addressees, while access is limited to the user's own mailbox, which in turn is well protected against access by strangers. The principle which has been adopted is that the sender drops the message in the addressee's mailbox and the latter collects the message. Everything, however, takes place using a controllable procedure which can simulate automatic message 'traffic'. For every message sent, a charge will be related to the duration of the message and the number of characters transmitted.

Gateways

In a later stage of the project the users will be able to communicate with other systems and networks via specifi⌐ ports, known as gateways. This will offer the possibility to use additional network facilities such as databases, mailing lists and so on. Gateways are already in place with the port authorities (APICS), Customs (SADBEL), financial institutions (banks), insurance, rail (NMBS) and several transport organisations.

Value added function

The gateway function can be combined with a value added function, if for instance an indirect relation, another network or system should use a special protocol, or should fail to use international standards, or use them incompletely. In such cases a one-off additional translation applicable to the entire SEAGHA network could be added to that gateway (special gate). This can of course also apply in the opposite direction.

SEAGHA-Manual

Apart from containing instructions for the use of the system and the procedures and regulations to be adopted, the SEAGHA Manual contains detailed information about the international standards used. These international standards are those recommended by the United Nations Economic Commission for Europe (UNECE). They contain among other things: the syntax to be applied for the composition of electronic messages (EDIFACT); a list of data elements to be used—United Nations Trade Data Elements Directory (UNTDED); general provisions for the interchange of data—United Nations Guidelines for Trade Data Interchange (UNGTDI).

Use is made of Universal Standard Messages (UNSM) for the interchange itself. The universal standard messages used in SEAGHA, which are composed of data segments, are described in detail in the manual. These messages are the result of the discussions and preparations of various working committees both beyond and within SEAGHA. To this end SEAGHA participates in various national and international working groups. As a result SEAGHA will be able to interchange data internationally.

Methodology

All the working groups meet regularly in order to prepare electronic messages which will be tested in a pilot project. SEAGHA coordinates and processes the results for inclusion in the manual. The chosen standards are, as has already been explained, standards which have been recommended by the UNECE in order to facilitate commercial procedures.

Parallel to the work of the 'standards' working group, the AGHA steering committee has been involved with the foundation of the SEAGHA cooperative company, and has taken an option on the architecture of the projected system.

In principle SEAGHA will do everything on its own, including system construction, management, and operation, bearing in mind the rule 'make it or buy it'. During construction internal tests will be made. This will be followed by external testing in a pilot project, in which pilot companies will participate. Pilot companies are those companies who are prepared to assist with the starting up and the debugging of the SEAGHA system, and are willing to make their knowledge and infrastructure available to the port community, as represented by SEAGHA. Nevertheless a pilot company must meet certain requirements.

SEAGHA has been assisted by external consultants for the drawing up of an overall project plan, namely the Antwerp branch of Coopers & Lybrand on the functional design and the determination of network topologies.

Timetable

The overall project plan was finalised early February 1987, and by mid-March a start was made to drawing up the data model, immediately followed by the functional and technical analysis. SEAGHA-Bridge and SEAGHA-Clearing were started from October 1987. SEAGHA-Clearing should be available in the second half of 1988.

The pilot project was started in the first half of 1988 between about 30 companies. From March 1988 the sending of electronic messages within the pilot project started. The pilot project has been split up into a number of steps. At every stage the electronic message interchange between various operational functions will be checked against the everyday situation and the practicability of the system. From the end of 1988, the horizontal expansion, that is the marketing of the SEAGHA system, will be started.

Initially only those companies who are directly involved (about 400), will be served. These are the members of the professional associations, promoting the project. Gateways and additional facilities will be dealt with and added to the system as demand for them becomes apparent, if at all possible in parallel with the other developments. In this way the gateway with SADBEL is planned to begin mid-1988 and the gateway with APICS will start around the end of 1988.

Cost Of Implementation

The costs for the construction of the SEAGHA system until the end of 1988, have been estimated at about BEF 70 million. This will be financed by the funds contributed by the founding professional associations, a loan and supplemented by an early call for subscriptions on capital by the member-users of the cooperative company. SEAGHA will recover the investment by claiming from the users a one-off start-up fee, charges for using the network, and maintenance fees for the programs, the code tables, the international standards and the manuals. Moreover for every message sent, a charge will be related to the duration of the message and the number of characters transmitted. Special rates will be applied for the use of the system beyond normal business hours and for large volumes.

The user has to bear the cost for the required machinery but he will get support from SEAGHA which will organise a joint purchase in order to obtain the most favourable terms for the member-users. Users with small volumes could start by using SEAGHA-Bridge in conjunction with an IBM-compatible personal computer linked to SEAGHA-Clearing by means of a modem. This can be regarded as a very low cost solution.

Finally every user will have to bear the cost for the line connection with SEAGHA-Clearing. There are a number of possible solutions for this, depending on the volume of messages transmitted or received, and the geographical location of the user. SEAGHA will assist the user on the best decision, by applying economic models in order to determine the most favourable price/performance ratio.

Further information concerning SEAGHA may be obtained from: Louis Soudan, General Manager, SEAGHA CV, Brouwersvliet 33/8, B-2000 Antwerp, Belgium. Telephone: 010 323 22737. Telex: 35678. Fax: 010 323 16728.

SHIPNET

SHIPNET was an initiative of 40 companies in the freight industry, together with IBM, to improve the speed and accuracy of data-transfer between trading partners. The balance of participation was markedly different from that of DISH—most of the trading companies were medium-sized or small and there is a substantial proportion of forwarders. The project's data-base included some special features, such as access to shipping schedules.

Originally launched in the UK, SHIPNET is confident of expansion into Europe and beyond, over the next few years. IBM, which has committed itself to using EDIFACT for SHIPNET, estimates the potential, overall trading community EDI market in Europe at some 500,000 companies. Further information concerning SHIPNET may be obtained from The EDI Association.

SITPRO

Simplification of International Trade Procedures Board

SITPRO was established by the Department of Trade & Industry in 1970 as the UK's trade facilitation body. Its current mission is to make British companies more competitive in world trade by attacking red tape, by developing the skills of those involved and by encouraging the use of information technology in the trading, distribution and payment processes.

In EDI, SITPRO has led the development of standards in Europe. In 1978 it published the SITPRO syntax rules for data exchange and a directory of data elements. The syntax rules subsequently became the basis of the UN/ECE Guidelines for Trade Data Interchange (GTDI). In 1985 SITPRO led the European team in the UN-JEDI initiative which produced the EDIFACT standard and has contributed significantly to the subsequent EDIFACT developments through the EDIFACT Board.

To help finance its standards work SITPRO markets through distributors an EDI translation package, Interbridge, which will translate messages in both the GTDI and EDIFACT syntaxes.

For further information on EDI Standards please contact: The EDI Standards Section, SITPRO, 26 King Street, London SW1Y 6QW.

SOFI 1 & SOFI 2

Systeme d'Ordinateurs pour le traitement du Fret International

This cooperative, Customs/agents/importers, computerised system was commissioned by French Customs to speed up international freight clearance. SOFI 1 had no automated interface between airlines and Customs and no automated cargo inventory control. Inventory control will be included in SOFI 2. In the longer term, French Customs may wish to establish an automated interface with other Customs EDI systems in, for example, the UK.

SOFI currently processes more than 40 per cent of the national entry volume. The processing centre at Osny (Oise) is linked to airports at Roissy and Orly, the Customs Directorate General in Paris and a large number of local Customs offices. Apart from Customs clearance routines, SOFI also performs such off-line operations as the preparation of foreign trade statistics and the printing of account statements for Customs collections.

It is planned to extend SOFI to all Customs offices, and to link up with private systems for inventory control and preparation of Customs declarations.

SWIFT

Society for World Interbank Financial Telecommunications

This is a major, perhaps the most important, truly international data interchange system. It serves more than 2,000 banks in over 50 countries, and is a leading example of electronic funds transfer (EFT). It was formed by banks themselves to provide a secure, completely confidential inter-bank message-transfer service. The Society has defined standard message formats to suit all types of exchanges and transactions required by the members. It handles over 850,000 messages daily. SWIFT was constructed some years before there was any sign of the emergence of international standards, such as EDIFACT, and is now considering what should be its future strategy, not only in relation to the core inter-bank activity, but also to any extensions of the SWIFT to other international trade participants.

The Message Text Standards

One of SWIFT's greatest strengths is undoubtedly its involvement in the development of message text standards. These allow financial institutions worldwide to communicate using a common language. Whenever it is possible

SWIFT uses existing international standards such as those developed by the International Organisation for Standardisation (ISO), or the International Chamber of Commerce (ICC). Yet the majority of message text standards are developed specifically for use in the SWIFT system. Despite their proprietary character they are increasingly being used by outside organisations and are thus recognised as de facto standards for financial messages. In addition to easing communication, standards facilitate the automation of operations, in the process helping to improve productivity, reduce costs and eliminate errors.

The standards are drawn up by groups composed of specialists nominated from the banks and SWIFT staff. Their purpose is to enhance existing standards and develop new ones in order to broaden the range of message types available to the network users. Each group is composed of eight to 10 people and meets roughly three times a year.

Permanent working groups exist for payments, financial trading, and documentary services whilst provisional groups are often set up to examine ad hoc issues: securities, travellers cheques, syndications, and gold and precious metals trading are some examples.

The development of internationally-approved banking standards has moved a step further with ISO's recognition of SWIFT as the registration authority for Bank Identifier Codes (BIC codes). The BIC code is a universal standard for identifying banks in telecommunications messages and is based on the methodology established by SWIFT to identify its users. BIC codes are allocated automatically to SWIFT banks and to non-SWIFT banks which request them. They are published by SWIFT in the 'Bank Identifier Code Directory' which is available to all banks upon request.

There are currently seven message categories covering more than 70 message types, each designed to meet the very precise data requirements of the transaction it represents. The text is organised into fields, some of which are mandatory and some optional. Mandatory fields contain information essential for the message to be processed. The optional fields are needed for complex transactions or when additional instructions are necessary. The seven message categories are as follows: customer transfers; bank transfers; foreign exchange; collections; securities; documentary credits; special messages.

System messages are also available to allow users to communicate with the system and vice versa. They are used to request certain system functions and special reports, for message retrieval, for training purposes and by SWIFT to respond to user requests and to inform them of system upgrades and new services. Each message is made up of a header, the message text, an authenticator and a trailer. The message is automatically encrypted when it enters the network to ensure secrecy. The message also contains an authenticator which guarantees that the message text has not been modified during transmission.

The Network

After 10 years of activity, the SWIFT telecommunications network covers all continents and has become an indispensable financial tool worldwide. The demands put on this fast, reliable and secure communication system are increasing daily.

The technical infrastructure of the present system consists of computer centres located around the world interconnected by high speed lines leased from national or commercial communications carriers. The hub of the network is made up of two Operating Centres, in the Netherlands and the United States, which connect to autonomous regional processing centres, usually one per connected country.

Users link to the network through computer-based terminals, called 'interfaces', installed on their own premises. Users are free to use any compatible interface they prefer, from small microprocessor-driven terminals to large mainframe systems. The present SWIFT I network has been operational since 1977 and despite being continually upgraded it has gradually reached its full capacity. Therefore it will be replaced by a new system called SWIFT II on a country-by-country basis, starting towards mid-1989. Further technical information concerning the two networks is available from SWIFT.

Support

SWIFT is a service organisation not just a provider of technological tools, hence a comprehensive range of support services is available to ensure that each user derives maximum benefits from the system. Such support services include: on-line support; implementation support; educational support; technical support; special projects support; user group support; roadshows; seminars; information/ documentation; regional support. In addition SWIFT offers SWIFT Terminal Services (STS), a wholly owned SWIFT subsidiary, which was created in 1980 to help users to benefit fully from the network through the provision of turnkey computerised interface devices. Since then, STS has grown rapidly and widened its product portfolio to offer a full range of network interface systems and application packages for every type and size of international financial institution.

STS is now the leading connection to SWIFT in two ways. Firstly, its unique relationship with SWIFT guarantees that all its products are immediately compatible with the network and all new functions.

Secondly, STS has won a major share of the market through superior service and cost-effective products. Over 70 per cent of all users have chosen STS products to interface to the network. The emphasis at STS is on customer support and service. STS offices worldwide assist SWIFT users to find the most suitable system and on-site consultancy provides unbiased technical advice and installation assistance. Furthermore, local user groups maintain a constant dialogue between STS and individual users in different geographical areas, whilst a regular newsletter, Interface, contains information about new product releases, technical updates and the experiences of users. Regular training courses are also held, giving practical advice on the use of STS products. For further information on products and services, contact STS at: Chausee de La Hulpe 164, 1170 Brussels, Belgium. Telephone: 010 322 674 2411. Telex: 617731.

Security

For SWIFT, a quality service implies safety, privacy, accuracy, reliability and timeliness. To achieve this, security is considered inherent to the system, from software to terminals, and from the physical installations right through to the staff in contact with the network.

Ensuring security at SWIFT is one of the responsibilities of the Chief Inspector's Office, a group of specialists whose task is to audit activities throughout the company and its subsidiaries. In order to ensure them total freedom in their investigations, they can report directly to the Board of Directors. Regular security checks are also undertaken by external auditors. Security is ensured by: maintaining a high level of site security; restricted system access; message checks; message privacy by encryption techniques; message authenticity procedures. Because of the extremely high level of security, SWIFT assumes financial liability for the accuracy, completeness, and timely delivery of all validated messages between the moment they enter and leave the network at the regional processor level. Further information concerning the organisational structure, membership requirements and technical details may be obtained from: The Marketing Director, SWIFT SC, avenue Ernest Solvay 81, 1310 La Hulpe, Belgium. Telephone: 010 322 656 3111. Telex: 26532. Fax: 010 322 656 3226.

TEDIS

The Trade Electronic Data Interchange Systems Programme

The Role Of The European Community

The European Community has recognised the strategic importance of rapid and coordinated development of EDI to improve trading relations between partners within the community. Within DGXIII of the European Commission there are several programmes focussed on the improvement of the European data communications networks, and already much work has been done in the area of standards and development to provide a common IT infrastructure. In particular there have been a number of programmes and projects involving the transfer of data between users.

An integrated services inter-institutional information system (INSIS) was launched in 1982. The Cooperation in Automation of Data and Documentation for Import/Export and Agriculture programme (CADDIA) has led on to the Coordinated Development (CD) project, which will standardise computerised customs clearance for transactions within the Community, and also with external countries. The Mercator project was set up to test out the practical difficulties of implementing EDI within the UN guidelines. It highlighted areas where more work is needed both at the communication network level and in terms of incompatible software implementations.

TEDIS programme

Following these several studies and initiatives a complete programme for expanding the use of EDI in a coordinated fashion within the Community was planned. The Council of Ministers approved these plans as the TEDIS programme on 5 October 1987 and it was launched early in 1988. TEDIS has two main objectives: coordination of the activities of the various groups actively involved with EDI in different industry sectors and an awareness campaign, to stimulate the demand for EDI from potential users and foster the provision of EDI software and services by public network providers or European VADS suppliers.

Coordination

The coordination activities of the TEDIS programme support the standardisation activities of the EDIFACT Board for Europe. DGXIII of the Commission provides the secretariat for the Board's activities, and for its various subgroups. These subgroups are composed of the different groups active in EDI within their respective industrial sectors. For example the Trade subgroup might comprise ODETTE within the automotive industry, CEFIC for the chemical industry and EDIFICE in the electronic sector. Subgroups to cover transport, banking and insurance are also to be set up.

As part of its technical support activity the TEDIS programme will also maintain a database of standard message types, segments, code sets and data elements in current use, so that potential users can avoid reinventing the wheel and readily make use of messages which have already been developed. In addition to these vertical sector-specific groups the TEDIS programme will coordinate issues of common interest across all sectors by means of so-called horizontal groups considering issues of telecommunications, message standardisation, security, legal aspects and software provision.

Awareness campaign

In parallel with its coordinating role, the TEDIS programme will encourage businesses throughout the Community to take an active interest in EDI. This will be achieved by the dissemination of appropriate information, the promotion of relevant seminars or conferences and by supporting EDI initiatives either by suppliers or by groups of users, particularly amongst small and medium sized enterprises.

Raising awareness is a gradual and many sided activity. TEDIS can give help to potential users either at a general or a specific level. It can put users in touch with their appropriate industry EDI group, or help them find other users with similar needs. It will keep EDI service or software suppliers abreast of current progress in developments. Finally it will offer specific help to small or medium-sized firms to become part of the EDI community.

What To Do Now

If you are currently using EDI and would like to be kept informed of developments, if you are thinking of implementing it within your own organisation, or simply if you are interested in EDI developments, get in touch with the TEDIS programme. Further information concerning the TEDIS programme may be obtained from: The TEDIS Programme, Commission of the European Communities, Directorate-General for Telecommunications, Information Industries and Innovation, DG XIII-D4, 200 Rue de la Loi, B-1040 Brussels, Belgium. Telephone: 010 322 235 7330. Fax: 010 322 236 0029.

TELEVAS SPA

Televas was formed at the end of 1985 as a joint venture between STET (the Italian holding for telecommunications services—51 per cent) and Montedison (the largest Italian chemical group—49 per cent). The intention of Televas is to provide EDI services and the relevant support to the users.

Working Structure

Televas is based in Milan, but has correspondent offices within the Italian STET offices. In Milan Televas employs 60 people: six administrative, 10 commercial, 44 programmers of which 70 per cent are dedicated to system engineering and the rest to application software.

Service Structure

All the EDI services of Televas are provided via public networks (Itapac, dial-up, videotex). Televas has a virtual network on Itapac allowing users to connect the EDI services from 100 Italian locations paying dial-up charges. The services are provided error-free (even if dial-up access is used) by means of a proprietary Televas software.

The central mainframe is formed by a Tandem VLX with 20 mips power, the applications are developed with a Tandem ETX system. A second Tandem VLX will be soon installed in a site whose location has yet to be disclosed. Protocols supported include: RJE 2780; 3780; SDLC 3777; X.25; BSC. Televas provides EDI services for the retail, transport, financial and pharmaceutical industries.

Service Profile

At the end of last year Televas launched Teledis, the first Italian EDI service for the retail industry (it is also believed to be the first European EDI service running on public networks). The service is aimed at interconnecting retail chains with their suppliers and with transporters. Teledis is an around-the-clock service supporting both EDIFACT and TRADACOMS standards. Televas can interconnect either the customer's mainframe or a PC. The local software provided by Televas gives the user many facilities.The telecommunication software provided enables the user to automatically switch between the best available Itapac node and the dial-up access. Other services provided include Telefin, aimed at interconnecting financial institution agents to their head-quarters via a secure network. Approximate costs of the service are as follows:

Once-off installation charge	Lire 3 million
Yearly fixed minimum	Lire 3 million
cost per character sent	Lire 0.3

Further information concerning Televas and the EDI services it offers on a European scale may be obtained from: Achille de Tommaso, General Manager, Televas SpA, Via Cernaia 2, 20100 Milano, Italy. Telephone: 010 392 265 56202. Telex: 353183. Fax: 010 392 265 90883.

TRADANET

Further information concerning Tradanet may be found in Appendix A.

TRADANET INTERNATIONAL

Further information concerning Tradanet International may be found in Appendix A.

TRANSNET

Dutch EDI initiative developed under the supervision of the national EAN Numbering Organisation in conjunction with GE Information Services. This organisation promotes and coordinates the development of the universal EAN product numbering and symbol marking system. About 90 per cent of all food products are included. Purchase orders, delivery and confirmation messages, invoices, product descriptions are all circulated electronically. The service has grown to include DIY products and pharmaceuticals and uses GTDI and TDED standards. Further information concerning Transnet may be obtained from: Philip de Roos, GE Information Services BV, Kabelweg 37, 1014 BA Amsterdam, The Netherlands. Telephone: 010 31 208 46825.

TRANSPOTEL

International electronic information system for the transport industry

Developments in modern transport make it necessary for all the parties involved to use the best of the electronic systems available in order to stay competitive. Whether running internal optimisation programmes or exchanging information with colleagues electronically, companies need to work to an integrated and efficient plan. In this context Transpotel's EDI service offers the European freighting industry a unique package of products and support. This has grown as a direct response to what Transpotel sees as the needs of its existing clients in the transport sector. In order to understand this better, it is worth taking a brief look at Transpotel's current products and history.

Transpotel And The Central Application

The Transpotel concept was developed by Transpotel International (TI). TI is a joint venture between a number of leading figures in the European freighting information business. Transpotel has developed its own range of on-line interactive, international database services for the European freighting market. Foremost among these is the road application—a database of freight consignments and empty trucks available by selected route into which the end-users themselves are able to input the information. Each announcement gives details of the points of departure and arrival, of weight, volume and contact data which can then be called up by all other users of the system.

The shipping application offers a database of liner sailings from key European ports, giving full schedules with arrival and sailing dates, again with the facility of end-users to input their own information. This application is supported by port information, such as local conditions and delays, and conference data. These cover the currency and bunkerage adjustment factors (CAF/BAF) and latest notices to shippers.

The system also includes mailbox facilities. Transpotel users can send each other messages in either free format or by using a reply card. A number of standard layouts are available which can be adapted to customers' designs. Free-formatted messages can be sent on a one-to-one basis or using a mailing list. Since its pilot phase Transpotel has marketed these services through national franchises, refining them and extending access from the original international videotex network to IBM's 3270 and, in some markets, asynchronous protocols. Today it has a user base of some 1000 companies, mainly road hauliers and freight forwarders, across 10 European countries.

However, it is clear that electronics can offer the Transpotel community more than central database applications. Through a joint venture with the Maritime Cargo Processing (MCP) group in the UK, Transpotel have extended their services to cover EDI.

This 450-strong community of forwarders, agents and customs brokers in 10 UK ports already operates with a high degree of sophisticated automation, including direct links to UK Customs computers (through Direct Trader Input). In collaboration with Transpotel this group is now seeking to increase the benefits of telecommunications by linking up with their continental trading partners. Further information concerning MCP is available in this information section.

Transpotel's Role In EDI

However, the experiences gained with the original Transpotel services have shown that acceptance and integration of electronics varies greatly across Europe. Nowhere is this more true than in the field of EDI. Although much of the groundwork in the freighting industry has already been laid by organisations such as SITPRO and a number of trial communities have been established, in practice EDI is not as simple as it might appear. Quite apart from issues such as the absence of internationally standardised documents and a universally accepted electronic language for their transmission, major hurdles have to be overcome by companies wishing to embrace EDI.

To send documents electronically the user must have appropriate software packages on his in-house computer which will generate the document and an editor to put it into an accepted form for transmission via a network. Having selected his editor packages the user must ensure that not only his own organisation but also his trading partners are installed on an electronic mailbox service and are fully equipped to work with it. In all these vital areas Transpotel has a service to offer current users and other interested communities.

One thing that Transpotel is not and should not aim to be is an author or co-author of standardised documents. There are already quite clearly established working groups among the parties involved who are tackling these issues. Running a network itself, too, lies outside Transpotel's terms of reference. In this area, IBM, GE Information Services and the PTTs are increasingly active. However, the networks are not yet interlinked (and are unlikely to be so in the short term), nor can any one network be said to be predominant. Users are therefore faced with a choice of networks and with the additional problem of which network their trading partners have opted for. To make matters more complicated GE Information Services and IBM have also developed their own software packages. With the increasing array of sources the small to medium-sized players will need some form of mass distribution services to be able to handle international electronic documentation. This function could always be provided by the major VADS themselves, but Transpotel is filling the gap that the VADS created in their present approach to the market.

Just as importantly, before a company can get the benefits of sending its documents electronically, it has to have its relevant trading partners linked in to the same EDI service. With tens of thousands of separate enterprises—be they shippers, forwarders, agents, ports, customs or hauliers—making up the European freighting market, this will be a considerable undertaking, again, this is where Transpotel comes in. Transpotel will take on the problem of linking any company's trading partners into the Transpotel EDI Service anywhere within its growing network. For this purpose Transpotel has developed a workstation to allow end-users to perform EDI and access Transpotel's range of database services via PCs. The workstation itself can be divided into three parts, the workstation manager, EDI services and the original database applications.

The Workstation Manager

Transpotel's workstation manager allows: easy access to different services via simple menus; maintenance of an 'access code file' of telephone number and ids for all registered services; automatic dial-up procedures.

EDI services

Transpotel offers a number of services relevant to EDI. Firstly it offers installation facilities for specific editor packages to accept and create data files from or for other computers. Data files can be re-edited and stored in the workstation. Files can be addressed to specific trading partners by network and built up into batches for transmission. Secondly, Transpotel offers translation of batch files into EDIFACT standard for transmission to each installed network and retrieval of EDIFACT—standard batch files and transmission back into data files for access through existing editor packages. Additionally an 'address book' of trading partners with network details is available.

This list briefly outlines some of the key functionality that is built into the workstation. One of its unique features is the ability to access multiple networks. Additional network links will be able to be added modularly.

Since it is very unlikely that IBM, GE Information Services and the PTTs will interconnect in the short/medium term, a minimum of three different network links will be necessary. Although Transpotel may only be offering an international EDI service via one network, its customers will need to handle EDI nationally as well and hence need the flexibility of being able to access more than one network. This can be done using the Transpotel service using whatever network Transpotel contracts with. Further information concerning Transpotel may be obtained from: Mike Ratcliffe, Managing Director, Transpotel, Koopmansstraat 9, 2288 BC Rijswijk, The Netherlands. Telephone: 010 31 709 03730. Telex: 7032695. Fax: 010 31 701 90654.

UNCID

Uniform Rules of Conduct for Interchange of Trade Data by Teletransmission

The UNCID rules are meant to provide a background for users of EDIFACT and other systems of EDI. They lay down minimum standards of professional care and behaviour for commercial parties engaged in a trade deal involving EDI by teletransmission. The UNCID rules contain provisions on the obligation of the parties to follow agreed interchange standards, duty of care in respect of correctness of transmission, identification of transmissions, acknowledgement of transmissions, confirmation of content, protection of trade data and storage of data.

Though voluntary like all ICC Codes, Rules and Guidelines, UNCID provide a foundation on which the business parties involved can build a 'communications agreement', a contract with legally binding effect. Copies of the guide may be obtained from: The ICC, Centrepoint, 103 New Oxford Street, London WC1A 1QB. Telephome: 01 240 5558.

UNICORN

United Nations EDI for Cooperation in Reservation Networks

The UNICORN group exists to promote the use of interactive EDI for reservation and similar functions within the travel, leisure and associated industries. It is of particular interest since it is concerned solely with an interactive system. It does not run as a batch system and has not been developed from a batch system base. UNICORN is an acronym for United Nations EDI for Cooperation in Reservation Networks, and has migrated from initial development under UNTDI to an EDIFACT system.

The system was set up in 1985 when START, the travel agents multi-access network provider in West Germany, and based in Frankfurt, circulated ferry companies in Europe that it was interested in making connections for reservations and on-line price calculations. It had no particular wish to define or impose the Application level, but did require that the German user's screen displays which had been developed over a number of years as part of a ticketing and accounting system taking manually-keyed data from a reservation made by telephone remained unchanged. This is a different approach to that normally found in travel systems, where it is the norm for a principal's reservation system to drive agent's screens directly (often through viewdata) and thus display the principal's format on the agent's screen.

Seting Up The Project

Three ferry companies responded positively—North Sea Ferries, Sealink British Ferries and Townsend Thoresen (now P&O European Ferries). It seemed pointless for each ferry company to define a different interface when there was a prospect of cooperation reducing costs at the West German end. The three companies resolved to try and overcome differences in computer systems and end-user screen displays by adopting a common interface if that were possible.

A search of existing standards produced the conclusion that the United Nations Trade Data Interchange Standard was the right solution even though up to that time it was related to the store-and-forward end of data processing. The Group considered that many of the control messages would work in real-time, albeit with a reduced vocabulary, but that the addition of system state conditions to ensure the two systems were kept in step would need to be described. It was envisaged that the general concept would be that each participating ferry operator would write one incoming request decoder and one response compiler and each agent (in this case the remote START computer) would write one request compiler and one incoming response decoder. There were no standard messages within the EDI community for the system that was being developed, therefore the definition was UNICORN's own. It was found necessary to add both flow charts and state tables to the user described messages in order to ensure sequential continuity and maintenance of each system's understanding of the position of the conversation. It was also necessary to provide detailed rules defining the procedures to be followed in the event of an abnormal end to a transaction, such as would be occasioned through a line failure, or a non-standard termination by the user, and which would maintain the integrity of the host computer database.

The messages defined are composed, where possible, of elements drawn from the United Nations Trade Data Elements Directory. It is hoped that the acceptance by both SITPRO in the UK and by the ISO of the additional elements and the respective messages as used in UNICORN will be achieved. Work is currently under way through the Travel Industry System Standards Group (TISSG) in the UK to develop the messages necessary for interactive reservation of other modes of travel, and particularly for inclusive tours.

Membership

At present, the group has no formal constitution, but exists as a focal point for discussions between present members on matters of common interest, and to promulgate the concept and standard to other parties within the travel and leisure industry. However, as membership, which is open to anyone involved with the design or usage of systems in these industries, grows, it is expected that a formal structure will be put in place. Other members of the group are: Automobile Association (Basingstoke, UK); Caravan Club (East Grinstead, UK); Libra Logic (Wokingham, UK); North Sea Ferries (Rotterdam, The Netherlands); START (Frankfurt, W Germany); Travellog Systems Ltd (Haywards Heath, UK).

Copies of the UNICORN specification have been distributed, widely but on a controlled circulation, throughout the UK and Western Europe, but may be obtained from either of the of the two following organisations: R E Parsons, Management Services Department, Sealink British Ferries, Sea Containers House, 20 Upper Ground, London SE1 9PF. Telephone: 01 928 5550. Telex: 8955803. Fax: 01 928 1469; P Hough, Head of Department, P&O European Ferries Ltd, Channel House, Channel View Road, Dover, Kent CT17. Telephone: 0304 223126. Telex: 965104. Fax: 0304 223223.

23
Classification of EDI Development Groups in Europe

Below is a list of the development groups described in chapter 22, giving the industry in which they are active in addition to an indication of the community type. Some of the groups shown do not happily fall into any one category, it is therefore advisable to consult the descriptive notes provided in the previous chapter. The coding used is as follows:

* E—EDI Users Community

* N—Network Provider

* P—Supplier of EDI Products

* S—Support Body

Group	Industry	Community type
ACP 90	Airport Customs Clearance	E
ALFA	Airport Customs Clearance	E
ANA	Retail	E
ASTI	Freight Transportation	E
BACS	Banking	E
BEDIS	Booktrade/Publishing	E
BROKERNET	Insurance VADS	N
BTAT	VADS Provider	N
CARGONAUT	Airport Cargo Clearance	E
CCC	European Customs	S
CD	European Community Initiative	S
CEFIC	Chemical Industry	E
CHAMBERNET	European Community Initiative	S
COST 306	Transportation	E
DAKOSY	Port Administration	P
DANNET	VADS Provider	N
DEDIST	Inter-Nordic Communications	E
DEPS	Customs Clearance System	N
DISH	Shipping	E
DOCIMEL	Railways	E
EAN	Retail	E
EDIA	Transportation	E
EDICON	Construction	E
EDICT	VADS Provider	N

Group	Industry	Community type
EDIFICE	Electronics	E
ERTIS	Road Transportation	E
FCP 80	Port Customs Clearance	E
GBA	Administration	E
IBM IES	VADS Provider	N
INS	VADS Provider	N
INTIS	Port Communications	N
ISTEL	VADS Provider	N
KOMPASS	Port Information System	N
LOG	Transportation	E
MCP	Port Communications	N
MOTORNET	Motor Industry VADS	N
ODETTE	Motor Industry	E
PACE	Port Communications	N
PERIOD ENTRY USERS ASSN	Customs Entries	E
PHARMNET	Pharmaceuticals VADS	N
RINET	Reinsurance/Insurance	E
SADBEL	Customs Clearance System	N
SEAGHA	Port Communications	N
SHIPNET	Shipping	E
SITPRO	Trade	S
SOFI 1 & SOFI 2	Customs Clearance System	N
SWIFT	Banking	N
TEDIS	European Community Initiative	S
TELEVAS	VADS Provider	N
TRADANET	Retail VADS	N
TRADANET INTERNATIONAL	Retail VADS	N
TRANSNET	Retail VADS	N
TRANSPOTEL	Transportation	N
UNCID	Legal	S
UNICORN	Ferries	E

24
Computer Data Interchange Guidelines for Users Exchanging Invoice & Accounting Information

Issued by The Computer Audit Branch of HM Customs & Excise

Introduction

The use of computer data interchange does not, in principle, change the obligations of VAT registered bodies to fulfil the normal requirements of VAT Law as enacted under the Value Added Tax Act 1983. There are, however, certain additional requirements imposed under Schedule 7, paragraph 3, of this Act upon organisations who exchange VAT invoice information between computer systems.

General requirements

An overview of the requirements imposed under Schedule 7, paragraph 3, of the Value Added Tax Act 1983 are set out in Appendix 1 to this guideline. These are advised to each organisation concerned by letter before the commencement of any system. The requirements vary slightly, depending on whether invoices are being transmitted or received, and there are slightly differing requirements for exchanges on computer media (tape, diskette) and direct electronic transmission.

It should be noted that, for VAT purposes, the two parties that are legally responsible for the proper accounting for the tax are the initial sender (*viz supplier*) and the ultimate receiver (*viz customer*) of tax invoice information and it is upon both these parties that the requirements specifically apply.

Where VADS are used as intermediaries between the sender and receiver, there is a requirement upon them to be able to store and forward file VAT control information as required by HM Customs & Excise. Provided that this can be achieved and maintained, the normal requirements imposed upon the sender and the receiver do not apply to the VADS themselves. VADS operators are also required to provide the undertakings as at paragraph 7 of Appendix 1— experience has found that these undertakings are usually given as part of the standard contract between the VAD operators and their principals, but intending users should confirm that this is the case.

It should be noted that these requirements apply only to the exchange of VAT invoices (*viz: tax invoices*) where there is a positive rate of VAT (currently 15 per cent) chargeable on the supplies. In the case of zero rated supplies (eg certain foodstuffs, exports), there is no legal obligation to issue a tax invoice for such transactions and they are therefore outside the scope of the requirements. Unless the Law and all the conditions are met in full, any documents issued by Computer Data Interchange will not be acceptable as tax invoices for VAT purposes and could result in input tax being disallowed in the *receiver's* records.

Further Guidance

VAT registered bodies who are considering the use of Computer Data Interchange should initially advise their local VAT Office of the circumstances. In the case of persons making zero-rated supplies only, HM Customs & Excise should still be advised, as future Budget changes could impose positive rates of VAT on these supplies and bring them within the sphere of the regulations.

More detailed guidance may also be obtained from The Computer Audit Unit, HM Customs & Excise.

The Requirements Regarding Computer Data Interchange of Invoice for Value Added Tax Purposes

A Guidance Note as Supplied to Trade Organisations

A The Law Requires:

1 Notice of intention

Before any system for transmitted tax invoices can be accepted as operational, each organisation involved must give the Commissioners of Customs & Excise at least one month's notice in writing. This should be sent to your local VAT office. It should be borne in mind that the longer the period of notice, then the greater the time that will be available to sort out any problems.

2 Compliance with requirements

The organisations involved must comply with the Requirements imposed by the Commissioners of Customs & Excise. Please note that these requirements may be amended or supplemented from time to time.

B The Requirements

A summary of the conditions imposed by the Department:

1 System trials

The parties concerned must first trial the system and provide Customs & Excise with the opportunity of attending one or more of these trials to observe the trial and inspect the results.

2 System changes

Any significant change in the system, such as a change from exchange on magnetic tape to exchange via electronic mail system, or a major change in the computerised accounting system which produces the invoice information, must be advised to Customs & Excise at least one month before implementation. Again, the earlier, the better.

3 Control information and reports

3.1 The sender

For each invoice file created for transmission purposes, the sender must produce a control document on paper for retention in his records. This must show, among other things:

(a) the full name and address of the recipient of the invoice file and the sender's name, address and VAT registration number

(b) the unique transmission reference (see paragraph 4), or other unique reference allocated to the invoice file, and the transmission date

(c) the total numbers and types of invoices (or other documents) on the file

(d) for each tax rate, the total tax exclusive value of supplies mentioned in the file

(e) the total tax charged at each rate on the above

(f) the total value of any exempt supplies in the file.

All the above information must also be included as control data within the transmitted invoice file and provided that the receiver can fulfil certain other requirements, a copy of the control document need not be sent to the recipient.

3.2 The receiver

On receipt of a transmission, the file will be deformatted from the transmission message standard to the installation's own transaction file format.

The data and values at (a)-(f) in paragraph 3.1 must be printed out on a control report. The values at paragraph 3.1 (c)-(f) must now be re-calculated by totalling the relevant values from the invoice file at transaction level again and the calculated totals must be printed out. Providing the two sets of values agree exactly, then the file may be processed normally as purchase invoices received. If, however, a discrepancy is identified at this stage, then the file must be rejected (either partly or wholly) and a copy of the control/discrepancy report(s) must be forwarded to the sender to take corrective action. Copies of all control and discrepancy reports must be retained as part of the business records.

If, for technical reasons, it is not possible to receive or read a transmission, then the transmission may be treated as not received and a control document need not be raised. The sender should, of course, be advised to re-transmit.

If, for any other reason, it is not possible to read and print the control information at para 3.1 (a)-(f) but the file is accepted for processing, a copy of the sender's control document must be obtained and the control totals thereon verified by totalling the requisite values at invoice transaction level.

4 Unique identification of invoice files

Each invoice file must be uniquely identified by data within the transmission. This identification is usually the generation and version number of the file related to the customer and supplier details. The sender will normally maintain a discrete generation number series for each customer, the generation number being incremented by one for each file transmitted. Installations are, of course, free to agree on some other suitably unique identification if they so choose.

5 Monitoring to ensure no duplication

The recipient of an invoice file must set up a system which will detect and report the receipt of a duplicated transmission. The monitoring of the generation number and version number series would seem to be a suitable method for most systems, but, an additional control on the value of transmission files received could also be used. This should provide:

(a) a control to ensure that all invoice files transmitted have been received;

(b) an appropriate means of identifying a duplicate invoice file.

6 Provision of Evidence (in accordance with Section 5(4) of Civil Evidence Act 1968/Law Reform (Miscellaneous Provisions) (Scotland) Act 1948)

You must provide, or arrange for the provision of a certificate in accordance with section 5(4) of the Civil Evidence Act 1968 should this be requested by Customs & Excise.

7 Computer Bureau Services

If you are using a computer bureau or similar organisation for any part of the procedure, then you must obtain an undertaking that the company involved:

(a) is aware that the provisions of the Finance Act 1985, Section 10, apply in respect of any computer used for such purposes;

(b) will provide a certificate in accordance with Section 5(4) of the Civil Evidence Act 1968 (or the relevant Scottish or Northern Ireland legislation where applicable) if so required by the Commissioners.

8 Names and addresses on invoices

The full name and address and VAT registration number of the supplier and the full name and address of the receiver may be recorded once per invoice file, eg in the header record, provided all the conditions are met in full.

9 Shortened names and addresses

Alternatively to 8—Shortened names and addresses may be shown on each invoice record providing Customs & Excise have been given prior notice, the name and address records may be reduced, eg to a shortened version of the name and full post code on condition that:

(a) the file control report shows the full names and addresses;

(b) the same shortened version must not be used by two or more companies separately registered for VAT or re-allocated to another user.

10 Preservation of documents and audit trail

You must retain copies of all documents related to a particular transmitted file for the statutory period required by VAT legislation unless a shorter period has been approved by your local VAT office.

The historic record of the invoice data must contain all the invoice details and may be stored on paper, magnetic media or similar or on microform. It is desirable from an audit viewpoint that where possible a record of the constitution of the file at transaction level be maintained. For instance the constitution of the transmitted file may be recorded within summary reports, eg a listing of invoice numbers, values, etc, associated with the unique file reference or the invoice records are retained in such a way that the transmitted file content can be reproduced either manually or on magnetic media for audit purposes.

11 Changes in requirements

In order to meet changes in legislation, or in order to make changes found to be necessary in the light of experience, the Commissioners of Customs & Excise reserve the right to amend or change these requirements as they see fit.

For further information, please contact: David Watt, HM Customs & Excise, Computer Audit Unit, Burton House, Church Street, Wilmslow, Cheshire SK9 1DP. Tel: 0625 532131

Appendix A

Guide to UK EDI Suppliers

BROKERNET

International Network Services

INS House
Station Road
Sunbury-On-Thames
Middlesex TW16 6SB

Telephone: 0932 761020
Fax. 0932 761020

Managing Director: Mr Lee Tate
Marketing Manager: Mr Brian Morgan
Sales Contact: Mr Steven Wigmore

Company Founded 1987
Number of Employees 100

DESCRIPTION OF SERVICE

Brokernet is run on the Mercury Data
Network
Contact: Mr Brian Morgan

Application description

The Brokernet service offers a facility to
brokers, insurance companies and
syndicates to revolutionise the
communications of the insurance world.
Using a nationwide network, Brokernet
links the computers of insurance
companies, syndicates and service
providers not only to each other but to
intermediaries wherever they may be.

Technical description

Brokernet avoids the headaches of
connecting with many insurers'
computers and dealing with the technical
intricacies of different internal systems.
With Brokernet, brokers can use a simple
set of standard instructions and do
business when it suits them.

Number of users

Number of users is available from INS

Service history

First full year of commissioned service in
UK 1986

Electronic data interchange equipment & software

The following specialist equipment and
software is required to utilise Brokernet:
Name: Trada-Start Products
Function: User interface products
Supplied solely by INS Ltd

Maintenance

Maintenance is provided by the service
operator

Communications protocols supported by network

The following protocols are presently
supported:
2780, 3780, X.25, SNA, CO3, Asynch,
Synch

Access

Method of access

United Kingdom
Local call to third party network

Western Europe
Local call direct dial-up in all major
European cities

USA
Local call direct dial-up

Worldwide
Local call direct dial-up, a list of cities is
available from INS

Other methods of access
Videotex is available on the network
worldwide

Delivery times

97.5 per cent of messages/documents are
delivered concurrently with 100 per cent
delivered within 60 minutes.

Interconnection with other EDI services

Brokernet is interconnected with EDI
Express (GE Information Services)

Data or document formats

Data & documentation Standards
Employed:
Brokernet data standards are based on
TRADACOMS format and Brokernet
supports EDIFACT

Documents transferred

All aspects of private motor business,
also moving into other areas such as
household and life document transfer.

HM Customs & Excise/Inland Revenue Requirements

The following provisions have been
made for Customs and Inland Revenue
requirements:
Generation and retention of control
documentation for each transmission
The control of duplicate transmissions

Electronic data interchange service operation

The Brokernet service is available to
customers for 24 hours a day, 365 days of
the year with the help desk being
available 24 hours a day, seven days a
week.

SERVICE CHARGES

Service charges vary and are available
on request from INS

CUSTOMER SERVICES

Services available

Electronic Mail: Quik-Comm
Electronic Data Interchange: Tradanet,
Tradanet International, Pharmnet,
Motornet Electronic Funds Transfer:
Paynet
Drug Marketing Survey (Videotex):
Drugwatch

Consultative arrangements

INS has a range of EDI consulting
services available.

Customer list

A customer list is available on request
from INS

Reference customers

Reference customers will be provided on
request to INS

EDICT

Istel Limited

Grosvenor House
Redditch
Worcestershire
B97 4DQ

Telephone: 0527 64274
Telex: 339954

Managing Director: Mr J P Leighfield
Marketing Manager: Mr Phil Coathup

Company Founded 1979
Number of Employees 1,400

DESCRIPTION OF SERVICE

Edict is run on the Infotrac Network

Application description

Full EDI service for manufacturing,
distribution, health, finance, travel and
mining industries.

Technical description

Edict offers a flexible service of network
access, a maintenance centre and full
support. Edict supports all UK approved
standards with national and international
access, synchronous and asynchronous
access dial-up or leased line, or by other
networks such as BT's PSS.

Number of users

Number of users not given

Service history

First full year of commissioned service in
UK 1985
First full year of commissioned service in
USA, Europe and Japan 1987

Communications protocols supported by network

Most common protocols are presently
supported

Maintenance

Maintenance is provided by the service
operator and the equipment supplier.

Access

Method of access

United Kingdom
Local call to third party network

Western Europe
Local call direct dial-up via local PTT
service which is connected to Infotrac.

USA
Local call direct dial-up via PTT network
which is connected to Infotrac

Rest of World
Local call direct dial-up. All via local PTT
service which is connected to Infotrac.

Data or document formats

Data & documentation standards
employed:
All approved standards, eg.
TRADACOMS, ODETTE.

International standards:
All approved standards eg. EDIFACT

Documents transferred

Purchase Orders
Acceptance/Rejection Advice
Invoices
Shipment Information
Status Details
Plan Schedule with Release
Warranty Claims
Travel Information
Finance Information

HM Customs & Excise/Inland Revenue requirements

The following provisions have been
made to cater for Inland Revenue and
Customs & Excise requirements:

Generation and retention of control documentation for each transmission
Retention of invoice data received
Production of summary reporting mechanism for invoice information
The control of duplicate transmissions

Electronic data interchange service operation

The Edict service is available to customers from 7am Monday to Saturday. The service is not available during English Bank Holidays

SERVICE CHARGES

Registration charge

There is an minimum subscription charge of £1,750

Minimum charges

Dial-up: £1,500 per year
Leased line: £3,000 for up to 36 million characters a year

CUSTOMER SERVICES

Services available

Electronic Mail: Comet
Viewdata Bureau: Viewshare
Viewdata Travel Service: Travelshare
File Transfer: Edict—FTS
Late holiday availability: Travelbank
Insurance Quotation Service: Inview

Customer List

A customer list is available on request

Reference customers

A list of reference customers is available from the service provider

IBM Information Exchange (IE)

IBM United Kingdom Limited

PO Box 41
North Harbour
Portsmouth
Hampshire PO6 3AU

Telephone: 0705 321212
Telex: 86741
E-Mail: Screenmail

Business Network Services Head Office
PO Box 117
Mountbatten House
Basingstoke
Hampshire RG21 1EJ

Telephone: 0256 56144
Telex: 858043

BNS Industry Networks Branch
389 Chiswick High Road
London W4 4AL

Telephone: 01 995 1441
Telex: 23295

Sales Contact: BNS Branch Manager

BNS Financial Networks Branch
IBM Southbank
76 Upper Ground
London SE1 9PZ

Telephone: 01 928 1777
Telex: 919039

Sales Contact: BNS Branch Manager

DESCRIPTION OF SERVICE

The IBM Information Exchange Service is
run on the IBM Managed Network Service

Application description

The IBM Information Exchange Service is
a store-and-forward service allowing
customer computer systems to exchange
business transactions or data files.
Typical business transactions are
purchase orders, confirmations, shipping
notices and invoices. Access for
customers in the UK, for both national and
international applications, is achieved
through connection to the IBM Managed
Network Service.

Technical description

The IBM Information Exchange Service
includes the following functions:
Send/receive data on a store-and-forward
basis
Connectivity options for IBM PC
(asynchronous communications), SNA
host, and Remote Job Entry (RJE) devices.
Archiving
Administrative and profile maintenance
tool

Number of users

Number of users not given

Service history

First full year of commissioned service in
UK 1986/87

Electronic data interchange equipment & software

Please contact IBM Business Network
Services (BNS) for information concerning
requisite equipment and software

Communications protocols supported by network

The following protocols are presently
supported for connection to EDI services:
IBM SNA/SDLC: leased line or dial-up
connections Synchronous: BSC 2780
[3780], leased line or dial-up connections
Asynchronous: including TTY and
videotex

A wider range of connectivity is
supported to other services including:
X.25
OSI: to layer 5
Refer to IBM for current support

Access

Method of access

PSTN, private circuits, IPSS, IBM's international network

International coverage

See under the IBM Managed Network Service

Data or document formats

Data & documentation standards employed:
The IBM Information Exchange Service provides support for the UNTDI data format, the ANSI X12 data format and the ISO EDIFACT format.

Electronic data interchange service operation

The IBM Managed Network Service is available to customers for 20 hours a day, 365 days of the year excluding Christmas Day

SERVICE CHARGES

Network charges

Standard MNS charges apply, please refer to IBM BNS for details

Message charges—National (sender and receiver are in the same country)

Primary segment sent: 16.5 pence
Primary segment received: 16.5 pence
Secondary segment sent: 6 pence
Secondary segment received: 6 pence
Acknowledgement: 21 pence

Message charges—European (sender and receiver not in the same country)

Primary segment sent: 19.5 pence
Primary segment received: 19.5 pence
Secondary segment sent: 9 pence
Secondary segment received: 9 pence
Acknowledgement: 21 pence

Storage charges

Storage MB/hour: 43 pence
Archiving MB/day: 2.72
Retrieval from archive: 2.5 pence

Software—once off charges

PC/IE Network Interface Program: £129
SNA/Host Network Interface Program: £2,857
ExpEDIte/36 Interface Program: £205

Further application software support for EDI is provided by Edilink which is currently announced for PC, MVS, S/36, and which in conjunction with Interbridge (available from SITPRO), provides formatting and distribution services.

LTMC

IE segment charges, acknowledgement, storage and archiving charges will be eligible for LTMC at the standard rates applicable to IBM's IPS.
PC Interface and SNA/Host Interface are not eligible for LTMC.

CUSTOMER SERVICES

Services available

Electronic Mail: Screenmail
Electronic Data Interchange: Information Exchange (IE), IBM Data Transfer Service (IDTS)
Electronic Funds Transfer: Supporting a number of closed user groups
Videotex: IBM Videotex Service (IVS)
Office Support: IBM International PROFS, IBM MVS/AS Application System Service
Information Services: Exbond, Exshare and access to information providers
Bulk data transfers: IBM Data Transfer Service

Consultative arrangements

A wide range of support is available. Refer to IBM for details

Customer list

A customer list is available on request

Reference customers

IBM will supply reference customers on request

MOTORNET

International Network Services

INS House
Station Road
Middlesex
TW1 6SB

Telephone 0932 761020
Fax 0932 761020
E-Mail Quik-Comm INS LOND

Managing Director Mr Lee Tate
Marketing Manager Mr John Jenkins
Sales Contact: Mr Malcolm Miller

Company Founded 1987
Number of Employees 100

DESCRIPTION OF SERVICE

Motornet is run on the Mercury Managed
Data Network

Contact: Mr Malcolm Miller

Application description

Commercial document exchange for
automotive industry. Primarily UK but
some international usage. Endorsed by
Society of Motor Manufacturers and
Traders (SMMT). Main documents carried
are: invoices, schedule releases, and
advice notes. Use ODETTE formats,
based on GTDI and EDIFACT syntax.

Technical description

Store and forward data service with
nodal access throughout UK. Service
access guaranteed during normal
operations. All major protocols
supported. Full implementation service
and technical consultancy provided.

Number of users

Number of user is available from INS

Service history

First full year of commissioned service in
the UK and worldwide 1986

Electronic data interchange equipment & software

The following specialist equipment and
software is required to utilise Motornet:

Name: Trada-Start Products
Function: User interface packages
Supplied solely by INS

Maintenance

Maintenance is provided by the
equipment supplier

Communication protocols supported by network

The following protocols are presently
supported:
2780, 3780, X.25, SNA, CO3,
asynchronous, synchronous, OFTP

Access

Method of access

United Kingdom
Local call direct dial-up (Local PSTN)

Western Europe
Local call direct dial-up from all major
cities

USA
Local call direct dial-up

Worldwide
Local call direct dial-up from 750 cities in
85 countries

Other methods of access

Worldwide
Videotex is available on the network
worldwide

Delivery times

97.5 per cent of messages/documents are
delivered concurrently and all messages
are delivered within 60 minutes

International coverage

Motornet is linked to the worldwide EDI Express service operated by GE Information Services

Interconnection with other EDI services

The Motornet service is interconnected with the Tradanet, EDI Express and Pharmnet service

Data or document standards

Participating Trade Associations/ Institutions:
Society of Motor Manufacturers & Traders (SMMT)

Data & documentation standards employed:
ODETTE

International standards employed:
OSI standards are implemented within the network

Documents transferred

Purchase Orders
Purchase Order Acknowledgements
Purchase Order Change Requests
Acceptance/Rejection Advice
Functional Acknowledgements
Invoices
Freight Details, Invoices
Shipment Information
Status Details
Plan Schedule with Release
All other documents as defined by the ODETTE standards

HM Customs & Excise/Inland Revenue requirements:

The following provisions have been made to cater for Inland Revenue and Customs & Excise requirements:
Generation and retention of control documentation for each transmission
The control of duplicate transmissions

Electronic data interchange service operation

The Motornet service is available to customers for 24 hours a day, 365 days of the year

SERVICE CHARGES

Service charges vary and are available on request from INS

CUSTOMER SERVICES

Services available

Electronic Mail: Quik-Comm
Electronic Data Interchange: Tradanet, Tradanet International, Brokernet, Pharmnet
Electronic Funds Transfer: Paynet
Drug Marketing Survey (Videotex): Drugwatch

Consultative arrangements

INS has a range of consulting services available

Customer list

A customer list is available on request from INS

PHARMNET

International Network Services

INS House
Station Road
Sunbury-On-Thames
Middlesex
TW16 6SB

Telephone: 0932 761020
Fax: 0932 761020

Managing Director: Mr Lee Tate
Marketing Manager: Mr Perminder Dale
Sales Contact: Mr Jim Wallace

Company Founded 1987
Number of Employees 100

DESCRIPTION OF SERVICE

Pharmnet is run on the Mercury Data
Network
Contact: Mr Jim Wallace

Application description

This INS service provides a way for
Regional Health Authorities, wholesalers,
suppliers and pharmaceutical companies
to transfer documents electronically. The
net result is a faster, cheaper and more
reliable way of communicating orders
within the health industry

Technical description

Pharmnet provides access to a variety of
different types of computer from BBC
micros, through IBM, ICL PC's to minis
and mainframes. It also provides for
access speeds from 1200bps to 48 kb. It's
technical and security facilities have been
validated by independent consultants and
the service has the five year exclusive
endorsement of the ANA.

Number of users

A list is available from INS

Service history

First full year of commissioned service in
the UK 1985
First full year of commissioned service
worldwide 1987

Electronic data interchange equipment & software

The following specialist equipment and
software is required to utilise Pharmnet:

Name: Trada-Start
Function: User interface packages
Supplied solely by INS Ltd

Maintenance

Maintenance is provided by the service
operator

Communications protocols supported by network

The following protocols are presently
supported:
2780, 3780, X.25, SNA, CO3, synchronous,
asynchronous

Access

Method of access

United Kingdom
Local call direct dial-up

Western Europe
Local call direct dial-up in all major cities

USA
Local call direct dial-up

Worldwide
Local call direct dial-up covering 750
cities in 85 countries

Other methods of access
Videotex is available on the network
worldwide

Delivery times

97.5 per cent of messages/documents are

delivered concurrently with 100 per cent delivered within 60 minutes

International coverage

Pharmnet is linked to the worldwide EDI Express service operated by GE information Services

Interconnection with other EDI services

Pharmnet is interconnected with Tradanet, EDI Express and Motornet utilising a full application to application bridge

Data or document formats

Participating Trade Associations/ Institutions:
Association of the British Pharmaceutical Industry (ABPI)

Data or documentation standards employed:
TRADACOMS. EDIFACT standards are supported worldwide, OSI standards are implemented within the network

Documents transferred

Purchase Orders
Purchase Order Acknowledgements
Purchase Order Change Requests
Acceptance/Rejection Advice
Invoices

HM Customs & Excise/Inland Revenue requirements

Generation and retention of control documentation for each transmission
The control of duplicate transmissions

Electronic data interchange service operation

The Pharmnet service is available 24 hours a day, 365 days a year with the INS service desk available for 24 hours a day seven days a week

SERVICE CHARGES

Service charges vary and are available on request from INS

CUSTOMER SERVICES

Services available

Electronic Mail: Quik-Comm
Electronic Data Interchange: Tradanet, Tradanet International, Brokernet, Motornet
Electronic Funds Transfer: Paynet
Drug Marketing Survey (Videotex): Drugwatch

Consultative arrangements

INS has a range of EDI consulting services available

Customer list

A customer list is available on request from INS

Reference customers

Reference customers are available on request from INS

TRADANET

International Network Services

INS House
Station Road
Sunbury-On-Thames
Middlesex
TW16 6SB

Telephone: 0932 761020
Fax: 0932 761020

Managing Director: Mr Lee Tate
Marketing Manager: Mr John Jenkins
Sales Contact: Mr Malcolm Miller

Company Founded 1987
Number of Employees 100

DESCRIPTION OF SERVICE

Tradanet is run on the Mercury Data Network
Contact: Mr Malcolm Miller

Application description

Tradanet is the leading UK EDI service with more than 600 customers. It provides a store-and-forward service in the following market areas: food, clothing, chemicals, mail order, stores, pharmaceutical, white goods, electronics, public utilities and authorities, distribution, DIY, brewing, leisure, oil and petroleum, opticians, music, fast food and publishing.

Technical description

Tradanet provides access to a variety of different types of computer from BBC micros, through IBM, ICL PC's to minis and mainframes. It also provides for access speeds from 1200bps to 48kb. It's technical and security facilities have been validated by independent consultants and the service has the five year exclusive endorsement of the ANA.

Number of users

Number of users 600

Service history

First full year of commissioned service in the UK 1985
First full year of commissioned service worldwide 1987

Electronic data interchange equipment & software

The following specialist equipment and software is required to utilise Tradanet:
Name: Trada-Start
Function: User interface packages
Supplied solely by INS Ltd

There are more than 65 different types of computer equipment and software connected to Tradanet available from INS and third party suppliers

Maintenance

Maintenance is provided by the service operator

Communications protocols supported by network

The following protocols are presently supported:
2780, 3780, X.25, SNA, CO3, asynchronous, synchronous

Access

Method of access

United Kingdom
Local call direct dial-up (Local PSTN)

Western Europe
Local call direct dial-up in all major cities

USA
Local call direct dial-up

Worldwide
Local call direct dial-up in 750 cities covering 85 countries

Other methods

Videotex is available on the network worldwide

Delivery times

97.5 per cent of messages/documents are delivered concurrently with 100 per cent delivered within 60 seconds

International coverage

Tradanet is linked to EDI Express run by GE Information Services

Interconnection with other EDI services

Tradanet is linked with EDI Express, Motornet and Pharmnet. The interconnection is a full application to application bridge. No specialist equipment or software is required by potential users since the bridge is transparent to the end user.

Data or document formats

Participating Trade Associations/ Institutions:
Article Numbering Association (ANA), SMMT, AMDEA, ECIF, AFDEC, DISH, EDICON

Data & documentation standards employed
TRADACOMS, ODETTE, EDIFACT

International standards
EDIFACT standards are supported world-wide. OSI standards are implemented within the network.

Documents transferred

Purchase Orders
Purchase Order Acknowledgements
Purchase Order Change Requests
Acceptance/Rejection Advice
Functional Acknowledgements
Invoices
Freight Details, Invoices
Shipment Information
T5 Status Details
Plan Schedule with Release
30 other document types—all documents used in the national and international trade cycles

HM Customs & Excise/Inland Revenue requirements

The following provisions have been made to cater for Inland Revenue and Customs & Excise requirements:
Generation and retention of control documentation for each transmission
The control of duplicate transmissions
Tradanet has full clearance by HM Customs—refer to the Article Numbering Association (ANA)

Electronic data interchange service operation

The Tradanet service is available to customers for 24 hours a day, 365 days of the year. The service desk is available 24 hours a day for seven days a week

SERVICE CHARGES

Service charges vary and are dependent on the type of access and the volume of usage. Charges are available on request.

CUSTOMER SERVICES

Services available

Electronic Mail: Quik-Comm
Electronic Data Interchange: Motornet, Tradanet International, Brokernet, Pharmnet
Electronic Funds Transfer: Paynet Drug Marketing Survey (Videotex): Drugwatch

Consultative arrangements

INS has a range of EDI consulting services available

Customer list

A customer list is available on request from INS

Reference customers

Reference customers are available on request from INS

TRADANET INTERNATIONAL

International Network Services

INS House
Station Road
Sunbury-On-Thames
Middlesex
TW16 6SB

Telephone: 0932 761020
Fax: 0932 761020

Managing Director: Mr Lee Tate
Marketing Manager: Mr Chris Nelson
Sales Contact: Mr Lance Spencer

DESCRIPTION OF SERVICE

Tradanet International is run on the GE
Information Services Data Network
Contact: Mr Lance Spencer

Application description

Tradanet International is a network
service that allows processing and
exchange of shipment data electronically
with shippers, consignees, freight
forwarders, carriers, banks and others in
the UK or worldwide.

Technical description

Store-and-forward data service with
nodal access in 85 countries worldwide.
All major protocols and message
standards supported. Full international
implementation and local country support
service available.

Number of users

A list of users is available from INS

Service history

First full year of commissioned service in
the UK 1988
First full year of commissioned service
worldwide 1988

Electronic data interchange equipment & software

The following specialist equipment and
software is required to utilise Tradanet
International:
Name: Trada-Start
Function: User interface packages
Supplied solely by INS Ltd

Communications protocols supported by network

The following protocols are presently
supported:
2780, 3780, X.25, SNA, CO3, OFTP,
asynchronous, synchronous

Access

Method of access

United Kingdom
Local call direct dial-up (Local PSTN)

Western Europe
Local call direct dial-up in all major cities

USA
Local call direct dial-up

Worldwide
Local call direct dial-up in 750 cities in 85
countries

Other methods of access

United Kingdom
Videotex is available on the network
worldwide

Delivery times

97.5 per cent of messages/documents are
delivered concurrently with 100 per cent
delivered within 60 minutes

International coverage

Dial-out connections provided to several
US-based third party services

Interconnection with other EDI services

Tradanet International is linked with Tradanet, Pharmnet, Motornet. The link is a full application to application bridge.

Data or document standards

Participating Trade Associations/ Institutions:
Data Interchange for Shipping (DISH), ODETTE, CEFIC

Data & documentation standards employed:
EDIFACT

International standards:
ISO data standards. OSI standards are implemented within the network

Documents transferred

Freight Details,
Invoices
Shipment Information
Bookings/Confirmation
Maritime Transport Contract
Schedule Charges

HM Customs & Excise/Inland Revenue requirements

The following provisions have been made to cater for Inland Revenue and Customs & Excise requirements:
Generation and retention of control documentation for each transmission The control of duplicate transmissions

Electronic Data Interchange service operation

The Tradanet service is available to customers for 24 hours a day, 365 days of the year. Customer service desks are available in all main countries with network support centres in 26 countries.

SERVICE CHARGES

Service charges vary and are available on request

CUSTOMER SERVICES

Services available

Electronic Mail: Quik-Comm, Businesstalk
Electronic Data Interchange: Motornet, Tradanet, Brokernet, Pharmnet
Electronic Funds Transfer: Paynet
Drug Marketing Survey (Videotex): Drugwatch

Consultative arrangements

INS has a range of EDI consulting services available

Customer list

A customer list is available on request from INS

Reference customers

Reference customers are available on request from INS

Appendix B

Guide to Interbridge

THE EDIFACT TRANSLATOR

The new EDIFACT standard (ISO 9735) has created a great deal of excitement in the world of electronic data interchange. Systems Designers were already suppliers of the most successful translation software for the previous United Nations TDI standard—Interbridge 3. SITPRO have now launched Interbridge 4 which will provide a powerful, reliable and cost effective solution to companies planning to use EDIFACT messages. The new package builds on SITPRO's extensive experience in international standards work, and can bring benefits to users in all trades and with computers ranging from micros to the largest mainframes.

HOW IT WORKS

Interbridge is message independent. Messages are embodied in tables which drive the software. It is thus far cheaper and easier to install and maintain than message-dependent routines, particularly as the user progresses beyond the first few message types. The package maintains a clean interface with in-house applications. Whether the user is sending or receiving electronic messages, or both, Interbridge allows a great deal of flexibility in designing the interface file. The extensive validation checks militate against the, normally easy, dissemination of bad data. Where interchange messages are defined in ways which are inconvenient to internal applications, Interbridge helps by adjusting data formats and converting between interchange codes and qualifiers and those used in-house. It also has some (fancy) facilities for handling generic EDIFACT segments.

Interbridge maintains a clean interface with communications media. It can be used with store-and-forward networks, direct connections (X.25 or proprietary) or even magnetic media exchange (diskette or tape).

WHY USE IT?

For existing TDI TRADACOMS users, including those who have put billions of characters through Interbridge 3, there is not really any question. Interbridge 4 handles both TDI/TRADACOMS and EDIFACT formats. Furthermore, it comes with an automatic table converter to help manage the transition period. The EDIFACT side of Interbridge 4 also contains numerous enhancements.

For those com- panies and organisations moving straight to EDIFACT interchanges the choice of software should be obvious. Interbridge possesses all the aces—the main ones being its long-standing pedigree and its continuing user support.

Above all, the potential user should think carefully about the costs of writing and maintaining in-house routines to link with particular messages. This can seem superficially attractive, yet prove extremely expensive as messages change and multiply. Interbridge, being table driven, makes message changes relatively minor events.

Any standard is subject to further development and EDIFACT is no exception. SITPRO is ideally placed to anticipate the continuing process of standards clarification. Interbridge 4 is not merely good—it is state-of-the-art in EDIFACT translation.

WHO WILL IT SUIT?

Interbridge has been proven as a reliable and efficient product by many users, on over 50 types of mainframes, minis and micros and across many application areas. Whilst its major uses have been for messages containing commercial, transportation of official data, Interbridge 4 will handle all messages written to EDIFACT standards. Some new users will find that they have little choice but to use Interbridge. Often they will find that the EDIFACT conversion within a specialist application package is in fact a licenced copy of Interbridge utilised by a large customer fed up with testing bug-ridden one-off message routines.

MAJOR INTERBRIDGE FACILITIES

The following are all major Interbridge facilities: level A EDIFACT compatibility; automatic conversion between in-house and transmitted codes; conversion of Qualifier codes, and mandatory Qualifier checks, this helps the user avoid any direct contact with qualifiers; control of each item of data through facilities such as optional case conversion, compression and fixed data, accessed from (or checked against) the table itself; an 'append option', so that different EDI or TDI/EDI transmission can be stored in the same file prior to actual transmission; facility to translate mixed TDI and EDI messages if required; powerful Menu for Micro version; better error recovery and a better user manual.

Further information concerning Interbridge may be obtained from: David Palmer, SD-Scicon, EDI Group, Haw Bank House, 2 High Street, Cheadle, Cheshire SK8 1AL. Telephone: 061 428 0811. Telex: 666189 SYSDES G.

Appendix C

About the authors

Anthony ALLEN

Tony Allen is Systems Development Manager of Sealink (UK) Limited. Although originally qualifying as a Chartered Accountant, he spent 3 post qualifying years as a professional accountant, engaged in the audit and appraisal of client's computer systems, which provided a breadth of exposure to systems of different styles and to many different manufacturer's hardware. He then moved into the commercial area, and spent eight years in air freight forwarding, primarily designing and controlling system applications in accounting and operational areas, and led a team developing an interactive real-time freight control system.

His next career step took him into the ferry industry, which has been his home for the past 12 years. His involvement in systems has covered the full range of activities in the travel industry, from accounting to freight and from on-board retailing to his major interest for reservation systems, where he has been heavily involved with the design and implementation of a number of real-time systems having significant number of access points, both internal and external. He has also undertaken a number of consultancy projects for other ferry companies both in Europe and North America.

Alison BIDGOOD

Alison Bidgood is a senior consultant with Coopers & Lybrand, one of the leading international firms of consultants, auditors and business advisors.

After reading languages at Durham University, she joined Plessey where she worked in a number of functions involving market analysis, business development and strategic planning. Alison moved to C&L four years ago. As a member of the London-based communications division she has specialised in business issues relating to telecommunications. A particular focus has been the way in which changing market conditions are creating opportunities for both suppliers and users in areas such as EDI.

Keith BLACKER

Keith Blacker is the EDI Coordinator for Lucas Industries. He is a Chartered Electrical Engineer with wide business and systems experience around the Lucas Group. He currently leads the ODETTE Engineering Groups in the UK and in Europe and is a member of the Council of the EDI Association. He has contributed to and edited a number of ODETTE books published by The Society of Motor Manufacturers & Traders (SMMT).

Phil COATHUP

Phil Coathup is Marketing Director for the EDI Services Division (Istel). He joined Istel in 1984, working in the Strategic Planning Department of the company. One of the areas he identified for the future growth of the company was EDI.

Before joining Istel, Mr Coathup was a Senior Consultant with the International Data Corporation, and was responsible for European software and services market research. Mr Coathup is a graduate of the University of Reading, and also has an M.Sc. in Civil Engineering from the University of Leeds.

Paul DAWKINS

Dr Paul Dawkins is a senior consultant with Scicon Limited which is the civil business within the SD-Scicon group of companies. He graduated in Electronics from Kent University and later obtained a Ph.D. at Aston University, sponsored by GEC. His thesis was concerned with ways of speeding up the development cycle for new products. After some years in GEC, which included a strategic role in planning and implementing an office automation strategy, he became a product planner in ITL with special responsibility for office automation products. Whilst there he worked on ITL's successful submission for the government's IDEM project, which uses X.400 protocols. Since joining Scicon Limited in 1986 he has been concerned with X.400 messaging systems. He has led the marketing of Scicon's messaging products.

Christopher EAGLEN

Dr Christopher Eaglen works in the Business Evaluation and Planning Unit of the Business Development Department at BACS Limited. In 1986 after 10 years in the consultancy sector he joined BACS Ltd to work on the promotion of automated payment methods in the UK. His specialist areas are the development and application of Electronic Funds Transfer and Automated Payment Clearance Systems.

Nigel FENTON

Nigel Fenton has been executive secretary of the Article Number Association for 5 years. His particular responsibility within the Association is for the TRADACOMS standards for electronic data exchange, currently the most widely used standard in the UK.

Mr Fenton is also involved in several industry projects aimed at coordinating EDI developments. He chairs the UK EDI Standards Working Group, and is a member of the BSI EDI Standards Committee.

Mike GIFKINS

Dr Mike Gifkins has held a variety of positions in computing and tele-communications. After a brief academic career he worked on several software engineering projects which included a flight simulator. During five years with ITT he was involved in the development of business systems and their supporting technology, which included two years working on the operating system for a novel microprocessor in Intel, Oregon. After returning to the UK he became product manager for a range of software tools used for building large public exchanges. He joined Scicon Limited in 1985. Amongst his assignments for Scicon he was responsible for the telecommunications aspects of a multi-national project in a major oil company. His interest in EDI developed as he led Scicon's contribution to the Government's Vanguard programme. At present his main professional interest is in the relationship between information technology and the law. He is currently training to act as an expert arbitrator in commercial disputes.

David HITCHCOCK

Having gained an honours degree from the University of London in Natural Sciences David Hitchcock entered publishing. David has held various editorial appointments, joining Blenheim Online in November 1986 as the editor of Online Publications. He commissions and edits works across a broad spectrum of high technology areas which include data and telecommunications. He was co-editor of *The VANS Handbook* (Online Publications, London, 1987) and whilst com-piling that work he appreciated the pressing business requirement for a book devoted to a subset of VADS, EDI. It is expected that *The EDI Handbook* will be the introductory work in a series of books commissioned in the field of EDI and paperless trade.

David JACKSON

David Jackson is Programme Director with Management Centre Europe, where he is responsible for developing and managing a range of leading-edge conferences and training programmes in the information systems and operations management disciplines.

He joined Management Centre Europe from the School of Management at Derbyshire College of Higher Education. He was actively involved in the development of a unique Masters degree on the management of advanced manufacturing. He was also responsible for all programmes in the field of purchasing and logistics management. His lecturing experience covers a wide variety of undergraduate and postgraduate programmes as well as lecturing on short programmes in the UK and mainland Europe. David also consulted with a number of companies on procurement issues, including the implementation of EDI projects.

David's previous experience has included nine years with a major public sector energy corporation where he held a number of posts in the purchasing and logistics fields. Specific responsibilities included handling and storage facility for a greenfield site and the development of computer systems to improve management decision and reporting processes. David holds a Master of Science degree in computing and is a Corporate Member of the Institute of Purchasing and Supply. Before leaving the UK he acted as Chief Examiner for the IPS. His published work includes: coeditor and contributor, *The Management of Manufacturing—the competitive edge*, IFS (Publications) Ltd, 1987; Information Systems and Corporate Strategy, *The International Management Development Review*, 1988.

John JENKINS

John Jenkins joined ICL in May 1975 as a Senior Systems Analyst in the Software Development unit of ICL's bureau operation, Baric Computing Services Ltd. Subsequently he has held a number of senior positions and was responsible for a number of systems developments.

In the autumn of 1983 John joined International Network Services as Project Manager of the development of Tradanet, the UK's first electronic data interchange service. In 1985 he became Tradanet Marketing & Develop- ment Manager, a position he retained after the formation of International Network Services Ltd by ICL and G E Information Services at the beginning of 1987.

Edmund LEE

Edmund Lee is the product manager for British Telecom's Public Data Network. His responsibilities encompass the marketing and product management of all aspects of the PDN services which include among others PSS, MultiStream and Cardway. Previously he pioneered the development and marketing of BT's insurance value added services. He has, from 1978, been closely associated with BT's development in data networks and packet switching.

Tom McGUFFOG

Tom McGuffog graduated in economics at the Universities of Glasgow and Massachusetts, where he was elected to the National Honor Society, Phi Kappa Phi. Following which he worked as an economist with the Electricity Council in London and the Merseyside and North Wales Electricity Board in Liverpool.

Tom joined Rowntree in 1967 in Operational Research and worked on models and systems in most parts of the company, becoming Head of Systems Development (Systems Analysis, Programming, OR, O&M, Information Services). In 1981, he was made responsible for coordinating business systems development in Rowntree Mackintosh Confectionery UK, and in North America. In 1985 he became Managing Director of the Rowntree Transport and Distribution Division, becoming Director of Purchasing and Logistics in Rowntree Mackintosh Confectionery Ltd in 1987.

Tom is Chairman of the TRADACOMS Working Party of the Article Number Association, and he has been involved with the development of the TRADACOMS standard messages and the Tradanet network since 1979. TRADACOMS-Tradanet represent the largest and fastest growing general electronic trading data interchange community in the world.

David PALMER

David has 15 years experience in the computer industry and has wide-ranging experience in the development, installation and support of computer based systems. He has been working exclusively in the EDI arena for two and a half years. During this time he has had direct involvement with many EDI installations as a consultant. He is the manager of SD-Scicon's Customer Services in its EDI Group.

Gil PATRICK

Gil Patrick holds a BSc from the University of London and a Masters degree in Business Administration from the University of Washington. Gil held a number of management positions in industry before joining Booz, Allen & Hamilton as an Associate/Consultant. Following five years of managing and participating in client assignments, primarily involving organistion development, manufacturing industries and local government, Gil joined the Plessey Company. Having joined as a strategic planning executive in 1977, he became General Manager Plessey Satellite Communications in 1978. Since 1981 Gil has been involved in running his own independent businesses, including Patrick Consulting Associates which offers management consultancy in the communications and data processing environment. The company has played leading roles in strategic assignments for BT, Shell Chemicals and the Department of Trade & Industry.

Nick POPE

Nick Pope is a senior consultant with Logica Consultancy Limited. He has 12 years experience in computer communications and over the last four years has been involved in standardisation in the EDI field. He recently completed a study for the joint UK Government/Industry initiative, Vanguard, investigating the use of X.400 for EDI. He contributed to the development of the security aspects of the 1988 X.400 Recommendations and has input the results of the Vanguard study into the next round of CCITT activities covering message handling for EDI.

Prior to joining Logica he worked for GEC at their Marconi Research Centre on advanced data communication projects such as Project Admiral, for which he was project manager, and Project Universe. Publications include, *Vanguard—EDI and X.400 Study* (HMSO, London, 1988).

John SANDERS

John Sanders is EDI Development Manager within the Group Services function of Trafalgar House plc, a major international company based in the UK. John has played a major role in the formation of the UK Construction Industry's EDI Community, EDICON, of which he is the founder Chairman.

He is Chairman of the EDIFACT Board's Special Projects Message Development Group with particular responsibility for the requirements of the Construction Industry and Tourism within Western Europe.

John is also Chairman of the UK EDI Association's Message Coordination Group responsible for monitoring the varied International Trade and Transport Message Requirements in Great Britain. As Chairman of the EDIA-DEDIST-INTIS-SEAGHA International Transport Message Working Group he has managed the development of the International Transport Messages Scenario.

To use his own words John is an 'EDI Revolutionary' with a strong belief that the future success of business demands the successful introduction of EDI.

Ray SMITHERS

Ray Smithers is a graduate of Oxford University with an MA in Natural Sciences and was employed for five years as a science and industrial talks producer in the World Service of the BBC. He joined IBM United Kingdom Limited in 1967 where the first part of his career was spent in management development and personnel management. Ray joined the newly formed Network Services Department in 1984 and for the past two years has held the position of Special Projects Manager with responsibility for promoting IBM's VADS services. He is married with two daughters and has written a book called *Your Book of the Earth* (Faber, London) and written several radio programmes on scientific and industrial subjects.

Paul TURNBULL

Since joining OASiS in 1987 as a consultant specialising in the business application of communications, Paul Turnbull has undertaken a number of assignments which have included establishing the telecommunications networking options available to an international textile manufacturing client, and designing a networking architecture capable of supporting business strategy for an international pharmaceutical company. He has also managed consultancy projects including determining those factors which accelerate the uptake of value added and data services and assisted in establishing a cross-industry VADS user community.

Paul Turnbull spent the early part of his career in New Zealand, providing marketing consultancy services in industry and agriculture. He subsequently returned to the academic world as a tutor in the business studies faculty at the University of Otago. In 1977 he joined Carter Wilkes & Fane Ltd (Lloyds Brokers), where he was initially involved in financial accounting but increasingly involved in developing information systems. In 1982 he became Project Manager at BIS Insurance Ltd. He was responsible for the specification and management of a number of software developoment projects for clients in the UK and North America.

In 1984 he joined Ernst & Whinney Management Consultancy where he undertook a range if IT and telecommunications assignments in insurance, finance, industry, transport and the public sector. Consultancy assignments included: formulating a number of telecommunications and office automation strategies supporting the more effective use of voice, data, image and text communications; establishing the causes of failure in the design and implementation of a major packet switched VAD network which supported international air cargo freight forwarding; reviewing the arrangements for a public sector client in providing mobile radio communications systems throughout England and Wales. During this period he was responsible for developing Ernst & Whinney's telecommunications consultancy services in the United Kingdom.

Paul holds a BCom in Marketing and Management, a BSc in Biochemistry and an MSc in Computer Science.

Douglas TWEDDLE

Douglas Tweddle is the Assistant Secretary within Customs and Excise Headquarters responsible for the development of customs freight processing systems. He has played a major role in the implementation of direct trader input systems which now cover the electronic transfer of nearly 90 per cent of import declarations. He is heavily involved in the development of new customs systems and represents the United Kingdom on European Community committees looking at the introduction of EDI links between traders and Member States.

He has worked for Customs and Excise for over 20 years except for a two year secondment to a major British Shipping company and six months working for Lord Rayner, Head of Marks and Spencer, as part of the Government's drive to improve efficiency within the Civil Service.

Ray WALKER

Ray Walker has been a SITPRO Board Member since 1976 and its Chief Executive since 1983. He was the Co-Chairman of the UN-JEDI team which produced the UN-EDIFACT standard and is currently the Western European UN-EDIFACT rapporteur and Vice-Chairman of the EDIFACT Board.

In 1986 he received the ANSI X12 award for outstanding contribution to International Data Exchange and in 1988 became the first holder of IDEA's *Man of the Year* award. Before joining SITPRO in 1983, he spent 14 years in senior management positions in a major textile company with responsibility for exports. He is 45 and has a degree in International Economics and Chemistry.

Terence WESTGATE

Terence Westgate was born in Sussex in 1944 and educated at East Grinstead County Grammar School, Bristol Polytechnic, University College London and the Cranfield School of Management. His professional experience includes 10 years in manufacturing, two years as a systems consultant with Coopers & Lybrand, and three years as an independent consultant in computer communications.

Terence's involvement with computer-based message systems dates from 1973 when he commenced field stduies into the psychological and operational aspects of implementing this type of communication.

From 1977 to 1981 he was assistant professor of systems analysis and management science at Mount Allison University in Canada and a visiting lecturer at McGill University and the University of Quebec in Monteal. He held a Canadian Social Sciences & Humanitities Research Council Fellowship at the department of computer science at University College London, 1980-1981, and was a research consultant with the Man-Computer Interaction Group at the National Physical Laboratory. His experiments in cognition and applications of computer-mediated teleconferencing, sponsored by the long range system strategy group of British Telecom, were the first in the world and paved the way for his market study which resulted in the establishment of Telecom Gold in 1982.

During the same period Terence became a founder member of the International Federation for Information Processing's Working Group 6.5 and took part in the development of the theoretical model for computer-based message services which later became the CCITT X.400 Standards.

From 1982-1984 he represented ITT in over 35 countries introducing electronic messaging as public services to PTTs around the world. He also sat on the CCITT Study Group VII (Question 5), which produced the X.400 Standards. In 1984 he founded l'Association de Services Transport Informatiques, ASTI.

Bernard WHEBLE, CBE

Bernard S. Wheble is a former merchant banker and was awarded the CBE in 1972 for, 'services to international trade'. In the same year he was also made an Honorary Fellow of the Chartered Institute of Bankers for, 'services to the practice and law of international banking'. Bernard is a member of the UK's Simplification of Trade Procedures Board (SITPRO) and also acts as the legal co-rapporteur of the United Nations Economic Commission for Europe Trade Facilitation Working Party with reference to EDI.

From 1963 to 1984 he was Chairman of the International Chamber of Commerce Commission on Banking Technique & Practice being made Honorary Chairman thereafter. Bernard has published widely with articles covering such areas as: international trade and finance; law and practice of document credits; combined transport documentation; international trade facilitation; documentary fraud; legal aspects of EDI.

Appendix D

A selective bibliography

This bibliography has been assembled during the research of *The EDI Handbook* and can in no way be viewed as exhaustive. It does however list the major texts available concerned with electronic data interchange (EDI) and the allied subject of value added and data services (VADS). The bibliography concentrates on those publications whose primary editorial aim is discussion of paperless trading techniques and technologies. Specialist bibliographies based on papers published in a wide range of periodicals are available from the OFTEL library in the UK and EDI, spread the word! in the US. This bibliography lists the title of the publication and the publisher. A list of the publishers' addresses and telephone numbers is given at the end of this Appendix.

BEDIS (Book Trade Electronic Data Interchange Standards) Report
J. Whitaker & Sons Ltd.
Published recommendations for the role of EDI in the publishing and booktrades. Published in association with the MARC User Group.

The Economic Effects of Value Added & Data Services
HMSO Books
Vanguard sponsored study of the likely economic effects of widespread VADS implementation.

The EDI Executive (US)
EDI, spread the word!
US Newsletter published in association with Electronic Cash Management Inc.

EDI & Paperless Trade: The Implementation Guide
Euromatica SA
Booklet giving an overview of the problems associated with EDI implementation

EDI: A Selected Bibliography (US)
EDI, spread the word!
Extensive bibliography of articles concerned with EDI/paperless trade which have been published in a wide variety of periodicals. Primarily US based although some European references are given.

The EDI Reporter (US)
Input
US Newsletter with a small European section

EDI in Western Europe
Input Market research report

EDI Software Markets (US)
Input Market research report concerned with the US market

EDI Yellow Pages (US)
EDI, spread the word!
Yellow Pages containing numbers of all the companies and divisions that use EDI in the US.

Electronic Data Interchange
Online Publications Limited
Proceedings of the conference held in London in 1987.

Electronic Data Interchange
Butler Cox Foundation
Market research report

Electronic Data Interchange for Administration, Commerce & Transport (EDIFACT) Standards for Electronic Data Interchange
SITPRO
Manual of the international standard, in a condensed form, including the rules on application level for the structuring of the user data and of the associated service data in the interchange of messages in an

open environment. The rules have been agreed by the United Nations Economic Commission for Europe (UN/ECE) as syntax rules for EDIFACT and are part of the ECE Trade Data Interchange Directory which also includes Message Design Guidelines. The Guidelines should be used in conjunction with this standard.

Electronic Document Interchange
Link Resources Limited
Market research report

Electronic Message Systems 86, 87 and 88
Online Publications Limited
Proceedings of the conferences held in London in 1986, 1987, and 1988.

Electronic Messaging
Link Resources Limited
Market research report

International EDI (US)
Input
Market research report

Prospects for Paperless Government Procurement (US)
Input
Market research report

TRADACOMS: Standards for Electronic Data Interchange
ANA Limited
Manual of standards for implementation of TRADACOMS standards

Trade Facilitation
Elsevier Science Publishers
Journal concentrating on paperless trading and transport

Tradeflash
Euromatica SA
Monthly European newsletter solely concerned with reporting news concerning EDI and paperless trade in Europe.

UNCID (Uniform Rules of Conduct for Interchange of Trade Data by Teletransmission)
International Chamber of Commerce (ICC)
Booklet outlining rules and guidelines for business parties considering EDI implementation thereby allowing the formulation of a communication agreement and a contract with a legally binding effect.

Value Added & Data Services—A Select Reading List
OFTEL Library
Bibliography concerned with VADS

Value Added and Data Services Interworking Study
HMSO Books
Published study commissioned during the Vanguard initiative concerned with interworking of VADS.

Value Added Network & Data Services—European Market Directions
Input
Market research

The Value Added Network Services Handbook
Online Publications Limited
Complete guide to selecting and setting-up value added and data services. Further information under entry for **The VANS Handbook**.

Value Added Networks & Services—Risks & Rewards
Online Publications Limited
Proceedings of the conference held in London in 1986

Value Added Networks in Europe
Frost & Sullivan
Market research report

Vanguard
Marathon Publishing Limited
Bi-monthly magazine concerned with VADS.

The VANS Handbook
Online Publications Limited
Complete guide to selecting and setting-up value added and data services. The structure of the book may be simply defined as explanatory editorial linked to comprehensive factual directory information. The editorial gives complete coverage of the VADS field as it stands at present and how it is likely to develop in the future drawing on user experience of existing VADS by way of illustration in the text. **The VANS Handbook** should be purchased as a complementary volume to **The EDI Handbook**.

VANS in the Automotive Industry
Link Resources Limited
Market research report

VANS in the Travel Industry
Link Resources Limited
Market research report

Who's Who & What's What in Electronic Data Interchange
Euromatica SA
List of individuals and companies active in the EDI field in Europe with brief descriptions of type of involvement.

Publishers' addresses

Listed below are the names and telephone numbers of the publishers of the preceeding publications.

ANA Limited
The Article Number Association Limited
6 Catherine Street
London WC2B 5JJ
Telephone: 01 836 2460

Blenheim Euromatica SA
68 Avenue d'Auderghem
Bte 29
1040 Brussels
Belgium
Telephone: 010 322 736 9821

Blenheim Online Ltd
Blenheim House
Ash Hill Drive
Pinner
Middlesex HA5 2AE
Telephone: 01 868 4466

Butler Cox Foundation
Butler Cox House
12 Bloomsbury Square
London WC1A 2LL
Telephone: 01 831 0101

EDI, spread the word!
3527 Oak Lawn Avenue
Box Number 506
Dallas
Texas 75219—8089
USA
Telephone: 0101 214 855 1406

Elsevier Science Publishers bv
PO Box 1991
1000 BZ Amsterdam
The Netherlands
Telephone: 010 020 586 2911

Euromatica SA
—*see Blenheim Euromatica SA*

Frost and Sullivan
Sullivan House
4 Grosvenor Gardens
London SW1W 0DH
Telephone: 01 730 3438

HMSO Books
HMSO Publications Centre
PO Box 276
London SW8 5DT
Telephone: 01 622 3310

ICC
International Chamber of Commerce
C/O Centrepoint
103 New Oxford Street
London WC1A 1QB
Telephone: 01 240 5558

Input
41 Dover Street
London W1X 3RB
Telephone: 01 493 9335

Link Resources Limited
2 Bath Road
London W4 1LN
Telephone: 01 995 8082

Marathon Publishing Limited
Queens House
2 Holly Road
Twickenham
Middlesex TW1 4EG
Telephone: 01 891 1155

OFTEL
Office of Telecommunications
Atlantic House
Holborn Viaduct
London EC1N 2HQ
Telephone: 01 353 4020

Online Publications Limited
— *see Blenheim Online*

SITPRO
Simplification of Trade Procedures Board
Almack House
26-28 King Street
London SW1Y 6QW
Telephone: 01 930 0532

J. Whitaker & Sons Ltd.
12 Dyott Street
London WC1A 1DF
Telephone: 01 836 8911

Appendix E

Guide to acronyms

ABI	Automated Broker Interface
ABPI	Association of British Pharmaceutical Industry
ACH	Automated Clearing House
ACL	Atlantic Container Line
ACS	Automated Commercial System
ACP 90	Air Cargo Processing in the Nineties
ADMD	Administrative Management Domain
ADP	Automated Data Processing
AECMA	Association Européene des Constructeurs de Matériel Aerospatiale
AFDEC	Association of Franchised Distributors of Electronic Components
AGHA	Antwerp Port Community
ALCS	Airline Control System
ANA	The Article Number Association
ANNA	American National Numbering Authority
ANSI	American National Standards Institution
APACS	Association of Payment & Clearing Services
ARPA	Advanced Research Projects Association
ARPANET	Advanced Research Projects Association Network
ASCII	American Standard Code for Information Interchange
ASN. 1	Abstract Syntax Notation 1
ASTI	L'Association de Services Transports Informatique
ATM	Automatic Teller Machine
ATTIS	American Telephone & Telegraph Information Services
BABT	British Approvals Board for Telecommunications
BBA	British Bankers Association
BACS	Bankers Automated Clearing Service
BAF	Bunkerage Adjustment Figures
BDI	Batch Data Interchange
BEDIS	Booktrade Electronic Data Interchange Standards
BIA	British Insurance Association
BIBA	Brish Insurance Brokers Association
BIC	Bank Identifier Code
BISAC	Book Industry Systems Advisory Committee
Bit	Binary digit
Bps	Bits per second
BS	British Standard
BSC	Binary Synchronous Communications
BSGL	Branch Systems General Licence

BSI	British Standards Institute
BT	British Telecom
BTAT	British Telecom Applied Technology
CAD/CAM	Computer Aided Design/Computer Aided Manufacturing
CADDIA	Cooperation in the Automation of Data & Documentation for Imports/Exports in Agriculture
CAF	Currency Adjustment Factors
CARF	Common Access Reference
CASE	Common Application Service Elements
CAT	Credit Authorisation Telephone
CBI	Confederation of British Industry
CBMS	Computer Based Message Service
CCC	Customs Cooperation Council
CCITT	Comité Consultatif International Télégraphique et Téléphonique
CCRS	Community Cargo Release System
CD	Coordinated Development of Computerised Administrative Procedures Project
CEC	Commission of European Communities
CEFIC	Conseil Européen des Fédérations de l'Industrie Chimique
CEN	European Standards Committee
CEPT	Committee of European Postal & Telecommunications Administrations
CGM	Compagnie Générale Maritime (CGM)
CHIEF	Customs Handling of Import & Export Freight
CMP	Communications Management Processor
COGS	Customs and Other Governmental Issues
CPE	Customer Premises Equipment
CPT	Customs Project Team
CSA	Computer Services Association
CTI	Commission Technical & Industrial
CUG	Closed User Group
DACOM	Description and Classification of Meetings
DCA	Document Content Architecture
DEPS	Departmental Entry Processing System
DES	Data Encryption Standard
DIA	Document Interchange Architecture
DIS	Draft International Standard
DISH	Data Interchange for Shipping
DP	Data Processing
DTI	Department of Trade & Industry
DTI	Direct Trader Input
EAN	International Article Number Association
EBDI	Electronic Business Data Interchange
EC	European Community
EC	European Communications
ECE	Economic Commission for Europe
ECIF	Electronic Components Industry Federation
ECMA	European Computer Manufacturers Association
ECU	European Currency Unit

EDI	Electronic Data Interchange
EDIA	Electronic Data Interchange Association
EDICON	Electronic Data Interchange in Construction
EDIFACT	Electronic Data Interchange for Administration, Commerce & Trade
EDIFICE	Electronic Data Interchange Forum for Companies Interested in Computing & Electronics
EDIMS	Electronic Data Interchange Messaging System
EFT	Electronic Funds Transfer
EFTA	European Free Trade Association
EFTPOS	Electronic Funds Transfer at Point of Sale
E-MAIL	Electronic Mail
EP	Electronic Publishing
EPOS	Electronic Point of Sale
EPSS	Experimental Packet Switched System
ERTIS	European Road Transport Information Services
ETDI	Electronic Trade Data Interchange
FCC	Federal Communications Commission (FCC)
FCP 80	Felixstowe Cargo Processing 80
FEP	Front End Processor
FTAM	File Transfer Access & Management
FX	Foreign Exchange
GBA	Gemeentelijk Bevolkings Administratie
GDP	Gross Domestic Product
GOSIP	Government OSI Protocol
HMSO	HM Stationary Office
IATA	International Air Transport Authority
IBM IES	IBM Information Exchange Service
IBC	Integrated Broadband Communications
IBRO	Inter-Bank Research Organisation
ICC	International Chamber of Commerce
ICL	International Computers Limited
ICS	International Chamber of Shipping
IFIP	International Federation of Information Processing
IFIP WG	International Federation of Information Processing Working Group
IGES	Initial Graphics Exchange Specification
IMS	Integrated Message Services
INS	International Network Services
INSIS	Inter-Institutional Information System
INTIS	International Transport Information System
IPM	Interpersonal Message
IPMS	Interpersonal Messaging System
IPSS	International Packet Switched Service
ISDN	Integrated Services Digital Network
ISO	International Standards Organisation
IT	Information Technology
ITMA	Nesting Element
ITO	International Transport Order
ITMS	International Transport Messages Scenario

JEDI	Joint Electronic Data Interchange
JIT	Just-In-Time
JTM	Job Transfer & Manipulation
LACES	London Airport Cargo EDP Scheme
LAN	Local Area Network
LAPB	Link Access Protocol Type B
LOG	Logistik & Kommunikation
LSI	Large Scale Integration
MAC	Message Authentication Code
MDN	Managed Data Network
MDNS	Managed Data Network Service
MAP	Manufacturing Automation Protocol
MARC	Machine Readable Cataloguing
MCP	Maritime Cargo Processing
MHD	Message Header
MHS	Message Handling Service
MI	Multi-Invoice
MIDA	Message Interchange Distributed Application Standard
MOTIS	Message Orientated Text Interchange System
MPD	Multilingual Product Description
MRN	Multipayments Reference Number (EFT)
MS	Messaging Services
MTA	Message Transfer Agent
MTS	Message Transfer System
NAPLP	North American Presentation Layer Protocol
NBS	National Bureau of Standards
NCC	National Computing Centre
NCCL	National Commission for Communications & Liberalisation
NCP	Network Control Program
NDPS	National Data Processing Service (see BTAT)
NHS	National Health Service
NPL	National Physical Laboratory
NPP	Network Protocol Processors
OCR	Optical Code Reader
ODA	Office Document Architecture
ODETTE	Organisation for Data Exchange by Teletransmission in Europe
OFTEL	Office of Telecommunications
OFTP	ODETTE File Transfer Protocol
OIS	Office Information System
O/R	Originator/Recipient
OSI	Open Systems Interconnection
P1	Message Transfer Protocol
P2	Interpersonal Messaging Protocol
P3	Submission & Delivery Protocol
PABX	Private Automatic Branch Exchange
PACE	Ports Automated Cargo Environment
PAD	Packet Assembler & Disassembler
PDDI	Products Definition Data Interchange
PDN	Public Data Network

PC	Personal Computer
PCM	Pulse Code Modulation
P/E	Price/Earnings Ratio
PE	Period Entry
PIN	Personal Identification Number
PRMD	Private Management Domain
PSA	Property Services Agency
PSS	Packet Switch Service
PSTN	Public Switched Telephone Network
PTT	Postal, Telegraph and Telephone Administration
PTO	Public Telephone Operator
PVS	Private Videotex System
PVV	PIN Verification Values
RINET	Reinsurance & Insurance Network
RJE	Remote Job Entry
RO-RO	Roll-on/Roll-off
SAD	Single Administrative Document
SASE	Specific Application Service Elements
SDLC	Synchronous Data Link Control
SEA	Studycentre for the Expansion of Antwerp
SEAGHA	Systems Electronic and Adapted Data Interchange in the Port of Antwerp
SET	Standard Exchange et de Transfer (SET)
SGML	Standard Generalised Markup Language
SISAC	Serials Industry Systems Advisory Committee
SITA	Society of International Airline Telecommunications
SITPRO	Simplification of International Trade Procedures Board
SMMT	Society of Motor Manufacturers and Traders
SNA	Systems Network Architecture
SPC	Stored Program Control
SOFI 1 & SOFI 2	Systeme d'Ordinateurs pour le traitement du Fret International
SPAG	Standards Promotion and Applications Group
STAT	Status of Transfer
STX	Long Transmission Header
SWIFT	Society for World Interbank Financial, Telecommunications
TARIC	European Integrated Tariff
TDCC	Transportation Data Coordinating Committee
TDI	Trade Data Interchange
TEDIS	Trade Electronic Data Interchange Systems Programme
TISSG	Travel Industry System Standards Group
TMA	Telecommunications Managers Association
TOP	Technical & Office Protocols
TRADACOMS	Trading Data Communications Standard
TRANSPOTEL	International electronic information system for the transport industry
TS	Transaction Services
TTY	Teletype
TUA	Telecommunications Users Association
UA	User Agent

UCS	Uniform Communications System
UNCID	Uniform Rules of Conduct for Interchange of Trade Data by Teletransmission
UNCITRAL	United Nations Commission on International Trade Law
UNECE	United Nations Economic Commission for Europe
UNICORN	United Nations Interactive (message) Concept Over Reservation Networks
UNJEDI	United Nations Joint Electronic Data Interchange
UNSM	Universal Standard Messages
UNTDED	United Nations Trade Data Elements Directory
UNTDI	United Nations Trade Data Interchange
VADS	Value Added & Data Service
VAN	Value Added Network
VANS	Value Added Network Service
VAT	Value Added Tax
VDA	German Automotive Trade Associations
VDU	Video Display Unit
VTP	Virtual Terminal Protocol
WAN	Wide Area Network
WORM	Write Once Read Multiple

Appendix F

Glossary of Terms

Acoustic Coupler
A portable device which couples its model to the telephone line without a hard-wired connection.

Adaptor
A device designed to link a TV set to the telephone network allowing communication with videotex and viewdata systems.

Analogue Transmission
Transmission of continuously variable signal which directly represents the physical quantity being communicated. Digital data is converted to an analogue signal by a modem.

Architecture
The parameters by which computer or communications systems are defined.

ASCII
The USA standard code for information interchange.

Asynchronous Transmission
Each character transmitted is preceded by a start signal and followed by a stop signal. The reciever is switched on by the start signal and switched off by the stop signal, ready to receive the next character.

Auto-answer
The facility to answer whilst unattended.

Bandwidth
Indicates the information carrying capacity of a communications channel.

Baud
Unit of discrete signalling speed per second, approximates bits per second.

Bit
Binary digit, used in representing a number in binary notation

Bits per second (Bps)
Measurement used to denote the transmission rate possible over digital networks.

Bridge
Similar to a gateway however it does not support protocol conversion.

Byte
A measure synonymous with a character.

Used to represent computer storage capacity.

Coaxial Cable
Cable consisting of a central copper core surrounded by a cylindrical conductor and an insulating cover, able to support high transmission bandwidth.

Database
A collection of related data which may be utilised to serve one or more functions. The data is independent of the programs which utilise it.

Dial-up Link
Dialed-up link over the switched telephone network

Digital Transmission
Transmission of a series of discrete signal pulses representing coded values. Pulse code modulation (PCM) is used to digitise speech for transmission.

Electronic Data Interchange (EDI)
The electronic exchange of structured information between different locations over a network. Usually refers to business documentation.

Electronic Funds Transfer (EFT)
Electronic payment where transfer of funds from transaction parties' bank accounts is automatic.

Electronic Funds Transfer at Point of Sale (EFTPOS)
Electronic Funds Transfer initiated in retail establishment, via specialised terminal.

Electonic Mail (e-mail)
The distribution of addressed messages. Users retrieve mail when convenient.

End-user
The person who uses the terminal equipment on an information processing system.

Gateway
A computer exchange which allows access from one network to another, in addition to supporting protocol conversion.

Half Duplex Transmission
Two way transmission, but not both ways simultaneously.

INCOTERMS
A widely-used standard set of rules for the interpretation of trade terms by buyers and sellers.

Integrated Services Digital Network (ISDN)
Based on digital transmission, a network which will allow voice and data traffic to utilise the same digital links and exchanges.

Leased Line
Dedicated telecomms link between two points leased from the PTT for the exclusive user of the subscriber.

Local Area Network (LAN)
A network with limited geographical coverage, often a single building, interconnecting different types of computers and terminals.

Megabyte (Mbyte)
One million bytes

Modem
MOdulator/DEModulator. In transmission mode accepts data in a digital form converting it into an analogue signal for transmission over a telecoms link. Modem and the receiving end converts the analogue data back to the digital form.

Modulation
Modification of an analogue signal—usually changing its frequency range.

Multiplexer
A multiplexer divides a single data channel into several data channels of lower speed.

Network
The interconnection of computers and terminals placed in different locations.

Network Architecture
Reference used for the definition and development of protocols and products for interworking between data processing systems, often used to define a hierarchy of communication function layers.

Node
A computer or switching device situated at the point where two or more communications lines meet.

Managed Data Network (MDN)
Sometimes called third party network, where network owner sells spare network capacity to interested parties. Additional network services are often available.

Off-line
Pertaining to data processing equipment that is not connected to a computer or network, or the operations performed on such equipment.

On-line
Pertaining to data processing equipment that is connected to a communications line or a computer.

Open Systems Interconnection (OSI)
Agreed standard procedures for information exchange between previously incompatible systems.

Open Systems Interconnection Model
Reference model for the definition of OSI. Devloped by the International Telephony and Telegraphy Consultative Committee (CCITT) and the International Standards Organisation (ISO) the model defines seven layers of communications functions in end systems.

Packet
Block of data with a well defined format which allows it to be handled by a network designed to route such packets.

Packet Assembler Disassembler (PAD)
Interfaces terminals direct to a packet switched network by converting usual data flow to and from packets, setting-up calls and addressing packets.

Packet Switching
The switching of data in individual packets ensuring acceptance by the network and subsequent delivery. Packet sequence and destination is determined by control information passed from the originating terminal and the network.

Prestel
Videotex service operated by British Telecom

Private Automatic Branch Exchange (PABX)
Computer-based controller of a branch telephone system.

Protocol
A set of rules which governs the way a computer conversation is set up and conducted.

Protocol Conversion
For computers with different protocols to understand each other, meaningful conversation needs to take place. Many VADS are equipped to allow conversations between different 'tongues'.

Pulse Code Modulation
The method of transmitting analogue speech in a digital form.

Real-time

Computer functions carried out at a time demanded by the user—usually refers to present time.

Switched Network

Shared network where users have the potential to communicate over the network with each other at any time.

Switching

Allows the routing of data to the necessary recipient over communications networks.

Synchronous Transmission

Data flows at a fixed rate between the sender and receiver.

System

Term applied to the range of component parts which allow information processing to take place.

Systems Architecture

The defined arrangement of the various components to provide a working computer system.

Teletext

Viewdata service broadcast with TV transmissions, displayed on suitable receivers.

Telex

Public switched low speed data network allowing message transmission.

V.24

List of definitions for interchange circuits between data terminal equipment (DTE) and data circuit-terminating equipment (DCE).

V.35

Data transmission at 48 kbs using 60 to 108 kHz group band circuits.

Value Added Data Service (VADS) or Value Added Network Service (VANS)

A service which adds value to the telecommunications network above and beyond basic conveyance.

Video Conferencing

Conferences held between people at geographically different locations alowing sight and sound.

Videotex

Includes both viewdata and teletext.

Viewdata

System which displays information sent via a telephone line.

Wide Area Network (WAN)

National or international network connecting points of wide geographical coverage.

X.21bis

The use on the public data network of data terminal equipment (DTE) which is designed for interfacing to synchronous V-series modems.

X.25

The international standard formulated by CCITT for assembling and transmitting data in a packet switched network.

X.28

Data terminal equipment (DTE) and data circuit-terminating equipment (DCE) interface for start/stop mode of terminal equipment accessing the PAD facility in a public data network

X.32

Interface between DTE and DCE for terminals operating in the packet mode and accessing a packet switched data network through the PSTN or a circuit switched network.

X.400

Message handling facility